Workshop on Statistical Machine Translation 2006

(WMT 06)

Held at HLT/NAACL 2006

New York, New York, USA
8-9 June 2006

ISBN: 978-1-61738-493-6

Printed from e-media with permission by:

Curran Associates, Inc.
57 Morehouse Lane
Red Hook, NY 12571
www.proceedings.com

Some format issues inherent in the e-media version may also appear in this print version.

Printed by Curran Associates, Inc. (2010)

Association for Computational Linguistics
209 N. Eighth Street
Stroudsburg, Pennsylvania 18360

Phone: 1-570-476-8006
Fax: 1-570-476-0860

acl@aclweb.org

Introduction

The HLT-NAACL 2006 Workshop on Statistical Machine Translation (WMT-06) took place on Thursday, June 8 and Friday, June 9 in New York City, immediately following the *Human Language Technology Conference — North American Chapter of the Association for Computational Linguistics Annual Meeting*, which was hosted by New York University.

This is the second time that this workshop has been held. The first time was last year as part of the *ACL 2005 Workshop on Building and Using Parallel Texts: Data-Driven Machine Translation and Beyond*, which was a merger of two workshops that were originally proposed as independent events.

The focus of our workshop was to use parallel corpora for machine translation. Recent experimentation has shown that the performance of SMT systems varies greatly with the source and target language. In this workshop we encouraged researchers to investigate ways to improve the performance of SMT systems for diverse languages, including morphologically more complex languages and languages with partial free word order.

Prior to the workshop, in addition to soliciting relevant papers for review and possible presentation, we conducted a shared task that brought together machine translation systems for an evaluation on previously unseen data. This year's task resembled the one from last year's in many ways, but also included a manual evaluation of MT system output and focused on translation *from* English into other languages, whereas most other evaluations focus on translation *into* English.

The results of the shared task were announced at the workshop, and these proceedings also include an overview paper for the shared task that summarizes the results, as well as provides information about the data used and any procedures that were followed in conducting or scoring the task. In addition, there are short papers from each participating team that describe their underlying system in some detail.

The first day of the workshop, Thursday, June 8 was dedicated to full paper presentations, whereas the second day, Friday June 9 was mainly dedicated to system descriptions and discussions from teams that have participated in the shared task.

The workshop attracted a considerably larger number of submissions compared to last year's workshop. In total, WMT-06 featured 13 full paper oral presentations and 12 shared task presentations. The invited talk was given by Kevin Knight of the Information Sciences Institute/University of Southern California.

We would like to thank the members of the Program Committee for their timely reviews. We are also indebted to the many volunteers who served as judges in the manual evaluation of the shared task.

Philipp Koehn and Christof Monz

Co-Chairs

Organizers:

Philipp Koehn, Univeristy of Edinburgh, UK
Christof Monz, Queens Mary, Univeristy of London, UK

Program Committee:

Yaser Al-Onaizan, IBM, USA
Bill Byrne, University of Cambridge, UK
Chris Callison-Burch, University of Edinburgh, UK
Francisco Casacuberta, University of Valencia, Spain
David Chiang, ISI/University of Southern California, UK
Stephen Clark, Oxford University, UK
Marcello Federico, ITC-IRST, Italy
George Foster, Canada National Research Council, Canada
Alexander Fraser, ISI/University of Southern California, USA
Ulrich Germann, University of Toronto, Canada
Jan Hajic, Charles University, Czech Republic
Kevin Knight, ISI/University of Southern California, USA
Greg Kondrak, University of Alberta, Canada
Shankar Kumar, Google, USA
Philippe Langlais, University of Montreal, Canada
Daniel Marcu, ISI/University of Southern California, USA
Dan Melamed, New York University, USA
Franz-Josef Och, Google, USA
Miles Osborne, University of Edinburgh, UK
Philip Resnik, University of Maryland, USA
Libin Shen, University of Pennsylvania, USA
Wade Shen, MIT-Lincoln Labs, USA
Michel Simard, Canada National Research Council, Canada
Eiichiro Sumita, ATR Spoken Language Translation Research Laboratories, Japan
Joerg Tiedemann, University of Groningen, Netherlands
Christoph Tillmann, IBM, USA
Taro Watanabe, NTT, Japan
Dekai Wu, HKUST, China
Richard Zens, RWTH Aachen, Germany

Additional Reviewers:

Colin Cherry, University of Alberta, Canada
Fatiha Sadat, Canada National Research Council, Canada
Tarek Sherif, University of Alberta, Canada

Invited Speaker:

Kevin Knight, ISI/University of Southern California, USA

Table of Contents

Conference Program

Thursday, June 8, 2006

8:45–9:00	Opening Remarks
	Session 1: Paper Presentations
9:00–9:30	*Morpho-syntactic Information for Automatic Error Analysis of Statistical Machine Translation Output* Maja Popovic, Adrià de Gispert, Deepa Gupta, Patrik Lambert, Hermann Ney, José B. Mariño, Marcello Federico and Rafael Banchs
9:30–10:00	*Initial Explorations in English to Turkish Statistical Machine Translation* ilknur Durgar El-Kahlout and Kemal Oflazer
10:00–10:30	*Morpho-syntactic Arabic Preprocessing for Arabic to English Statistical Machine Translation* Anas El Isbihani, Shahram Khadivi, Oliver Bender and Hermann Ney
10:30–11:00	Coffee Break
	Session 2: Paper Presentations
11:00–11:30	*Quasi-Synchronous Grammars: Alignment by Soft Projection of Syntactic Dependencies* David Smith and Jason Eisner
11:30–12:00	*Why Generative Phrase Models Underperform Surface Heuristics* John DeNero, Dan Gillick, James Zhang and Dan Klein
12:00–12:30	*Phrase-Based SMT with Shallow Tree-Phrases* Philippe Langlais and Fabrizio Gotti
12:30–14:00	Lunch

Thursday, June 8, 2006 (continued)

Session 3: Paper Presentations

14:00–14:30 *Searching for alignments in SMT. A novel approach based on an Estimation of Distribution Algorithm*
Luis Rodríguez, Ismael García-Varea and Jose A. Gámez

14:30–15:30 Invited Talk by Kevin Knight

15:30–16:00 Coffee Break

Session 4: Paper Presentations

16:00–16:30 *Discriminative Reordering Models for Statistical Machine Translation*
Richard Zens and Hermann Ney

16:30–17:00 *Generalized Stack Decoding Algorithms for Statistical Machine Translation*
Daniel Ortiz-Martínez, Ismael García-Varea and Francisco Casacuberta

17:00–17:30 *N-Gram Posterior Probabilities for Statistical Machine Translation*
Richard Zens and Hermann Ney

Friday, June 9, 2006

Session 5: Paper Presentations

9:00–9:30 *Partitioning Parallel Documents Using Binary Segmentation*
Jia Xu, Richard Zens and Hermann Ney

9:30–10:00 *Contextual Bitext-Derived Paraphrases in Automatic MT Evaluation*
Karolina Owczarzak, Declan Groves, Josef Van Genabith and Andy Way

10:00–10:30 *How Many Bits Are Needed To Store Probabilities for Phrase-Based Translation?*
Marcello Federico and Nicola Bertoldi

10:30–11:00 Coffee Break

Friday, June 9, 2006 (continued)

Session 6: Shared Task

11:00–11:30 *Manual and Automatic Evaluation of Machine Translation between European Languages*
Philipp Koehn and Christof Monz

11:30–11:45 *NTT System Description for the WMT2006 Shared Task*
Taro Watanabe, Hajime Tsukada and Hideki Isozaki

11:45–12:00 *Mood at work: Ramses versus Pharaoh*
Alexandre Patry, Fabrizio Gotti and Philippe Langlais

12:00–14:00 Lunch

Session 7: Shared Task

14:00–14:15 *Stochastic Inversion Transduction Grammars for Obtaining Word Phrases for Phrase-based Statistical Machine Translation*
Joan Andreu Sánchez and José Miguel Benedí

14:15–14:30 *PORTAGE: with Smoothed Phrase Tables and Segment Choice Models*
Howard Johnson, Fatiha Sadat, George Foster, Roland Kuhn, Michel Simard, Eric Joanis and Samuel Larkin

14:30–14:45 *Syntax Augmented Machine Translation via Chart Parsing*
Andreas Zollmann and Ashish Venugopal

14:45–15:00 *TALP Phrase-based statistical translation system for European language pairs*
Marta R. Costa-jussà, Josep M. Crego, Adrià de Gispert, Patrik Lambert, Maxim Khalilov, José B. Mariño, José A. R. Fonollosa and Rafael Banchs

15:00–15:15 *Phramer - An Open Source Statistical Phrase-Based Translator*
Marian Olteanu, Chris Davis, Ionut Volosen and Dan Moldovan

15:15–15:30 *Language Models and Reranking for Machine Translation*
Marian Olteanu, Pasin Suriyentrakorn and Dan Moldovan

15:30–16:00 Coffee Break

Friday, June 9, 2006 (continued)

Session 8: Shared Task

Morpho-syntactic Information for Automatic Error Analysis of Statistical Machine Translation Output

Maja Popović[⋆] **Hermann Ney**[⋆]
Adrià de Gispert[†] **José B. Mariño**[†]
Deepa Gupta[⊥] **Marcello Federico**[⊥]
Patrik Lambert[†] **Rafael Banchs**[†]

[⋆] Lehrstuhl für Informatik VI - Computer Science Department, RWTH Aachen University, Aachen, Germany
[†] TALP Research Center, Universitat Politècnica de Catalunya (UPC), Barcelona, Spain
[⊥] ITC-irst, Centro per la Ricerca Scientifica e Tecnologica, Trento, Italy
{popovic,ney}@informatik.rwth-aachen.de {agispert,canton}@gps.tsc.upc.es
{gupta,federico}@itc.it {lambert,banchs}@gps.tsc.upc.es

Abstract

Evaluation of machine translation output is an important but difficult task. Over the last years, a variety of automatic evaluation measures have been studied, some of them like Word Error Rate (WER), Position Independent Word Error Rate (PER) and BLEU and NIST scores have become widely used tools for comparing different systems as well as for evaluating improvements within one system. However, these measures do not give any details about the nature of translation errors. Therefore some analysis of the generated output is needed in order to identify the main problems and to focus the research efforts. On the other hand, human evaluation is a time consuming and expensive task. In this paper, we investigate methods for using of morpho-syntactic information for automatic evaluation: standard error measures WER and PER are calculated on distinct word classes and forms in order to get a better idea about the nature of translation errors and possibilities for improvements.

1 Introduction

The evaluation of the generated output is an important issue for all natural language processing (NLP) tasks, especially for machine translation (MT). Automatic evaluation is preferred because human evaluation is a time consuming and expensive task. A variety of automatic evaluation measures have been proposed and studied over the last years, some of them are shown to be a very useful tool for comparing different systems as well as for evaluating improvements within one system. The most widely used are Word Error Rate (WER), Position Independent Word Error Rate (PER), the BLEU score (Papineni et al., 2002) and the NIST score (Doddington, 2002). However, none of these measures give any details about the nature of translation errors. A relationship between these error measures and the actual errors in the translation outputs is not easy to find. Therefore some analysis of the translation errors is necessary in order to define the main problems and to focus the research efforts. A framework for human error analysis and error classification has been proposed in (Vilar et al., 2006), but like human evaluation, this is also a time consuming task.

The goal of this work is to present a framework for automatic error analysis of machine translation output based on morpho-syntactic information.

2 Related Work

There is a number of publications dealing with various automatic evaluation measures for machine translation output, some of them proposing new measures, some proposing improvements and extensions of the existing ones (Doddington, 2002; Papineni et al., 2002; Babych and Hartley, 2004; Matusov et al., 2005). Semi-automatic evaluation measures have been also investigated, for example in (Nießen et al., 2000). An automatic metric which uses base forms and synonyms of the words in order to correlate better to human judgements has been

Proceedings of the Workshop on Statistical Machine Translation, pages 1–6,
New York City, June 2006.

proposed in (Banerjee and Lavie, 2005). However, error analysis is still a rather unexplored area. A framework for human error analysis and error classification has been proposed in (Vilar et al., 2006) and a detailed analysis of the obtained results has been carried out. Automatic methods for error analysis to our knowledge have not been studied yet.

Many publications propose the use of morpho-syntactic information for improving the performance of a statistical machine translation system. Various methods for treating morphological and syntactical differences between German and English are investigated in (Nießen and Ney, 2000; Nießen and Ney, 2001a; Nießen and Ney, 2001b). Morphological analysis has been used for improving Arabic-English translation (Lee, 2004), for Serbian-English translation (Popović et al., 2005) as well as for Czech-English translation (Goldwater and McClosky, 2005). Inflectional morphology of Spanish verbs is dealt with in (Popović and Ney, 2004; de Gispert et al., 2005). To the best of our knowledge, the use of morpho-syntactic information for error analysis of translation output has not been investigated so far.

3 Morpho-syntactic Information and Automatic Evaluation

We propose the use of morpho-syntactic information in combination with the automatic evaluation measures WER and PER in order to get more details about the translation errors.

We investigate two types of potential problems for the translation with the Spanish-English language pair:

- syntactic differences between the two languages considering nouns and adjectives
- inflections in the Spanish language considering mainly verbs, adjectives and nouns

As any other automatic evaluation measures, these novel measures will be far from perfect. Possible POS-tagging errors may introduce additional noise. However, we expect this noise to be sufficiently small and the new measures to be able to give sufficiently clear ideas about particular errors.

3.1 Syntactic differences

Adjectives in the Spanish language are usually placed after the corresponding noun, whereas in English is the other way round. Although in most cases the phrase based translation system is able to handle these local permutations correctly, some errors are still present, especially for unseen or rarely seen noun-adjective groups. In order to investigate this type of errors, we extract the nouns and adjectives from both the reference translations and the system output and then calculate WER and PER. If the difference between the obtained WER and PER is large, this indicates reordering errors: a number of nouns and adjectives is translated correctly but in the wrong order.

3.2 Spanish inflections

Spanish has a rich inflectional morphology, especially for verbs. Person and tense are expressed by the suffix so that many different full forms of one verb exist. Spanish adjectives, in contrast to English, have four possible inflectional forms depending on gender and number. Therefore the error rates for those word classes are expected to be higher for Spanish than for English. Also, the error rates for the Spanish base forms are expected to be lower than for the full forms. In order to investigate potential inflection errors, we compare the PER for verbs, adjectives and nouns for both languages. For the Spanish language, we also investigate differences between full form PER and base form PER: the larger these differences, more inflection errors are present.

4 Experimental Settings

4.1 Task and Corpus

The corpus analysed in this work is built in the framework of the TC-Star project. It contains more than one million sentences and about 35 million running words of the Spanish and English European Parliament Plenary Sessions (EPPS). A description of the EPPS data can be found in (Vilar et al., 2005). In order to analyse effects of data sparseness, we have randomly extracted a small subset referred to as 13k containing about thirteen thousand sentences and 370k running words (about 1% of the original

Training corpus:		Spanish	English
full	Sentences	1281427	
	Running Words	36578514	34918192
	Vocabulary	153124	106496
	Singletons [%]	35.2	36.2
13k	Sentences	13360	
	Running Words	385198	366055
	Vocabulary	22425	16326
	Singletons [%]	47.6	43.7
Dev:	Sentences	1008	
	Running Words	25778	26070
	Distinct Words	3895	3173
	OOVs (full) [%]	0.15	0.09
	OOVs (13k) [%]	2.7	1.7
Test:	Sentences	840	1094
	Running Words	22774	26917
	Distinct Words	4081	3958
	OOVs (full) [%]	0.14	0.25
	OOVs (13k) [%]	2.8	2.6

Table 1: Corpus statistics for the Spanish-English EPPS task (running words include punctuation marks)

corpus). The statistics of the corpora can be seen in Table 1.

4.2 Translation System

The statistical machine translation system used in this work is based on a log-linear combination of seven different models. The most important ones are phrase based models in both directions, additionally IBM1 models at the phrase level in both directions as well as phrase and length penalty are used. A more detailed description of the system can be found in (Vilar et al., 2005; Zens et al., 2005).

4.3 Experiments

The translation experiments have been done in both translation directions on both sizes of the corpus. In order to examine improvements of the baseline system, a new system with POS-based word reorderings of nouns and adjectives as proposed in (Popović and Ney, 2006) is also analysed. Adjectives in the Spanish language are usually placed after the corresponding noun, whereas for English it is the other way round. Therefore, local reorderings of nouns and adjective groups in the source language have been applied. If the source language is Spanish, each noun is moved behind the corresponding adjective group. If the source language is English, each adjective group is moved behind the corresponding noun. An adverb followed by an adjective (e.g. "more important") or two adjectives with a coordinate conjunction in between (e.g. "economic and political") are treated as an adjective group. Standard translation results are presented in Table 2.

Spanish→English		WER	PER	BLEU
full	baseline	34.5	25.5	54.7
	reorder	33.5	25.2	56.4
13k	baseline	41.8	30.7	43.2
	reorder	38.9	29.5	48.5

English→Spanish		WER	PER	BLEU
full	baseline	39.7	30.6	47.8
	reorder	39.6	30.5	48.3
13k	baseline	49.6	37.4	36.2
	reorder	48.1	36.5	37.7

Table 2: Translation Results [%]

5 Error Analysis

5.1 Syntactic errors

As explained in Section 3.1, reordering errors due to syntactic differences between two languages have been measured by the relative difference between WER and PER calculated on nouns and adjectives. Corresponding relative differences are calculated also for verbs as well as adjectives and nouns separately.

Table 3 presents the relative differences for the English and Spanish output. It can be seen that the PER/WER difference for nouns and adjectives is relatively high for both language pairs (more than 20%), and for the English output is higher than for the Spanish one. This corresponds to the fact that the Spanish language has a rather free word order: although the adjective usually is placed behind the noun, this is not always the case. On the other hand, adjectives in English are always placed before the corresponding noun. It can also be seen that the difference is higher for the reduced corpus for both outputs indicating that the local reordering problem

English output		$1 - \frac{PER}{WER}$
full	nouns+adjectives	24.7
	+reordering	20.8
	verbs	4.1
	adjectives	10.2
	nouns	20.1
13k	nouns+adjectives	25.7
	+reordering	20.1
	verbs	4.6
	adjectives	8.4
	nouns	19.1

Spanish output		$1 - \frac{PER}{WER}$
full	nouns+adjectives	21.5
	+reordering	20.3
	verbs	3.3
	adjectives	5.6
	nouns	16.9
13k	nouns+adjectives	22.9
	+reordering	19.8
	verbs	3.9
	adjectives	5.4
	nouns	19.3

Table 3: Relative difference between PER and WER [%] for different word classes

is more important when only small amount of training data is available. As mentioned in Section 3.1, the phrase based translation system is able to generate frequent noun-adjective groups in the correct word order, but unseen or rarely seen groups introduce difficulties.

Furthermore, the results show that the POS-based reordering of adjectives and nouns leads to a decrease of the PER/WER difference for both outputs and for both corpora. Relative decrease of the PER/WER difference is larger for the small corpus than for the full corpus. It can also be noted that the relative decrease for both corpora is larger for the English output than for the Spanish one due to free word order - since the Spanish adjective group is not always placed behind the noun, some reorderings in English are not really needed.

For the verbs, PER/WER difference is less than 5% for both outputs and both training corpora, indicating that the word order of verbs is not an important issue for the Spanish-English language pair. PER/WER difference for adjectives and nouns is higher than for verbs, for the nouns being significantly higher than for adjectives. The reason for this is probably the fact that word order differences involving only the nouns are also present, for example "export control = control de exportación".

English output		PER
full	verbs	44.8
	adjectives	27.3
	nouns	23.0
13k	verbs	56.1
	adjectives	38.1
	nouns	31.7

Spanish output		PER
full	verbs	61.4
	adjectives	41.8
	nouns	28.5
13k	verbs	73.0
	adjectives	50.9
	nouns	37.0

Table 4: PER [%] for different word classes

5.2 Inflectional errors

Table 4 presents the PER for different word classes for the English and Spanish output respectively. It can be seen that all PERs are higher for the Spanish output than for the English one due to the rich inflectional morphology of the Spanish language. It can be also seen that the Spanish verbs are especially problematic (as stated in (Vilar et al., 2006)) reaching 60% of PER for the full corpus and more than 70% for the reduced corpus. Spanish adjectives also have a significantly higher PER than the English ones, whereas for the nouns this difference is not so high.

Results of the further analysis of inflectional errors are presented in Table 5. Relative difference between full form PER and base form PER is significantly lower for adjectives and nouns than for verbs, thus showing that the verb inflections are the main source of translation errors into the Spanish language.

Furthermore, it can be seen that for the small cor-

Spanish output		$1 - \frac{PERb}{PERf}$
full	verbs	26.9
	adjectives	9.3
	nouns	8.4
13k	verbs	23.7
	adjectives	15.1
	nouns	6.5

Table 5: Relative difference between PER of base forms and PER of full forms [%] for the Spanish output

pus base/full PER difference for verbs and nouns is basically the same as for the full corpus. Since nouns in Spanish only have singular and plural form as in English, the number of unseen forms is not particularly enlarged by the reduction of the training corpus. On the other hand, base/full PER difference of adjectives is significantly higher for the small corpus due to an increased number of unseen adjective full forms.

As for verbs, intuitively it might be expected that the number of inflectional errors for this word class also increases by reducing the training corpus, even more than for adjectives. However, the base/full PER difference is not larger for the small corpus, but even smaller. This is indicating that the problem of choosing the right inflection of a Spanish verb apparently is not related to the number of unseen full forms since the number of inflectional errors is very high even when the translation system is trained on a very large corpus.

6 Conclusion

In this work, we presented a framework for automatic analysis of translation errors based on the use of morpho-syntactic information. We carried out a detailed analysis which has shown that the results obtained by our method correspond to those obtained by human error analysis in (Vilar et al., 2006). Additionally, it has been shown that the improvements of the baseline system can be adequately measured as well.

This work is just a first step towards the development of linguistically-informed evaluation measures which provide partial and more specific information of certain translation problems. Such measures are very important to understand what are the weaknesses of a statistical machine translation system, and what are the best ways and methods for improvements.

For our future work, we plan to extend the proposed measures in order to carry out a more detailed error analysis, for example examinating different types of inflection errors for Spanish verbs. We also plan to investigate other types of translation errors and other language pairs.

Acknowledgements

This work was partly supported by the TC-STAR project by the European Community (FP6-506738) and partly by the Generalitat de Catalunya and the European Social Fund.

References

Bogdan Babych and Anthony Hartley. 2004. Extending bleu mt evaluation method with frequency weighting. In *Proc. of the 42nd Annual Meeting of the Association for Computational Linguistics (ACL)*, Barcelona, Spain, July.

Satanjeev Banerjee and Alon Lavie. 2005. Meteor: An automatic metric for mt evaluation with improved correlation with human judgements. In *43rd Annual Meeting of the Assoc. for Computational Linguistics: Proc. Workshop on Intrinsic and Extrinsic Evaluation Measures for MT and/or Summarization*, pages 65–72, Ann Arbor, MI, June.

Adrià de Gispert, José B. Mariño, and Josep M. Crego. 2005. Improving statistical machine translation by classifying and generalizing inflected verb forms. In *Proc. of the 9th European Conf. on Speech Communication and Technology (Interspeech)*, pages 3185–3188, Lisbon, Portugal, September.

George Doddington. 2002. Automatic evaluation of machine translation quality using n-gram co-occurrence statistics. In *Proc. ARPA Workshop on Human Language Technology*, pages 128–132, San Diego.

Sharon Goldwater and David McClosky. 2005. Improving stastistical machine translation through morphological analysis. In *Proc. of the Conf. on Empirical Methods for Natural Language Processing (EMNLP)*, Vancouver, Canada, October.

Young-suk Lee. 2004. Morphological analysis for statistical machine translation. In *Proc. 2004 Meeting of the North American chapter of the Association for Computational Linguistics (HLT-NAACL)*, Boston, MA, May.

Evgeny Matusov, Gregor Leusch, Oliver Bender, and Hermann Ney. 2005. Evaluating machine translation output with automatic sentence segmentation. In *Proceedings of the International Workshop on Spoken Language Translation (IWSLT)*, pages 148–154, Pittsburgh, PA, October.

Sonja Nießen and Hermann Ney. 2000. Improving SMT quality with morpho-syntactic analysis. In *COLING '00: The 18th Int. Conf. on Computational Linguistics*, pages 1081–1085, Saarbrücken, Germany, July.

Sonja Nießen and Hermann Ney. 2001a. Morpho-syntactic analysis for reordering in statistical machine translation. In *Proc. MT Summit VIII*, pages 247–252, Santiago de Compostela, Galicia, Spain, September.

Sonja Nießen and Hermann Ney. 2001b. Toward hierarchical models for statistical machine translation of inflected languages. In *Data-Driven Machine Translation Workshop*, pages 47–54, Toulouse, France, July.

Sonja Nießen, Franz J. Och, Gregor Leusch, and Hermann Ney. 2000. An evaluation tool for machine translation: Fast evaluation for mt research. In *Proc. Second Int. Conf. on Language Resources and Evaluation (LREC)*, pages 39–45, Athens, Greece, May.

Kishore Papineni, Salim Roukos, Todd Ward, and Wie-Jing Zhu. 2002. BLEU: a method for automatic evaluation of machine translation. In *Proc. of the 40th Annual Meeting of the Association for Computational Linguistics (ACL)*, pages 311–318, Philadelphia, PA, July.

Maja Popović and Hermann Ney. 2004. Towards the use of word stems & suffixes for statistical machine translation. In *Proc. 4th Int. Conf. on Language Resources and Evaluation (LREC)*, pages 1585–1588, Lissabon, Portugal, May.

Maja Popović and Hermann Ney. 2006. POS-based word reorderings for statistical machine translation. In *Proc. of the Fifth Int. Conf. on Language Resources and Evaluation (LREC)*, Genova, Italy, May.

Maja Popović, David Vilar, Hermann Ney, Slobodan Jovičić, and Zoran Šarić. 2005. Augmenting a small parallel text with morpho-syntactic language resources for Serbian–English statistical machine translation. In *43rd Annual Meeting of the Assoc. for Computational Linguistics: Proc. Workshop on Building and Using Parallel Texts: Data-Driven Machine Translation and Beyond*, pages 41–48, Ann Arbor, MI, June.

David Vilar, Evgeny Matusov, Saša Hasan, Richard Zens, and Hermann Ney. 2005. Statistical machine translation of european parliamentary speeches. In *Proc. MT Summit X*, pages 259–266, Phuket, Thailand, September.

David Vilar, Jia Xu, Luis Fernando D'Haro, and Hermann Ney. 2006. Error analysis of statistical machine translation output. In *Proc. of the Fifth Int. Conf. on Language Resources and Evaluation (LREC)*, page to appear, Genova, Italy, May.

Richard Zens, Oliver Bender, Saša Hasan, Shahram Khadivi, Evgeny Matusov, Jia Xu, Yuqi Zhang, and Hermann Ney. 2005. The RWTH phrase-based statistical machine translation system. In *Proceedings of the International Workshop on Spoken Language Translation (IWSLT)*, pages 155–162, Pittsburgh, PA, October.

Initial Explorations in English to Turkish Statistical Machine Translation

İlknur Durgar El-Kahlout
Faculty of Enginering
and
Natural Sciences
Sabancı University
Istanbul, 34956, Turkey
ilknurdurgar@su.sabanciuniv.edu

Kemal Oflazer
Faculty of Engineering
and
Natural Sciences
Sabancı University
Istanbul, 34956, Turkey
oflazer@sabanciuniv.edu

Abstract

This paper presents some very preliminary results for and problems in developing a statistical machine translation system from English to Turkish. Starting with a baseline word model trained from about 20K aligned sentences, we explore various ways of exploiting morphological structure to improve upon the baseline system. As Turkish is a language with complex agglutinative word structures, we experiment with morphologically segmented and disambiguated versions of the parallel texts in order to also uncover relations between morphemes and function words in one language with morphemes and functions words in the other, in addition to relations between open class content words. Morphological segmentation on the Turkish side also conflates the statistics from allomorphs so that sparseness can be alleviated to a certain extent. We find that this approach coupled with a simple grouping of most frequent morphemes and function words on both sides improve the BLEU score from the baseline of 0.0752 to 0.0913 with the small training data. We close with a discussion on why one should not expect distortion parameters to model word-local morpheme ordering and that a new approach to handling complex morphotactics is needed.

1 Introduction

The availability of large amounts of so-called parallel texts has motivated the application of statistical techniques to the problem of machine translation starting with the seminal work at IBM in the early 90's (Brown et al., 1992; Brown et al., 1993). Statistical machine translation views the translation process as a noisy-channel signal recovery process in which one tries to recover the input "signal" e, from the observed output signal f.[1]

Early statistical machine translation systems used a purely word-based approach without taking into account any of the morphological or syntactic properties of the languages (Brown et al., 1993). Limitations of basic word-based models prompted researchers to exploit morphological and/or syntactic/phrasal structure (Niessen and Ney, (2004), Lee,(2004), Yamada and Knight (2001), Marcu and Wong (2002), Och and Ney (2004),Koehn et al. (2003), among others.)

In the context of the agglutinative languages similar to Turkish (in at least morphological aspects) , there has been some recent work on translating from and to Finnish with the significant amount of data in the Europarl corpus. Although the BLEU (Papineni et al., 2002) score from Finnish to English is 21.8, the score in the reverse direction is reported as 13.0 which is one of the lowest scores in 11 European languages scores (Koehn, 2005). Also, reported *from* and *to* translation scores for Finnish are the lowest on average, even with the large number of

[1]Denoting *English* and *French* as used in the original IBM Project which translated from French to English using the parallel text of the Hansards, the Canadian Parliament Proceedings.

Proceedings of the Workshop on Statistical Machine Translation, pages 7–14,
New York City, June 2006. ©2006 Association for Computational Linguistics

sentences available. These may hint at the fact that standard alignment models may be poorly equipped to deal with translation from a poor morphology language like English to an complex morphology language like Finnish or Turkish.

This paper presents results from some very preliminary explorations into developing an English-to-Turkish statistical machine translation system and discusses the various problems encountered. Starting with a baseline word model trained from about 20K aligned sentences, we explore various ways of exploiting morphological structure to improve upon the baseline system. As Turkish is a language with agglutinative word structures, we experiment with morphologically segmented and disambiguated versions of the parallel text, in order to also uncover relations between morphemes and function words in one language with morphemes and functions words in the other, in addition to relations between open class content words; as a cursory analysis of sentence aligned Turkish and English texts indicates that translations of certain English words are actually morphemes embedded into Turkish words. We choose a morphological segmentation representation on the Turkish side which abstracts from word-internal morphological variations and conflates the statistics from allomorphs so that data sparseness can be alleviated to a certain extent.

This paper is organized as follows: we start with the some of the issues of building an SMT system into Turkish followed by a short overview Turkish morphology to motivate its effect on the word alignment problem with English. We then present results from our explorations with a baseline system and with morphologically segmented parallel aligned texts, and conclude after a short discussion.

2 Issues in building a SMT system for Turkish

The first step of building an SMT system is the compilation of a large amount of parallel texts which turns out to be a significant problem for the Turkish and English pair. There are not many sources of such texts and most of what is electronically available are parallel texts diplomatic or legal domains from NATO, EU, and foreign ministry sources. There is also a limited amount data parallel news corpus available from certain news sources. Although we have collected about 300K sentence parallel texts, most of these require significant clean-up (from HTML/PDF sources) and we have limited our training data in this paper to about 22,500 sentence subset of these parallel texts which comprises the subset of sentences of 40 words or less from the 30K sentences that have been cleaned-up and sentence aligned.[2,3]

The main aspect that would have to be seriously considered first for Turkish in SMT is the productive inflectional and derivational morphology. Turkish word forms consist of morphemes concatenated to a root morpheme or to other morphemes, much like "beads on a string" (Oflazer, 1994). Except for a very few exceptional cases, the surface realizations of the morphemes are conditioned by various local regular morphophonemic processes such as vowel harmony, consonant assimilation and elisions. Further, most morphemes have phrasal scopes: although they attach to a particular stem, their syntactic roles extend beyond the stems. The morphotactics of word forms can be quite complex especially when multiple derivations are involved. For instance, the derived modifier `sağlamlaştırdığımızdaki` [4] would be broken into surface morphemes as follows:

`sağlam+laş+tır+dığ+ımız+da+ki`

Starting from an adjectival root *sağlam*, this word form first derives a verbal stem *sağlamlaş*, meaning "to become strong". A second suffix, the causative surface morpheme *+tır* which we treat as a verbal derivation, forms yet another verbal stem meaning "to cause to become strong" or "to make strong (fortify)". The immediately following participle suffix

[2]We are rapidly increasing our cleaned-up text and expect to clean up and sentence align all within a few months.

[3]As the average Turkish word in running text has between 2 and 3 morphemes we limited ourselves to 40 words in the parallel texts in order not to exceed the maximum number of words recommended for GIZA++ training.

[4]Literally, "(the thing existing) at the time we caused (something) to become strong". Obviously this is not a word that one would use everyday, but already illustrates the difficulty as one Turkish "word" would have to be aligned to a possible discontinues sequence of English words if we were to attempt a word level alignment. Turkish words (excluding noninflecting frequent words such as conjunctions, clitics, etc.) found in typical running text average about 10 letters in length. The average number of bound morphemes in such words is about 2.

+dığ, produces a participial nominal, which inflects in the normal pattern for nouns (here, for 1st person plural possessor which marks agreement with the subject of the verb, and locative case). The final suffix, *+ki*, is a relativizer, producing a word which functions as a modifier in a sentence, modifying a noun somewhere to the right.

However, if one further abstracts from the morphophonological processes involved one could get a lexical form

`sağlam+lAş+DHr+DHk+HmHz+DA+ki`

In this representation, the lexical morphemes except the lexical root utilize meta-symbols that stand for a set of graphemes which are selected on the surface by a series of morphographemic processes which are rooted in morphophonological processes some of which are discussed below, but have nothing whatsoever with any of the syntactic and semantic relationship that word is involved in. For instance, `A` stands for back and unrounded vowels *a* and *e*, in orthography, `H` stands for high vowels *ı*, *i*, *u* and *ü*, and `D` stands for *d* and *t*, representing alveolar consonants. Thus, a lexical morpheme represented as `+DHr` actually represents 8 possible allomorphs, which appear as one of *+dır, +dir, +dur, +dür, +tır, +tir, +tur, +tür* depending on the local morphophonemic context. Thus at this level of representation words that look very different on the surface, look very similar. For instance, although the words *masasında* 'on his table' and *defterinde* 'in his notebook' in Turkish look quite different, the lexical morphemes except for the root are the same: *masasında* has the lexical structure `masa+sH+ndA`, while *defterinde* has the lexical structure `defter+sH+ndA`.

The use of this representation is particularly important for Turkish for the following reason. Allomorphs which differ because of local word-internal morphographemic and morphotactical constraints almost always correspond to the same words or units in English when translated. When such units are considered by themselves as the units in alignment, statistics get fragmented and the model quality suffers. On the other hand, this representation if directly used in a standard SMT model such as IBM Model 4, will most likely cause problems, since now, the distortion parameters will have to take on the task of generating the correct sequence of morphemes in a word (which is really a local word-internal problem to be solved) in addition to generating the correct sequence of words.

3 Aligning English–Turkish Sentences

If an alignment between the components of parallel Turkish and English sentences is computed, one obtains an alignment like the one shown in Figure 1, where it is clear that Turkish words may actually correspond to whole phrases in the English sentence.

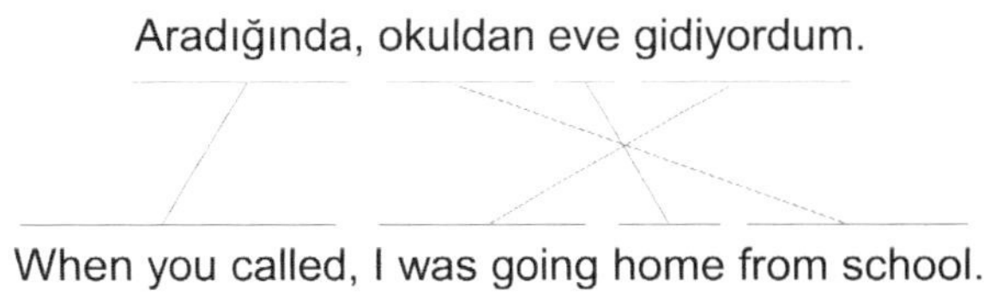

Figure 1: Word level alignment between a Turkish and an English sentence

One major problem with this situation is that even if a word occurs many times in the English side, the actual Turkish equivalent could be either missing from the Turkish part, or occur with a very low frequency, but many inflected variants of the form could be present. For example, Table 1 shows the occurrences of different forms for the root word *faaliyet* 'activity' in the parallel texts we experimented with. Although, many forms of the root word appear, none of the forms appear very frequently and one may even have to drop occurrences of frequency 1 depending on the word-level alignment model used, further worsening the sparseness problem.[5]

To overcome this problem and to get the maximum benefit from the limited amount of parallel texts, we decided to perform morphological analysis of both the Turkish and the English texts to be able to uncover relationships between root words, suffixes and function words while aligning them.

[5] A noun root in Turkish may have about hundred inflected forms and substantially more if productive derivations are considered, meanwhile verbs can have thousands of inflected and derived forms if not more.

Table 1: Forms of the word *faaliyet* 'activity'

Wordform	Count	Gloss
faaliyet	3	'activity'
faaliyete	1	'to the activity'
faaliyetinde	1	'in its activity'
faaliyetler	3	'activities'
faaliyetlere	6	'to the activities'
faaliyetleri	7	'their activities'
faaliyetlerin	7	'of the activities'
faaliyetlerinde	1	'in their activities'
faaliyetlerine	5	'to their activities'
faaliyetlerini	1	'their activities (acc.)'
faaliyetlerinin	2	'of their activities'
faaliyetleriyle	1	'with their activities'
faaliyette	2	'in (the) activity'
faaliyetteki	1	'that which is in activity'
Total	41	

On the Turkish side, we extracted the lexical morphemes of each word using a version of the morphological analyzer (Oflazer, 1994) that segmented the Turkish words along morpheme boundaries and normalized the root words in cases they were deformed due to a morphographemic process. So the word *faaliyetleriyle* when segmented into lexical morphemes becomes *faaliyet +lAr +sH +ylA*. Ambiguous instances were disambiguated statistically (Külekçi and Oflazer, 2005).

Similarly, the English text was tagged using TreeTagger (Schmid, 1994), which provides a lemma and a POS for each word. We augmented this process with some additional processing for handling derivational morphology. We then dropped any tags which did not imply an explicit morpheme (or an exceptional form). The complete set of tags that are used from the Penn-Treebank tagset is shown in Table 2.[6] To make the representation of the Turkish texts and English texts similar, tags are marked with a '+' at the beginning of all tags to indicate that such tokens are treated as "morphemes." For instance, the English word *activities* was segmented as *activity +NNS*. The alignments we expected to obtain are depicted in Figure 2 for the example sentence given earlier in Figure 1.

[6]The tagset used by the TreeTagger is a refinement of Penn-Treebank tagset where the second letter of the verb part-of-speech tags distinguishes between "be" verbs (B), "have" verbs (H) and other verbs (V),(Schmid, 1994).

Table 2: The set of tags used to mark explicit morphemes in English

Tag	Meaning
JJR	Adjective, comparative
JJS	Adjective, superlative
NNS	Noun, plural
POS	Possessive ending
RBR	Adverb, comparative
RBS	Adverb, superlative
VB	Verb, base form
VBD	Verb, past tense
VBG	Verb, gerund or present participle
VBN	Verb, past participle
VBP	Verb, non3rd person singular present
VBZ	Verb, 3rd person singular present

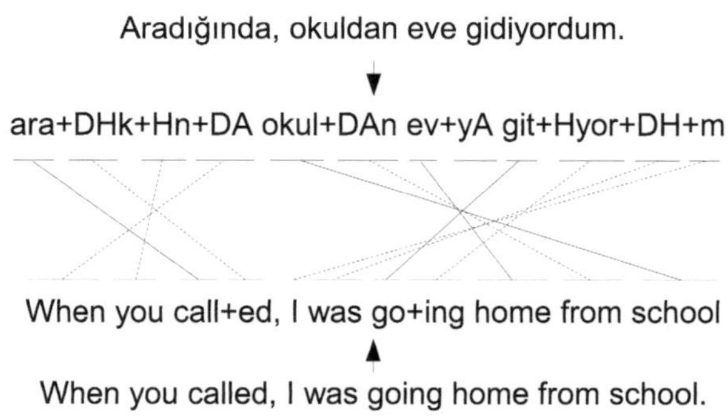

Figure 2: "Morpheme" alignment between a Turkish and an English sentence

4 Experiments

We proceeded with the following sequence of experiments:

(1) **Baseline:** As a baseline system, we used a pure word-based approach and used Pharaoh Training tool (2004), to train on the 22,500 sentences, and decoded using Pharaoh (Koehn et al., 2003) to obtain translations for a test set of 50 sentences. This gave us a baseline BLEU score of 0.0752.

(2) **Morpheme Concatenation:** We then trained the same system with the morphemic representation

of the parallel texts as discussed above. The decoder now produced the translations as a sequence of root words and morphemes. The surface words were then obtained by just concatenating all the morphemes following a root word (until the next root word) taking into just morphographemic rules but not any morphotactic constraints. As expected this "morpheme-salad" produces a "word-salad", as most of the time wrong morphemes are associated with incompatible root words violating many morphotactic constraints. The BLEU score here was 0.0281, substantially worse than the baseline in (1) above.

(3) **Selective Morpheme Concatenation:** With a small script we injected a bit of morphotactical knowledge into the surface form generation process and only combined those morphemes following a root word (in the given sequence), that gave rise to a valid Turkish word form as checked by a morphological analyzer. Any unused morphemes were ignored. This improved the BLEU score to 0.0424 which was still below the baseline.

(4) **Morpheme Grouping:** Observing that certain sequence of morphemes in Turkish texts are translations of some continuous sequence of functional words and tags in English texts, and that some morphemes should be aligned differently depending on the other morphemes in their context, we attempted a morpheme grouping. For example the morpheme sequence *+DHr +mA* marks infinitive form of a causative verb which in Turkish inflects like a noun; or the lexical morpheme sequence *+yAcAk +DHr* usually maps to "it/he/she will". To find such groups of morphemes and functional words, we applied a sequence of morpheme groupings by extracting frequently occuring n-grams of morphemes as follows (much like the grouping used by Chiang (2005): in a series of iterations, we obtained high-frequency bi-grams from the morphemic representation of parallel texts, of either morphemes, or of previously such identified morpheme groups and neighboring morphemes until up to four morphemes or one root 3 morpheme could be combined. During this process we ignored those combinations that contain punctuation or a morpheme preceding a root word. A similar grouping was done on the English side grouping function words and morphemes before and after root words.

The aim of this process was two-fold: it let frequent morphemes to behave as a single token and help Pharaoh with identification of some of the phrases. Also since the number of tokens on both sides were reduced, this enabled GIZA++ to produce somewhat better alignments.

The morpheme level translations that were obtained from training with this parallel texts were then converted into surface forms by concatenating the morphemes in the sequence produced. This resulted in a BLEU score of 0.0644.

(5) **Morpheme Grouping with Selective Morpheme Concatenation:** This was the same as (4) with the morphemes selectively combined as in (3). The BLEU score of 0.0913 with this approach was now above the baseline.

Table 3 summarizes the results in these five experiments:

Table 3: BLEU scores for experiments (1) to (4)

Exp.	*System*	*BLEU*
(1)	Baseline	0.0752
(2)	Morph. Concatenation.	0.0281
(3)	Selective Morph. Concat.	0.0424
(4)	Morph. Grouping and Concat.	0.0644
(5)	Morph. Grouping + (3)	**0.0913**

In an attempt to factor out and see if the translations were at all successful in getting the root words in the translations we performed the following: We morphologically analyzed and disambiguated the reference texts, and reduced all to sequences of root words by eliminating all the morphemes. We performed the same for the outputs of (1) (after morphological analysis and disambiguation), (2) and (4) above, that is, threw away the morphemes ((3) is the same as (2) and (5) same as (4) here). The translation root word sequences and the reference root word sequences were then evaluated using the BLEU (which would like to label here as BLEU-r for *BLEU root*, to avoid any comparison to previous results, which will be misleading. These scores are shown in Figure 4.

The results in Tables 3 and 4 indicate that with the standard models for SMT, we are still quite far from even identifying the correct root words in the trans-

Table 4: BLEU-r scores for experiments (1), (2) and (4)

Exp.	*System*	*BLEU*
(1)	Baseline	0.0955
(2)	Morph. Concatenation.	0.0787
(4)	Morph. Grouping	**0.1224**

lations into Turkish, let alone getting the morphemes and their sequences right. Although some of this may be due to the (relatively) small amount of parallel texts we used, it may also be the case that splitting the sentences into morphemes can play havoc with the alignment process by significantly increasing the number of tokens per sentence especially when such tokens align to tokens on the other side that is quite far away.

Nevertheless the models we used produce some quite reasonable translations for a small number of test sentences. Table 5 shows the two examples of translations that were obtained using the standard models (containing no Turkish specific manipulation except for selective morpheme concatenation). We have marked the *surface* morpheme boundaries in the translated and reference Turkish texts to indicate where morphemes are joined for exposition purposes here – they neither appear in the reference translations nor in the produced translations!

Table 5: Some good SMT results

Input: international terrorism also remains to be an important issue .
Baseline: ulus+lararası terörizm de önem+li kal+mış+tır . bir konu ol+acak+tır
Selective Morpheme Concatenation: ulus+lararası terörizm de ol+ma+ya devam et+mek+te+dir önem+li bir sorun+dur .
Morpheme Grouping: ulus+lararası terörizm de önem+li bir sorun ol+ma+ya devam et+mek+te+dir .
Reference Translation: ulus+lararası terörizm de önem+li bir sorun ol+ma+ya devam et+mek+te+dir .

Input: the initiation of negotiations will represent the beginning of a next phase in the process of accession
Baseline: müzakere+ler+in gör+üş+me+ler yap+ıl+acak bir der+ken aşama+nın hasar+ı sürec+i başlangıc+ı+nı 15+'i
Selective Morpheme Concatenation: initiation müzakere+ler temsil ed+il+me+si+nin başlangıc+ı bir aşama+sı+nda katılım süreс+i+nin ertesi
Morpheme Grouping: müzakere+ler+in başla+ma+sı+nın başlangıc+ı+nı temsil ed+ecek+tir katılım sürec+i+nin bir sonra+ki aşama
Reference Translation: müzakere+ler+in başla+ma+sı , katılım sürec+i+nin bir sonra+ki aşama+sı+nın başlangıc+ı+nı temsil ed+ecek+tir

5 Discussion

Although our work is only an initial exploration into developing a statistical machine translation system from English to Turkish, our experiments at least point out that using standard models to determine the correct sequence of morphemes within the words, using more powerful mechanisms meant to determine the (longer) sequence of words in sentences, is probably not a good idea. Morpheme ordering is a very local process and the correct sequence should be determined locally though the existence of morphemes could be postulated from sentence level features during the translation process. Furthermore, insisting on generating the exact sequence of morphemes could be an overkill. On the other hand, a morphological generator could take a *root word* and a *bag of morphemes* and generate possible legitimate surface words by taking into account morphotactic constraints and morphographemic constraints, possibly (and ambiguously) filling in any morphemes missing in the translation but actually required by the morphotactic paradigm. Any ambiguities from the morphological generation could then be filtered by a language model.

Such a bag-of-morphemes approach suggests that we do not actually try to determine exactly where the morphemes actually go in the translation but rather determine the root words (including any function words) and then *associate* translated morphemes with the (bag of the) right root word. The resulting sequence of root words and their bags-of-morpheme can be run through a morphological generator which can handle all the word-internal phenomena such as proper morpheme ordering, filling in morphemes or even ignoring spurious morphemes, handling local morphographemic phenomena such as vowel harmony, etc. However, this approach of not placing morphemes into specific position in the translated output but just associating them with certain root words requires that a significantly different alignment and decoding models be developed.

Another representation option that could be employed is to do away completely with morphemes on the Turkish side and just replace them with morphological feature symbols (much like we did here for English). This has the advantage of better handling allomorphy – all allomorphs including those that are not just phonological variants map to the same feature, and homograph morphemes which signal different features map to different features. So in a sense, this would provide a more accurate decomposition of the words on the Turkish side, but at the same time introduce a larger set of features since default feature symbols are produced for any morphemes that do not exist on the surface. Removing such redundant features from such a representation and then using reduced features could be an interesting avenue to pursue. Generation of surface words would not be a problem since, our morphological generator does not care if it is input morphemes or features.

6 Conclusions

We have presented the results of our initial explorations into statistical machine translation from English to Turkish. Using a relatively small parallel corpus of about 22,500 sentences, we have experimented with a baseline word-to-word translation model using the Pharaoh decoder. We have also experimented with a morphemic representation of the parallel texts and have aligned the sentences at the morpheme level. The decoder in this cases produces root word and morpheme sequences which are then selectively concatenated into surface words by possibly ignoring some morphemes which are redundant or wrong. We have also attempted a simple grouping of root words and morphemes to both help the alignment by reducing the number of tokens in the sentences and by already identifying some possible phrases. This grouping of morphemes and the use of selective morpheme concatenation in producing surface words has increased the BLEU score for our test set from 0.0752 to 0.0913. Current ongoing work involves increasing the parallel corpus size and the development of bag-of-morphemes modeling approach to translation to separate the sentence level word sequencing from word-internal morpheme sequencing.

7 Acknowledgements

This work was supported by TÜBİTAK (Turkish Scientific and Technological Research Foundation) project 105E020 "Building a Statistical Machine Translation for Turkish and English".

References

Peter F. Brown, Stephen A. Della Pietra, Vincent J. Della Pietra, John D. Lafferty, and Robert L. Mercer. 1992. Analysis, statistical transfer, and synthesis in machine translation. In *Proceeding of TMI: Fourth International Conference on Theoretical and Methodological Issues in MT*, pages 83–100.

Peter F Brown, Stephen A Della Pietra, Vincent J Della Pietra, and Robert L Mercer. 1993. The mathematics of statistical machine translation: Parameter estimation. *Computational Linguistics*, 19(2):263–311.

David Chiang. 2005. A hierarchical phrase-based model for statistical machine translation. In *Proceedings of the 43rd Annual Meeting of the Association for Computational Linguistics (ACL'05)*, pages 263–270, Ann Arbor, Michigan, June. Association for Computational Linguistics.

Philipp Koehn, Franz J. Och, and Daniel Marcu. 2003. Statistical phrase-based translation. In *Proceedings of HLT/NAACL*.

Philip Koehn. 2005. Europarl: A parallel corpus for statistical machine translation. In *MT Summit X*, Phuket, Thailand.

M. Oguzhan Külekçi and Kemal Oflazer. 2005. Pronunciation disambiguation in turkish. In Pinar Yolum, Tunga Güngör, Fikret S. Gürgen, and Can C. Özturan, editors, *ISCIS*, volume 3733 of *Lecture Notes in Computer Science*, pages 636–645. Springer.

Young-Suk Lee. 2004. Morphological analysis for statistical machine translation. In *Proceedings of HLT-NAACL 2004 - Companion Volume*, pages 57–60.

Daniel Marcu and William Wong. 2002. A phrase-based, joint probability model for statistical machine translation. In *In Proceedings of the Conference on Empirical Methods in Natural Language Processing (EMNLP-02)*, Philadelphia.

Sonja Niessen and Hermann Ney. 2004. Statistical machine translation with scarce resources using morpho-syntatic information. *Computational Linguistics*, 30(2):181–204.

Franz J. Och and Hermann Ney. 2004. The alignment template approach to statistical machine translation. *Computational Linguistics*, 30(4):417–449.

Kemal Oflazer. 1994. Two-level description of Turkish morphology. *Literary and Linguistic Computing*, 9(2):137–148.

Kishore Papineni, Todd Ward Salim Roukos, and Wei-Jing Zhu. 2002. Bleu: a method for automatic evaluation of machine translation. In *Proceedings of the 40th Annual Meeting of the Association for Computational Linguistics (ACL'02)*, pages 311–318, Philadelphia, July. Association for Computational Linguistics.

Helmut Schmid. 1994. Probabilistic part-of-speech tagging using decision trees. In *Proceedings of International Conference on New Methods in Language Processing*.

Kenji Yamada and Kevin Knight. 2001. A syntax-based statistical translation model. In *Proceedings of the 39th Annual Meeting of the Association for Computational Linguistics*, pages 00–00, Toulouse.

Morpho-syntactic Arabic Preprocessing for Arabic-to-English Statistical Machine Translation

Anas El Isbihani **Shahram Khadivi** **Oliver Bender** **Hermann Ney**
Lehrstuhl für Informatik VI - Computer Science Department
RWTH Aachen University
D-52056 Aachen, Germany
{isbihani,khadivi,bender,ney}@informatik.rwth-aachen.de

Abstract

The Arabic language has far richer systems of inflection and derivation than English which has very little morphology. This morphology difference causes a large gap between the vocabulary sizes in any given parallel training corpus. Segmentation of inflected Arabic words is a way to smooth its highly morphological nature. In this paper, we describe some statistically and linguistically motivated methods for Arabic word segmentation. Then, we show the efficiency of proposed methods on the Arabic-English BTEC and NIST tasks.

1 Introduction

Arabic is a highly inflected language compared to English which has very little morphology. This morphological richness makes statistical machine translation from Arabic to English a challenging task. A usual phenomenon in Arabic is the attachment of a group of words which are semantically dependent on each other. For instance, prepositions like "and" and "then" are usually attached to the next word. This applies also to the definite article "the". In addition, personal pronouns are attached to the end of verbs, whereas possessive pronouns are attached to the end of the previous word, which constitutes the possessed object. Hence, an Arabic word can be decomposed into "prefixes, stem and suffixes". We restrict the set of prefixes and suffixes to those showed in Table 1 and 2, where each of the prefixes and suffixes has at least one meaning which can be represented by a single word in the target language. Some prefixes can be combined. For example the word *wbAlqlm* (وبالقلم which means "and with the pen") has a prefix which is a combination of three prefixes, namely *w*, *b* and *Al*. The suffixes we handle in this paper can not be combined with each other. Thus, the compound word pattern handled here is "prefixes-stem-suffix".

All possible prefix combinations that do not contain *Al* allow the stem to have a suffix. Note that there are other suffixes that are not handled here, such as *At* (ات), *An* (ان) and *wn* (ون) which make the plural form of a word. The reason why we omit them is that they do not have their own meaning. The impact of Arabic morphology is that the vocabulary size and the number of singletons can be dramatically high, i.e. the Arabic words are not seen often enough to be learned by statistical machine translation models. This can lead to an inefficient alignment.

In order to deal with this problem and to improve the performance of statistical machine translation, each word must be decomposed into its parts. In (Larkey et al., 2002) it was already shown that word segmentation for Arabic improves information retrieval. In (Lee et al., 2003) a statistical approach for Arabic word segmentation was presented. It decomposes each word into a sequence of morphemes (prefixes-stem-suffixes), where all possible prefixes and suffixes (not only those we described in Table 1 and 2) are split from the original word. A comparable work was done by (Diab et al., 2004), where a POS tagging method for Arabic is also discussed. As we have access to this tool, we test its impact on the performance of our translation system. In

Proceedings of the Workshop on Statistical Machine Translation, pages 15–22,
New York City, June 2006.

Table 1: Prefixes handled in this work and their meanings.

Prefix	و	ف	ك	ل	ب	ال
Transliteration	*w*	*f*	*k*	*l*	*b*	*Al*
Meaning	and	and then	as, like	in order to	with, in	the

(Habash and Rambow, 2005) a morphology analyzer was used for the segementation and POS tagging. In contrast to the methods mentioned above, our segmentation method is unsupervised and rule based.

In this paper we first explain our statistical machine translation (SMT) system used for testing the impact of the different segmentation methods, then we introduce some preprocessing and normalization tools for Arabic and explain the linguistic motivation beyond them. Afterwards, we present three word segmentation methods, a supervised learning approach, a finite state automaton-based segmentation, and a frequency-based method. In Section 5, the experimental results are presented. Finally, the paper is summarized in Section 6 .

2 Baseline SMT System

In statistical machine translation, we are given a source language sentence $f_1^J = f_1 \ldots f_j \ldots f_J$, which is to be translated into a target language sentence $e_1^I = e_1 \ldots e_i \ldots e_I$. Among all possible target language sentences, we will choose the sentence with the highest probability:

$$\hat{e}_1^{\hat{I}} = \underset{I, e_1^I}{\operatorname{argmax}} \left\{ Pr(e_1^I | f_1^J) \right\} \quad (1)$$

The posterior probability $Pr(e_1^I | f_1^J)$ is modeled directly using a log-linear combination of several models (Och and Ney, 2002):

$$Pr(e_1^I | f_1^J) = \frac{\exp\left(\sum_{m=1}^{M} \lambda_m h_m(e_1^I, f_1^J)\right)}{\sum\limits_{e'^{I'}_1} \exp\left(\sum_{m=1}^{M} \lambda_m h_m(e'^{I'}_1, f_1^J)\right)} \quad (2)$$

The denominator represents a normalization factor that depends only on the source sentence f_1^J. Therefore, we can omit it during the search process. As a decision rule, we obtain:

$$\hat{e}_1^{\hat{I}} = \underset{I, e_1^I}{\operatorname{argmax}} \left\{ \sum_{m=1}^{M} \lambda_m h_m(e_1^I, f_1^J) \right\} \quad (3)$$

This approach is a generalization of the source-channel approach (Brown et al., 1990). It has the advantage that additional models $h(\cdot)$ can be easily integrated into the overall system. The model scaling factors λ_1^M are trained with respect to the final translation quality measured by an error criterion (Och, 2003).

We use a state-of-the-art phrase-based translation system including the following models: an n-gram language model, a phrase translation model and a word-based lexicon model. The latter two models are used for both directions: $p(f|e)$ and $p(e|f)$. Additionally, we use a word penalty and a phrase penalty. More details about the baseline system can be found in (Zens and Ney, 2004; Zens et al., 2005).

3 Preprocessing and Normalization Tools

3.1 Tokenizer

As for other languages, the corpora must be first tokenized. Here words and punctuations (except abbreviation) must be separated. Another criterion is that Arabic has some characters that appear only at the end of a word. We use this criterion to separate words that are wrongly attached to each other.

3.2 Normalization and Simplification

The Arabic written language does not contain vowels, instead diacritics are used to define the pronunciation of a word, where a diacritic is written under or above each character in the word. Usually these diacritics are omitted, which increases the ambiguity of a word. In this case, resolving the ambiguity of a word is only dependent on the context. Sometimes, the authors write a diacritic on a word to help the reader and give him a hint which word is really meant. As a result, a single word with the same meaning can be written in different ways. For example *$Eb* (شعب) can be read[1] as *sha'ab* (Eng. nation) or *sho'ab* (Eng. options). If the author wants to give the reader a hint that the second word is meant, he

[1] There are other possible pronunciations for the word *$Eb* than the two mentioned.

Table 2: Suffixes handled in this work and their meanings.

Suffix	ي	ني	ك	كما، كم، كن
Transliteration	*y*	*ny*	*k*	*kmA, km, kn*
Meaning	my	me	you, your (sing.)	you, your (pl.)
Suffix	نا	ه	ها	هما، هم، هن
Transliteration	*nA*	*h*	*hA*	*hmA, hm, hn*
Meaning	us, our	his, him	her	them, their

can write *$uEb* (شُعب) or *$uEab* (شُعَب). To avoid this problem we normalize the text by removing all diacritics.

After segmenting the text, the size of the sentences increases rapidly, where the number of the stripped article *Al* is very high. Not every article in an Arabic sentence matches to an article in the target language. One of the reasons is that the adjective in Arabic gets an article if the word it describes is definite. So, if a word has the prefix *Al*, then its adjective will also have *Al* as a prefix. In order to reduce the sentence size we decide to remove all these articles that are supposed to be attached to an adjective. Another way for determiner deletion is described in (Lee, 2004).

4 Word Segmentation

One way to simplify inflected Arabic text for a SMT system is to split the words in prefixes, stem and suffixes. In (Lee et al., 2003), (Diab et al., 2004) and (Habash and Rambow, 2005) three supervised segmentation methods are introduced. However, in these works the impact of the segmentation on the translation quality is not studied. In the next subsections we will shortly describe the method of (Diab et al., 2004). Then we present our unsupervised methods.

4.1 Supervised Learning Approach (SL)

(Diab et al., 2004) propose solutions to word segmentation and POS Tagging of Arabic text. For the purpose of training the Arabic TreeBank is used, which is an Arabic corpus containing news articles of the newswire agency AFP. In the first step the text must be transliterated to the Buckwalter transliteration, which is a one-to-one mapping to ASCII characters. In the second step it will be segmented and tokenized. In the third step a partial lemmatization is done. Finally a POS tagging is performed. We will test the impact of the step 3 (segmentation + lemmatization) on the translation quality using our phrase based system described in Section 2.

4.2 Frequency-Based Approach (FB)

We provide a set of all prefixes and suffixes and their possible combinations. Based on this set, we may have different splitting points for a given compound word. We decide whether and where to split the composite word based on the frequency of different resulting stems and on the frequency of the compound word, e.g. if the compound word has a higher frequency than all possible stems, it will not be split. This simple heuristic harmonizes the corpus by reducing the size of vocabulary, singletons and also unseen words from the test corpus. This method is very similar to the method used for splitting German compound words (Koehn and Knight, 2003).

4.3 Finite State Automaton-Based Approach (FSA)

To segment Arabic words into prefixes, stem and one suffix, we implemented two finite state automata. One for stripping the prefixes and the other for the suffixes. Then, we append the suffix automaton to the other one for stripping prefixes. Figure 1 shows the finite state automaton for stripping all possible prefix combinations. We add the prefix *s* (س), which changes the verb tense to the future, to the set of prefixes which must be stripped (see table 1). This prefix can only be combined with *w* and *f*. Our motivation is that the future tense in English is built by adding the separate word "will".

The automaton showed in Figure 1 consists of the following states:

- S: the starting point of the automaton.
- E: tne end state, which can only be achieved if

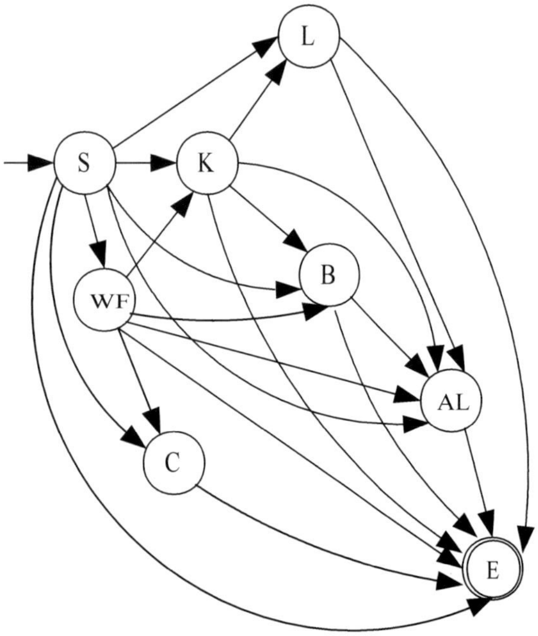

Figure 1: Finite state automaton for stripping prefixes off Arabic words.

the resulting stem exists already in the text.

- WF: is achieved if the word begins with *w* or *f*.
- And the states , K, L, B and AL are achieved if the word begins with *s, k, l, b* and *Al*, respectively.

To minimize the number of wrong segmentations, we restricted the transition from one state to the other to the condition that the produced stem occurs at least one time in the corpus. To ensure that most compound words are recognized and segmented, we run the segmenter itteratively, where after each iteration the newly generated words are added to the vocabulary. This will enable recognizing new compound words in the next iteration. Experiments showed that running the segmenter twice is sufficient and in higher iterations most of the added segmentations are wrong.

4.4 Improved Finite State Automaton-Based Approach (IFSA)

Although we restricted the finite state segmenter in such a way that words will be segmented only if the yielded stem already exists in the corpus, we still get some wrongly segmented words. Thus, some new stems, which do not make sense in Arabic, occur in the segmented text. Another problem is that the finite state segmenter does not care about ambiguities and splits everything it recognizes. For example let us examine the word *frd* (فرد). In one case, the character *f* is an original one and therefore can not be segmented. In this case the word means "person". In the other case, the word can be segmented to "*f rd*" (which means "and then he answers" or "and then an answer"). If the words *Alfrd, frd* and *rd*(فرد ، الفرد and رد) occur in the corpus, then the finite state segmenter will transform the *Alfrd* (which means "the person") to *Al f rd* (which can be translated to "the and then he answers"). Thus the meaning of the original word is distorted. To solve all these problems, we improved the last approach in a way that prefixes and suffixes are recognized simultaneously. The segmentation of the ambiguous word will be avoided. In doing that, we intend to postpone resolving such ambiguities to our SMT system.

The question now is how can we avoid the segmentation of ambiguous words. To do this, it is sufficient to find a word that contains the prefix as an original character. In the last example the word *Alfrd* contains the prefix *f* as an original character and therefore only *Al* can be stripped off the word. The next question we can ask is, how can we decide if a character belongs to the word or is a prefix. We can extract this information using the invalid prefix combinations. For example *Al* is always the last prefix that can occur. Therefore all characters that occur in a word after *Al* are original characters. This method can be applied for all invalid combinations to extract new rules to decide whether a character in a word is an original one or not.

On the other side, all suffixes we handle in this work are pronouns. Therefore it is not possible to combine them as a suffix. We use this fact to make a decision whether the end characters in a word are original or can be stripped. For example the word *trkhm* (تركهم) means "he lets them". If we suppose that *hm* is a suffix and therefore must be stripped, then we can conclude that *k* is an original character and not a suffix. In this way we are able to extract from the corpus itself decisions whether and how a word can be segmented.

In order to implement these changes the original automaton was modified. Instead of splitting a word we mark it with some properties which corespond to the states traversed untill the end state. On the other side, we use the technique described above to generate negative properties which avoid the corresponding kind of splitting. If a property and its negation belong to the same word then the property is removed and only the negation is considered. At the end each word is split corresponding to the properties it is marked with.

5 Experimental Results

5.1 Corpus Statistics

The experiments were carried out on two tasks: the corpora of the Arabic-English NIST task, which contain news articles and UN reports, and the Arabic-English corpus of the Basic Travel Expression Corpus (BTEC) task, which consists of typical travel domain phrases (Takezawa et al., 2002). The corpus statistics of the NIST and BTEC corpora are shown in Table 3 and 5. The statistics of the news part of NIST corpus, consisting of the Ummah, ATB, ANEWS1 and eTIRR corpora, is shown in Table 4. In the NIST task, we make use of the NIST 2002 evaluation set as a development set and NIST 2004 evaluation set as a test set. Because the test set contains four references for each senence we decided to use only the first four references of the development set for the optimization and evaluation. In the BTEC task, C-Star'03 and IWSLT'04 copora are considered as development and test sets, respectively.

5.2 Evaluation Metrics

The commonly used criteria to evaluate the translation results in the machine translation community are: WER (word error rate), PER (position-independent word error rate), BLEU (Papineni et al., 2002), and NIST (Doddington, 2002). The four criteria are computed with respect to multiple references. The number of reference translations per source sentence varies from 4 to 16 references. The evaluation is case-insensitive for BTEC and case-sensitive for NIST task. As the BLEU and NIST scores measure accuracy, higher scores are better.

5.3 Translation Results

To study the impact of different segmentation methods on the translation quality, we apply different word segmentation methods to the Arabic part of the BTEC and NIST corpora. Then, we make use of the phrase-based machine translation system to translate the development and test sets for each task.

First, we discuss the experimental results on the BTEC task. In Table 6, the translation results on the BTEC corpus are shown. The first row of the table is the baseline system where none of the segmentation methods is used. All segmentation methods improve the baseline system, except the SL segmentation method on the development corpus. The best performing segmentation method is IFSA which generates the best translation results based on all evaluation criteria, and it is consistent over both development and evaluation sets. As we see, the segmentation of Arabic words has a noticeable impact in improving the translation quality on a small corpus.

To study the impact of word segmentation methods on a large task, we conduct two sets of experiments on the NIST task using two different amounts of the training corpus: only news corpora, and full corpus. In Table 7, the translation results on the NIST task are shown when just the news corpora were used to train the machine translation models. As the results show, except for the FB method, all segmentation methods improve the baseline system. For the NIST task, the SL method outperforms the other segmentation methods, while it did not achieve good results when comparing to the other methods in the BTEC task.

We see that the SL, FSA and IFSA segmentation methods consistently improve the translation results in the BTEC and NIST tasks, but the FB method failed on the NIST task, which has a larger training corpus . The next step is to study the impact of the segmentation methods on a very large task, the NIST full corpus. Unfortunately, the SL method failed on segmenting the large UN corpus, due to the large processing time that it needs. Due to the negative results of the FB method on the NIST news corpora, and very similar results for FSA and IFSA, we were interested to test the impact of IFSA on the NIST full corpus. In Table 8, the translation results of the baseline system and IFSA segmentation method for the NIST full corpus are depicted. As it is shown in table, the IFSA method slightly improves the translation results in the development and test sets.

The IFSA segmentation method generates the best results among our proposed methods. It acheives consistent improvements in all three tasks over the baseline system. It also outperforms the SL

Table 3: BTEC corpus statistics, where the Arabic part is tokenized and segmented with the SL, FB, FSA and the IFSA methods.

		ARABIC					ENGLISH
		TOKENIZED	SL	FB	FSA	IFSA	
Train:	Sentences	20K					
	Running Words	159K	176.2K	185.5K	190.3K	189.1K	189K
	Vocabulary	18,149	14,321	11,235	11,736	12,874	7,162
Dev:	Sentences	506					
	Running Words	3,161	3,421	3,549	3,759	3,715	5,005
	OOVs (Running Words)	163	129	149	98	118	NA
Test:	Sentences	500					
	Running Words	3,240	3,578	3,675	3,813	3,778	4,986
	OOVs (Running Words)	186	120	156	92	115	NA

Table 4: Corpus statistics for the news part of the NIST task, where the Arabic part is tokenized and segmented with SL, FB, FSA and IFSA methods.

		ARABIC					ENGLISH
		TOKENIZED	SL	FB	FSA	IFSA	
Train:	Sentences	284.9K					
	Running Words	8.9M	9.7M	12.2M	10.9M	10.9M	10.2M
	Vocabulary	118.7K	90.5K	43.1K	68.4K	62.2K	56.1K
Dev:	Sentences	1,043					
	Running Words	27.7K	29.1K	37.3K	34.4K	33.5K	33K
	OOVs (Running Words)	714	558	396	515	486	NA
Test:	Sentences	1,353					
	Running Words	37.9K	41.7K	52.6K	48.6K	48.3K	48.3K
	OOVs (Running Words)	1,298	1,027	612	806	660	NA

segmentation on the BTEC task.

Although the SL method outperforms the IFSA method on the NIST tasks, the IFSA segmentation method has a few notable advantages over the SL system. First, it is consistent in improving the baseline system over the three tasks. But, the SL method failed in improving the BTEC development corpus. Second, it is fast and robust, and capable of being applied to the large corpora. Finally, it employs an unsupervised learning method, therefore can easily cope with a new task or corpus.

We observe that the relative improvement over the baseline system is decreased by increasing the size of the training corpus. This is a natural effect of increasing the size of the training corpus. As the larger corpus provides higher probability to have more samples per word, this means higher chance to learn the translation of a word in different contexts. Therefore, larger training corpus makes a better translation system, i.e. a better baseline, then it would be harder to outperform this better system. Using the same reasoning, we can realize why the FB method achieves good results on the BTEC task, but not on the NIST task. By increasing the size of the training corpus, the FB method tends to segment words more than the IFSA method. This over-segmentation can be compensated by using longer phrases during the translation, in order to consider the same context compared to the non-segmented corpus. Then, it would be harder for a phrase-based machine translation system to learn the translation of a word (stem) in different contexts.

6 Conclusion

We presented three methods to segment Arabic words: a supervised learning approach, a frequency-

Table 5: NIST task corpus statistics, where the Arabic part is tokenized and segmented with the IFSA method.

		ARABIC		ENGLISH
		TOKENIZED	IFSA	
Train:	Sentences	8.5M		
	Running Words	260.5M	316.8M	279.2M
	Vocabulary	510.3K	411.2K	301.2K
Dev:	Sentences	1043		
	Running Words	30.2K	33.3K	33K
	OOVs (Running Words)	809	399	NA
Test:	Sentences	1353		
	Running Words	40K	47.9K	48.3K
	OOVs (Running Words)	871	505	NA

Table 6: Case insensitive evaluation results for translating the development and test data of BTEC task after performing divers preprocessing.

	Dev				Test			
	mPER [%]	mWER [%]	BLEU [%]	NIST	mPER [%]	mWER [%]	BLEU [%]	NIST
Non-Segmented Data	21.4	24.6	63.9	10.0	23.5	27.2	58.1	9.6
SL Segmenter	21.2	24.4	62.5	9.7	23.4	27.4	59.2	9.7
FB Segmenter	20.9	24.4	65.3	10.1	22.1	25.8	59.8	9.7
FSA Segmenter	20.1	23.4	64.8	10.2	21.1	25.2	61.3	10.2
IFSA Segmenter	20.0	23.3	65.0	10.4	21.2	25.3	61.3	10.2

based approach and a finite state automaton-based approach. We explained that the best of our proposed methods, the improved finite state automaton, has three advantages over the state-of-the-art Arabic word segmentation method (Diab, 2000), supervised learning. They are: consistency in improving the baselines system over different tasks, its capability to be efficiently applied on the large corpora, and its ability to cope with different tasks.

7 Acknowledgment

This material is based upon work supported by the Defense Advanced Research Projects Agency (DARPA) under Contract No. HR0011-06-C-0023.

Any opinions, findings and conclusions or recommendations expressed in this material are those of the author(s) and do not necessarily reflect the views of the Defense Advanced Research Projects Agency (DARPA).

References

P. F. Brown, J. Cocke, S. A. Della Pietra, V. J. Della Pietra, F. Jelinek, J. D. Lafferty, R. L. Mercer, and P. S. Roossin. 1990. A statistical approach to machine translation. *Computational Linguistics*, 16(2):79–85, June.

M. Diab, K. Hacioglu, and D. Jurafsky. 2004. Automatic tagging of arabic text: From raw text to base phrase chunks. In D. M. Susan Dumais and S. Roukos, editors, *HLT-NAACL 2004: Short Papers*, Boston, Massachusetts, USA, May 2 - May 7. Association for Computational Linguistics.

M. Diab. 2000. An unsupervised method for multilingual word sense tagging using parallel corpora: A preliminary investigation. In *ACL-2000 Workshop on Word Senses and Multilinguality*, pages 1–9, Hong Kong, October.

G. Doddington. 2002. Automatic evaluation of machine translation quality using n-gram co-occurrence statistics. In *Proc. ARPA Workshop on Human Language Technology*.

Table 7: Case sensitive evaluation results for translating the development and test data of the news part of the NIST task after performing divers preprocessing.

	Dev				Test			
	mPER [%]	mWER [%]	BLEU [%]	NIST	mPER [%]	mWER [%]	BLEU [%]	NIST
Non-Segmented Data	43.7	56.4	43.6	9.9	46.1	58.0	37.4	9.1
SL Segmenter	42.0	54.7	45.1	10.2	44.3	56.3	39.9	9.6
FB Segmenter	43.4	56.1	43.2	9.8	45.6	57.8	37.2	9.2
FSA Segmenter	42.9	55.7	43.7	9.9	44.8	56.9	38.7	9.4
IFSA Segmenter	42.6	55.0	44.6	9.9	44.5	56.6	38.8	9.4

Table 8: Case-sensitive evaluation results for translating development and test data of NIST task.

	Dev				Test			
	mPER [%]	mWER [%]	BLEU [%]	NIST	mPER [%]	mWER [%]	BLEU [%]	NIST
Non-Segmented Data	41.5	53.5	46.4	10.3	42.5	53.9	42.6	10.0
IFSA Segmenter	41.1	53.2	46.7	10.2	42.1	53.6	43.4	10.1

N. Habash and O. Rambow. 2005. Arabic tokenization, part-of-speech tagging and morphological disambiguation in one fell swoop. In *Proc. of the 43rd Annual Meeting of the Association for Computational Linguistics (ACL'05)*, pages 573–580, Ann Arbor, Michigan, June. Association for Computational Linguistics.

P. Koehn and K. Knight. 2003. Empirical methods for compound splitting. In *Proc. 10th Conf. of the Europ. Chapter of the Assoc. for Computational Linguistics (EACL)*, pages 347–354, Budapest, Hungary, April.

L. S. Larkey, L. Ballesteros, and M. E. Connell. 2002. Improving stemming for arabic information retrieval: light stemming and co-occurrence analysis. In *Proc. of the 25th annual of the international Association for Computing Machinery Special Interest Group on Information Retrieval (ACM SIGIR)*, pages 275–282, New York, NY, USA. ACM Press.

Y. S. Lee, K. Papineni, S. Roukos, O. Emam, and H. Hassan. 2003. Language model based Arabic word segmentation. In E. Hinrichs and D. Roth, editors, *Proc. of the 41st Annual Meeting of the Association for Computational Linguistics*.

Y. S. Lee. 2004. Morphological analysis for statistical machine translation. In D. M. Susan Dumais and S. Roukos, editors, *HLT-NAACL 2004: Short Papers*, pages 57–60, Boston, Massachusetts, USA, May 2 - May 7. Association for Computational Linguistics.

F. J. Och and H. Ney. 2002. Discriminative training and maximum entropy models for statistical machine translation. In *Proc. of the 40th Annual Meeting of the Association for Computational Linguistics (ACL)*, pages 295–302, Philadelphia, PA, July.

F. J. Och. 2003. Minimum error rate training in statistical machine translation. In *Proc. of the 41th Annual Meeting of the Association for Computational Linguistics (ACL)*, pages 160–167, Sapporo, Japan, July.

K. Papineni, S. Roukos, T. Ward, and W. J. Zhu. 2002. Bleu: a method for automatic evaluation of machine translation. In *Proc. of the 40th Annual Meeting of the Association for Computational Linguistics (ACL)*, pages 311–318, Philadelphia, PA, July.

T. Takezawa, E. Sumita, F. Sugaya, H. Yamamoto, and S. Yamamoto. 2002. Toward a broad-coverage bilingual corpus for speech translation of travel conversations in the real world. In *Proc. of the Third Int. Conf. on Language Resources and Evaluation (LREC)*, pages 147–152, Las Palmas, Spain, May.

R. Zens and H. Ney. 2004. Improvements in phrase-based statistical machine translation. In *Proc. of the Human Language Technology Conf. (HLT-NAACL)*, pages 257–264, Boston, MA, May.

R. Zens, O. Bender, S. Hasan, S. Khadivi, E. Matusov, J. Xu, Y. Zhang, and H. Ney. 2005. The RWTH phrase-based statistical machine translation system. In *Proceedings of the International Workshop on Spoken Language Translation (IWSLT)*, pages 155–162, Pittsburgh, PA, October.

Quasi-Synchronous Grammars: Alignment by Soft Projection of Syntactic Dependencies

David A. Smith and **Jason Eisner**
Department of Computer Science
Center for Language and Speech Processing
Johns Hopkins University
Baltimore, MD 21218, USA
{dasmith,eisner}@jhu.edu

Abstract

Many syntactic models in machine translation are channels that transform one tree into another, or synchronous grammars that generate trees in parallel. We present a new model of the translation process: quasi-synchronous grammar (QG). Given a source-language parse tree T_1, a QG defines a *monolingual* grammar that generates translations of T_1. The trees T_2 allowed by this monolingual grammar are inspired by pieces of substructure in T_1 and aligned to T_1 at those points. We describe experiments learning quasi-synchronous context-free grammars from bitext. As with other monolingual language models, we evaluate the cross-entropy of QGs on unseen text and show that a better fit to bilingual data is achieved by allowing greater syntactic divergence. When evaluated on a word alignment task, QG matches standard baselines.

1 Motivation and Related Work

1.1 Sloppy Syntactic Alignment

This paper proposes a new type of syntax-based model for machine translation and alignment. The goal is to make use of syntactic formalisms, such as context-free grammar or tree-substitution grammar, without being overly constrained by them.

Let S_1 and S_2 denote the source and target sentences. We seek to model the conditional probability

$$p(T_2, A \mid T_1) \quad (1)$$

where T_1 is a parse tree for S_1, T_2 is a parse tree for S_2, and A is a node-to-node alignment between them. This model allows one to carry out a variety of alignment and decoding tasks. Given T_1, one can translate it by finding the T_2 and A that maximize (1). Given T_1 and T_2, one can align them by finding the A that maximizes (1) (equivalent to maximizing $p(A \mid T_2, T_1)$). Similarly, one can align S_1 and S_2 by finding the parses T_1 and T_2, and alignment A, that maximize $p(T_2, A \mid T_1) \cdot p(T_1 \mid S_1)$, where $p(T_1 \mid S_1)$ is given by a monolingual parser. We usually accomplish such maximizations by dynamic programming.

Equation (1) does not assume that T_1 and T_2 are isomorphic. For example, a model might judge T_2 and A to be likely, given T_1, provided that *many*—but not necessarily all—of the syntactic dependencies in T_1 are aligned with corresponding dependencies in T_2. Hwa et al. (2002) found that human translations from Chinese to English preserved only 39–42% of the unlabeled Chinese dependencies. They increased this figure to 67% by using more involved heuristics for aligning dependencies across these two languages. That suggests that (1) should be defined to consider more than one dependency at a time.

This inspires the key novel feature of our models: A does not have to be a "well-behaved" syntactic alignment. Any portion of T_2 can align to any portion of T_1, or to NULL. Nodes that are syntactically related in T_1 do *not* have to translate into nodes that are syntactically related in T_2—although (1) is usually higher if they do.

This property makes our approach especially promising for aligning freely, or erroneously, translated sentences, and for coping with syntactic **diver-**

Proceedings of the Workshop on Statistical Machine Translation, pages 23–30,
New York City, June 2006. ©2006 Association for Computational Linguistics

gences observed between even closely related languages (Dorr, 1994; Fox, 2002). We can patch together an alignment without accounting for all the details of the translation process. For instance, perhaps a source NP (figure 1) or PP (figure 2) appears "out of place" in the target sentence. A linguist might account for the position of the PP *auf diese Frage* either syntactically (by invoking scrambling) or semantically (by describing a deep analysis-transfer-synthesis process in the translator's head). But an MT researcher may not have the wherewithal to design, adequately train, and efficiently compute with "deep" accounts of this sort. Under our approach, it is possible to use a simple, tractable syntactic model, but with some contextual probability of "sloppy" transfer.

1.2 From Synchronous to Quasi-Synchronous Grammars

Because our approach will let anything align to anything, it is reminiscent of IBM Models 1–5 (Brown et al., 1993). It differs from the many approaches where (1) is defined by a stochastic synchronous grammar (Wu, 1997; Alshawi et al., 2000; Yamada and Knight, 2001; Eisner, 2003; Gildea, 2003; Melamed, 2004) and from transfer-based systems defined by context-free grammars (Lavie et al., 2003).

The synchronous grammar approach, originally due to Shieber and Schabes (1990), supposes that T_2 is generated in lockstep to T_1.[1] When choosing how to expand a certain VP node in T_2, a synchronous CFG process would observe that this node is aligned to a node VP′ in T_1, which had been expanded in T_1 by VP′ $\rightarrow$ NP′ V′. This might bias it toward choosing to expand the VP in T_2 as VP $\rightarrow$ V NP, with the new children V aligned to V′ and NP aligned to NP′. The process then continues recursively by choosing moves to expand these children.

One can regard this stochastic process as an instance of analysis-transfer-synthesis MT. Analysis chooses a parse T_1 given S_1. Transfer maps the context-free rules in T_1 to rules of T_2. Synthesis deterministically assembles the latter rules into an actual tree T_2 and reads off its yield S_2.

What is worrisome about the synchronous process is that it can only produce trees T_2 that are perfectly isomorphic to T_1. It is possible to relax this requirement by using synchronous grammar formalisms more sophisticated than CFG:[2] one can permit unaligned nodes (Yamada and Knight, 2001), duplicated children (Gildea, 2003)[3], or alignment between elementary trees of differing sizes rather than between single rules (Eisner, 2003; Ding and Palmer, 2005; Quirk et al., 2005). However, one would need rather powerful and slow grammar formalisms (Shieber and Schabes, 1990; Melamed et al., 2004), often with discontiguous constituents, to account for all the linguistic divergences that could arise from different movement patterns (scrambling, wh-*in situ*) or free translation. In particular, a synchronous grammar cannot practically allow S_2 to be any permutation of S_1, as IBM Models 1–5 do.

Our alternative is to define a "quasi-synchronous" stochastic process. It generates T_2 in a way that is not in thrall to T_1 but is "inspired by it." (A human translator might be imagined to behave similarly.) When choosing how to expand nodes of T_2, we are influenced both by the structure of T_1 and by monolingual preferences about the structure of T_2. Just as conditional Markov models can more easily incorporate global features than HMMs, we can look at the entire tree T_1 at every stage in generating T_2.

2 Quasi-Synchronous Grammar

Given an input S_1 or its parse T_1, a quasi-synchronous grammar (QG) constructs a monolingual grammar for parsing, or generating, the possible translations S_2—that is, a grammar for finding appropriate trees T_2. What ties this target-language grammar to the source-language input? The grammar provides for target-language words to take on

[1] The usual presentation describes a process that generates T_1 and T_2 jointly, leading to a joint model $p(T_2, A, T_1)$. Dividing by the marginal $p(T_1)$ gives a conditional model $p(T_2, A \mid T_1)$ as in (1). In the text, we directly describe an equivalent conditional process for generating T_2, A given T_1.

[2] When one moves beyond CFG, the derived trees T_1 and T_2 are still produced from a single derivation tree, but may be shaped differently from the derivation tree and from each other.

[3] For tree-to-tree alignment, Gildea proposed a *clone* operation that allowed subtrees of the source tree to be reused in generating a target tree. In order to preserve dynamic programming constraints, the identity of the cloned subtree is chosen independently of its insertion point. This breakage of monotonic tree alignment moves Gildea's alignment model from synchronous to quasi-synchronous.

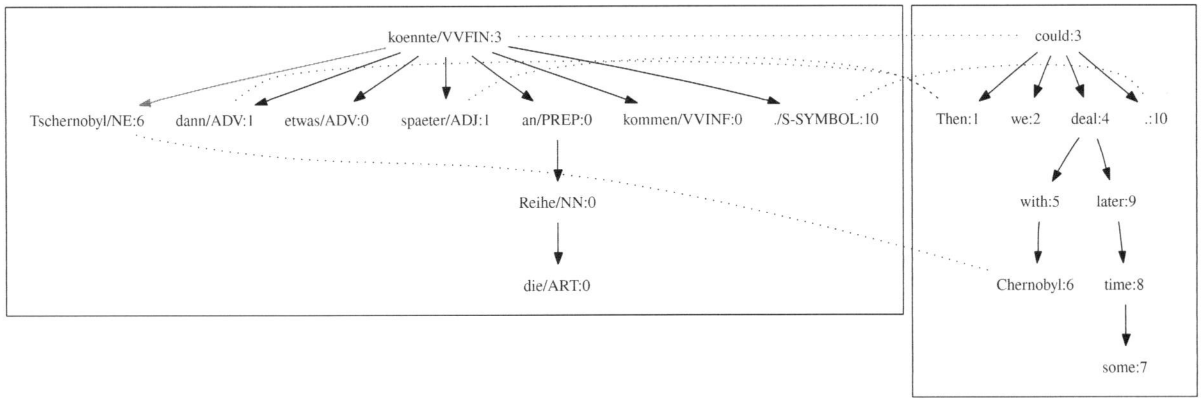

Figure 1: German and English dependency parses and their alignments from our system where German is the target language. *Tschernobyl* depends on *könnte* even though their English analogues are not in a dependency relationship. Note the parser's error in not attaching *etwas* to *später*.
German: *Tschernobyl könnte dann etwas später an die Reihe kommen .*
Literally: Chernobyl could then somewhat later on the queue come.
English: *Then we could deal with Chernobyl some time later .*

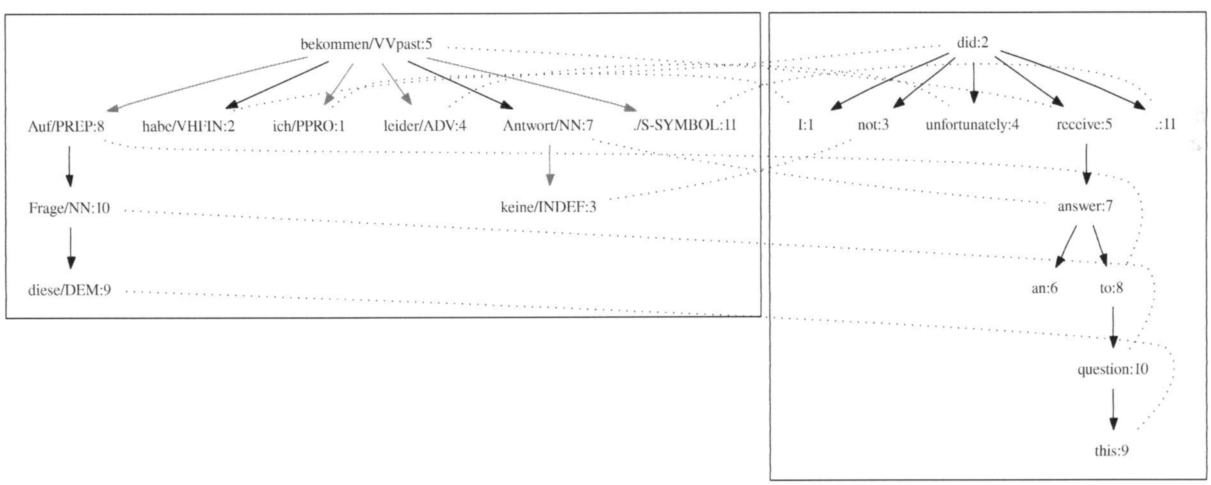

Figure 2: Here the German sentence exhibits scrambling of the phrase *auf diese Frage* and negates the object of *bekommen* instead of the verb itself.
German: *Auf diese Frage habe ich leider keine Antwort bekommen .*
Literally: To this question have I unfortunately no answer received.
English: *I did not unfortunately receive an answer to this question .*

multiple hidden "senses," which correspond to (possibly empty sets of) word tokens in S_1 or nodes in T_1. To take a familiar example, when parsing the English side of a French-English bitext, the word *bank* might have the sense *banque* (financial) in one sentence and *rive* (littoral) in another.

The QG[4] considers the "sense" of the former *bank* token to be a pointer to the particular *banque* token to which it aligns. Thus, a particular assignment of S_1 "senses" to word tokens in S_2 encodes a word alignment.

Now, selectional preferences in the monolingual grammar can be influenced by these T_1-specific senses. So they can encode preferences for how T_2 ought to copy the syntactic structure of T_1. For example, if T_1 contains the phrase *banque nationale*, then the QG for generating a corresponding T_2 may encourage any T_2 English noun whose sense is *banque* (more precisely, T_1's token of *banque*) to generate an adjectival English modifier with sense *nationale*. The exact probability of this, as well as the likely identity and position of that English modifier (e.g., *national bank*), may also be influenced by monolingual facts about English.

2.1 Definition

A quasi-synchronous grammar is a monolingual grammar that generates translations of a source-language sentence. Each state of this monolingual grammar is annotated with a "sense"—a set of zero or more nodes from the source tree or forest.

For example, consider a quasi-synchronous *context-free* grammar (QCFG) for generating translations of a source tree T_1. The QCFG generates the target sentence using nonterminals from the cross product $U \times 2^{V_1}$, where U is the set of monolingual target-language nonterminals such as NP, and V_1 is the set of nodes in T_1.

Thus, a binarized QCFG has rules of the form

$$\langle A, \alpha \rangle \rightarrow \langle B, \beta \rangle \langle C, \gamma \rangle \quad (2)$$

$$\langle A, \alpha \rangle \rightarrow w \quad (3)$$

where $A, B, C \in U$ are ordinary target-language nonterminals, $\alpha, \beta, \gamma \in 2^{V_1}$ are sets of source tree nodes to which A, B, C respectively align, and w is a target-language terminal.

Similarly, a quasi-synchronous tree-substitution grammar (QTSG) annotates the root and frontier nodes of its elementary trees with sets of source nodes from 2^{V_1}.

2.2 Taming Source Nodes

This simple proposal, however, presents two main difficulties. First, the number of possible senses for each target node is exponential in the number of source nodes. Second, note that the senses are sets of source tree nodes, not word types or absolute sentence positions as in some other translation models. Except in the case of identical source trees, source tree nodes will not recur between training and test.

To overcome the first problem, we want further restrictions on the set α in a QG state such as $\langle A, \alpha \rangle$. It should not be an *arbitrary* set of source nodes. In the experiments of this paper, we adopt the simplest option of requiring $|\alpha| \leq 1$. Thus each node in the target tree is aligned to a *single* node in the source tree, or to $\emptyset$ (the traditional NULL alignment). This allows one-to-many but not many-to-one alignments.

To allow many-to-many alignments, one could limit $|\alpha|$ to at most 2 or 3 source nodes, perhaps further requiring the 2 or 3 source nodes to fall in a particular configuration within the source tree, such as child-parent or child-parent-grandparent. With that configurational requirement, the number of possible senses α remains small—at most three times the number of source nodes.

We must also deal with the menagerie of different source tree nodes in different sentences. In other words, how can we tie the parameters of the different QGs that are used to generate translations of different source sentences? The answer is that the probability or weight of a rule such as (2) should depend on the specific nodes in α, β, and γ only through their properties—e.g., their nonterminal labels, their head words, and their grammatical relationship in the source tree. Such properties do recur between training and test.

For example, suppose for simplicity that $|\alpha| = |\beta| = |\gamma| = 1$. Then the rewrite probabilities of (2) and (3) could be log-linearly modeled using features that ask whether the single node in α has two children in the source tree; whether its children in the

[4] By abuse of terminology, we often use "QG" to refer to the T_1-specific monolingual grammar, although the QG is properly a recipe for constructing such a grammar from any input T_1.

source are the nodes in β and γ; whether its nonterminal label in the source is A; whether its fringe in the source translates as w; and so on. The model should also consider monolingual features of (2) and (3), evaluating in particular whether $A \rightarrow BC$ is likely in the target language.

Whether rule weights are given by factored generative models or by naive Bayes or log-linear models, we want to score QG productions with a small set of monolingual and bilingual features.

2.3 Synchronous Grammars Again

Finally, note that synchronous grammar is a special case of quasi-synchronous grammar. In the context-free case, a synchronous grammar restricts senses to single nodes in the source tree and the NULL node. Further, for any k-ary production

$$\langle X_0, \alpha_0 \rangle \rightarrow \qquad \langle X_1, \alpha_1 \rangle \ldots \langle X_k, \alpha_k \rangle$$

a synchronous context-free grammar requires that

1. $(\forall i \neq j)\ \alpha_i \neq \alpha_j$ unless $\alpha_i = \text{NULL}$,
2. $(\forall i > 0)\ \alpha_i$ is a child of α_0 in the source tree, unless $\alpha_i = \text{NULL}$.

Since NULL has no children in the source tree, these rules imply that the children of any node aligned to NULL are themselves aligned to NULL. The construction for synchronous tree-substitution and tree-adjoining grammars goes through similarly but operates on the derivation trees.

3 Parameterizing a QCFG

Recall that our goal is a conditional model of $p(T_2, A \mid T_1)$. For the remainder of this paper, we adopt a dependency-tree representation of T_1 and T_2. Each tree node represents a word of the sentence together with a part-of-speech tag. Syntactic dependencies in each tree are represented directly by the parent-child relationships.

Why this representation? First, it helps us concisely formulate a QG translation model where the source dependencies influence the generation of target dependencies (see figure 3). Second, for evaluation, it is trivial to obtain the word-to-word alignments from the node-to-node alignments. Third, the part-of-speech tags are useful backoff features, and in fact play a special role in our model below.

When stochastically generating a translation T_2, our quasi-synchronous generative process will be influenced by both fluency and adequacy. That is, it considers both the local well-formedness of T_2 (a monolingual criterion) and T_2's local faithfulness to T_1 (a bilingual criterion). We combine these in a simple generative model rather than a log-linear model. When generating the children of a node in T_2, the process first generates their tags using monolingual parameters (fluency), and then fills in in the words using bilingual parameters (adequacy) that select and translate words from T_1.[5]

Concretely, each node in T_2 is labeled by a triple (tag, word, aligned word). Given a parent node (p, h, h') in T_2, we wish to generate sequences of left and right child nodes, of the form (c, a, a').

Our *monolingual parameters* come from a simple generative model of syntax used for grammar induction: the Dependency Model with Valence (DMV) of Klein and Manning (2004). In scoring dependency attachments, DMV uses tags rather than words. The parameters of the model are:

1. $p_{choose}(c \mid p, dir)$: the probability of generating c as the next child tag in the sequence of dir children, where $dir \in \{left, right\}$.
2. $p_{stop}(s \mid h, dir, adj)$: the probability of generating no more child tags in the sequence of dir children. This is conditioned in part on the "adjacency" $adj \in \{true, false\}$, which indicates whether the sequence of dir children is empty so far.

Our *bilingual parameters* score word-to-word translation and aligned dependency configurations. We thus use the conditional probability $p_{trans}(a \mid a')$ that source word a', which may be NULL, translates as target word a. Finally, when a parent word h aligned to h' generates a child, we stochastically decide to align the child to a node a' in T_1 with one several possible relations to h'. A "monotonic" dependency alignment, for example, would have h' and a' in a parent-child relationship like their target-tree analogues. In different versions of the model, we allowed various dependency alignment configurations (figure 3). These configurations rep-

[5]This division of labor is somewhat artificial, and could be remedied in a log-linear model, Naive Bayes model, or deficient generative model that generates both tags and words conditioned on both monolingual and bilingual context.

resent cases where the parent-child dependency being generated by the QG in the target language maps onto source-language child-parent, for head swapping; the same source node, for two-to-one alignment; nodes that are siblings or in a c-command relationship, for scrambling and extraposition; or in a grandparent-grandchild relationship, e.g. when a preposition is inserted in the source language. We also allowed a "none-of-the-above" configuration, to account for extremely mismatched sentences.

The probability of the target-language dependency treelet rooted at h is thus:

$$P(D(h) \mid h, h', p) = \prod_{dir \in \{l,r\}} \prod_{c \in deps_D(p,dir)} P(D(c) \mid a, a', c) \times p_{stop}(nostop \mid p, dir, adj) \times p_{choose}(c \mid p, dir) \times p_{config}(config) \times p_{trans}(a \mid a') \; p_{stop}(stop \mid p, dir, adj)$$

4 Experiments

We claim that for modeling human-translated bitext, it is better to project syntax only loosely. To evaluate this claim, we train quasi-synchronous dependency grammars that allow progressively more divergence from monotonic tree alignment. We evaluate these models on cross-entropy over held-out data and on error rate in a word-alignment task.

One might doubt the use of dependency trees for alignment, since Gildea (2004) found that constituency trees aligned better. That experiment, however, aligned only the 1-best parse trees. We too will consider only the 1-best source tree T_1, but in constrast to Gildea, we will search for the target tree T_2 that aligns best with T_1. Finding T_2 and the alignment is simply a matter of parsing S_2 with the QG derived from T_1.

4.1 Data and Training

We performed our modeling experiments with the German-English portion of the Europarl European Parliament transcripts (Koehn, 2002). We obtained monolingual parse trees from the Stanford German and English parsers (Klein and Manning, 2003). Initial estimates of lexical translation probabilities came from the IBM Model 4 translation tables produced by GIZA++ (Brown et al., 1993; Och and Ney, 2003).

All text was lowercased and numbers of two or more digits were converted to an equal number of hash signs. The bitext was divided into training sets of 1K, 10K, and 100K sentence pairs. We held out one thousand sentences for evaluating the cross-entropy of the various models and hand-aligned 100 sentence pairs to evaluate alignment error rate (AER).

We trained the model parameters on bitext using the Expectation-Maximization (EM) algorithm. The T_1 tree is fully observed, but we parse the target language. As noted, the initial lexical translation probabilities came from IBM Model 4. We initialized the monolingual DMV parameters in one of two ways: using either simple tag co-occurrences as in (Klein and Manning, 2004) or "supervised" counts from the monolingual target-language parser. This latter initialization simulates the condition when one has a small amount of bitext but a larger amount of target data for language modeling. As with any monolingual grammar, we perform EM training with the Inside-Outside algorithm, computing inside probabilities with dynamic programming and outside probabilities through backpropagation.

Searching the full space of target-language dependency trees and alignments to the source tree consumed several seconds per sentence. During training, therefore, we constrained alignments to come from the union of GIZA++ Model 4 alignments. These constraints were applied only during training and not during evaluation of cross-entropy or AER.

4.2 Conditional Cross-Entropy of the Model

To test the explanatory power of our QCFG, we evaluated its conditional cross-entropy on held-out data (table 1). In other words, we measured how well a trained QCFG could predict the true translation of novel source sentences by summing over all parses of the target given the source. We trained QCFG models under different conditions of bitext size and parameter initialization. However, the principal independent variable was the set of dependency alignment configurations allowed.

From these cross-entropy results, it is clear that strictly synchronous grammar is unwise. We ob-

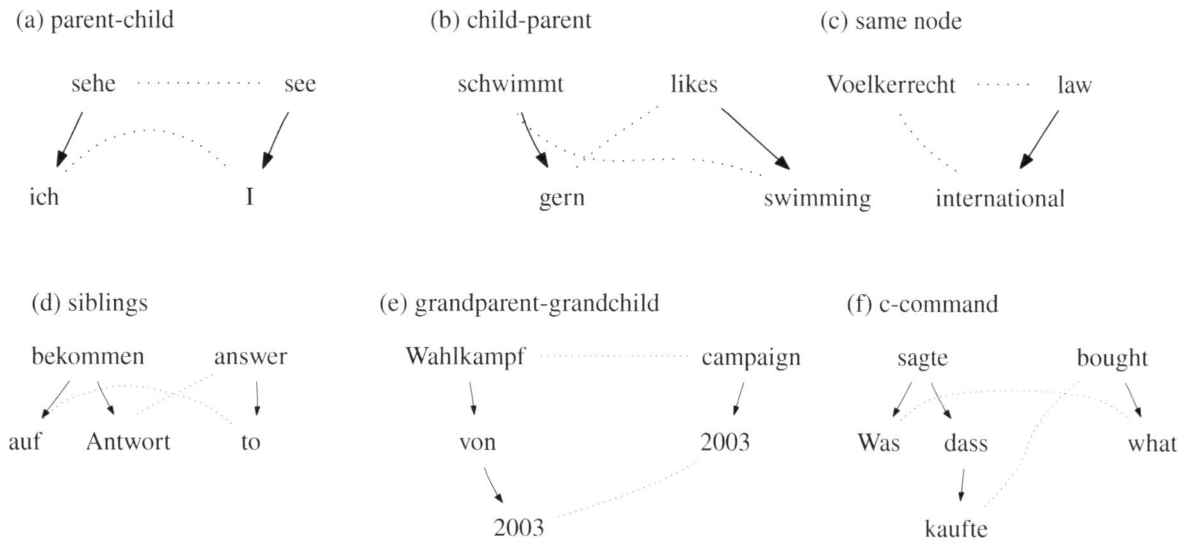

Figure 3: When a head h aligned to h' generates a new child a aligned to a' under the QCFG, h' and a' may be related in the source tree as, among other things, (a) parent–child, (b) child–parent, (c) identical nodes, (d) siblings, (e) grandparent–grandchild, (f) c-commander–c-commandee, (g) none of the above. Here German is the source and English is the target. Case (g), not pictured above, can be seen in figure 1, in English-German order, where the child-parent pair *Tschernobyl könnte* correspond to the words *Chernobyl* and *could*, respectively. Since *could* dominates *Chernobyl*, they are not in a c-command relationship.

Permitted configurations	CE at 1k	CE 10k	CE 100k
∅ or parent-child (a)	43.82	22.40	13.44
+ child-parent (b)	41.27	21.73	12.62
+ same node (c)	41.01	21.50	12.38
+ all breakages (g)	35.63	18.72	11.27
+ siblings (d)	34.59	18.59	11.21
+ grandparent-grandchild (e)	34.52	**18.55**	**11.17**
+ c-command (f)	**34.46**	18.59	11.27
No alignments allowed	60.86	53.28	46.94

Table 1: Cross-entropy on held-out data with different dependency configurations (figure 3) allowed, for 1k, 10k, and 100k training sentences. The big error reductions arrive when we allow arbitrary non-local alignments in condition (g). Distinguishing some common cases of non-local alignments improves performance further. For comparison, we show cross-entropy when every target language node is unaligned.

tain comparatively poor performance if we require parent-child pairs in the target tree to align to parent-child pairs in the source (or to parent-NULL or NULL-NULL). Performance improves as we allow and distinguish more alignment configurations.

4.3 Word Alignment

We computed standard measures of alignment precision, recall, and error rate on a test set of 100 hand-aligned German sentence pairs with 1300 alignment links. As with many word-alignment evaluations, we do not score links to NULL. Just as for cross-entropy, we see that more permissive alignments lead to better performance (table 2).

Having selected the best system using the cross-entropy measurement, we compare its alignment error rate against the standard GIZA++ Model 4 baselines. As Figure 4 shows, our QCFG for German → English consistently produces better alignments than the Model 4 channel model for the same direction, German → English. This comparison is the appropriate one because both of these models are forced to align each English word to at most one German word. [6]

5 Conclusions

With quasi-synchronous grammars, we have presented a new approach to syntactic MT: constructing a monolingual target-language grammar that describes the aligned translations of a source-language sentence. We described a simple parameterization

[6] For German → English MT, one would use a German → English QCFG as above, but an English → German channel model. In this arguably inappropriate comparison, Figure 4 shows, the Model 4 channel model produces slightly better word alignments than the QG.

Permitted configurations	AER at 1k	AER 10k	AER 100k
∅ or parent-child (a)	40.69	39.03	33.62
+ child-parent (b)	43.17	39.78	33.79
+ same node (c)	43.22	40.86	34.38
+ all breakages (g)	37.63	**30.51**	**25.99**
+ siblings (d)	37.87	33.36	29.27
+ grandparent-grandchild (e)	**36.78**	32.73	28.84
+ c-command (f)	37.04	33.51	27.45

Table 2: Alignment error rate (%) with different dependency configurations allowed.

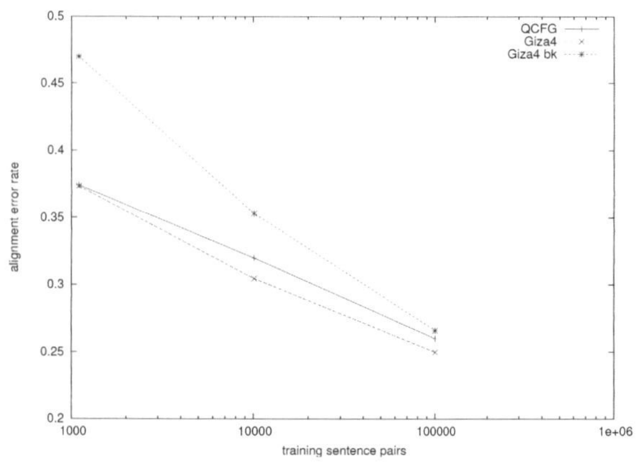

Figure 4: Alignment error rate with best model (all breakages). The QCFG consistently beat one GIZA++ model and was close to the other.

with gradually increasing syntactic domains of locality, and estimated those parameters on German-English bitext.

The QG formalism admits many more nuanced options for features than we have exploited. In particular, we now are exploring log-linear QGs that score overlapping elementary trees of T_2 while considering the syntactic configuration and lexical content of the T_1 nodes to which each elementary tree aligns.

Even simple QGs, however, turned out to do quite well. Our evaluation on a German-English word-alignment task showed them to be competitive with IBM model 4—consistently beating the German-English direction by several percentage points of alignment error rate and within 1% AER of the English-German direction. In particular, alignment accuracy benefited from allowing syntactic breakages between the two dependency structures.

We are also working on a translation decoding using QG. Our first system uses the QG to find optimal T_2 aligned to T_1 and then extracts a synchronous tree-substitution grammar from the aligned trees. Our second system searches a target-language vocabulary for the optimal T_2 given the input T_1.

Acknowledgements

This work was supported by a National Science Foundation Graduate Research Fellowship for the first author and by NSF Grant No. 0313193.

References

H. Alshawi, S. Bangalore, and S. Douglas. 2000. Learning dependency translation models as collections of finite state head transducers. *CL*, 26(1):45–60.

P. F. Brown, S. A. Della Pietra, V. J. Della Pietra, and R. L. Mercer. 1993. The mathematics of statistical machine translation: Parameter estimation. *CL*, 19(2):263–311.

Y. Ding and M. Palmer. 2005. Machine translation using probabilistic synchronous dependency insertion grammars. In *ACL*, pages 541–548.

B. J. Dorr. 1994. Machine translation divergences: A formal description and proposed solution. *Computational Linguistics*, 20(4):597–633.

J. Eisner. 2003. Learning non-isomorphic tree mappings for machine translation. In *ACL Companion Vol.*

H. J. Fox. 2002. Phrasal cohesion and statistical machine translation. In *EMNLP*, pages 392–399.

D. Gildea. 2003. Loosely tree-based alignment for machine translation. In *ACL*, pages 80–87.

D. Gildea. 2004. Dependencies vs. constituents for tree-based alignment. In *EMNLP*, pages 214–221.

R. Hwa, P. Resnik, A. Weinberg, and O. Kolak. 2002. Evaluating translational correspondence using annotation projection. In *ACL*.

D. Klein and C. D. Manning. 2003. Accurate unlexicalized parsing. In *ACL*, pages 423–430.

D. Klein and C. D. Manning. 2004. Corpus-based induction of syntactic structure: Models of dependency and constituency. In *ACL*, pages 479–486.

P. Koehn. 2002. Europarl: A multilingual corpus for evaluation of machine translation. http://www.iccs.informatics.ed.ac.uk/~pkoehn/-publications/europarl.ps.

A. Lavie, S. Vogel, L. Levin, E. Peterson, K. Probst, A. F. Llitjós, R. Reynolds, J. Carbonell, and R. Cohen. 2003. Experiments with a Hindi-to-English transfer-based MT system under a miserly data scenario. *ACM Transactions on Asian Language Information Processing*, 2(2):143 – 163.

I. D. Melamed, G. Satta, and B. Wellington. 2004. Generalized multitext grammars. In *ACL*, pages 661–668.

I. D. Melamed. 2004. Statistical machine translation by parsing. In *ACL*, pages 653–660.

F. J. Och and H. Ney. 2003. A systematic comparison of various statistical alignment models. *CL*, 29(1):19–51.

C. Quirk, A. Menezes, and C. Cherry. 2005. Dependency treelet translation: Syntactically informed phrasal SMT. In *ACL*, pages 271–279.

S. M. Shieber and Y. Schabes. 1990. Synchronous tree-adjoining grammars. In *ACL*, pages 253–258.

D. Wu. 1997. Stochastic inversion transduction grammars and bilingual parsing of parallel corpora. *CL*, 23(3):377–403.

K. Yamada and K. Knight. 2001. A syntax-based statistical translation model. In *ACL*.

Why Generative Phrase Models Underperform Surface Heuristics

John DeNero, Dan Gillick, James Zhang, Dan Klein
Department of Electrical Engineering and Computer Science
University of California, Berkeley
Berkeley, CA 94705
{denero, dgillick, jyzhang, klein}@eecs.berkeley.edu

Abstract

We investigate why weights from generative models underperform heuristic estimates in phrase-based machine translation. We first propose a simple generative, phrase-based model and verify that its estimates are inferior to those given by surface statistics. The performance gap stems primarily from the addition of a hidden segmentation variable, which increases the capacity for overfitting during maximum likelihood training with EM. In particular, while word level models benefit greatly from re-estimation, phrase-level models do not: the crucial difference is that distinct word alignments cannot all be correct, while distinct segmentations can. Alternate segmentations rather than alternate alignments compete, resulting in increased determinization of the phrase table, decreased generalization, and decreased final BLEU score. We also show that interpolation of the two methods can result in a modest increase in BLEU score.

1 Introduction

At the core of a phrase-based statistical machine translation system is a *phrase table* containing pairs of source and target language phrases, each weighted by a conditional translation probability. Koehn et al. (2003a) showed that translation quality is very sensitive to how this table is extracted from the training data. One particularly surprising result is that a simple heuristic extraction algorithm based on surface statistics of a word-aligned training set outperformed the phrase-based generative model proposed by Marcu and Wong (2002).

This result is surprising in light of the reverse situation for word-based statistical translation. Specifically, in the task of word alignment, heuristic approaches such as the Dice coefficient consistently underperform their re-estimated counterparts, such as the IBM word alignment models (Brown et al., 1993). This well-known result is unsurprising: re-estimation introduces an element of *competition* into the learning process. The key virtue of competition in word alignment is that, to a first approximation, only one source word should generate each target word. If a good alignment for a word token is found, other plausible alignments are explained away and should be discounted as incorrect for that token.

As we show in this paper, this effect does not prevail for phrase-level alignments. The central difference is that phrase-based models, such as the ones presented in section 2 or Marcu and Wong (2002), contain an element of *segmentation*. That is, they do not merely learn correspondences between phrases, but also segmentations of the source and target sentences. However, while it is reasonable to suppose that if one alignment is right, others must be wrong, the situation is more complex for segmentations. For example, if one segmentation subsumes another, they are not necessarily incompatible: both may be equally valid. While in some cases, such as idiomatic vs. literal translations, two segmentations may be in true competition, we show that the most common result is for different segmentations to be recruited for different examples, overfitting the training data and overly determinizing the phrase translation estimates.

In this work, we first define a novel (but not radical) generative phrase-based model analogous to IBM Model 3. While its exact training is intractable, we describe a training regime which uses word-level alignments to constrain the space of feasible segmentations down to a manageable number. We demonstrate that the phrase analogue of the Dice coefficient is superior to our generative model (a result also echoing previous work). In the primary contribution of the paper, we present a series of experiments designed to elucidate what re-estimation learns in this context. We show that estimates are overly determinized because segmentations are used

Proceedings of the Workshop on Statistical Machine Translation, pages 31–38,
New York City, June 2006.

in unintuitive ways for the sake of data likelihood. We comment on both the beneficial instances of segment competition (idioms) as well as the harmful ones (most everything else). Finally, we demonstrate that interpolation of the two estimates can provide a modest increase in BLEU score over the heuristic baseline.

2 Approach and Evaluation Methodology

The generative model defined below is evaluated based on the BLEU score it produces in an end-to-end machine translation system from English to French. The top-performing *diag-and* extraction heuristic (Zens et al., 2002) serves as the baseline for evaluation.[1] Each approach – the generative model and heuristic baseline – produces an estimated conditional distribution of English phrases given French phrases. We will refer to the distribution derived from the baseline heuristic as ϕ_H. The distribution learned via the generative model, denoted ϕ_{EM}, is described in detail below.

2.1 A Generative Phrase Model

While our model for computing ϕ_{EM} is novel, it is meant to exemplify a class of models that are not only clear extensions to generative word alignment models, but also compatible with the statistical framework assumed during phrase-based decoding.

The generative process we modeled produces a phrase-aligned English sentence from a French sentence where the former is a translation of the latter. Note that this generative process is opposite to the translation direction of the larger system because of the standard noisy-channel decomposition. The learned parameters from this model will be used to translate sentences from English to French. The generative process modeled has four steps:[2]

1. Begin with a French sentence **f**.
2. Segment **f** into a sequence of I multi-word phrases that span the sentence, $\bar{f}_1^I$.
3. For each phrase $\bar{f}_i \in \bar{f}_1^I$, choose a corresponding position j in the English sentence and establish the alignment $a_j = i$, then generate exactly one English phrase $\bar{e}_j$ from $\bar{f}_i$.
4. The sequence $\bar{e}_j$ ordered by a describes an English sentence **e**.

The corresponding probabilistic model for this generative process is:

$$P(\mathbf{e}|\mathbf{f}) = \sum_{\bar{f}_1^I, \bar{e}_1^I, a} P(\mathbf{e}, \bar{f}_1^I, \bar{e}_1^I, a|\mathbf{f})$$
$$= \sum_{\bar{f}_1^I, \bar{e}_1^I, a} \sigma(\bar{f}_1^I|\mathbf{f}) \prod_{\bar{f}_i \in \bar{f}_1^I} \phi(\bar{e}_j|\bar{f}_i) d(a_j = i|\mathbf{f})$$

where $P(\mathbf{e}, \bar{f}_1^I, \bar{e}_1^I, a|\mathbf{f})$ factors into a segmentation model σ, a translation model ϕ and a distortion model d. The parameters for each component of this model are estimated differently:

- The segmentation model $\sigma(\bar{f}_1^I|\mathbf{f})$ is assumed to be uniform over all possible segmentations for a sentence.[3]
- The phrase translation model $\phi(\bar{e}_j|\bar{f}_i)$ is parameterized by a large table of phrase translation probabilities.
- The distortion model $d(a_j = i|\mathbf{f})$ is a discounting function based on absolute sentence position akin to the one used in IBM model 3.

While similar to the joint model in Marcu and Wong (2002), our model takes a conditional form compatible with the statistical assumptions used by the Pharaoh decoder. Thus, after training, the parameters of the phrase translation model ϕ_{EM} can be used directly for decoding.

2.2 Training

Significant approximation and pruning is required to train a generative phrase model and table – such as ϕ_{EM} – with hidden segmentation and alignment variables using the expectation maximization algorithm (EM). Computing the likelihood of the data

[1] This well-known heuristic extracts phrases from a sentence pair by computing a word-level alignment for the sentence and then enumerating all phrases compatible with that alignment. The word alignment is computed by first intersecting the directional alignments produced by a generative IBM model (e.g., model 4 with minor enhancements) in each translation direction, then adding certain alignments from the union of the directional alignments based on local growth rules.

[2] Our notation matches the literature for phrase-based translation: e is an English word, $\bar{e}$ is an English phrase, and $\bar{e}_1^I$ is a sequence of I English phrases, and **e** is an English sentence.

[3] This segmentation model is deficient given a maximum phrase length: many segmentations are disallowed in practice.

for a set of parameters (the e-step) involves summing over exponentially many possible segmentations for each training sentence. Unlike previous attempts to train a similar model (Marcu and Wong, 2002), we allow information from a word-alignment model to inform our approximation. This approach allowed us to directly estimate translation probabilities even for rare phrase pairs, which were estimated heuristically in previous work.

In each iteration of EM, we re-estimate each phrase translation probability by summing fractional phrase counts (soft counts) from the data given the current model parameters.

$$\phi_{new}(\bar{e}_j|\bar{f}_i) = \frac{c(\bar{f}_i, \bar{e}_j)}{c(\bar{f}_i)} =$$

$$\sum_{(\mathbf{f},\mathbf{e})} \frac{\sum_{\bar{f}_1^I:\bar{f}_i \in \bar{f}_1^I} \sum_{\bar{e}_1^I:\bar{e}_j \in \bar{e}_1^I} \sum_{a:a_j=i} P(\mathbf{e}, \bar{f}_1^I, \bar{e}_1^I, a|\mathbf{f})}{\sum_{\bar{f}_1^I:\bar{f}_i \in \bar{f}_1^I} \sum_{\bar{e}_1^I} \sum_{a} P(\mathbf{e}, \bar{f}_1^I, \bar{e}_1^I, a|\mathbf{f})}$$

This training loop necessitates approximation because summing over all possible segmentations and alignments for each sentence is intractable, requiring time exponential in the length of the sentences. Additionally, the set of possible phrase pairs grows too large to fit in memory. Using word alignments, we can address both problems.[4] In particular, we can determine for any aligned segmentation $(\bar{f}_1^I, \bar{e}_1^I, a)$ whether it is compatible with the word-level alignment for the sentence pair. We define a phrase pair to be compatible with a word-alignment if no word in either phrase is aligned with a word outside the other phrase (Zens et al., 2002). Then, $(\bar{f}_1^I, \bar{e}_1^I, a)$ is compatible with the word-alignment if each of its aligned phrases is a compatible phrase pair.

The training process is then constrained such that, when evaluating the above sum, only compatible aligned segmentations are considered. That is, we allow $P(\mathbf{e}, \bar{f}_1^I, \bar{e}_1^I, a|\mathbf{f}) > 0$ only for aligned segmentations $(\bar{f}_1^I, \bar{e}_1^I, a)$ such that a provides a one-to-one mapping from $\bar{f}_1^I$ to $\bar{e}_1^I$ where all phrase pairs $(\bar{f}_{a_j}, \bar{e}_j)$ are compatible with the word alignment.

This constraint has two important effects. First, we force $P(\bar{e}_j|\bar{f}_i) = 0$ for all phrase pairs not compatible with the word-level alignment for some sentence pair. This restriction successfully reduced the total legal phrase pair types from approximately 250 million to 17 million for 100,000 training sentences. However, some desirable phrases were eliminated because of errors in the word alignments.

Second, the time to compute the e-step is reduced. While in principle it is still intractable, in practice we can compute most sentence pairs' contributions in under a second each. However, some spurious word alignments can disallow all segmentations for a sentence pair, rendering it unusable for training. Several factors including errors in the word-level alignments, sparse word alignments and non-literal translations cause our constraint to rule out approximately 54% of the training set. Thus, the reduced size of the usable training set accounts for some of the degraded performance of ϕ_{EM} relative to ϕ_H. However, the results in figure 1 of the following section show that ϕ_{EM} trained on twice as much data as ϕ_H still underperforms the heuristic, indicating a larger issue than decreased training set size.

2.3 Experimental Design

To test the relative performance of ϕ_{EM} and ϕ_H, we evaluated each using an end-to-end translation system from English to French. We chose this nonstandard translation direction so that the examples in this paper would be more accessible to a primarily English-speaking audience. All training and test data were drawn from the French/English section of the Europarl sentence-aligned corpus. We tested on the first 1,000 unique sentences of length 5 to 15 in the corpus and trained on sentences of length 1 to 60 starting after the first 10,000.

The system follows the structure proposed in the documentation for the Pharaoh decoder and uses many publicly available components (Koehn, 2003b). The language model was generated from the Europarl corpus using the SRI Language Modeling Toolkit (Stolcke, 2002). Pharaoh performed decoding using a set of default parameters for weighting the relative influence of the language, translation and distortion models (Koehn, 2003b). A maximum phrase length of three was used for all experiments.

To properly compare ϕ_{EM} to ϕ_H, all aspects of the translation pipeline were held constant except for the parameters of the phrase translation table. In particular, we did not tune the decoding hyperparameters for the different phrase tables.

[4] The word alignments used in approximating the e-step were the same as those used to create the heuristic *diag-and* baseline.

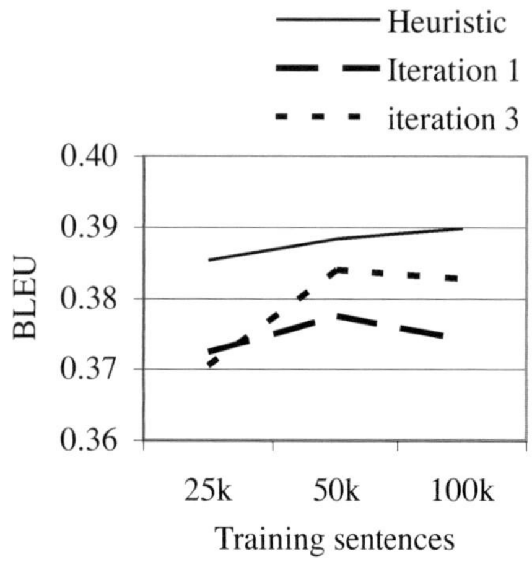

Figure 1: Statistical re-estimation using a generative phrase model degrades BLEU score relative to its heuristic initialization.

3 Results

Having generated ϕ_H heuristically and ϕ_{EM} with EM, we now compare their performance. While the model and training regimen for ϕ_{EM} differ from the model from Marcu and Wong (2002), we achieved results similar to Koehn et al. (2003a): ϕ_{EM} slightly underperformed ϕ_H. Figure 1 compares the BLEU scores using each estimate. Note that the expectation maximization algorithm for training ϕ_{EM} was initialized with the heuristic parameters ϕ_H, so the heuristic curve can be equivalently labeled as iteration 0.

Thus, the first iteration of EM increases the observed likelihood of the training sentences while simultaneously degrading translation performance on the test set. As training proceeds, performance on the test set levels off after three iterations of EM. The system never achieves the performance of its initialization parameters. The pruning of our training regimen accounts for part of this degradation, but not all; augmenting ϕ_{EM} by adding back in all phrase pairs that were dropped during training does not close the performance gap between ϕ_{EM} and ϕ_H.

3.1 Analysis

Learning ϕ_{EM} degrades translation quality in large part because EM learns overly determinized segmentations and translation parameters, overfitting the training data and failing to generalize. The primary increase in richness from generative word-level models to generative phrase-level models is due to the additional latent segmentation variable. Although we impose a uniform distribution over segmentations, it nonetheless plays a crucial role during training. We will characterize this phenomenon through aggregate statistics and translation examples shortly, but begin by demonstrating the model's capacity to overfit the training data.

Let us first return to the motivation behind introducing and learning phrases in machine translation. For any language pair, there are contiguous strings of words whose collocational translation is non-compositional; that is, they translate together differently than they would in isolation. For instance, *chat* in French generally translates to *cat* in English, but *appeler un chat un chat* is an idiom which translates to *call a spade a spade*. Introducing phrases allows us to translate *chat un chat* atomically to *spade a spade* and vice versa.

While introducing phrases and parameterizing their translation probabilities with a surface heuristic allows for this possibility, statistical re-estimation would be required to learn that *chat* should never be translated to *spade* in isolation. Hence, translating *I have a spade* with ϕ_H could yield an error.

But enforcing competition among segmentations introduces a new problem: true translation ambiguity can also be spuriously explained by the segmentation. Consider the french fragment *carte sur la table*, which could translate to *map on the table* or *notice on the chart*. Using these two sentence pairs as training, one would hope to capture the ambiguity in the parameter table as:

French	English	$\phi(e\|f)$
carte	*map*	0.5
carte	*notice*	0.5
carte sur	*map on*	0.5
carte sur	*notice on*	0.5
sur	*on*	1.0
...	...	...
table	*table*	0.5
table	*chart*	0.5

Assuming we only allow non-degenerate segmentations and disallow non-monotonic alignments, this parameter table yields a marginal likelihood $P(\mathbf{f}|\mathbf{e}) = 0.25$ for both sentence pairs – the intuitive result given two independent lexical ambiguities. However, the following table yields a likelihood of 0.28 for both sentences:[5]

French	English	$\phi(e\|f)$
carte	*map*	1.0
carte sur	*notice on*	1.0
carte sur la	*notice on the*	1.0
sur	*on*	1.0
sur la table	*on the table*	1.0
la	*the*	1.0
la table	*the table*	1.0
table	*chart*	1.0

Hence, a higher likelihood can be achieved by allocating some phrases to certain translations while reserving overlapping phrases for others, thereby failing to model the real ambiguity that exists across the language pair. Also, notice that the phrase *sur la* can take on an arbitrary distribution over any english phrases without affecting the likelihood of either sentence pair. Not only does this counterintuitive parameterization give a high data likelihood, but it is also a fixed point of the EM algorithm.

The phenomenon demonstrated above poses a problem for generative phrase models in general. The ambiguous process of translation can be modeled either by the latent segmentation variable or the phrase translation probabilities. In some cases, optimizing the likelihood of the training corpus adjusts for the former when we would prefer the latter. We next investigate how this problem manifests in ϕ_{EM} and its effect on translation quality.

3.2 Learned parameters

The parameters of ϕ_{EM} differ from the heuristically extracted parameters ϕ_H in that the conditional distributions over English translations for some French words are sharply peaked for ϕ_{EM} compared to flatter distributions generated by ϕ_H. This determinism – predicted by the previous section's example – is not atypical of EM training for other tasks.

To quantify the notion of peaked distributions over phrase translations, we compute the entropy of the distribution for each French phrase according to the standard definition.

$$H(\phi(\bar{e}|\bar{f})) = \sum_{\bar{e}} \phi(\bar{e}|\bar{f}) \log_2 \phi(\bar{e}|\bar{f})$$

The average entropy, weighted by frequency, for the most common 10,000 phrases in the learned table was 1.55, comparable to 3.76 for the heuristic table. The difference between the tables becomes much more striking when we consider the histogram of entropies for phrases in figure 2. In particular, the learned table has many more phrases with entropy near zero. The most pronounced entropy differences often appear for common phrases. Ten of the most common phrases in the French corpus are shown in figure 3.

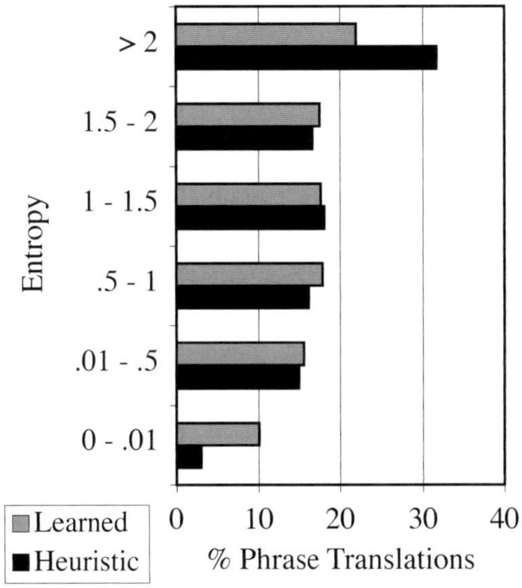

Figure 2: Many more French phrases have very low entropy under the learned parameterization.

As more probability mass is reserved for fewer translations, many of the alternative translations under ϕ_H are assigned prohibitively small probabilities. In translating 1,000 test sentences, for example, no phrase translation with $\phi(\bar{e}|\bar{f})$ less than 10^{-5} was used by the decoder. Given this empirical threshold, nearly 60% of entries in ϕ_{EM} are unusable, compared with 1% in ϕ_H.

3.3 Effects on Translation

While this determinism of ϕ_{EM} may be desirable in some circumstances, we found that the ambiguity in ϕ_H is often preferable at decoding time.

[5]For example, summing over the first translation expands to $\frac{1}{7}(\phi(map \mid carte)\phi(on\ the\ table \mid sur\ la\ table) + \phi(map \mid carte)\phi(on \mid sur)\phi(the\ table \mid la\ table))$.

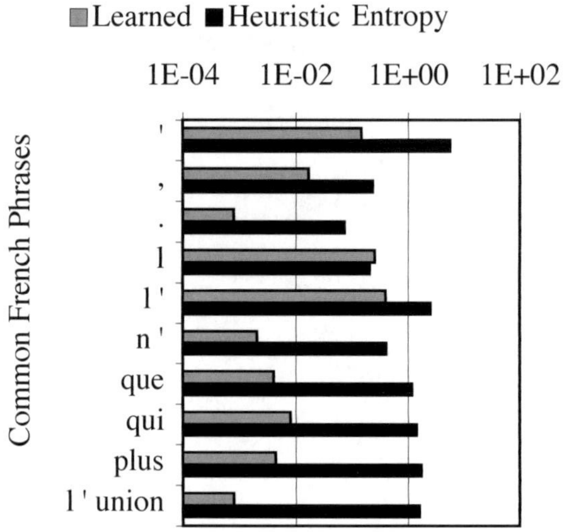

Figure 3: Entropy of 10 common French phrases. Several learned distributions have very low entropy.

In particular, the pattern of translation-ambiguous phrases receiving spuriously peaked distributions (as described in section 3.1) introduces new translation errors relative to the baseline. We now investigate both positive and negative effects of the learning process.

The issue that motivated training a generative model is sometimes resolved correctly: for a word that translates differently alone than in the context of an idiom, the translation probabilities can more accurately reflect this. Returning to the previous example, the phrase table for *chat* has been corrected through the learning process. The heuristic process gives the incorrect translation *spade* with 61% probability, while the statistical learning approach gives *cat* with 95% probability.

While such examples of improvement are encouraging, the trend of spurious determinism overwhelms this benefit by introducing errors in four related ways, each of which will be explored in turn.

1. Useful phrase pairs can be assigned very low probabilities and therefore become unusable.
2. A proper translation for a phrase can be overridden by another translation with spuriously high probability.
3. Error-prone, common, ambiguous phrases become active during decoding.
4. The language model cannot distinguish between different translation options as effectively due to deterministic translation model distributions.

The first effect follows from our observation in section 3.2 that many phrase pairs are unusable due to vanishingly small probabilities. Some of the entries that are made unusable by re-estimation are helpful at decoding time, evidenced by the fact that pruning the set of ϕ_{EM}'s low-scoring learned phrases from the original heuristic table reduces BLEU score by 0.02 for 25k training sentences (below the score for ϕ_{EM}).

The second effect is more subtle. Consider the sentence in figure 4, which to a first approximation can be translated as a series of cognates, as demonstrated by the decoding that follows from the heuristic parameterization ϕ_H.[6] Notice also that the translation probabilities from heuristic extraction are non-deterministic. On the other hand, the translation system makes a significant lexical error on this simple sentence when parameterized by ϕ_{EM}: the use of *caractérise* in this context is incorrect. This error arises from a sharply peaked distribution over English phrases for *caractérise*.

This example illustrates a recurring problem: errors do not necessarily arise because a correct translation is not available. Notice that a preferable translation of degree as *degré* is available under both parameterizations. *Degré* is not used, however, because of the peaked distribution of a competing translation candidate. In this way, very high probability translations can effectively block the use of more appropriate translations at decoding time.

What is furthermore surprising and noteworthy in this example is that the learned, near-deterministic translation for *caractérise* is not a common translation for the word. Not only does the statistical learning process yield low-entropy translation distributions, but occasionally the translation with undesirably high conditional probability does not have a strong surface correlation with the source phrase. This example is not unique; during different initializations of the EM algorithm, we noticed such pat-

[6] While there is some agreement error and awkwardness, the heuristic translation is comprehensible to native speakers. The learned translation incorrectly translates *degree*, degrading the translation quality.

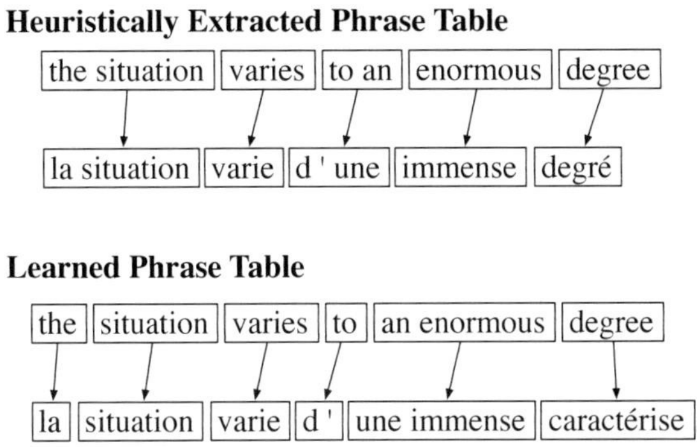

Heuristically extracted — caractérise

English	• (e|f)
characterises	0.49
characterised	0.21
permeate	0.05
features	0.05
typifies	0.05

Heuristically extracted — degré

English	• (e|f)
degree	0.49
level	0.38
extent	0.02
amount	0.02
how	0.01

Learned — caractérise

English	• (e|f)
degree	0.998
characterises	0.001
characterised	0.001

Learned — degré

English	• (e|f)
degree	0.64
level	0.26
extent	0.10

Figure 4: Spurious determinism in the learned phrase parameters degrades translation quality.

terns even for common French phrases such as *de* and *ne*.

The third source of errors is closely related: common phrases that translate in many ways depending on the context can introduce errors if they have a spuriously peaked distribution. For instance, consider the lone apostrophe, which is treated as a single token in our data set (figure 5). The shape of the heuristic translation distribution for the phrase is intuitively appealing, showing a relatively flat distribution among many possible translations. Such a distribution has very high entropy. On the other hand, the learned table translates the apostrophe to *the* with probability very near 1.

Heuristic		Learned	
English	$\phi_H(e\|f)$	English	$\phi_{EM}(e\|f)$
our	0.10	*the*	0.99
that	0.09	*,*	$4.1 \cdot 10^{-3}$
is	0.06	*is*	$6.5 \cdot 10^{-4}$
we	0.05	*to*	$6.3 \cdot 10^{-4}$
next	0.05	*in*	$5.3 \cdot 10^{-4}$

Figure 5: Translation probabilities for an apostrophe, the most common french phrase. The learned table contains a highly peaked distribution.

Such common phrases whose translation depends highly on the context are ripe for producing translation errors. The flatness of the distribution of ϕ_H ensures that the single apostrophe will rarely be used during decoding because no one phrase table entry has high enough probability to promote its use. On the other hand, using the peaked entry $\phi_{EM}(the|')$ incurs virtually no cost to the score of a translation.

The final kind of errors stems from interactions between the language and translation models. The selection among translation choices via a language model – a key virtue of the noisy channel framework – is hindered by the determinism of the translation model. This effect appears to be less significant than the previous three. We should note, however, that adjusting the language and translation model weights during decoding does not close the performance gap between ϕ_H and ϕ_{EM}.

3.4 Improvements

In light of the low entropy of ϕ_{EM}, we could hope to improve translations by retaining entropy. There are several strategies we have considered to achieve this. Broadly, we have tried two approaches: combining ϕ_{EM} and ϕ_H via heuristic interpolation methods and modifying the training loop to limit determinism.

The simplest strategy to increase entropy is to interpolate the heuristic and learned phrase tables. Varying the weight of interpolation showed an improvement over the heuristic of up to 0.01 for 100k sentences. A more modest improvement of 0.003 for 25k training sentences appears in table 1.

In another experiment, we interpolated the output of each iteration of EM with its input, thereby maintaining some entropy from the initialization parameters. BLEU score increased to a maximum of 0.394 using this technique with 100k training sentences, outperforming the heuristic by a slim margin of 0.005.

We might address the determinization in ϕ_{EM} without resorting to interpolation by modifying the training procedure to retain entropy. By imposing a non-uniform segmentation model that favors shorter phrases over longer ones, we hope to prevent the error-causing effects of EM training outlined above. In principle, this change will encourage EM to explain training sentences with shorter sentences. In practice, however, this approach has not led to an improvement in BLEU.

Another approach to maintaining entropy during the training process is to smooth the probabilities generated by EM. In particular, we can use the following smoothed update equation during the training loop, which reserves a portion of probability mass for unseen translations.

$$\phi_{new}(\bar{e}_j|\bar{f}_i) = \frac{c(\bar{f}_i, \bar{e}_j)}{c(\bar{f}_i) + k^{l-1}}$$

In the equation above, l is the length of the French phrase and k is a tuning parameter. This formulation not only serves to reduce very spiked probabilities in ϕ_{EM}, but also boosts the probability of short phrases to encourage their use. With $k = 2.5$, this smoothing approach improves BLEU by .007 using 25k training sentences, nearly equaling the heuristic (table 1).

4 Conclusion

Re-estimating phrase translation probabilities using a generative model holds the promise of improving upon heuristic techniques. However, the combinatorial properties of a phrase-based generative model have unfortunate side effects. In cases of true ambiguity in the language pair to be translated, parameter estimates that explain the ambiguity using segmentation variables can in some cases yield higher data likelihoods by determinizing phrase translation estimates. However, this behavior in turn leads to errors at decoding time.

We have also shown that some modest benefit can be obtained from re-estimation through the blunt instrument of interpolation. A remaining challenge is to design more appropriate statistical models which tie segmentations together unless sufficient evidence of true non-compositionality is present; perhaps such models could properly combine the benefits of both current approaches.

Estimate	BLEU
ϕ_H	0.385
ϕ_H phrase pairs that also appear in ϕ_{EM}	0.365
ϕ_{EM}	0.374
ϕ_{EM} with a non-uniform segmentation model	0.374
ϕ_{EM} with smoothing	0.381
ϕ_{EM} with gaps filled in by ϕ_H	0.374
ϕ_{EM} interpolated with ϕ_H	0.388

Table 1: BLEU results for 25k training sentences.

5 Acknowledgments

We would like to thank the anonymous reviewers for their valuable feedback on this paper.

References

Peter F. Brown, Stephen A. Della Pietra, Vincent J. Della Pietra, and Robert L. Mercer. The mathematics of statistical machine translation: Parameter estimation. *Computational Linguistics*, 19(2), 1993.

Philipp Koehn. *Europarl: A Multilingual Corpus for Evaluation of Machine Translation.* USC Information Sciences Institute, 2002.

Philipp Koehn, Franz Josef Och, and Daniel Marcu. Statistical phrase-based translation. *HLT-NAACL*, 2003.

Philipp Koehn. *Pharaoh: A Beam Search Decoder for Phrase-Based Statisical Machine Translation Models.* USC Information Sciences Institute, 2003.

Daniel Marcu and William Wong. A phrase-based, joint probability model for statistical machine translation. *Conference on Empirical Methods in Natual Language Processing*, 2002.

Franz Josef Och and Hermann Ney. A systematic comparison of various statistical alignment models. *Computational Linguistics*, 29(1):19–51, 2003.

Franz Josef Och, Christoph Tillmann, and Hermann Ney. Improved alignment models for statistical machine translation. *ACL Workshops*, 1999.

Andreas Stolcke. Srilm – an extensible language modeling toolkit. *Proceedings of the International Conference on Statistical Language Processing*, 2002.

Richard Zens, Franz Josef Och and Hermann Ney. Phrase-Based Statistical Machine Translation. *Annual German Conference on AI*, 2002.

Phrase-Based SMT with Shallow Tree-Phrases

Philippe Langlais and Fabrizio Gotti

RALI – DIRO

Université de Montréal,
C.P. 6128 Succ. Centre-Ville
H3C 3J7, Montréal, Canada

{felipe,gottif}@iro.umontreal.ca

Abstract

In this article, we present a translation system which builds translations by gluing together Tree-Phrases, i.e. associations between simple syntactic dependency treelets in a source language and their corresponding phrases in a target language. The Tree-Phrases we use in this study are syntactically informed and present the advantage of gathering source and target material whose words do not have to be adjacent. We show that the phrase-based translation engine we implemented benefits from Tree-Phrases.

1 Introduction

Phrase-based machine translation is now a popular paradigm. It has the advantage of naturally capturing local reorderings and is shown to outperform word-based machine translation (Koehn et al., 2003). The underlying unit (a pair of phrases), however, does not handle well languages with very different word orders and fails to derive generalizations from the training corpus.

Several alternatives have been recently proposed to tackle some of these weaknesses. (Matusov et al., 2005) propose to reorder the source text in order to mimic the target word order, and then let a phrase-based model do what it is good at. (Simard et al., 2005) detail an approach where the standard phrases are extended to account for "gaps" either on the target or source side. They show that this representation has the potential to better exploit the training corpus and to nicely handle differences such as negations in French and English that are poorly handled by standard phrase-based models.

Others are considering translation as a synchronous parsing process e.g. (Melamed, 2004; Ding and Palmer, 2005)) and several algorithms have been proposed to learn the underlying production rule probabilities (Graehl and Knight, 2004; Ding and Palmer, 2004). (Chiang, 2005) proposes an heuristic way of acquiring context free transfer rules that significantly improves upon a standard phrase-based model.

As mentioned in (Ding and Palmer, 2005), most of these approaches require some assumptions on the level of isomorphism (lexical and/or structural) between two languages. In this work, we consider a simple kind of unit: a Tree-Phrase (TP), a combination of a fully lexicalized treelet (TL) and an elastic phrase (EP), the tokens of which may be in non-contiguous positions. TPs capture some syntactic information between two languages and can easily be merged with standard phrase-based engines.

A TP can be seen as a simplification of the treelet pairs manipulated in (Quirk et al., 2005). In particular, we do not address the issue of projecting a source treelet into a target one, but take the bet that collecting (without structure) the target words associated with the words encoded in the nodes of a treelet will suffice to allow translation. This set of target words is what we call an elastic phrase.

We show that these units lead to (modest) improvements in translation quality as measured by automatic metrics. We conducted all our experiments

Proceedings of the Workshop on Statistical Machine Translation, pages 39–46,
New York City, June 2006.

on an in-house version of the French-English Canadian Hansards.

This paper is organized as follows. We first define a Tree-Phrase in Section 2, the unit with which we built our system. Then, we describe in Section 3 the phrase-based MT decoder that we designed to handle TPs. We report in Section 4 the experiments we conducted combining standard phrase pairs and TPs. We discuss this work in Section 5 and then conclude in Section 6.

2 Tree-Phrases

We call *tree-phrase* (TP) a bilingual unit consisting of a source, fully-lexicalized *treelet* (TL) and a target *phrase* (EP), that is, the target words associated with the nodes of the treelet, in order. A treelet can be an arbitrary, fully-lexicalized subtree of the parse tree associated with a source sentence. A phrase can be an arbitrary sequence of words. This includes the standard notion of phrase, popular with phrased-based SMT (Koehn et al., 2003; Vogel et al., 2003) as well as sequences of words that contain gaps (possibly of arbitrary size).

In this study, we collected a repository of tree-phrases using a robust syntactic parser called SYNTEX (Bourigault and Fabre, 2000). SYNTEX identifies syntactic dependency relations between words. It takes as input a text processed by the TREETAGGER part-of-speech tagger.[1] An example of the output SYNTEX produces for the source (French) sentence "on a demandé des crédits fédéraux" (request for federal funding) is presented in Figure 1.

We parsed with SYNTEX the source (French) part of our training bitext (see Section 4.1). From this material, we extracted all dependency subtrees of depth 1 from the complete dependency trees found by SYNTEX. An elastic phrase is simply the list of tokens aligned with the words of the corresponding treelet as well as the respective offsets at which they were found in the target sentence (the first token of an elastic phrase always has an offset of 0).

For instance, the two treelets in Figure 2 will be collected out of the parse tree in Figure 1, yielding 2 tree-phrases. Note that the TLs as well as the EPs might not be contiguous as is for instance the case

[1]www.ims.uni-stuttgart.de/projekte/corplex/.

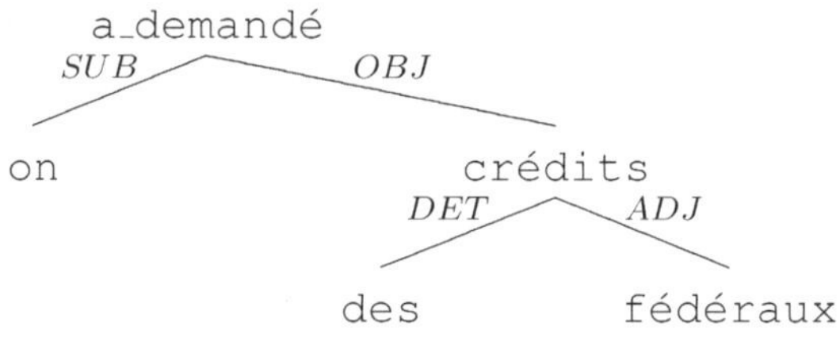

Figure 1: Parse of the sentence "on a demandé des crédits fédéraux" (request for federal funding). Note that the 2 words "a" and "demandé" (literally "have" and "asked") from the original sentence have been merged together by SYNTEX to form a single token. These tokens are the ones we use in this study.

with the first pair of structures listed in the example.

3 The Translation Engine

We built a translation engine very similar to the statistical phrase-based engine PHARAOH described in (Koehn, 2004) that we extended to use tree-phrases. Not only does our decoder differ from PHARAOH by using TPs, it also uses direct translation models. We know from (Och and Ney, 2002) that not using the noisy-channel approach does not impact the quality of the translation produced.

3.1 The maximization setting

For a source sentence f, our engine incrementally generates a set of translation hypotheses $\mathcal{H}$ by combining tree-phrase (TP) units and phrase-phrase (PP) units.[2] We define a hypothesis in this set as $h = \{U_i \equiv (F_i, E_i)\}_{i\in[1,u]}$, a set of u pairs of source (F_i) and target sequences (E_i) of n_i and m_i words respectively:

$$F_i \equiv \{f_{j^i_n} : j^i_n \in [1, |f|]\}_{n\in[1,n_i]}$$
$$E_i \equiv \{e_{l^i_m} : l^i_m \in [1, |e|]\}_{m\in[1,m_i]}$$

under the constraints that for all $i \in [1,u]$, $j^i_n < j^i_{n+1}, \forall n \in [1, n_i[$ for a source *treelet* (similar constraints apply on the target side), and $j^i_{n+1} = j^i_n + 1, \forall n \in [1, n_i[$ for a source *phrase*. The way the hypotheses are built imposes additional constraints between units that will be described in Section 3.3. Note that, at decoding time, $|e|$, the number of words

[2]What we call here a phrase-phrase unit is simply a pair of source/target sequences of words.

alignment:

a_demandé ≡ request for, fédéraux ≡ federal, crédits ≡ funding

treelets:

tree-phrases:

TL*	`{{on@-1} a_demandé {crédits@2}}`
EP*	`|request@0||for@1||funding@3|`
TL	`{{des@-1} crédits {fédéraux@1}}`
EP	`|federal@0||funding@1|`

Figure 2: The Tree-Phrases collected out of the SYNTEX parse for the sentence pair of Figure 1. Non-contiguous structures are marked with a star. Each dependent node of a given governor token is displayed as a list surrounding the governor node, e.g. {governor {right-dependent}}. Along with the tokens of each node, we present their respective offset (the governor/root node has the offset 0 by definition). The format we use to represent the treelets is similar to the one proposed in (Quirk et al., 2005).

of the translation is unknown, but is bounded according to $|f|$ (in our case, $|e|_{max} = 2 \times |f| + 5$).

We define the source and target projection of a hypothesis h by the $proj$ operator which collects *in order* the words of a hypothesis along one language:

$$proj_F(h) = \left\{ f_p : p \in \bigcup_{i=1}^{u} \{j_n^i\}_{n \in [1,n_i]} \right\}$$
$$proj_E(h) = \left\{ e_p : p \in \bigcup_{i=1}^{u} \{l_m^i\}_{m \in [1,m_i]} \right\}$$

If we denote by $\mathcal{H}_f$ the set of hypotheses that have f as a source projection (that is, $\mathcal{H}_f = \{h : proj_F(h) \equiv f\}$), then our translation engine seeks $\hat{e} = proj_E(\hat{h})$ where:

$$\hat{h} = \underset{h \in \mathcal{H}_f}{\text{argmax}}\, s(h)$$

The function we seek to maximize $s(h)$ is a log-linear combination of 9 components, and might be better understood as the numerator of a maximum entropy model popular in several statistical MT systems (Och and Ney, 2002; Bertoldi et al., 2004; Zens and Ney, 2004; Simard et al., 2005; Quirk et al., 2005). The components are the so-called feature functions (described below) and the weighting coefficients (λ) are the parameters of the model:

$$\begin{aligned} s(h) = \; & \lambda_{pp_{rf}} \log p_{pp_{rf}}(h) + \lambda_p |h| + \\ & \lambda_{tp_{rf}} \log p_{tp_{rf}}(h) + \lambda_t |h| + \\ & \lambda_{pp_{ibm}} \log p_{pp_{ibm}}(h) + \\ & \lambda_{tp_{ibm}} \log p_{tp_{ibm}}(h) + \\ & \lambda_{lm} \log p_{lm}(proj_E(h)) + \\ & \lambda_d\, d(h) + \lambda_w |proj_E(h)| \end{aligned}$$

3.2 The components of the scoring function

We briefly enumerate the features used in this study.

Translation models Even if a tree-phrase is a generalization of a standard phrase-phrase unit, for investigation purposes, we differentiate in our MT system between two kinds of models: a TP-based model p_{tp} and a phrase-phrase model p_{pp}. Both rely on conditional distributions whose parameters are learned over a corpus. Thus, each model is assigned its own weighting coefficient, allowing the tuning process to bias the engine toward a special kind of unit (TP or PP).

We have, for $k \in \{\text{rf}, \text{ibm}\}$:

$$\begin{aligned} p_{pp_k}(h) &= \textstyle\prod_{i=1}^{u} p_{pp}(E_i|F_i) \\ p_{tp_k}(h) &= \textstyle\prod_{i=1}^{u} p_{tp}(E_i|F_i) \end{aligned}$$

with $p_{\bullet_{rf}}$ standing for a model trained by relative frequency, whereas $p_{\bullet_{ibm}}$ designates a non-normalized score computed by an IBM model-1 translation model p, where f_0 designates the so-called NULL word:

$$p_{\bullet_{ibm}}(E_i|F_i) = \prod_{m=1}^{m_i} \sum_{n=1}^{n_i} p(e_{l_m^i}|f_{j_n^i}) + p(e_{k_m^i}|f_0)$$

Note that by setting $\lambda_{tp_{rf}}$ and $\lambda_{tp_{ibm}}$ to zero, we revert back to a standard phrase-based translation engine. This will serve as a reference system in the experiments reported (see Section 4).

The language model Following a standard practice, we use a trigram target language model $p_{lm}(proj_E(h))$ to control the fluency of the translation produced. See Section 3.3 for technical subtleties related to their use in our engine.

Distortion model d This feature is very similar to the one described in (Koehn, 2004) and only depends on the offsets of the source units. The only difference here arises when TPs are used to build a translation hypothesis:

$$d(h) = -\sum_{i=1}^{n} abs(1 + \overline{F}_{i-1} - \underline{F}_i)$$

where:

$$\overline{F}_i = \begin{cases} \sum_{n\in[1,n_i]} j^i_n / n_i & \text{if } F_i \text{ is a treelet} \\ j^i_{n_i} & \text{otherwise} \end{cases}$$
$$\underline{F}_i = j^i_1$$

This score encourages the decoder to produce a monotonous translation, unless the language model strongly privileges the opposite.

Global bias features Finally, three simple features help control the translation produced. Each TP (resp. PP) unit used to produce a hypothesis receives a fixed weight λ_t (resp. λ_p). This allows the introduction of an artificial bias favoring either PPs or TPs during decoding. Each target word produced is furthermore given a so-called word penalty λ_w which provides a weak way of controlling the preference of the decoder for long or short translations.

3.3 The search procedure

The search procedure is described by the algorithm in Figure 3. The first stage of the search consists in collecting all the units (TPs or PPs) whose source part matches the source sentence f. We call U the set of those matching units.

In this study, we apply a simple match policy that we call *exact match* policy. A TL t matches a source sentence f if its root matches f at a source position denoted r and if all the other words w of t satisfy:

$$f_{o_w+r} = w$$

where o_w designates the offset of w in t.

Hypotheses are built synchronously along with the target side (by appending the target material to the right of the translation being produced) by progressively covering the positions of the source sentence f being translated.

Require: a source sentence f
  $U \leftarrow \{u : \text{s-match}(u, f)\}$
  FUTURECOST(U)
  for $s \leftarrow 1$ to $|f|$ **do**
    $S[s] \leftarrow \emptyset$

  $S[0] \leftarrow \{(\emptyset, \epsilon, 0)\}$
  for $s \leftarrow 0$ to $|f| - 1$ **do**
    PRUNE($S[s], \beta$)
    for all hypotheses alive $h \in S[s]$ **do**
      for all $u \in U$ **do**
        if EXTENDS(u, h) **then**
          $h' \leftarrow$ UPDATE(u, h)
          $k \leftarrow |proj_F(h')|$
          $S[k] \leftarrow S[k] \cup \{h'\}$

  return $\text{argmax}_{h\in S[|f|]}\, \rho : h \rightarrow (p_s, t, \rho)$

Figure 3: The search algorithm. The symbol $\leftarrow$ is used in place of assignments, while $\rightarrow$ denotes unification (as in languages such as Prolog).

The search space is organized into a set S of $|f|$ stacks, where a stack $S[s]$ ($s \in [1, |f|]$) contains all the hypotheses covering exactly s source words. A hypothesis $h = (p_s, t, \rho)$ is composed of its target material t, the source positions covered p_s as well as its score ρ. The search space is initialized with an empty hypothesis: $S[0] = \{(\emptyset, \epsilon, 0)\}$.

The search procedure consists in extending each partial hypothesis h with every unit that can continue it. This process ends when all partial hypotheses have been expanded. The translation returned is the best one contained in $S[|f|]$:

$$\hat{e} = proj_E(\underset{h\in S[|f|]}{\text{argmax}}\, \rho : h \rightarrow (p_s, t, \rho))$$

PRUNE — In order to make the search tractable, each stack $S[s]$ is pruned before being expanded. Only the hypotheses whose scores are within a fraction (controlled by a meta-parameter β which typically is 0.0001 in our experiments) of the score of the best hypothesis in that stack are considered for expansion. We also limit the number of hypotheses maintained in a given stack to the top `maxStack` ones (`maxStack` is typically set to 500).

Because beam-pruning tends to promote in a stack partial hypotheses that translate easy parts (i.e. parts that are highly scored by the translation and language models), the score considered while pruning not only involves the cost of a partial hypothesis so far, but also an estimation of the future cost that will be incurred by fully expanding it.

FUTURECOST — We followed the heuristic described in (Koehn, 2004), which consists in computing for each source range $[i, j]$ the minimum cost $c(i, j)$ with which we can translate the source sequence f_i^j. This is pre-computed efficiently at an early stage of the decoding (second line of the algorithm in Figure 3) by a bottom-up dynamic programming scheme relying on the following recursion:

$$c(i,j) = min \begin{cases} min_{k \in [i,j[} c(i,k) + c(k,j) \\ min_{u \in U / u_s \cap f_i^j = u_s} score(u_s) \end{cases}$$

where u_s stands for the projection of u on the target side ($u_s \equiv proj_E(u)$), and $score(u)$ is computed by considering the language model and the translation components p_{pp} of the $s(h)$ score. The future cost of h is then computed by summing the cost $c(i, j)$ of all its empty source ranges $[i, j]$.

EXTENDS — When we simply deal with standard (contiguous) phrases, extending a hypothesis h by a unit u basically requires that the source positions of u be empty in h. Then, the target material of u is appended to the current hypothesis h.

Because we work with treelets here, things are a little more intricate. Conceptually, we are confronted with the construction of a (partial) source dependency tree while collecting the target material in order. Therefore, the decoder needs to check whether a given TL (the source part of u) is compatible with the TLs belonging to h. Since we decided in this study to use depth-one treelets, we consider that two TLs are *compatible* if either they do not share any source word, or, if they do, this shared word must be the governor of one TL and a dependent in the other TL.

So, for instance, in the case of Figure 2, the two treelets are deemed compatible (they obviously should be since they both belong to the same original parse tree) because `crédit` is the governor in the right-hand treelet while being the dependent in the left-hand one. On the other hand, the two treelets in Figure 4 are not, since `président` is the governor of both treelets, even though `mr. le président suppléant` would be a valid source phrase. Note that it might be the case that the treelet `{{mr.@-2} {le@-1} président {suppléant@1}}` has been observed during training, in which case it will compete with the treelets in Figure 2.

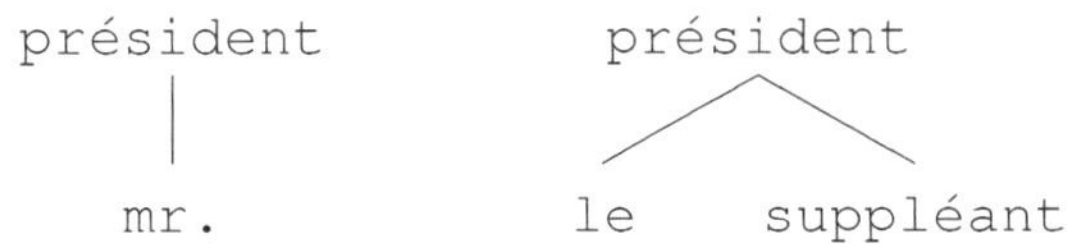

Figure 4: Example of two incompatible treelets. `mr. speaker` and `the acting speaker` are their respective English translations.

Therefore, extending a hypothesis containing a treelet with a new treelet consists in merging the two treelets (if they are compatible) and combining the target material accordingly. This operation is more complicated than in a standard phrase-based decoder since we allow gaps on the target side as well. Moreover, the target material of two compatible treelets may intersect. This is for instance the case for the two TPs in Figure 2 where the word `funding` is common to both phrases.

UPDATE — Whenever u extends h, we add a new hypothesis h' in the corresponding stack $S[|proj_F(h')|]$. Its score is computed by adding to that of h the score of each component involved in $s(h)$. For all but the one language model component, this is straightforward. However, care must be taken to update the language model score since the target material of u does not come necessarily right after that of h as would be the case if we only manipulated PP units.

Figure 5 illustrates the kind of bookkeeping required. In practice, the target material of a hypothesis is encoded as a vector of triplets $\{\langle w_i, \log p_{lm}(w_i|c_i), l_i\rangle\}_{i \in [1, |e|_{max}]}$ where w_i is the word at position i in the translation, $\log p_{lm}(w_i|c_i)$ is its score as given by the language model, c_i denotes the largest conditioning context possible, and l_i indicates the length (in words) of c_i (0 means a unigram probability, 1 a bigram probability and 2 a trigram probability). This vector is updated at each extension.

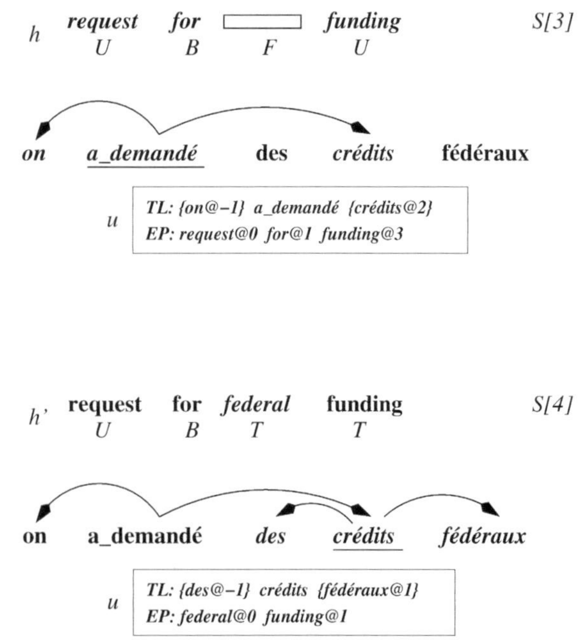

Figure 5: Illustration of the language model updates that must be made when a new target unit (circles with arrows represent dependency links) extends an existing hypothesis (rectangles). The tag inside each occupied target position shows whether this word has been scored by a **U**nigram, a **B**igram or a **T**rigram probability.

4 Experimental Setting

4.1 Corpora

We conducted our experiments on an in-house version of the Canadian Hansards focussing on the translation of French into English. The split of this material into train, development and test corpora is detailed in Table 1. The TEST corpus is subdivided in 16 (disjoints) slices of 500 sentences each that we translated separately. The vocabulary is atypically large since some tokens are being merged by SYNTEX, such as `étaient#financées` (`were financed` in English).

The training corpus has been aligned at the word level by two Viterbi word-alignments (*French2English* and *English2French*) that we combined in a heuristic way similar to the *refined* method described in (Och and Ney, 2003). The parameters of the word models (IBM model 2) were trained with the GIZA++ package (Och and Ney, 2000).

	TRAIN	DEV	TEST
sentences	1 699 592	500	8000
e-toks	27 717 389	8 160	130 192
f-toks	30 425 066	8 946	143 089
e-toks/sent	16.3 ($\pm$ 9.0)	16.3 ($\pm$ 9.1)	16.3 ($\pm$ 9.0)
f-toks/sent	17.9 ($\pm$ 9.5)	17.9 ($\pm$ 9.5)	17.9 ($\pm$ 9.5)
e-types	164 255	2 224	12 591
f-types	210 085	2 481	15 008
e-hapax	68 506	1 469	6 887
f-hapax	90 747	1 704	8 612

Table 1: Main characteristics of the corpora used in this study. For each language *l*, *l*-toks is the number of tokens, *l*-toks/sent is the average number of tokens per sentence ($\pm$ the standard deviation), *l*-types is the number of different token forms and *l*-hapax is the number of tokens that appear only once in the corpus.

4.2 Models

Tree-phrases Out of 1.7 million pairs of sentences, we collected more than 3 million different kinds of TLs from which we projected 6.5 million different kinds of EPs. Slightly less than half of the treelets are contiguous ones (i.e. involving a sequence of adjacent words); 40% of the EPs are contiguous. When the respective frequency of each TL or EP is factored in, we have approximately 11 million TLs and 10 million EPs. Roughly half of the treelets collected have exactly two dependents (three word long treelets).

Since the word alignment of non-contiguous phrases is likely to be less accurate than the alignment of adjacent word sequences, we further filter the repository of TPs by keeping the most likely EPs for each TL according to an estimate of $p(EP|TL)$ that do not take into account the offsets of the EP or the TL.

PP-model We collected the PP parameters by simply reading the alignment matrices resulting from the word alignment, in a way similar to the one described in (Koehn et al., 2003). We use an in-house tool to collect pairs of phrases of up to 8 words. Freely available packages such as THOT (Ortiz-Martínez et al., 2005) could be used as well for that purpose.

Language model We trained a Kneser-Ney trigram language model using the SRILM toolkit (Stolcke, 2002).

4.3 Protocol

We compared the performances of two versions of our engine: one which employs TPs ans PPs (TP-ENGINE hereafter), and one which only uses PPs (PP-ENGINE). We translated the 16 disjoint subcorpora of the TEST corpus with and without TPs.

We measure the quality of the translation produced with three automatic metrics. Two error rates: the sentence error rate (SER) and the word error rate (WER) that we seek to minimize, and BLEU (Papineni et al., 2002), that we seek to maximize. This last metric was computed with the `multi-bleu.perl` script available at `www.statmt.org/wmt06/shared-task/`.

We separately tuned both systems on the DEV corpus by applying a brute force strategy, i.e. by sampling uniformly the range of each parameter (λ) and picking the configuration which led to the best BLEU score. This strategy is inelegant, but in early experiments we conducted, we found better configurations this way than by applying the Simplex method with multiple starting points. The tuning roughly takes 24 hours of computation on a cluster of 16 computers clocked at 3 GHz, but, in practice, we found that one hour of computation is sufficient to get a configuration whose performances, while subobptimal, are close enough to the best one reachable by an exhaustive search.

Both configurations were set up to avoid distortions exceeding 3 (`maxDist = 3`). Stacks were allowed to contain no more than 500 hypotheses (`maxStack = 500`) and we further restrained the number of hypotheses considered by keeping for each matching unit (treelet or phrase) the 5 best ranked target associations. This setting has been fixed experimentally on the DEV corpus.

4.4 Results

The scores for the 16 slices of the test corpus are reported in Table 2. TP-ENGINE shows slightly better figures for all metrics.

For each system and for each metric, we had 16 scores (from each of the 16 slices of the test corpus) and were therefore able to test the statistical significance of the difference between the TP-ENGINE and PP-ENGINE using a Wilcoxon signed-rank test for paired samples. This test showed that the difference observed between the two systems is significant at the 95% probability level for BLEU and significant at the 99% level for WER and SER.

Engine	WER%	SER%	BLEU%
PP	52.80 ± 1.2	94.32 ± 0.9	29.95 ± 1.2
TP	51.98 ± 1.2	92.83 ± 1.3	30.47 ± 1.4

Table 2: Median WER, SER and BLEU scores (± value range) of the translations produced by the two engines on a test set of 16 disjoint corpora of 500 sentences each. The figures reported are percentages.

On the DEV corpus, we measured that, on average, each source sentence is covered by 39 TPs (their source part, naturally), yielding a source coverage of approximately 70%. In contrast, the average number of covering PPs per sentence is 233.

5 Discussion

On a comparable test set (Canadian Hansard texts), (Simard et al., 2005) report improvements by adding non-contiguous bi-phrases to their engine without requiring a parser at all. At the same time, they also report negative results when adding non-contiguous phrases computed from the refined alignment technique that we used here.

Although the results are not directly comparable, (Quirk et al., 2005) report much larger improvements over a phrase-based statistical engine with their translation engine that employs a source parser. The fact that we consider only depth-one treelets in this work, coupled with the absence of any particular treelet projection algorithm (which prevents us from training a syntactically motivated reordering model as they do) are other possible explanations for the modest yet significant improvements we observe in this study.

6 Conclusion

We presented a pilot study aimed at appreciating the potential of Tree-Phrases as base units for example-based machine translation.

We developed a translation engine which makes use of tree-phrases on top of pairs of source/target sequences of words. The experiments we conducted suggest that TPs have the potential to improve translation quality, although the improvements we measured are modest, yet statistically significant.

We considered only one simple form of tree in this study: depth-one subtrees. We plan to test our engine on a repository of treelets of arbitrary depth. In theory, there is not much to change in our engine to account for such units and it would offer an alternative to the system proposed recently by (Liu et al., 2005), which performs translations by recycling a collection of tree-string-correspondence (TSC) examples.

References

Nicola Bertoldi, Roldano Cattoni, Mauro Cettolo, and Marcello Federico. 2004. The ITC-irst statistical machine translation system for IWSLT-2004. In *IWSLT*, pages 51–58, Kyoto, Japan.

Didier Bourigault and Cécile Fabre. 2000. Approche linguistique pour l'analyse syntaxique de corpus. *Cahiers de Grammaire*, (25):131–151. Toulouse le Mirail.

David Chiang. 2005. A hierarchical phrase-based model for statistical machine translation. In *43rd ACL*, pages 263–270, Ann Arbor, Michigan, USA.

Yuang Ding and Martha Palmer. 2004. Automatic learning of parallel dependency treelet pairs. In *Proceedings of the first International Joint Conference on NLP*.

Yuan Ding and Martha Palmer. 2005. Machine translation using probabilistic synchronous dependency insertion grammars. In *43rd ACL*, pages 541–548, Ann Arbor, Michigan, June.

Jonathan Graehl and Kevin Knight. 2004. Training tree transducers. In *HLT-NAACL 2004*, pages 105–112, Boston, Massachusetts, USA, May 2 - May 7. Association for Computational Linguistics.

Philipp Koehn, Franz Joseph Och, and Daniel Marcu. 2003. Statistical Phrase-Based Translation. In *Proceedings of HLT*, pages 127–133.

Philipp Koehn. 2004. Pharaoh: a Beam Search Decoder for Phrase-Based SMT. In *Proceedings of AMTA*, pages 115–124.

Zhanyi Liu, Haifeng Wang, and Hua Wu. 2005. Example-based machine translation based on tsc and statistical generation. In *Proceedings of MT Summit X*, pages 25–32, Phuket, Thailand.

Evgeny Matusov, Stephan Kanthak, and Hermann Ney. 2005. Efficient statistical machine translation with constraint reordering. In *10th EAMT*, pages 181–188, Budapest, Hongary, May 30-31.

I. Dan Melamed. 2004. Statistical machine translation by parsing. In *42nd ACL*, pages 653–660, Barcelona, Spain.

Franz Joseph Och and Hermann Ney. 2000. Improved Statistical Alignment Models. In *Proceedings of ACL*, pages 440–447, Hongkong, China.

Franz Joseph Och and Hermann Ney. 2002. Discriminative training and maximum entropy models for statistical machine translation. In *Proceedings of the ACL*, pages 295–302.

Franz Joseph Och and Hermann Ney. 2003. A Systematic Comparison of Various Statistical Alignment Models. *Computational Linguistics*, 29:19–51.

Daniel Ortiz-Martínez, Ismael Garciá-Varea, and Francisco Casacuberta. 2005. Thot: a toolkit to train phrase-based statistical translation models. In *Proceedings of MT Summit X*, pages 141–148, Phuket, Thailand, Sep.

Kishore Papineni, Salim Roukos, Todd Ward, and Wei-Jing Zhu. 2002. Bleu: a method for automatic evaluation of machine translation. In *40th ACL*, pages 311–318, Philadelphia, Pennsylvania.

Chris Quirk, Arul Menezes, and Colin Cherry. 2005. Dependency treelet translation: Syntactically informed phrasal SMT. In *43rd ACL*, pages 271–279, Ann Arbor, Michigan, June.

Michel Simard, Nicola Cancedda, Bruno Cavestro, Marc Dymetman, Eric Gaussier, Cyril Goutte, Kenji Yamada, Philippe Langlais, and Arne Mauser. 2005. Translating with non-contiguous phrases. In *HLT/EMNLP*, pages 755–762, Vancouver, British Columbia, Canada, Oct.

Andreas Stolcke. 2002. Srilm - an Extensible Language Modeling Toolkit. In *Proceedings of ICSLP*, Denver, Colorado, Sept.

Stephan Vogel, Ying Zhang, Fei Huang, Alicai Tribble, Ashish Venugopal, Bing Zao, and Alex Waibel. 2003. The CMU Statistical Machine Translation System. In *Machine Translation Summit IX*, New Orleans, Louisina, USA, Sep.

Richard Zens and Hermann Ney. 2004. Improvements in phrase-based statistical machine translation. In *Proceedings of the HLT/NAACL*, pages 257–264, Boston, MA, May.

Searching for alignments in SMT. A novel approach based on an Estimation of Distribution Algorithm *

Luis Rodríguez, Ismael García-Varea, José A. Gámez
Departamento de Sistemas Informáticos
Universidad de Castilla-La Mancha
luisr@dsi.uclm.es, ivarea@dsi.uclm.es, jgamez@dsi.uclm.es

Abstract

In statistical machine translation, an alignment defines a mapping between the words in the source and in the target sentence. Alignments are used, on the one hand, to train the statistical models and, on the other, during the decoding process to link the words in the source sentence to the words in the partial hypotheses generated. In both cases, the quality of the alignments is crucial for the success of the translation process. In this paper, we propose an algorithm based on an Estimation of Distribution Algorithm for computing alignments between two sentences in a parallel corpus. This algorithm has been tested on different tasks involving different pair of languages. In the different experiments presented here for the two word-alignment shared tasks proposed in the HLT-NAACL 2003 and in the ACL 2005, the EDA-based algorithm outperforms the best participant systems.

1 Introduction

Nowadays, statistical approach to machine translation constitutes one of the most promising approaches in this field. The rationale behind this approximation is to learn a statistical model from a parallel corpus. A parallel corpus can be defined as a set of sentence pairs, each pair containing a sentence in a source language and a translation of this sentence in a target language. Word alignments are necessary to link the words in the source and in the target sentence. Statistical models for machine translation heavily depend on the concept of alignment, specifically, the well known IBM word based models (Brown et al., 1993). As a result of this, different task on aligments in statistical machine translation have been proposed in the last few years (HLT-NAACL 2003 (Mihalcea and Pedersen, 2003) and ACL 2005 (Joel Martin, 2005)).

In this paper, we propose a novel approach to deal with alignments. Specifically, we address the problem of searching for the best word alignment between a source and a target sentence. As there is no efficient exact method to compute the optimal alignment (known as *Viterbi alignment*) in most of the cases (specifically in the IBM models 3,4 and 5), in this work we propose the use of a recently appeared meta-heuristic family of algorithms, *Estimation of Distribution Algorithms* (EDAs). Clearly, by using a heuristic-based method we cannot guarantee the achievement of the optimal alignment. Nonetheless, we expect that the global search carried out by our algorithm will produce high quality results in most cases, since previous experiments with this technique (Larrañaga and Lozano, 2001) in different optimization task have demonstrated. In addition to this, the results presented in section 5 support the approximation presented here.

This paper is structured as follows. Firstly, Statistical word alignments are described in section 2. Estimation of Distribution Algorithms (EDAs) are

*This work has been supported by the Spanish Projects JCCM (PBI-05-022) and HERMES 05/06 (Vic. Inv. UCLM)

Proceedings of the Workshop on Statistical Machine Translation, pages 47–54,
New York City, June 2006. ©2006 Association for Computational Linguistics

introduced in section 3. An implementation of the search for alignments using an EDA is described in section 4. In section 5, we discuss the experimental issues and show the different results obtained. Finally, some conclussions and future work are discussed in section 6.

2 Word Alignments In Statistical Machine translation

In statistical machine translation, a word alignment between two sentences (a source sentence $\mathbf{f}$ and a target sentence $\mathbf{e}$) defines a mapping between the words $f_1...f_J$ in the source sentence and the words $e_1..e_I$ in the target sentence. The search for the optimal alignment between the source sentence $\mathbf{f}$ and the target sentence $\mathbf{e}$ can be stated as:

$$\hat{\mathbf{a}} = \underset{\mathbf{a} \in A}{\text{argmax}}\, Pr(\mathbf{a}|\mathbf{f}, \mathbf{e}) = \underset{\mathbf{a} \in A}{\text{argmax}}\, Pr(\mathbf{f}, \mathbf{a}|\mathbf{e}) \quad (1)$$

being A the set of all the possible alignments between $\mathbf{f}$ and $\mathbf{e}$.

The transformation made in Eq. (1) allows us to address the alignment problem by using the statitistical approach to machine translation described as follows. This approach can be stated as: a source language string $\mathbf{f} = f_1^J = f_1 \dots f_J$ is to be translated into a target language string $\mathbf{e} = e_1^I = e_1 \dots e_I$. Every target string is regarded as a possible translation for the source language string with maximum a-posteriori probability $Pr(\mathbf{e}|\mathbf{f})$. According to Bayes' decision rule, we have to choose the target string that maximizes the product of both the target language model $Pr(\mathbf{e})$ and the string translation model $Pr(\mathbf{f}|\mathbf{e})$. Alignment models to structure the translation model are introduced in (Brown et al., 1993). These alignment models are similar to the concept of Hidden Markov models (HMM) in speech recognition. The alignment mapping is $j \rightarrow i = a_j$ from source position j to target position $i = a_j$. In statistical alignment models, $Pr(\mathbf{f}, \mathbf{a}|\mathbf{e})$, the alignment $\mathbf{a}$ is usually introduced as a hidden variable. Nevertheless, in the problem described in this article, the source and the target sentences are given, and we are focusing on the optimization of the aligment $\mathbf{a}$.

The translation probability $Pr(\mathbf{f}, \mathbf{a}|\mathbf{e})$ can be rewritten as follows:

$$\begin{aligned} Pr(\mathbf{f}, \mathbf{a}|\mathbf{e}) &= \prod_{j=1}^{J} Pr(f_j, a_j | f_1^{j-1}, a_1^{j-1}, e_1^I) \\ &= \prod_{j=1}^{J} Pr(a_j | f_1^{j-1}, a_1^{j-1}, e_1^I) \\ &\quad \cdot Pr(f_j | f_1^{j-1}, a_1^{j}, e_1^I) \end{aligned} \quad (2)$$

The probability $Pr(\mathbf{f}, \mathbf{a}|\mathbf{e})$ can be estimated by using the word-based IBM statistical alignment models (Brown et al., 1993). These models, however, constrain the set of possible alignments so that each word in the source sentence can be aligned at most to one word in the target sentence. Of course, "real" alignments, in most of the cases, do not follow this limitation. Hence, the alignments obtained from the IBM models have to be extended in some way to achieve more realistic alignments. This is usually performed by computing the alignments in both directions (i.e, first from $\mathbf{f}$ to $\mathbf{e}$ and then from $\mathbf{e}$ to $\mathbf{f}$) and then combining them in a suitable way (this process is known as symmetrization).

3 Estimation of Distribution Algorithms

Estimation of Distribution Algorithms (EDAs) (Larrañaga and Lozano, 2001) are metaheuristics which has gained interest during the last five years due to their high performance when solving combinatorial optimization problems. EDAs, as well as genetics algorithms (Michalewicz, 1996), are population-based evolutionary algorithms but, instead of using genetic operators are based on the estimation/learning and posterior sampling of a probability distribution, which relates the variables or genes forming and individual or chromosome. In this way the dependence/independence relations between these variables can be explicitly modelled in the EDAs framework. The operation mode of a canonical EDA is shown in Figure 1.

As we can see, the algorithm maintains a population of m individuals during the search. An individual is a candidate or potential solution to the problem being optimized, e.g., in the problem considered here an individual would be a possible alignment. Usually, in combinatorial optimization problems an individual is represented as a vector of integers $\mathbf{a} = \langle a_1, \dots, a_J \rangle$, where each position a_j can

1. $D_0 \leftarrow$ Generate the initial population (m individuals)
2. Evaluate the population D_0
3. $k = 1$
4. Repeat
   (a) $D_{tra} \leftarrow$ Select $s \leq m$ individuals from D_{k-1}
   (b) Estimate/learn a new model $\mathcal{M}$ from D_{tra}
   (c) $D_{aux} \leftarrow$ Sample m individuals from $\mathcal{M}$
   (d) Evaluate D_{aux}
   (e) $D_k \leftarrow$ Select m individuals from $D_{k-1} \cup D_{aux}$
   (f) $k = k + 1$

   Until stop condition

Figure 1: A canonical EDA

take a set of finite values $\Omega_{a_j} = \{0, \ldots, I\}$. The first step in an evolutionary algorithm is to generate the initial population D_0. Although D_0 is usually generated randomly (to ensure diversity), prior knowledge can be of utility in this step.

Once we have a population our next step is to evaluate it, that is, we have to measure the goodness or fitness of each individual with respect to the problem we are solving. Thus, we use a fitness function $f(\mathbf{a}) = Pr(\mathbf{f}, \mathbf{a}|\mathbf{e})$ (see Eq. (3)) to score individuals. Evolutionary algorithms in general and EDAs in particular seek to improve the quality of the individuals in the population during the search. In genetic algorithms the main idea is to build a new population from the current one by copying some individuals and constructing new ones from those contained in the current population. Of course, as we aim to improve the quality of the population with respect to fitness, the best/fittest individuals have more chance to be copied or selected for recombination.

In EDAs, the transition between populations is quite different. The basic idea is to summarize the properties of the individuals in the population by learning a probability distribution that describes them as much as possible. Since the quality of the population should be improved in each step, only the s fittest individuals are selected to be included in the dataset used to learn the probability distribution $Pr(\mathbf{a}_1, \ldots, \mathbf{a}_J)$, in this way we try to discover the common regularities among good individuals. The next step is to obtain a set of new individuals by sampling the learnt distribution. These individuals are scored by using the fitness function and added to the ones forming the current population. Finally, the new population is formed by selecting n individuals from the $2n$ contained in the current one. A common practice is to use some kind of fitness-based elitism during this selection, in order to guarantee that the best(s) individual(s) is/are retained.

The main problem in the previous description is related to the estimation/learning of the probability distribution, since estimating the joint distribution is intractable in most cases. In the practice, what is learnt is a probabilistic model that consists in a factorization of the joint distribution. Different levels of complexity can be considered in that factorization, from univariate distributions to n-variate ones or Bayesian networks (see (Larrañaga and Lozano, 2001, Chapter 3) for a review). In this paper, as this is the first approximation to the alignment problem with EDAs and, because of some questions that will be discussed later, we use the simplest EDA model: the *Univariate Marginal Distribution Algorithm* or UMDA (Muhlenbein, 1997). In UMDA it is assumed that all the variables are marginally independent, thus, the n-dimensional probability distribution, $Pr(a_1, \ldots, a_J)$, is factorized as the product of J marginal/unidimensional distributions: $\prod_{j=1}^{J} Pr(a_j)$. Among the advantages of UMDA we can cite the following: no structural learning is needed; parameter learning is fast; small dataset can be used because only marginal probabilities have to be estimated; and, the sampling process is easy because each variable is independently sampled.

4 Design of an EDA to search for alignments

In this section, an EDA algorithm to align a source and a target sentences is described.

4.1 Representation

One of the most important issues in the definition of a search algorithm is to properly represent the space of solutions to the problem. In the problem considered here, we are searching for an "optimal" alignment between a source sentence $\mathbf{f}$ and a target sentence $\mathbf{e}$. Therefore, the space of solutions can be stated as the set of possible alignments between both sentences. Owing to the constraints imposed by the IBM models (a word in $\mathbf{f}$ can be aligned at most to one word in $\mathbf{e}$), the most natural way to represent a solution to this problem consists in storing each possible alignment in a vector $\mathbf{a} = a_1 ... a_J$, being J the length of **f**. Each position of this vector can take the value of "0" to represent a NULL alignment (that is, a word in the source sentence that is aligned to no words in the target sentence) or an index representing any position in the target sentence. An example of alignment is shown in Figure 4.1.

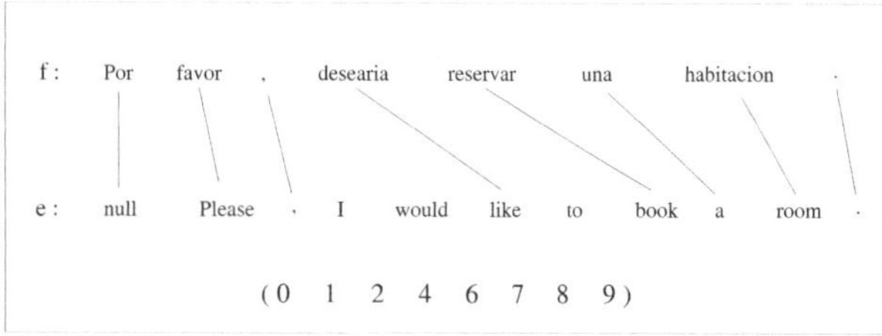

Figure 2: Example of alignment and its representation as a vector

4.2 Evaluation function

During the search process, each individual (search hypothesis) is scored using the fitness function described as follows. Let $\mathbf{a} = a_1 \cdots a_J$ be the alignment represented by an individual. This alignment **a** is evaluated by computing the probability $p(\mathbf{f}, \mathbf{a}|\mathbf{e})$. This probability is computed by using the IBM model 4 as:

$$
\begin{aligned}
p(\mathbf{f}, \mathbf{a}|\mathbf{e}) = & \sum_{(\tau,\pi)\in\langle\mathbf{f},\mathbf{a}\rangle} p(\tau, \pi|\mathbf{e}) \\
& \prod_{i=1}^{I} n(\phi_i|e_i) \times \prod_{i=1}^{I}\prod_{k=1}^{\phi_i} t(\tau_{ik}|e_i) \times \\
& \prod_{i=1,\phi_i>0}^{I} d_{=1}(\pi_{i1} - c_{\rho_i}|\mathcal{E}_c(e_{\rho_i}), \mathcal{F}_c(\tau_{i1})) \times \\
& \prod_{i=1}^{I}\prod_{k=2}^{\phi_i} d_{>1}(\pi_{ik} - \pi_{i(k-1)}|\mathcal{F}_c(\tau_{ik})) \times \\
& \binom{J-\phi_0}{\phi_0} p_0^{J-2\phi_0} p_1^{\phi_0} \times \prod_{k=1}^{\phi_0} t(\tau_{0k}|e_0)
\end{aligned} \quad (3)
$$

where the factors separated by $\times$ symbols denote fertility, translation, head permutation, non-head permutation, null-fertility, and null-translation probabilities[1].

This model was trained using the GIZA++ toolkit (Och and Ney, 2003) on the material available for the different alignment tasks described in section 5.1

4.3 Search

In this section, some specific details about the search are given. As was mentioned in section 3, the algorithm starts by generating an initial set of hypotheses (initial population). In this case, a set of randomly generated alignments between the source and the target sentences are generated. Afterwards, all the individuals in this population (a fragment of a real population is shown in figure 3) are scored using the function defined in Eq.(4.2). At this point, the actual search starts by applying the scheme shown in section 3, thereby leading to a gradual improvement in the hypotheses handled by the algorithm in each step of the search.

This process finishes when some finalization criterium (or criteria) is reached. In our implementation, the algorithm finishes when it passes a certain number of generations without improving the quality of the hypotheses (individuals). Afterwards, the best individual in the current population is returned as the final solution.

Regarding the EDA model, as commented before, our approach rely on the UMDA model due mainly to the size of the search space defined by the task. The algorithm has to deal with individuals of length J, where each position can take $(I + 1)$ possible values. Thus, in the case of UMDA, the number of free parameters to be learnt for each position is I (e.g., in the English-French task $avg(J) = 15$ and $avg(I) = 17.3$). If more complex models were considered, the size of the probability tables would have grown exponentially. As an example, in a bivariate model, each variable (position) is conditioned on another variable and thus the probability tables $P(.|.)$ to be learnt have $I(I + 1)$ free parameters. In order to properly estimate the probabilty distributions, the size of the populations has to be increased considerably. As a result, the computational resources

[1]The symbols in this formula are: J (the length of $\mathbf{e}$), I (the length of $\mathbf{f}$), e_i (the i-th word in e_1^I), e_0 (the NULL word), ϕ_i (the fertility of e_i), τ_{ik} (the k-th word produced by e_i in $\mathbf{a}$), π_{ik} (the position of τ_{ik} in $\mathbf{f}$), ρ_i (the position of the first fertile word to the left of e_i in $\mathbf{a}$), c_{ρ_i} (the ceiling of the average of all $\pi_{\rho_i k}$ for ρ_i, or 0 if ρ_i is undefined).

1 1 5 3 2 0 6 0	(-60.7500)
1 6 5 2 3 0 0 5	(-89.7449)
1 2 2 6 4 0 5 0	(-90.2221)
1 2 3 5 0 3 6 2	(-99.2313)
0 6 0 2 4 6 3 5	(-99.7786)
2 0 0 2 2 0 3 4	(-100.587)
1 0 1 6 3 6 0 5	(-101.335)

Figure 3: Part of one population generated during the search for the alignments between the English sentence *and then he tells us the correct result !* and the Romanian sentence *si ne spune noua rezultatul corect !*. These sentences are part of the HLT-NAACL 2005 shared task. Some individuals and their scores (fitness) are shown.

required by the algorithm rise dramatically.

Finally, as was described in section 3, some parameters have to be fixed in the design of an EDA. On the one hand, the size of each population must be defined. In this case, this size is proportional to the length of the sentences to be aligned. Specifically, the size of the population adopted is equal to the length of source sentence $\mathbf{f}$ multiplied by a factor of ten.

On the other hand, as we mentioned in section 3 the probability distribution over the individuals is not estimated from the whole population. In the present task about 20% of the best individuals in each population are used for this purpose.

As mentioned above, the fitness function used in the algorithm just allows for unidirectional alignments. Therefore, the search was conducted in both directions (i.e, from $\mathbf{f}$ to $\mathbf{e}$ and from $\mathbf{e}$ to $\mathbf{f}$) combining the final results to achieve bidirectional alignments. To this end, diffferent approaches (symmetrization methods) were tested. The results shown in section 5.2 were obtained by applying the *refined method* proposed in (Och and Ney, 2000).

5 Experimental Results

Different experiments have been carried out in order to assess the correctness of the search algorithm. Next, the experimental metodology employed and the results obtained are described.

5.1 Corpora and evaluation

Three different corpora and four different test sets have been used. All of them are taken from the two shared tasks in word alignments developed in HLT/NAACL 2003 (Mihalcea and Pedersen, 2003) and ACL 2005 (Joel Martin, 2005). These two tasks involved four different pair of languages, English-French, Romanian-English, English-Inuktitut and English-Hindi. English-French and Romanian-English pairs have been considered in these experiments (owing to the lack of timeto properly preprocess the Hindi and the Inuktitut). Next, a brief description of the corpora used is given.

Regarding the Romanian-English task, the test data used to evaluate the alignments consisted in 248 sentences for the 2003 evaluation task and 200 for the 2005 evaluation task. In addition to this, a training corpus, consisting of about 1 million Romanian words and about the same number of English word has been used. The IBM word-based alignment models were training on the whole corpus (training + test). On the other hand, a subset of the Canadian Hansards corpus has been used in the English-French task. The test corpus consists of 447 English-French sentences. The training corpus contains about 20 million English words, and about the same number of French words. In Table 1, the features of the different corpora used are shown.

To evaluate the quality of the final alignments obtained, different measures have been taken into account: *Precision*, *Recall*, *F-measure*, and *Alignment Error Rate*. Given an alignment A and a reference alignment G (both A and G can be split into two subsets A_S,A_P and G_S, G_P, respectively representing *Sure* and *Probable* alignments) *Precision* (P_T), *Recall* (R_T), *F-measure* (F_T) and *Alignment Error Rate* (AER) are computed as (where T is the alignment type, and can be set to either S or P):

$$
\begin{aligned}
P_T &= \frac{|A_T \bigcap G_T|}{|A_T|} \\
R_T &= \frac{|A_T \bigcap G_T|}{|G_T|} \\
F_T &= \frac{|2 P_T R_T|}{|P_T + R_T|} \\
AER &= \frac{1 - |A_S \bigcap G_S| + |A_P \bigcap G_P|}{|A_P| + |G_S|}
\end{aligned}
$$

Table 1: Features of the corpora used in the different alignment task

	En-Fr	Ro-En 03	Ro-En 05
Training size	1M	97K	97K
Vocabulary	68K / 86K	48K / 27K	48K / 27K
Running words	20M / 23M	1.9M / 2M	1.9M / 2M
Test size	447	248	200

It is important to emphasize that EDAs are non-deterministics algorithms. Because of this, the results presented in section 5.2 are actually the mean of the results obtained in ten different executions of the search algorithm.

5.2 Results

In Tables 2, 3 and 4 the results obtained from the different tasks are presented. The results achieved by the technique proposed in this paper are compared with the best results presented in the shared tasks described in (Mihalcea and Pedersen, 2003) (Joel Martin, 2005). The results obtained by the GIZA++ hill-climbing algorithm are also presented. In these tables, the mean and the variance of the results obtained in ten executions of the search algorithm are shown. According to the small variances observed in the results we can conclude that the non-deterministic nature of this approach it is not statistically significant.

According to these results, the proposed EDA-based search is very competitive with respect to the best result presented in the two shared task.

In addition to these results, additional experiments were carried out in to evaluate the actual behavior of the search algorithm. These experiments were focused on measuring the quality of the algorithm, distinguishing between the errors produced by the search process itself and the errors produced by the model that leads the search (i.e, the errors introduced by the fitness function). To this end, the next approach was adopted. Firstly, the (bidirectional) reference alignments used in the computation of the Alignment Error Rate were split into two sets of unidirectional alignments. Owing to the fact that there is no exact method to perform this decomposition, we employed the method described in the following way. For each reference alignment, all the possible decompositions into unidirectional alignments were perfomed, scoring each of them with the evaluation function $F(\mathbf{a}) = p(\mathbf{f}, \mathbf{a}|\mathbf{e})$ defined in section (3), and being selected the best one, $\mathbf{a}_{ref}$. Afterwards, this alignment was compared with the solution provided by the EDA, $\mathbf{a}_{eda}$. This comparison was made for each sentence in the test set, being measuried the AER for both alignments as well as the value of the fitness function. At this point, we can say that a model-error is produced if $F(\mathbf{a}_{eda}) > F(\mathbf{a}_{ref})$. In addition, we can say that a search-error is produced if $F(\mathbf{a}_{eda}) < F(\mathbf{a}_{ref})$. In table 5, a summary for both kinds of errors for the English-Romanian 2005 task is shown. In this table we can also see that these results correlate with the AER figures.

These experiments show that most of the errors were not due to the search process itself but to another different factors. From this, we can conclude that, on the one hand, the model used to lead the search should be improved and, on the other, different techniques for symmetrization should be explored.

6 Conclusions and Future Work

In this paper, a new approach, based on the use of an Estimation of Distribution Algorithm has been presented. The results obtained with this technique are very promising even with the simple scheme here considered.

According to the results presented in the previous section, the non-deterministic nature of the algorithm has not a real influence in the performance of this approach. Therefore, the main theoretical drawback of evolutionary algorithms have been proven not to be an important issue for the task we have addressed here.

Finally, we are now focusing on the influence of these improved alignments in the statistical models for machine translation and on the degree of accu-

Table 2: Alignment quality (%) for the English-French task with NULL alignments

System	P_s	R_s	F_s	P_p	R_p	F_p	AER
EDA	**73.82**	82.76	**78.04**	**83.91**	29.50	43.36	**13.61** ±0.03
GIZA++	73.61	82.56	77.92	79.94	32.96	46.67	15.89
Ralign.EF1	72.54	80.61	76.36	77.56	**36.79**	**49.91**	18.50
XRCE.Nolem.EF.3	55.43	**93.81**	69.68	72.01	36.00	48.00	21.27

Table 3: Alignment quality (%) for the Romanian-English 2003 task with NULL aligments

System	P_s	R_s	F_s	P_p	R_p	F_p	AER
EDA	94.22	49.67	65.05	76.66	60.97	**67.92**	**32.08** ±0.05
GIZA++	**95.20**	48.54	64.30	**79.89**	57.82	67.09	32.91
XRCE.Trilex.RE.3	80.97	53.64	64.53	63.64	**61.58**	62.59	37.41
XRCE.Nolem-56k.RE.2	82.65	**54.12**	**65.41**	61.59	61.50	61.54	38.46

Table 4: Alignment quality (%) for the Romanian-English 2005 task

System	P_s	R_s	F_s	P_p	R_p	F_p	AER
EDA	95.37	54.90	69.68	80.61	67.83	**73.67**	**26.33** ±0.044
GIZA++	**95.68**	53.29	68.45	81.46	65.83	72.81	27.19
ISI.Run5.vocab.grow	87.90	63.08	**73.45**	87.90	63.08	73.45	26.55
ISI.Run4.simple.intersect	94.29	57.42	71.38	**94.29**	57.42	71,38	28.62
ISI.Run2.simple.union	70.46	**71.31**	70.88	70.46	**71.31**	70.88	29.12

Table 5: Comparison between reference aligments (decomposed into two unidirectional alignments) and the alignments provided by the EDA. Search errors and model errors for EDA and GIZA++ algorithms are presented. In addition, the AER for the unidirectional EDA and reference alignments is also shown. These result are obtained on the Romanian-English 05 task

	Romanian-English	**English-Romanian**
EDA search errors (%)	35 (17.5 %)	18 (9 %)
EDA model errors (%)	165 (82.5 %)	182 (91 %)
GIZA++ search errors (%)	87 (43 %)	81 (40 %)
GIZA++ model errors (%)	113 (57 %)	119 (60 %)
AER-EDA	29.67 %	30.66 %
AER-reference	12.77 %	11.03 %

racy that could be achieved by means of these aligments. In addition to this, the integration of the aligment algorithm into the training process of the statistical translation models is currently being performed.

References

P. F. Brown, S. A. Della Pietra, V. J. Della Pietra, and R. L. Mercer. 1993. The mathematics of statistical machine translation: Parameter estimation. *Comp. Linguistics*, 19(2):263–311.

Ted Pedersen Joel Martin, Rada Mihalcea. 2005. Word alignment for languages with scarce resources. In Rada Mihalcea and Ted Pedersen, editors, *Proceedings of the ACL Workshop on Building and Exploiting Parallel Texts: Data Driven Machine Translation and Beyond*, pages 1–10, Michigan, USA, June 31. Association for Computational Linguistics.

P. Larrañaga and J.A. Lozano. 2001. *Estimation of Distribution Algorithms. A New Tool for Evolutionary Computation*. Kluwer Academic Publishers.

Z. Michalewicz. 1996. *Genetic Algorithms + Data Structures = Evolution Programs*. Springer-Verlag.

Rada Mihalcea and Ted Pedersen. 2003. An evaluation exercise for word alignment. In Rada Mihalcea and Ted Pedersen, editors, *HLT-NAACL 2003 Workshop: Building and Using Parallel Texts: Data Driven Machine Translation and Beyond*, pages 1–10, Edmonton, Alberta, Canada, May 31. Association for Computational Linguistics.

Heinz Muhlenbein. 1997. The equation for response to selection and its use for prediction. *Evolutionary Computation*, 5(3):303–346.

Franz J. Och and Hermann Ney. 2000. Improved statistical alignment models. In *ACL00*, pages 440–447, Hongkong, China, October.

Franz Josef Och and Hermann Ney. 2003. A systematic comparison of various statistical alignment models. *Computational Linguistics*, 29(1):19–51.

Discriminative Reordering Models for Statistical Machine Translation

Richard Zens and Hermann Ney

Human Language Technology and Pattern Recognition
Lehrstuhl für Informatik 6 – Computer Science Department
RWTH Aachen University, D-52056 Aachen, Germany
{zens,ney}@cs.rwth-aachen.de

Abstract

We present discriminative reordering models for phrase-based statistical machine translation. The models are trained using the maximum entropy principle. We use several types of features: based on words, based on word classes, based on the local context. We evaluate the overall performance of the reordering models as well as the contribution of the individual feature types on a word-aligned corpus. Additionally, we show improved translation performance using these reordering models compared to a state-of-the-art baseline system.

1 Introduction

In recent evaluations, phrase-based statistical machine translation systems have achieved good performance. Still the fluency of the machine translation output leaves much to desire. One reason is that most phrase-based systems use a very simple reordering model. Usually, the costs for phrase movements are linear in the distance, e.g. see (Och et al., 1999; Koehn, 2004; Zens et al., 2005).

Recently, in (Tillmann and Zhang, 2005) and in (Koehn et al., 2005), a reordering model has been described that tries to predict the orientation of a phrase, i.e. it answers the question 'should the next phrase be to the left or to the right of the current phrase?' This phrase orientation probability is conditioned on the current source and target phrase and relative frequencies are used to estimate the probabilities.

We adopt the idea of predicting the orientation, but we propose to use a maximum-entropy based model. The relative-frequency based approach may suffer from the data sparseness problem, because most of the phrases occur only once in the training corpus. Our approach circumvents this problem by using a combination of phrase-level and word-level features and by using word-classes or part-of-speech information. Maximum entropy is a suitable framework for combining these different features with a well-defined training criterion.

In (Koehn et al., 2005) several variants of the orientation model have been tried. It turned out that for different tasks, different models show the best performance. Here, we let the maximum entropy training decide which features are important and which features can be neglected. We will see that additional features do not hurt performance and can be safely added to the model.

The remaining part is structured as follows: first we will describe the related work in Section 2 and give a brief description of the baseline system in Section 3. Then, we will present the discriminative reordering model in Section 4. Afterwards, we will evaluate the performance of this new model in Section 5. This evaluation consists of two parts: first we will evaluate the prediction capabilities of the model on a word-aligned corpus and second we will show improved translation quality compared to the baseline system. Finally, we will conclude in Section 6.

2 Related Work

As already mentioned in Section 1, many current phrase-based statistical machine translation systems use a very simple reordering model: the costs

Proceedings of the Workshop on Statistical Machine Translation, pages 55–63,
New York City, June 2006.

for phrase movements are linear in the distance. This approach is also used in the publicly available Pharaoh decoder (Koehn, 2004). The idea of predicting the orientation is adopted from (Tillmann and Zhang, 2005) and (Koehn et al., 2005). Here, we use the maximum entropy principle to combine a variety of different features.

A reordering model in the framework of weighted finite state transducers is described in (Kumar and Byrne, 2005). There, the movements are defined at the phrase level, but the window for reordering is very limited. The parameters are estimated using an EM-style method.

None of these methods try to generalize from the words or phrases by using word classes or part-of-speech information.

The approach presented here has some resemblance to the bracketing transduction grammars (BTG) of (Wu, 1997), which have been applied to a phrase-based machine translation system in (Zens et al., 2004). The difference is that, here, we do not constrain the phrase reordering. Nevertheless the inverted/monotone concatenation of phrases in the BTG framework is similar to the left/right phrase orientation used here.

3 Baseline System

In statistical machine translation, we are given a source language sentence $f_1^J = f_1 \ldots f_j \ldots f_J$, which is to be translated into a target language sentence $e_1^I = e_1 \ldots e_i \ldots e_I$. Among all possible target language sentences, we will choose the sentence with the highest probability:

$$\hat{e}_1^{\hat{I}} = \underset{I,e_1^I}{\operatorname{argmax}} \left\{ Pr(e_1^I|f_1^J) \right\} \quad (1)$$

The posterior probability $Pr(e_1^I|f_1^J)$ is modeled directly using a log-linear combination of several models (Och and Ney, 2002):

$$Pr(e_1^I|f_1^J) = \frac{\exp\left(\sum_{m=1}^M \lambda_m h_m(e_1^I, f_1^J)\right)}{\sum\limits_{I',e'^{I'}_1} \exp\left(\sum_{m=1}^M \lambda_m h_m(e'^{I'}_1, f_1^J)\right)} \quad (2)$$

The denominator represents a normalization factor that depends only on the source sentence f_1^J. Therefore, we can omit it during the search process. As a decision rule, we obtain:

$$\hat{e}_1^{\hat{I}} = \underset{I,e_1^I}{\operatorname{argmax}} \left\{ \sum_{m=1}^M \lambda_m h_m(e_1^I, f_1^J) \right\} \quad (3)$$

This approach is a generalization of the source-channel approach (Brown et al., 1990). It has the advantage that additional models $h(\cdot)$ can be easily integrated into the overall system. The model scaling factors λ_1^M are trained with respect to the final translation quality measured by an error criterion (Och, 2003).

We use a state-of-the-art phrase-based translation system (Zens and Ney, 2004; Zens et al., 2005) including the following models: an n-gram language model, a phrase translation model and a word-based lexicon model. The latter two models are used for both directions: $p(f|e)$ and $p(e|f)$. Additionally, we use a word penalty and a phrase penalty. The reordering model of the baseline system is distance-based, i.e. it assigns costs based on the distance from the end position of a phrase to the start position of the next phrase. This very simple reordering model is widely used, for instance in (Och et al., 1999; Koehn, 2004; Zens et al., 2005).

4 The Reordering Model

4.1 Idea

In this section, we will describe the proposed discriminative reordering model.

To make use of word level information, we need the word alignment within the phrase pairs. This can be easily stored during the extraction of the phrase pairs from the bilingual training corpus. If there are multiple possible alignments for a phrase pair, we use the most frequent one.

The notation is introduced using the illustration in Figure 1. There is an example of a left and a right phrase orientation. We assume that we have already produced the three-word phrase in the lower part. Now, the model has to predict if the start position of the next phrase j' is to the left or to the right of the current phrase. The reordering model is applied only at the phrase boundaries. We assume that the reordering within the phrases is correct.

In the remaining part of this section, we will describe the details of this reordering model. The classes our model predicts will be defined in Section 4.2. Then, the feature functions will be defined

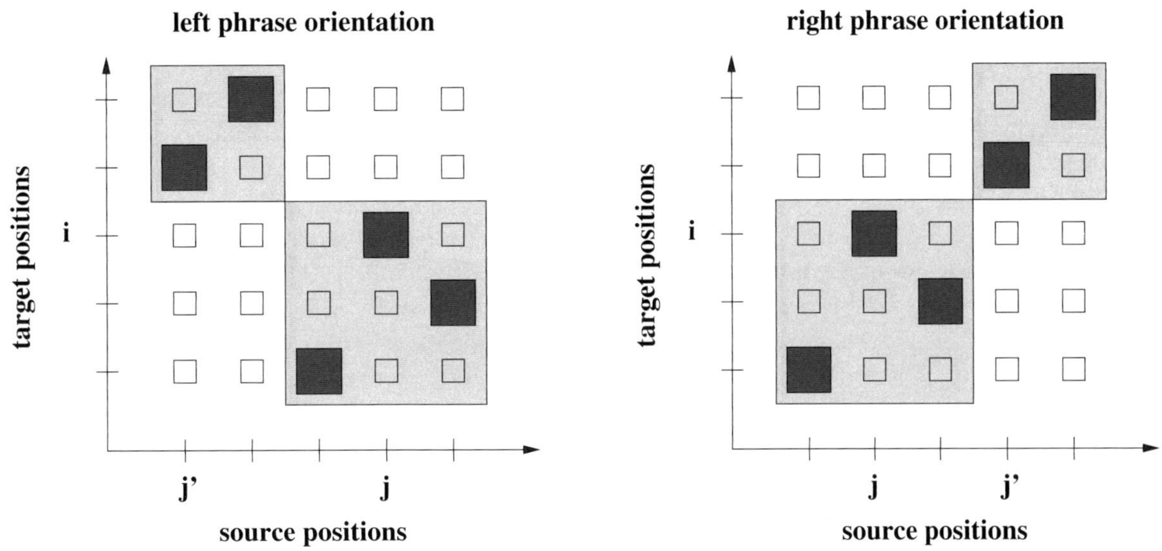

Figure 1: Illustration of the phrase orientation.

in Section 4.3. The training criterion and the training events of the maximum entropy model will be described in Section 4.4.

4.2 Class Definition

Ideally, this model predicts the start position of the next phrase. But as predicting the exact position is rather difficult, we group the possible start positions into classes. In the simplest case, we use only two classes. One class for the positions to the left and one class for the positions to the right. As a refinement, we can use four classes instead of two: 1) one position to the left, 2) more than one positions to the left, 3) one position to the right, 4) more than one positions to the right.

In general, we use a parameter D to specify $2 \cdot D$ classes of the types:

- exactly d positions to the left, $d = 1, ..., D - 1$
- at least D positions to the left
- exactly d positions to the right, $d = 1, ..., D - 1$
- at least D positions to the right

Let $c_{j,j'}$ denote the orientation class for a movement from source position j to source position j' as illustrated in Figure 1. In the case of two orientation classes, $c_{j,j'}$ is defined as:

$$c_{j,j'} = \begin{cases} \text{left}, & \text{if } j' < j \\ \text{right}, & \text{if } j' > j \end{cases} \quad (4)$$

Then, the reordering model has the form

$$p(c_{j,j'} | f_1^J, e_1^I, i, j)$$

A well-founded framework for directly modeling the probability $p(c_{j,j'} | f_1^J, e_1^I, i, j)$ is maximum entropy (Berger et al., 1996). In this framework, we have a set of N feature functions $h_n(f_1^J, e_1^I, i, j, c_{j,j'}), n = 1, \ldots, N$. Each feature function h_n is weighted with a factor λ_n. The resulting model is:

$$p_{\lambda_1^N}(c_{j,j'} | f_1^J, e_1^I, i, j) = \frac{\exp\left(\sum_{n=1}^{N} \lambda_n h_n(f_1^J, e_1^I, i, j, c_{j,j'})\right)}{\sum_{c'} \exp\left(\sum_{n=1}^{N} \lambda_n h_n(f_1^J, e_1^I, i, j, c')\right)} \quad (5)$$

The functional form is identical to Equation 2, but here we will use a large number of binary features, whereas in Equation 2 usually only a very small number of real-valued features is used. More precisely, the resulting reordering model $p_{\lambda_1^N}(c_{j,j'} | f_1^J, e_1^I, i, j)$ is used as an additional component in the log-linear combination of Equation 2.

4.3 Feature Definition

The feature functions of the reordering model depend on the last alignment link (j, i) of a phrase. Note that the source position j is not necessarily the end position of the source phrase. We use the source position j which is aligned to the last word of the target phrase in target position i. The illustration in Figure 1 contains such an example.

To introduce generalization capabilities, some of the features will depend on word classes or part-of-speech information. Let F_1^J denote the word class sequence that corresponds to the source language sentence f_1^J and let E_1^I denote the target word class sequence that corresponds to the target language sentence e_1^I. Then, the feature functions are of the form $h_n(f_1^J, e_1^I, F_1^J, E_1^I, i, j, j')$. We consider the following binary features:

1. source words within a window around the current source position j

$$h_{f,d,c}(f_1^J, e_1^I, F_1^J, E_1^I, i, j, j') = \delta(f_{j+d}, f) \cdot \delta(c, c_{j,j'}) \quad (6)$$

2. target words within a window around the current target position i

$$h_{e,d,c}(f_1^J, e_1^I, F_1^J, E_1^I, i, j, j') = \delta(e_{i+d}, e) \cdot \delta(c, c_{j,j'}) \quad (7)$$

3. word classes or part-of-speech within a window around the current source position j

$$h_{F,d,c}(f_1^J, e_1^I, F_1^J, E_1^I, i, j, j') = \delta(F_{j+d}, F) \cdot \delta(c, c_{j,j'}) \quad (8)$$

4. word classes or part-of-speech within a window around the current target position i

$$h_{E,d,c}(f_1^J, e_1^I, F_1^J, E_1^I, i, j, j') = \delta(E_{i+d}, E) \cdot \delta(c, c_{j,j'}) \quad (9)$$

Here, $\delta(\cdot, \cdot)$ denotes the Kronecker-function. In the experiments, we will use $d \in \{-1, 0, 1\}$. Many other feature functions are imaginable, e.g. combinations of the described feature functions, n-gram or multi-word features, joint source and target language feature functions.

4.4 Training

As training criterion, we use the maximum class posterior probability. This corresponds to maximizing the likelihood of the maximum entropy model. Since the optimization criterion is convex, there is only a single optimum and no convergence problems occur. To train the model parameters λ_1^N, we use the Generalized Iterative Scaling (GIS) algorithm (Darroch and Ratcliff, 1972).

In practice, the training procedure tends to result in an overfitted model. To avoid overfitting, (Chen and Rosenfeld, 1999) have suggested a smoothing method where a Gaussian prior distribution of the parameters is assumed.

This method tried to avoid very large lambda values and prevents features that occur only once for a specific class from getting a value of infinity.

We train IBM Model 4 with GIZA++ (Och and Ney, 2003) in both translation directions. Then the alignments are symmetrized using a refined heuristic as described in (Och and Ney, 2003). This word-aligned bilingual corpus is used to train the reordering model parameters, i.e. the feature weights λ_1^N. Each alignment link defines an event for the maximum entropy training. An exception are the one-to-many alignments, i.e. one source word is aligned to multiple target words. In this case, only the top-most alignment link is considered because the other ones cannot occur at a phrase boundary. Many-to-one and many-to-many alignments are handled in a similar way.

5 Experimental Results

5.1 Statistics

The experiments were carried out on the *Basic Travel Expression Corpus* (BTEC) task (Takezawa et al., 2002). This is a multilingual speech corpus which contains tourism-related sentences similar to those that are found in phrase books. We use the Arabic-English, the Chinese-English and the Japanese-English data. The corpus statistics are shown in Table 1.

As the BTEC is a rather clean corpus, the preprocessing consisted mainly of tokenization, i.e., separating punctuation marks from words. Additionally, we replaced contractions such as *it's* or *I'm* in the English corpus and we removed the case information. For Arabic, we removed the diacritics and we split common prefixes: Al, w, f, b, l. There was no special preprocessing for the Chinese and the Japanese training corpora.

To train and evaluate the reordering model, we

Table 1: Corpus statistics after preprocessing for the BTEC task.

		Arabic	Chinese	Japanese	English
Train	Sentences	20 000			
	Running Words	180 075	176 199	198 453	189 927
	Vocabulary	15 371	8 687	9 277	6 870
C-Star'03	Sentences	506			
	Running Words	3 552	3 630	4 130	3 823

Table 2: Statistics of the training and test word alignment links.

	Ara-Eng	Chi-Eng	Jap-Eng
Training	144K	140K	119K
Test	16.2K	15.7K	13.2K

use the word aligned bilingual training corpus. For evaluating the classification power of the reordering model, we partition the corpus into a training part and a test part. In our experiments, we use about 10% of the corpus for testing and the remaining part for training the feature weights of the reordering model with the GIS algorithm using YASMET (Och, 2001). The statistics of the training and test alignment links is shown in Table 2. The number of training events ranges from 119K for Japanese-English to 144K for Arabic-English.

The word classes for the class-based features are trained using the `mkcls` tool (Och, 1999). In the experiments, we use 50 word classes. Alternatively, one could use part-of-speech information for this purpose.

Additional experiments were carried out on the large data track of the Chinese-English NIST task. The corpus statistics of the bilingual training corpus are shown in Table 3. The language model was trained on the English part of the bilingual training corpus and additional monolingual English data from the GigaWord corpus. The total amount of language model training data was about 600M running words. We use a fourgram language model with modified Kneser-Ney smoothing as implemented in the SRILM toolkit (Stolcke, 2002). For the four English reference translations of the evaluation sets, the accumulated statistics are presented.

Table 3: Chinese-English NIST task: corpus statistics for the bilingual training data and the NIST evaluation sets of the years 2002 to 2005.

			Chinese	English
Train	Sentence Pairs		7M	
	Running Words		199M	213M
	Vocabulary Size		223K	351K
	Dictionary Entry Pairs		82K	
Eval	2002	Sentences	878	3 512
		Running Words	25K	105K
	2003	Sentences	919	3 676
		Running Words	26K	122K
	2004	Sentences	1788	7 152
		Running Words	52K	245K
	2005	Sentences	1082	4 328
		Running Words	33K	148K

5.2 Classification Results

In this section, we present the classification results for the three language pairs. In Table 4, we present the classification results for two orientation classes.

As baseline we always choose the most frequent orientation class. For Arabic-English, the baseline is with 6.3% already very low. This means that the word order in Arabic is very similar to the word order in English. For Chinese-English, the baseline is with 12.7% about twice as large. The most differences in word order occur for Japanese-English. This seems to be reasonable as Japanese has usually a different sentence structure, subject-object-verb compared to subject-verb-object in English.

For each language pair, we present results for several combination of features. The three columns per language pair indicate if the features are based on the words (column label 'Words'), on the word classes (column label 'Classes') or on both (column label

Table 4: Classification error rates [%] using two orientation classes.

		Arabic-English			Chinese-English			Japanese-English		
Baseline		6.3			12.7			26.2		
Lang.	Window	Words	Classes	W+C	Words	Classes	W+C	Words	Classes	W+C
Tgt	$d = 0$	4.7	5.3	4.4	9.3	10.4	8.9	13.6	15.1	13.4
	$d \in \{0, 1\}$	4.5	5.0	4.3	8.9	9.9	8.6	13.7	14.9	13.4
	$d \in \{-1, 0, 1\}$	4.5	4.9	4.3	8.6	9.5	8.3	13.5	14.6	13.3
Src	$d = 0$	5.6	5.0	3.9	7.9	8.3	7.2	12.2	11.8	11.0
	$d \in \{0, 1\}$	3.2	3.0	2.6	4.7	4.7	4.2	10.1	9.7	9.4
	$d \in \{-1, 0, 1\}$	2.9	2.5	2.3	3.9	3.5	3.3	9.0	8.0	7.8
Src	$d = 0$	4.3	3.9	3.7	7.1	7.8	6.5	10.8	10.9	9.8
+	$d \in \{0, 1\}$	2.9	2.6	2.5	4.6	4.5	4.1	9.3	9.1	8.6
Tgt	$d \in \{-1, 0, 1\}$	2.8	2.1	2.1	3.9	3.4	3.3	8.7	7.7	7.7

'W+C'). We also distinguish if the features depend on the target sentence ('Tgt'), on the source sentence ('Src') or on both ('Src+Tgt').

For Arabic-English, using features based only on words of the target sentence the classification error rate can be reduced to 4.5%. If the features are based only on the source sentence words, a classification error rate of 2.9% is reached. Combining the features based on source and target sentence words, a classification error rate of 2.8% can be achieved. Adding the features based on word classes, the classification error rate can be further improved to 2.1%. For the other language pairs, the results are similar except that the absolute values of the classification error rates are higher.

We observe the following:

- The features based on the source sentence perform better than features based on the target sentence.
- Combining source and target sentence features performs best.
- Increasing the window always helps, i.e. additional context information is useful.
- Often the word-class based features outperform the word-based features.
- Combining word-based and word-class based features performs best.
- In general, adding features does not hurt the performance.

These are desirable properties of an appropriate reordering model. The main point is that these are fulfilled not only on the training data, but on unseen test data. There seems to be no overfitting problem.

In Table 5, we present the results for four orientation classes. The final error rates are a factor 2-4 larger than for two orientation classes. Despite that we observe the same tendencies as for two orientation classes. Again, using more features always helps to improve the performance.

5.3 Translation Results

For the translation experiments on the BTEC task, we report the two accuracy measures BLEU (Papineni et al., 2002) and NIST (Doddington, 2002) as well as the two error rates: word error rate (WER) and position-independent word error rate (PER). These criteria are computed with respect to 16 references.

In Table 6, we show the translation results for the BTEC task. In these experiments, the reordering model uses two orientation classes, i.e. it predicts either a left or a right orientation. The features for the maximum-entropy based reordering model are based on the source and target language words within a window of one. The word-class based features are not used for the translation experiments. The maximum-entropy based reordering model achieves small but consistent improvement for all the evaluation criteria. Note that the baseline system, i.e. using the distance-based reordering, was among the best systems in the IWSLT 2005 evalua-

Table 5: Classification error rates [%] using four orientation classes.

		Arabic-English			Chinese-English			Japanese-English		
Baseline		31.4			44.9			59.0		
Lang.	Window	Words	Classes	W+C	Words	Classes	W+C	Words	Classes	W+C
Tgt	$d = 0$	24.5	27.7	24.2	30.0	34.4	29.7	28.9	31.4	28.7
	$d \in \{0, 1\}$	23.9	27.2	23.7	29.2	32.9	28.9	28.7	30.6	28.3
	$d \in \{-1, 0, 1\}$	22.1	25.3	21.9	27.6	31.4	27.4	28.3	30.1	28.2
Src	$d = 0$	22.1	23.2	20.4	25.9	27.7	20.4	24.1	24.9	22.3
	$d \in \{0, 1\}$	11.9	12.0	10.8	14.0	14.9	13.2	18.6	19.5	17.7
	$d \in \{-1, 0, 1\}$	10.1	8.7	8.0	11.4	11.1	10.5	15.6	15.6	14.5
Src	$d = 0$	20.9	21.8	19.6	24.1	26.8	19.6	22.3	23.4	21.1
+	$d \in \{0, 1\}$	11.8	11.5	10.6	13.5	14.5	12.8	18.6	18.8	17.1
Tgt	$d \in \{-1, 0, 1\}$	9.6	7.7	7.6	11.3	10.1	10.1	15.6	15.2	14.2

Table 6: Translation Results for the BTEC task.

Language Pair	Reordering	WER [%]	PER [%]	NIST	BLEU [%]
Arabic-English	Distance-based	24.1	20.9	10.0	63.8
	Max-Ent based	23.6	20.7	10.1	64.8
Chinese-English	Distance-based	50.4	43.0	7.67	44.4
	Max-Ent based	49.3	42.4	7.36	45.8
Japanese-English	Distance-based	32.1	25.2	8.96	56.2
	Max-Ent based	31.2	25.2	9.00	56.8

tion campaign (Eck and Hori, 2005).

Some translation examples are presented in Table 7. We observe that the system using the maximum-entropy based reordering model produces more fluent translations.

Additional translation experiments were carried out on the large data track of the Chinese-English NIST task. For this task, we use only the BLEU and NIST scores. Both scores are computed case-insensitive with respect to four reference translations using the mteval-v11b tool[1].

For the NIST task, we use the BLEU score as primary criterion which is optimized on the NIST 2002 evaluation set using the Downhill Simplex algorithm (Press et al., 2002). Note that only the eight or nine model scaling factors of Equation 2 are optimized using the Downhill Simplex algorithm. The feature weights of the reordering model are trained using the GIS algorithm as described in Section 4.4. We use a state-of-the-art baseline system which would have obtained a good rank in the last NIST evaluation (NIST, 2005).

[1]http://www.nist.gov/speech/tests/mt/resources/scoring.htm

The translation results for the NIST task are presented in Table 8. We observe consistent improvements of the BLEU score on all evaluation sets. The overall improvement due to reordering ranges from 1.2% to 2.0% absolute. The contribution of the maximum-entropy based reordering model to this improvement is in the range of 25% to 58%, e.g. for the NIST 2003 evaluation set about 58% of the improvement using reordering can be attributed to the maximum-entropy based reordering model.

We also measured the classification performance for the NIST task. The general tendencies are identical to the BTEC task.

6 Conclusions

We have presented a novel discriminative reordering model for statistical machine translation. This model is trained on the word aligned bilingual corpus using the maximum entropy principle. Several types of features have been used:

- based on the source and target sentence

Table 7: Translation examples for the BTEC task.

System	Translation
Distance-based	I would like to check out time one day before.
Max-Ent based	I would like to check out one day before the time.
Reference	I would like to check out one day earlier.
Distance-based	I hate pepper green.
Max-Ent based	I hate the green pepper.
Reference	I hate green peppers.
Distance-based	Is there a subway map where?
Max-Ent based	Where is the subway route map?
Reference	Where do they have a subway map?

Table 8: Translation results for several evaluation sets of the Chinese-English NIST task.

Evaluation set	2002 (dev)		2003		2004		2005	
Reordering	NIST	BLEU[%]	NIST	BLEU[%]	NIST	BLEU[%]	NIST	BLEU[%]
None	8.96	33.5	8.67	32.7	8.76	32.0	8.62	30.8
Distance-based	9.19	34.6	8.85	33.2	9.05	33.2	8.79	31.6
Max-Ent based	9.24	35.5	8.87	33.9	9.04	33.6	8.78	32.1

- based on words and word classes
- using local context information

We have evaluated the performance of the reordering model on a held-out word-aligned corpus. We have shown that the model is able to predict the orientation very well, e.g. for Arabic-English the classification error rate is only 2.1%.

We presented improved translation results for three language pairs on the BTEC task and for the large data track of the Chinese-English NIST task.

In none of the cases additional features have hurt the classification performance on the held-out test corpus. This is a strong evidence that the maximum entropy framework is suitable for this task.

Another advantage of our approach is the generalization capability via the use of word classes or part-of-speech information. Furthermore, additional features can be easily integrated into the maximum entropy framework.

So far, the word classes were not used for the translation experiments. As the word classes help for the classification task, we might expect further improvements of the translation results. Using part-of-speech information instead (or in addition) to the automatically computed word classes might also be beneficial. More fine-tuning of the reordering model toward translation quality might also result in improvements. As already mentioned in Section 4.3, a richer feature set could be helpful.

Acknowledgments

This material is partly based upon work supported by the Defense Advanced Research Projects Agency (DARPA) under Contract No. HR0011-06-C-0023, and was partly funded by the European Union under the integrated project TC-STAR (Technology and Corpora for Speech to Speech Translation, IST-2002-FP6-506738, http://www.tc-star.org).

References

A. L. Berger, S. A. Della Pietra, and V. J. Della Pietra. 1996. A maximum entropy approach to natural language processing. *Computational Linguistics*, 22(1):39–72, March.

P. F. Brown, J. Cocke, S. A. Della Pietra, V. J. Della Pietra, F. Jelinek, J. D. Lafferty, R. L. Mercer, and P. S. Roossin. 1990. A statistical approach to machine translation. *Computational Linguistics*, 16(2):79–85, June.

S. F. Chen and R. Rosenfeld. 1999. A gaussian prior for smoothing maximum entropy models. Technical Report CMUCS-99-108, Carnegie Mellon University, Pittsburgh, PA.

J. N. Darroch and D. Ratcliff. 1972. Generalized iterative scaling for log-linear models. *Annals of Mathematical Statistics*, 43:1470–1480.

G. Doddington. 2002. Automatic evaluation of machine translation quality using n-gram co-occurrence statistics. In *Proc. ARPA Workshop on Human Language Technology*.

M. Eck and C. Hori. 2005. Overview of the IWSLT 2005 evaluation campaign. In *Proc. International Workshop on Spoken Language Translation (IWSLT)*, Pittsburgh, PA, October.

P. Koehn, A. Axelrod, A. B. Mayne, C. Callison-Burch, M. Osborne, and D. Talbot. 2005. Edinburgh system description for the 2005 IWSLT speech translation evaluation. In *Proc. International Workshop on Spoken Language Translation (IWSLT)*, Pittsburgh, PA, October.

P. Koehn. 2004. Pharaoh: a beam search decoder for phrase-based statistical machine translation models. In *Proc. 6th Conf. of the Assoc. for Machine Translation in the Americas (AMTA)*, pages 115–124, Washington DC, September/October.

S. Kumar and W. Byrne. 2005. Local phrase reordering models for statistical machine translation. In *Proc. of the Human Language Technology Conf./Conf. on Empirical Methods in Natural Language Processing (HLT/EMNLP)*, pages 161–168, Vancouver, Canada, October.

NIST. 2005. NIST 2005 machine translation evaluation official results. `http://www.nist.gov/speech/tests/mt/mt05eval_official_results_release_20050801_v3.html`, August.

F. J. Och and H. Ney. 2002. Discriminative training and maximum entropy models for statistical machine translation. In *Proc. of the 40th Annual Meeting of the Assoc. for Computational Linguistics (ACL)*, pages 295–302, Philadelphia, PA, July.

F. J. Och and H. Ney. 2003. A systematic comparison of various statistical alignment models. *Computational Linguistics*, 29(1):19–51, March.

F. J. Och, C. Tillmann, and H. Ney. 1999. Improved alignment models for statistical machine translation. In *Proc. Joint SIGDAT Conf. on Empirical Methods in Natural Language Processing and Very Large Corpora*, pages 20–28, University of Maryland, College Park, MD, June.

F. J. Och. 1999. An efficient method for determining bilingual word classes. In *Proc. 9th Conf. of the Europ. Chapter of the Assoc. for Computational Linguistics (EACL)*, pages 71–76, Bergen, Norway, June.

F. J. Och. 2001. YASMET: Toolkit for conditional maximum entropy models. http://www-i6.informatik.rwth-aachen.de/web/Software/YASMET.html.

F. J. Och. 2003. Minimum error rate training in statistical machine translation. In *Proc. of the 41th Annual Meeting of the Assoc. for Computational Linguistics (ACL)*, pages 160–167, Sapporo, Japan, July.

K. Papineni, S. Roukos, T. Ward, and W. J. Zhu. 2002. Bleu: a method for automatic evaluation of machine translation. In *Proc. of the 40th Annual Meeting of the Assoc. for Computational Linguistics (ACL)*, pages 311–318, Philadelphia, PA, July.

W. H. Press, S. A. Teukolsky, W. T. Vetterling, and B. P. Flannery. 2002. *Numerical Recipes in C++*. Cambridge University Press, Cambridge, UK.

A. Stolcke. 2002. SRILM – an extensible language modeling toolkit. In *Proc. Int. Conf. on Spoken Language Processing (ICSLP)*, volume 2, pages 901–904, Denver, CO.

T. Takezawa, E. Sumita, F. Sugaya, H. Yamamoto, and S. Yamamoto. 2002. Toward a broad-coverage bilingual corpus for speech translation of travel conversations in the real world. In *Proc. of the Third Int. Conf. on Language Resources and Evaluation (LREC)*, pages 147–152, Las Palmas, Spain, May.

C. Tillmann and T. Zhang. 2005. A localized prediction model for statistical machine translation. In *Proc. of the 43rd Annual Meeting of the Assoc. for Computational Linguistics (ACL)*, pages 557–564, Ann Arbor, MI, June.

D. Wu. 1997. Stochastic inversion transduction grammars and bilingual parsing of parallel corpora. *Computational Linguistics*, 23(3):377–403, September.

R. Zens and H. Ney. 2004. Improvements in phrase-based statistical machine translation. In *Proc. Human Language Technology Conf. / North American Chapter of the Assoc. for Computational Linguistics Annual Meeting (HLT-NAACL)*, pages 257–264, Boston, MA, May.

R. Zens, H. Ney, T. Watanabe, and E. Sumita. 2004. Reordering constraints for phrase-based statistical machine translation. In *Proc. 20th Int. Conf. on Computational Linguistics (COLING)*, pages 205–211, Geneva, Switzerland, August.

R. Zens, O. Bender, S. Hasan, S. Khadivi, E. Matusov, J. Xu, Y. Zhang, and H. Ney. 2005. The RWTH phrase-based statistical machine translation system. In *Proc. International Workshop on Spoken Language Translation (IWSLT)*, pages 155–162, Pittsburgh, PA, October.

Generalized Stack Decoding Algorithms for Statistical Machine Translation*

Daniel Ortiz Martínez
Inst. Tecnológico de Informática
Univ. Politécnica de Valencia
46071 Valencia, Spain
dortiz@iti.upv.es

Ismael García Varea
Dpto. de Informatica
Univ. de Castilla-La Mancha
02071 Albacete, Spain
ivarea@info-ab.uclm.es

Francisco Casacuberta Nolla
Dpto. de Sist Inf. y Comp.
Univ. Politéc. de Valencia
46071 Valencia, Spain
fcn@dsic.upv.es

Abstract

In this paper we propose a generalization of the Stack-based decoding paradigm for Statistical Machine Translation. The well known single and multi-stack decoding algorithms defined in the literature have been integrated within a new formalism which also defines a new family of stack-based decoders. These decoders allows a tradeoff to be made between the advantages of using only one or multiple stacks. The key point of the new formalism consists in parameterizeing the number of stacks to be used during the decoding process, and providing an efficient method to decide in which stack each partial hypothesis generated is to be inserted-during the search process. Experimental results are also reported for a search algorithm for phrase-based statistical translation models.

1 Introduction

The translation process can be formulated from a statistical point of view as follows: A source language string $f_1^J = f_1 \ldots f_J$ is to be translated into a target language string $e_1^I = e_1 \ldots e_I$. Every target string is regarded as a possible translation for the source language string with maximum a-posteriori probability $Pr(e_1^I|f_1^J)$. According to Bayes' theorem, the target string $\hat{e}_1^I$ that maximizes[1] the product of both the target language model $Pr(e_1^I)$ and the string translation model $Pr(f_1^J|e_1^I)$ must be chosen. The equation that models this process is:

$$\hat{e}_1^I = \arg\max_{e_1^I}\{Pr(e_1^I) \cdot Pr(f_1^J|e_1^I)\} \qquad (1)$$

The search/decoding problem in SMT consists in solving the maximization problem stated in Eq. (1). In the literature, we can find different techniques to deal with this problem, ranging from heuristic and fast (as greedy decoders) to optimal and very slow decoding algorithms (Germann et al., 2001). Also, under certain circumstances, stack-based decoders can obtain optimal solutions.

Many works (Berger et al., 1996; Wang and Waibel, 1998; Germann et al., 2001; Och et al., 2001; Ortíz et al., 2003) have adopted different types of stack-based algorithms to solve the global search optimization problem for statistical machine translation. All these works follow two main different approaches according to the number of stacks used in the design and implementation of the search algorithm (the stacks are used to store partial hypotheses, sorted according to their partial score/probability, during the search process) :

- On the one hand, in (Wang and Waibel, 1998; Och et al., 2001) a single stack is used. In that case, in order to make the search feasible, the pruning of the number of partial hypotheses stored in the stack is needed. This causes many search errors due to the fact that hypotheses covering a different number of source (translated) words compete in the same conditions. Therefore, the greater number of covered words the higher possibility to be pruned.

- On the other hand (Berger et al., 1996; Germann et al., 2001) make use of multiple stacks

*This work has been partially supported by the Spanish project TIC2003-08681-C02-02, the *Agencia Valenciana de Ciencia y Tecnología* under contract GRUPOS03/031, the *Generalitat Valenciana*, and the project HERMES (Vicerrectorado de Investigación - UCLM-05/06)

[1]Note that the expression should also be maximized by I; however, for the sake of simplicity we suppose that it is known.

Proceedings of the Workshop on Statistical Machine Translation, pages 64–71,
New York City, June 2006. ©2006 Association for Computational Linguistics

(one for each set of source covered/translated words in the partial hypothesis) in order to solve the disadvantages of the single-stack approach. By contrast, the problem of finding the best hypothesis to be expanded introduces an exponential term in the computational complexity of the algorithm.

In (Ortíz et al., 2003) the authors present an empirical comparison (about efficiency and translation quality) of the two approaches paying special attention to the advantages and disadvantages of the two approaches.

In this paper we present a new formalism consisting of a generalization of the classical stack-based decoding paradigm for SMT. This new formalism defines a new family of stack-based decoders, which also integrates the well known stack-based decoding algorithms proposed so far within the framework of SMT, that is single and multi-stack decoders.

The rest of the paper is organized as follows: in section 2 the phrase-based approach to SMT is depicted; in section 3 the main features of classical stack-based decoders are presented; in section 4 the new formalism is presented and in section 5 experimental results are shown; finally some conclusions are drawn in section 6.

2 Phrase Based Statistical Machine Translation

Different *translation models* (TMs) have been proposed depending on how the relation between the source and the target languages is structured; that is, the way a target sentence is generated from a source sentence. This relation is summarized using the concept of *alignment*; that is, how the constituents (typically words or group-of-words) of a pair of sentences are aligned to each other. The most widely used single-word-based *statistical alignment models* (SAMs) have been proposed in (Brown et al., 1993; Ney et al., 2000). On the other hand, models that deal with structures or phrases instead of single words have also been proposed: the syntax translation models are described in (Yamada and Knight, 2001) , alignment templates are used in (Och, 2002), and the alignment template approach is re-framed into the so-called *phrase based translation* (PBT) in (Marcu and Wong, 2002; Zens et al., 2002; Koehn et al., 2003; Tomás and Casacuberta, 2003).

For the translation model ($Pr(f_1^J|e_1^I)$) in Eq. (1), PBT can be explained from a generative point of view as follows (Zens et al., 2002):

1. The target sentence e_1^I is segmented into K phrases ($\tilde{e}_1^K$).
2. Each target phrase $\tilde{e}_k$ is translated into a source phrase $\tilde{f}$.
3. Finally, the source phrases are reordered in order to compose the source sentence $\tilde{f}_1^K = f_1^J$.

In PBT, it is assumed that the relations between the words of the source and target sentences can be explained by means of the hidden variable $\tilde{a}_1^K$, which contains all the decisions made during the generative story.

$$\begin{aligned} Pr(f_1^J|e_1^I) &= \sum_{K,\tilde{a}_1^K} Pr(,\tilde{f}_1^K,\tilde{a}_1^K|\tilde{e}_1^K) \\ &= \sum_{K,\tilde{a}_1^K} Pr(\tilde{a}_1^K|\tilde{e}_1^K)Pr(\tilde{f}_1^K|\tilde{a}_1^K,\tilde{e}_1^K) \end{aligned} \quad (2)$$

Different assumptions can be made from the previous equation. For example, in (Zens et al., 2002) the following model is proposed:

$$p_\theta(f_1^J|e_1^I) = \alpha(e_1^I)\sum_{K,\tilde{a}_1^K}\prod_{k=1}^{K} p(\tilde{f}_k|\tilde{e}_{\tilde{a}_k}) \quad (3)$$

where $\tilde{a}_k$ notes the index of the source phrase $\tilde{e}$ which is aligned with the k-th target phrase $\tilde{f}_k$ and that all possible segmentations have the same probability. In (Tomás and Casacuberta, 2001; Zens et al., 2002), it also is assumed that the alignments must be monotonic. This led us to the following equation:

$$p_\theta(f_1^J|e_1^I) = \alpha(e_1^I)\sum_{K,\tilde{a}_1^K}\prod_{k=1}^{K} p(\tilde{f}_k|\tilde{e}_k) \quad (4)$$

In both cases the model parameters that have to be estimated are the translation probabilities between phrase pairs ($\theta = \{p(\tilde{f}|\tilde{e})\}$), which typically are estimated as follows:

$$p(\tilde{f}|\tilde{e}) = \frac{N(\tilde{f},\tilde{e})}{N(\tilde{e})} \quad (5)$$

where $N(\tilde{f}|\tilde{e})$ is the number of times that $\tilde{f}$ have been seen as a translation of $\tilde{e}$ within the training corpus.

3 Stack-Decoding Algorithms

The stack decoding algorithm, also called A^* algorithm, was first introduced by F. Jelinek in (Jelinek, 1969). The stack decoding algorithm attempts to generate partial solutions, called *hypotheses*, until a complete translation is found[2]; these hypotheses are stored in a stack and ordered by their *score*. Typically, this measure or score is the probability of the product of the translation and the language models introduced above. The A^* decoder follows a sequence of steps for achieving a complete (and possibly optimal) hypothesis:

1. Initialize the stack with an empty hypothesis.
2. Iterate
   (a) Pop h (the best hypothesis) off the stack.
   (b) If h is a complete sentence, output h and terminate.
   (c) Expand h.
   (d) Go to step 2a.

The search is started from a null string and obtains new hypotheses after an expansion process (step 2c) which is executed at each iteration. The expansion process consists of the application of a set of operators over the best hypothesis in the stack, as it is depicted in Figure 1. Thus, the design of stack decoding algorithms involves defining a set of operators to be applied over every hypothesis as well as the way in which they are combined in the expansion process. Both the operators and the expansion algorithm depend on the translation model that we use. For the case of the phrase-based translation models described in the previous section, the operator *add* is defined, which adds a sequence of words to the target sentence, and aligns it with a sequence of words of the source sentence.

The number of hypotheses to be stored during the search can be huge. In order then to avoid mem-

[2]Each hypothesis has associated a coverage vector of length J, which indicates the set of source words already covered/translated so far. In the following we will refer to this simply as coverage.

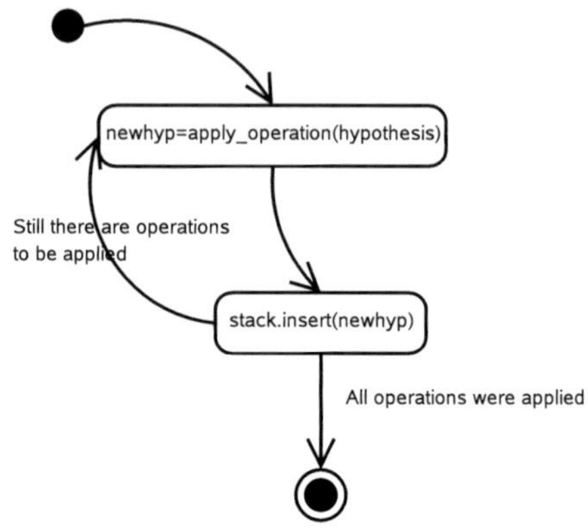

Figure 1: Flow chart associated to the expansion of a hypothesis when using an A^* algorithm.

ory overflow problems, the maximum number of hypotheses that a stack may store has to be limited. It is important to note that for a hypothesis, the higher the aligned source words, the worse the score. These hypotheses will be discarded sooner when an A^* search algorithm is used due to the stack length limitation. Because of this, the *multi-stack algorithms* were introduced.

Multi-stack algorithms store those hypotheses with different subsets of source aligned words in different stacks. That is to say, given an input sentence f_1^J composed of J words, multi-stack algorithms employes 2^J stacks to translate it. Such an organization improves the pruning of the hypotheses when the stack length limitation is exceeded, since only hypotheses with the same number of covered positions can compete with each other.

All the search steps given for A^* algorithm can also be applied here, except step 2a. This is due to the fact that multiple stacks are used instead of only one. Figure 2 depicts the expansion process that the multi-stack algorithms execute, which is slightly different than the one presented in Figure 1. Multi-stack algorithms have the negative property of spending significant amounts of time in selecting the hypotheses to be expanded, since at each iteration, the best hypothesis in a set of 2^J stacks must be searched for (Ortíz et al., 2003). By contrast, for the A^* algorithm, it is not possible to reduce the length of the stack in the same way as in the multi-stack case without loss of translation quality.

Additionally, certain translation systems, e.g. the Pharaoh decoder (Koehn, 2003) use an alternative

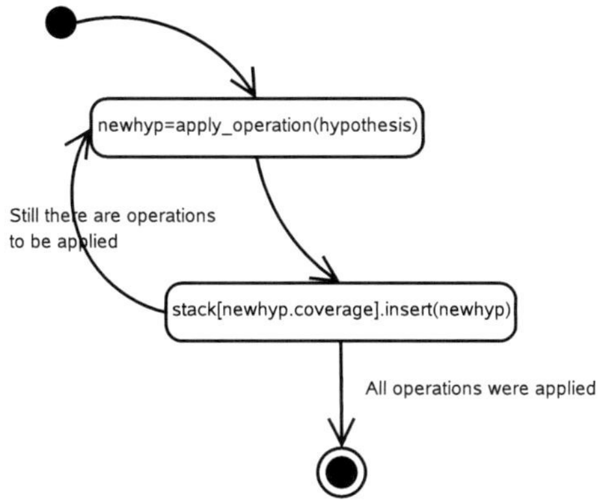

Figure 2: Flow chart associated to the expansion of a hypothesis when using a multi-stack algorithm.

approach which consists in assigning to the same stack, those hypotheses with the same number of source words covered.

4 Generalized Stack-Decoding Algorithms

As was mentioned in the previous section, given a sentence f_1^J to be translated, a single stack decoding algorithm employs only one stack to perform the translation process, while a multi-stack algorithm employs 2^J stacks. We propose a possible way to make a tradeoff between the advantages of both algorithms that introduces a new parameter which will be referred to as the *granularity* of the algorithm. The granularity parameter determines the number of stacks used during the decoding process.

4.1 Selecting the *granularity* of the algorithm

The granularity (G) of a generalized stack algorithm is an integer which takes values between 1 and J, where J is the number of words which compose the sentence to translate.

Given a sentence f_1^J to be translated, a generalized stack algorithm with a granularity parameter equal to g, will have the following features:

- The algorithm will use at most 2^g stacks to perform the translation
- Each stack will contain hypotheses which have 2^{J-g} different coverages of f_1^J
- If the algorithm can store at most $S = s$ hypotheses, then, the maximum size of each stack will be equal to $\frac{s}{2^g}$

4.2 Mapping hypotheses to stacks

Generalized stack-decoding algorithms require a mechanism to decide in which stack each hypothesis is to be inserted. As stated in section 4.1, given an input sentence f_1^J and a generalized stack-decoding algorithm with $G = g$, the decoder will work with 2^g stacks, and each one will contain 2^{J-g} different coverages. Therefore, the above mentioned mechanism can be expressed as a function which will be referred to as the μ function. Given a hypothesis coverage composed of J bits, the μ function return a stack identifier composed of only g bits:

$$\mu : (\{0,1\})^J \longrightarrow (\{0,1\})^g \quad (6)$$

Generalized stack algorithms are strongly inspired by multi-stack algorithms; however, both types of algorithms differ in the way the hypothesis expansion is performed. Figure 3 shows the expansion algorithm of a generalized stack decoder with a granularity parameter equal to g and a function μ which maps hypotheses coverages to stacks.

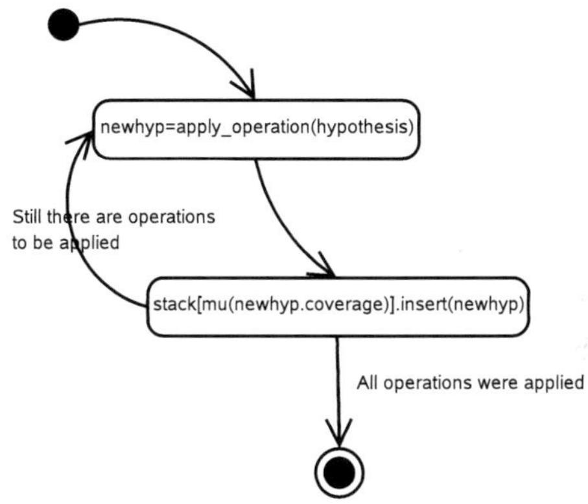

Figure 3: Flow chart associated to the expansion of a hypothesis when using a generalized-stack algorithm.

The function μ can be defined in many ways, but there are two essential principles which must be taken into account:

- The μ function must be efficiently calculated
- Hypotheses whose coverage have a similar number of bits set to one must be assigned to the same stack. This requirement allows the pruning of the stacks to be improved, since the

hypotheses with a similar number of covered words can compete fairly

A possible way to implement the μ function, namely μ_1, consists in simply shifting the coverage vector $J - g$ positions to the right, and then keeping only the first g bits. Such a proposal is very easy to calculate, however, it has a poor performance according to the second principle explained above.

A better alternative to implement the μ function, namely μ_2, can be formulated as a composition of two functions. A constructive definition of such a implementation is detailed next:

1. Let us suppose that the source sentence is composed by J words, we order the set of J bit numbers as follows: first the numbers which do not have any bit equal to one, next, the numbers which have only one bit equal to one, and so on

2. Given the list of numbers described above, we define a function which associates to each number of the list, the order of the number within this list

3. Given the coverage of a partial hypothesis, x, the stack on which this partial hypothesis is to be inserted is obtained by a two step process: First, we obtain the image of x returned by the function described above. Next, the result is shifted $J - g$ positions to the right, keeping the first g bits

Let β be the function that shifts a bit vector $J - g$ positions to the right, keeping the first g bits; and let α be the function that for each coverage returns its order:

$$\alpha : (\{0,1\})^J \longrightarrow (\{0,1\})^J \quad (7)$$

Then, μ_2 is expressed as follows:

$$\mu_2(x) = \beta \circ \alpha(x) \quad (8)$$

Table 1 shows an example of the values which returns the μ_1 and the μ_2 functions when the input sentence has 4 words and the granularity of the decoder is equal to 2. As it can be observed, μ_2 function performs better than μ_1 function according to the second principle described at the beginning of this section.

x	$\mu_1(x)$	$\alpha(x)$	$\mu_2(x)$
0000	00	0000	00
0001	00	0001	00
0010	00	0010	00
0100	01	0011	00
1000	10	0100	01
0011	00	0101	01
0101	01	0110	01
0110	01	0111	01
1001	10	1000	10
1010	10	1001	10
1100	11	1010	10
0111	01	1011	10
1011	10	1100	11
1101	11	1101	11
1110	11	1110	11
1111	11	1111	11

Table 1: Values returned by the μ_1 and μ_2 function defined as a composition of the α and β functions

4.3 Single and Multi Stack Algorithms

The classical single and multi-stack decoding algorithms can be expressed/instantiated as particular cases of the general formalism that have been proposed.

Given the input sentence f_1^J , a generalized stack decoding algorithm with $G = 0$ will have the following features:

- The algorithm works with $2^0 = 1$ stacks.

- Such a stack may store hypotheses with 2^J different coverages. That is to say, all possible coverages.

- The mapping function returns the same stack identifier for each coverage

The previously defined algorithm has the same features as a single stack algorithm.

Let us now consider the features of a generalized stack algorithm with a granularity value of J:

- The algorithm works with 2^J stacks

- Each stack may store hypotheses with only $2^0 = 1$ coverage.

- The mapping function returns a different stack identifier for each coverage

The above mentioned features characterizes the multi-stack algorithms described in the literature.

		EuTrans-I		Xerox	
		Spanish	**English**	**Spanish**	**English**
Training	Sentences	10,000		55,761	
	Words	97,131	99,292	753,607	665,400
	Vocabulary size	686	513	11,051	7,957
	Average sentence leng.	9.7	9.9	13.5	11.9
Test	Sentence	2,996		1,125	
	Words	35,023	35,590	10,106	8,370
	Perplexity (Trigrams)	–	3.62	–	48.3

Table 2: EuTrans-I and Xerox corpus statistics

5 Experiments and Results

In this section, experimental results are presented for two well-known tasks: the EuTrans-I (Amengual et al., 1996), a small size and easy translation task, and the Xerox (Cubel et al., 2004), a medium size and difficult translation task. The main statistics of these corpora are shown in Table 2. The translation results were obtained using a non-monotone generalized stack algorithm. For both tasks, the training of the different phrase models was carried out using the publicly available *Thot* toolkit (Ortiz et al., 2005).

Different translation experiments have been carried out, varying the value of G (ranging from 0 to 8) and the maximum number of hypothesis that the algorithm is allow to store for all used stacks (S) (ranging from 2^8 to 2^{12}). In these experiments the following statistics are computed: the average score (or logProb) that the phrase-based translation model assigns to each hypothesis, the translation quality (by means of WER and Bleu measures), and the average time (in secs.) per sentence[3].

In Figures 4 and 5 two plots are shown: the average time per sentence (left) and the average score (right), for EuTrans and Xerox corpora respectively. As can be seen in both figures, the bigger the value of G the lower the average time per sentence. This is true up to the value of $G = 6$. For higher values of G (keeping fixed the value of S) the average time per sentence increase slightly. This is due to the fact that at this point the algorithm start to spend more time to decide which hypothesis is to be expanded. With respect to the average score similar values are obtained up to the value of $G = 4$. Higher values of G slightly decreases the average score. In this case, as G increases, the number of hypotheses per stack decreases, taking into account that the value of S is fixed, then the "optimal" hypothesis can easily be pruned.

[3]All the experiments have been executed on a PC with a 2.60 Ghz Intel Pentium 4 processor with 2GB of memory. All the times are given in seconds.

In tables 3 and 4 detailed experiments are shown for a value of $S = 2^{12}$ and different values of G, for EuTrans and Xerox corpora respectively.

G	WER	Bleu	secsXsent	logprob
0	6.6	0.898	2.4	-18.88
1	6.6	0.898	1.9	-18.80
2	6.6	0.897	1.7	-18.81
4	6.6	0.898	1.3	-18.77
6	6.7	0.896	1.1	-18.83
8	6.7	0.896	1.5	-18.87

Table 3: Translation experiments for EuTrans corpus using a generalized stack algorithm with different values of G and a fixed value of $S = 2^{12}$

G	WER	Bleu	secsXsent	logProb
0	32.6	0.658	35.1	-33.92
1	32.8	0.657	20.4	-33.86
2	33.1	0.656	12.8	-33.79
4	32.9	0.657	7.0	-33.70
6	33.7	0.652	6.3	-33.69
8	36.3	0.634	13.7	-34.10

Table 4: Translation experiments for Xerox corpus using a generalized stack algorithm with different values of G and a fixed value of $S = 2^{12}$

According to the experiments presented here we can conclude that:

- The results correlates for the two considered tasks: one small and easy, and other larger and difficult.
- The proposed generalized stack decoding paradigm can be used to make a tradeoff be-

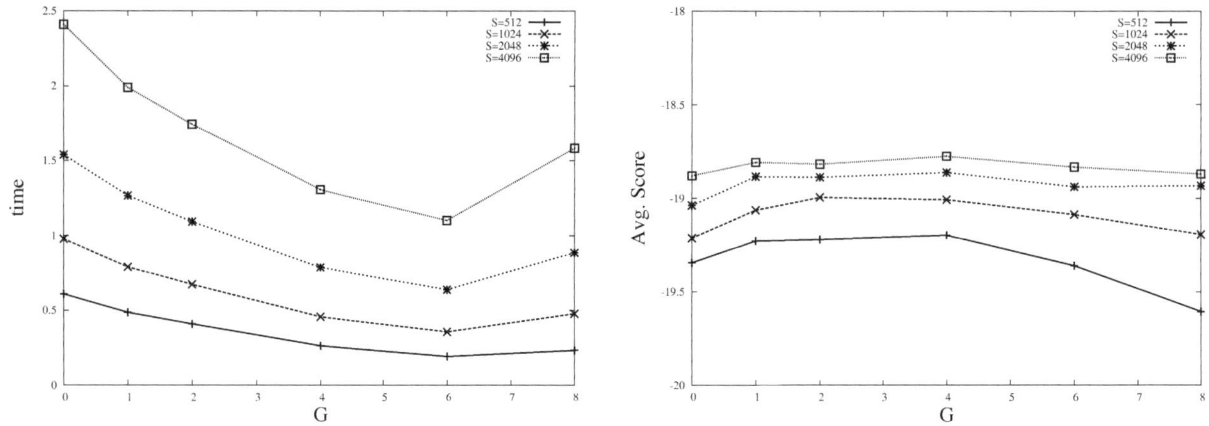

Figure 4: Average time per sentence (in secs.) and average score per sentence. The results are shown for different values of G and S for the EuTrans corpus.

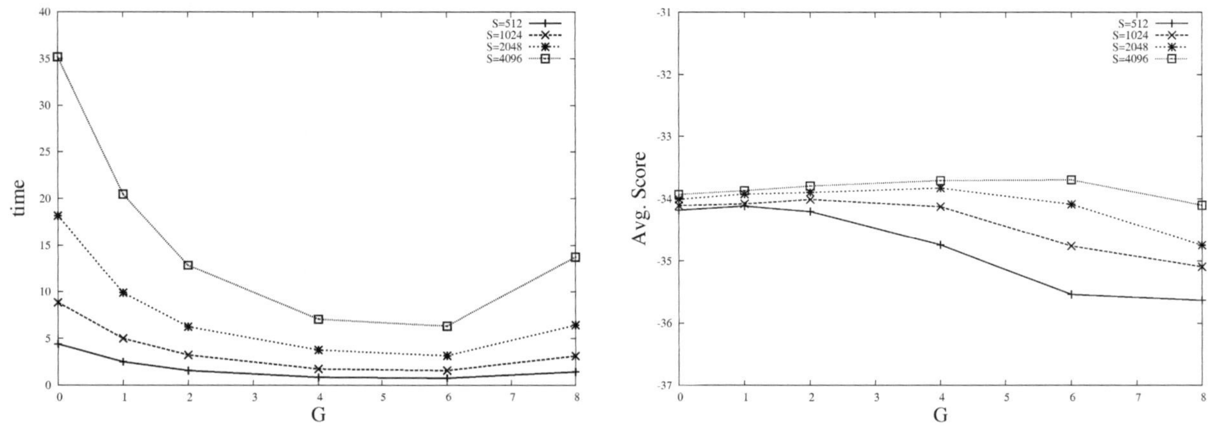

Figure 5: Average time per sentence (in secs.) and average score per sentence. The results are shown for different values of G and S for the Xerox corpus.

tween the advantages of classical single and multi-stack decoding algorithms.

- As we expected, better results (regarding efficiency and accuracy) are obtained when using a value of G between 0 and J.

6 Concluding Remarks

In this paper, a generalization of the stack-decoding paradigm has been proposed. This new formalism includes the well known single and multi-stack decoding algorithms and a new family of stack-based algorithms which have not been described yet in the literature.

Essentially, generalized stack algorithms use a parameterized number of stacks during the decoding process, and try to assign hypotheses to stacks such that there is "fair competition" within each stack, i.e., brother hypotheses should cover roughly the same number of input words (and the same words) if possible.

The new family of stack-based algorithms allows a tradeoff to be made between the classical single and multi-stack decoding algorithms. For this purpose, they employ a certain number of stacks between 1 (the number of stacks used by a single stack algorithm) and 2^J (the number of stacks used by a multiple stack algorithm to translate a sentence with J words.)

According to the experimental results, it has been proved that an appropriate value of G yields in a stack decoding algorithm that outperforms (in efficiency and acuraccy) the single and multi-stack algorithms proposed so far.

As future work, we plan to extend the experimentation framework presented here to larger and more complex tasks as HANSARDS and EUROPARL corpora.

References

J.C. Amengual, J.M. Benedí, M.A. Castao, A. Marzal, F. Prat, E. Vidal, J.M. Vilar, C. Delogu, A. di Carlo, H. Ney, and S. Vogel. 1996. Definition of a machine translation task and generation of corpora. Technical report d4, Instituto Tecnológico de Informática, September. ESPRIT, EuTrans IT-LTR-OS-20268.

Adam L. Berger, Peter F. Brown, Stephen A. Della Pietra, Vincent J. Della Pietra, John R. Gillett, A. S. Kehler, and R. L. Mercer. 1996. Language translation apparatus and method of using context-based translation models. United States Patent, No. 5510981, April.

Peter F. Brown, Stephen A. Della Pietra, Vincent J. Della Pietra, and R. L. Mercer. 1993. The mathematics of statistical machine translation: Parameter estimation. *Computational Linguistics*, 19(2):263–311.

E. Cubel, J. Civera, J. M. Vilar, A. L. Lagarda, E. Vidal, F. Casacuberta, D. Picó, J. González, and L. Rodríguez. 2004. Finite-state models for computer assisted translation. In *Proceedings of the 16th European Conference on Artificial Intelligence (ECAI04)*, pages 586–590, Valencia, Spain, August. IOS Press.

Ulrich Germann, Michael Jahr, Kevin Knight, Daniel Marcu, and Kenji Yamada. 2001. Fast decoding and optimal decoding for machine translation. In *Proc. of the 39th Annual Meeting of ACL*, pages 228–235, Toulouse, France, July.

F. Jelinek. 1969. A fast sequential decoding algorithm using a stack. *IBM Journal of Research and Development*, 13:675–685.

P. Koehn, F. J. Och, and D. Marcu. 2003. Statistical phrase-based translation. In *Proceedings of the HLT/NAACL*, Edmonton, Canada, May.

Phillip Koehn. 2003. Pharaoh: a beam search decoder for phrase-based statistical machine translation models. User manual and description. Technical report, USC Information Science Institute, December.

Daniel Marcu and William Wong. 2002. A phrase-based, joint probability model for statistical machine translation. In *Proceedings of the EMNLP Conference*, pages 1408–1414, Philadelphia, USA, July.

Hermann Ney, Sonja Nießen, Franz J. Och, Hassan Sawaf, Christoph Tillmann, and Stephan Vogel. 2000. Algorithms for statistical translation of spoken language. *IEEE Trans. on Speech and Audio Processing*, 8(1):24–36, January.

Franz J. Och, Nicola Ueffing, and Hermann Ney. 2001. An efficient A* search algorithm for statistical machine translation. In *Data-Driven Machine Translation Workshop*, pages 55–62, Toulouse, France, July.

Franz Joseph Och. 2002. *Statistical Machine Translation: From Single-Word Models to Alignment Templates*. Ph.D. thesis, Computer Science Department, RWTH Aachen, Germany, October.

D. Ortíz, Ismael García-Varea, and Francisco Casacuberta. 2003. An empirical comparison of stack-based decoding algorithms for statistical machine translation. In *New Advance in Computer Vision*, Lecture Notes in Computer Science. Springer-Verlag. 1st Iberian Conference on Pattern Recongnition and Image Analysis -IbPRIA2003- Mallorca. Spain. June.

D. Ortiz, I. Garca-Varea, and F. Casacuberta. 2005. Thot: a toolkit to train phrase-based statistical translation models. In *Tenth Machine Translation Summit*, pages 141–148, Phuket, Thailand, September.

J. Tomás and F. Casacuberta. 2001. Monotone statistical translation using word groups. In *Procs. of the Machine Translation Summit VIII*, pages 357–361, Santiago de Compostela, Spain.

J. Tomás and F. Casacuberta. 2003. Combining phrase-based and template-based models in statistical machine translation. In *Pattern Recognition and Image Analisys*, volume 2652 of *LNCS*, pages 1021–1031. Springer-Verlag. 1st bPRIA.

Ye-Yi Wang and Alex Waibel. 1998. Fast decoding for statistical machine translation. In *Proc. of the Int. Conf. on Speech and Language Processing*, pages 1357–1363, Sydney, Australia, November.

Kenji Yamada and Kevin Knight. 2001. A syntax-based statistical translation model. In *Proc. of the 39th Annual Meeting of ACL*, pages 523–530, Toulouse, France, July.

R. Zens, F.J. Och, and H. Ney. 2002. Phrase-based statistical machine translation. In *Advances in artificial intelligence. 25. Annual German Conference on AI*, volume 2479 of *Lecture Notes in Computer Science*, pages 18–32. Springer Verlag, September.

N-Gram Posterior Probabilities for Statistical Machine Translation

Richard Zens and Hermann Ney

Human Language Technology and Pattern Recognition
Lehrstuhl für Informatik 6 – Computer Science Department
RWTH Aachen University, D-52056 Aachen, Germany
{zens,ney}@cs.rwth-aachen.de

Abstract

Word posterior probabilities are a common approach for confidence estimation in automatic speech recognition and machine translation. We will generalize this idea and introduce n-gram posterior probabilities and show how these can be used to improve translation quality. Additionally, we will introduce a sentence length model based on posterior probabilities.

We will show significant improvements on the Chinese-English NIST task. The absolute improvements of the BLEU score is between 1.1% and 1.6%.

1 Introduction

The use of word posterior probabilities is a common approach for confidence estimation in automatic speech recognition, e.g. see (Wessel, 2002). This idea has been adopted to estimate confidences for machine translation, e.g. see (Blatz et al., 2003; Ueffing et al., 2003; Blatz et al., 2004). These confidence measures were used in the computer assisted translation (CAT) framework, e.g. (Gandrabur and Foster, 2003). The (simplified) idea is that the confidence measure is used to decide if the machine-generated prediction should be suggested to the human translator or not.

There is only few work on how to improve machine translation performance using confidence measures. The only work, we are aware of, is (Blatz et al., 2003). The outcome was that the confidence measures did not result in improvements of the translation quality measured with the BLEU and NIST scores. Here, we focus on how the ideas and methods commonly used for confidence estimation can be adapted and/or extended to improve translation quality.

So far, always word-level posterior probabilities were used. Here, we will generalize this idea to n-grams.

In addition to the n-gram posterior probabilities, we introduce a sentence-length model based on posterior probabilities. The common phrase-based translation systems, such as (Och et al., 1999; Koehn, 2004), do not use an explicit sentence length model. Only the simple word penalty goes into that direction. It can be adjusted to prefer longer or shorter translations. Here, we will explicitly model the sentence length.

The novel contributions of this work are to introduce n-gram posterior probabilities and sentence length posterior probabilities. Using these methods, we achieve significant improvements of translation quality.

The remaining part of this paper is structured as follows: first, we will briefly describe the baseline system, which is a state-of-the-art phrase-based statistical machine translation system. Then, in Section 3, we will introduce the n-gram posterior probabilities. In Section 4, we will define the sentence length model. Afterwards, in Section 5, we will describe how these novel models can be used for rescoring/reranking. The experimental results will be presented in Section 6. Future applications will be described in Section 7. Finally, we will conclude in Section 8.

Proceedings of the Workshop on Statistical Machine Translation, pages 72–77,
New York City, June 2006.

2 Baseline System

In statistical machine translation, we are given a source language sentence $f_1^J = f_1 \ldots f_j \ldots f_J$, which is to be translated into a target language sentence $e_1^I = e_1 \ldots e_i \ldots e_I$. Among all possible target language sentences, we will choose the sentence with the highest probability:

$$\hat{e}_1^{\hat{I}} = \operatorname*{argmax}_{I, e_1^I} \left\{ Pr(e_1^I | f_1^J) \right\} \quad (1)$$

The posterior probability $Pr(e_1^I|f_1^J)$ is modeled directly using a log-linear combination of several models (Och and Ney, 2002):

$$Pr(e_1^I|f_1^J) = \frac{\exp\left(\sum_{m=1}^M \lambda_m h_m(e_1^I, f_1^J)\right)}{\sum_{I', e'^{I'}_1} \exp\left(\sum_{m=1}^M \lambda_m h_m(e'^{I'}_1, f_1^J)\right)} \quad (2)$$

The denominator is a normalization factor that depends only on the source sentence f_1^J. Therefore, we can omit it during the search process. As a decision rule, we obtain:

$$\hat{e}_1^{\hat{I}} = \operatorname*{argmax}_{I, e_1^I} \left\{ \sum_{m=1}^M \lambda_m h_m(e_1^I, f_1^J) \right\} \quad (3)$$

This approach is a generalization of the source-channel approach (Brown et al., 1990). It has the advantage that additional models $h(\cdot)$ can be easily integrated into the overall system. The model scaling factors λ_1^M are trained with respect to the final translation quality measured by an error criterion (Och, 2003).

We use a state-of-the-art phrase-based translation system as described in (Zens and Ney, 2004; Zens et al., 2005). The baseline system includes the following models: an n-gram language model, a phrase translation model and a word-based lexicon model. The latter two models are used for both directions: $p(f|e)$ and $p(e|f)$. Additionally, we use a word penalty and a phrase penalty.

3 N-Gram Posterior Probabilities

The idea is similar to the word posterior probabilities: we sum the sentence posterior probabilities for each occurrence of an n-gram.

Let $\delta(\cdot, \cdot)$ denote the Kronecker function. Then, we define the fractional count $C(e_1^n, f_1^J)$ of an n-gram e_1^n for a source sentence f_1^J as:

$$C(e_1^n, f_1^J) = \sum_{I, e'^I_1} \sum_{i=1}^{I-n+1} p(e'^I_1|f_1^J) \cdot \delta(e'^{i+n-1}_i, e_1^n) \quad (4)$$

The sums over the target language sentences are limited to an N-best list, i.e. the N best translation candidates according to the baseline model. In this equation, the term $\delta(e'^{i+n-1}_i, e_1^n)$ is one if and only if the n-gram e_1^n occurs in the target sentence e'^I_1 starting at position i.

Then, the posterior probability of an n-gram is obtained as:

$$p(e_1^n|f_1^J) = \frac{C(e_1^n, f_1^J)}{\sum_{e'^n_1} C(e'^n_1, f_1^J)} \quad (5)$$

Note that the widely used word posterior probability is obtained as a special case, namely if n is set to one.

4 Sentence Length Posterior Probability

The common phrase-based translation systems, such as (Och et al., 1999; Koehn, 2004), do not use an explicit sentence length model. Only the simple word penalty goes into that direction. It can be adjusted to prefer longer or shorter translations.

Here, we will use the posterior probability of a specific target sentence length I as length model:

$$p(I|f_1^J) = \sum_{e_1^I} p(e_1^I|f_1^J) \quad (6)$$

Note that the sum is carried out only over target sentences e_1^I with the a specific length I. Again, the candidate target language sentences are limited to an N-best list.

5 Rescoring/Reranking

A straightforward application of the posterior probabilities is to use them as additional features in a rescoring/reranking approach (Och et al., 2004). The use of N-best lists in machine translation has several advantages. It alleviates the effects of the huge search space which is represented in word graphs by using a compact excerpt of the N best hypotheses generated by the system. N-best lists are suitable for easily applying several rescoring techniques since the hypotheses are already fully generated. In comparison, word graph rescoring techniques need specialized tools which can traverse the graph accordingly.

The n-gram posterior probabilities can be used similar to an n-gram language model:

$$h_n(f_1^J, e_1^I) = \frac{1}{I} \log \left(\prod_{i=1}^{I} p(e_i | e_{i-n+1}^{i-1}, f_1^J) \right) \quad (7)$$

with:

$$p(e_i | e_{i-n+1}^{i-1}, f_1^J) = \frac{C(e_{i-n+1}^{i}, f_1^J)}{C(e_{i-n+1}^{i-1}, f_1^J)} \quad (8)$$

Note that the models do not require smoothing as long as they are applied to the same N-best list they are trained on.

If the models are used for unseen sentences, smoothing is important to avoid zero probabilities. We use a linear interpolation with weights α_n and the smoothed $(n-1)$-gram model as generalized distribution.

$$p_n(e_i | e_{i-n+1}^{i-1}, f_1^J) = \alpha_n \cdot \frac{C(e_{i-n+1}^{i}, f_1^J)}{C(e_{i-n+1}^{i-1}, f_1^J)} + (1-\alpha_n) \cdot p_{n-1}(e_i | e_{i-n+2}^{i-1}, f_1^J) \quad (9)$$

Note that absolute discounting techniques that are often used in language modeling cannot be applied in a straightforward way, because here we have *fractional* counts.

The usage of the sentence length posterior probability for rescoring is even simpler. The resulting feature is:

$$h_L(f_1^J, e_1^I) = \log p(I | f_1^J) \quad (10)$$

Again, the model does not require smoothing as long as it is applied to the same N-best list it is trained on. If it is applied to other sentences, smoothing becomes important. We propose to smooth the sentence length model with a Poisson distribution.

$$p_\beta(I | f_1^J) = \beta \cdot p(I | f_1^J) + (1-\beta) \cdot \frac{\lambda^I \exp(-\lambda)}{I!} \quad (11)$$

We use a linear interpolation with weight β. The mean λ of the Poisson distribution is chosen to be identical to the mean of the unsmoothed length model:

$$\lambda = \sum_I I \cdot p(I | f_1^J) \quad (12)$$

6 Experimental Results

6.1 Corpus Statistics

The experiments were carried out on the large data track of the Chinese-English NIST task. The corpus statistics of the bilingual training corpus are shown in Table 1. The language model was trained on the English part of the bilingual training corpus and additional monolingual English data from the GigaWord corpus. The total amount of language model training data was about 600M running words. We use a fourgram language model with modified Kneser-Ney smoothing as implemented in the SRILM toolkit (Stolcke, 2002).

To measure the translation quality, we use the BLEU score (Papineni et al., 2002) and the NIST score (Doddington, 2002). The BLEU score is the geometric mean of the n-gram precision in combination with a brevity penalty for too short sentences. The NIST score is the arithmetic mean of a weighted n-gram precision in combination with a brevity penalty for too short sentences. Both scores are computed case-sensitive with respect to four reference translations using the mteval-v11b tool[1]. As the BLEU and NIST scores measure accuracy higher scores are better.

We use the BLEU score as primary criterion which is optimized on the development set using the Downhill Simplex algorithm (Press et al., 2002). As development set, we use the NIST 2002 evaluation set. Note that the baseline system is already well-tuned and would have obtained a high rank in the last NIST evaluation (NIST, 2005).

6.2 Translation Results

The translation results for the Chinese-English NIST task are presented in Table 2. We carried out experiments for evaluation sets of several years. For these rescoring experiments, we use the 10 000 best translation candidates, i.e. N-best lists of size N=10 000.

[1]http://www.nist.gov/speech/tests/mt/resources/scoring.htm

Table 1: Chinese-English NIST task: corpus statistics for the bilingual training data and the NIST evaluation sets of the years 2002 to 2005.

			Chinese	English
Train	Sentence Pairs		7M	
	Running Words		199M	213M
	Vocabulary Size		223K	351K
	Dictionary Entry Pairs		82K	
Eval	2002	Sentences	878	3 512
		Running Words	25K	105K
	2003	Sentences	919	3 676
		Running Words	26K	122K
	2004	Sentences	1788	7 152
		Running Words	52K	245K
	2005	Sentences	1082	4 328
		Running Words	33K	148K

Using the 1-gram posterior probabilities, i.e. the conventional word posterior probabilities, there is only a very small improvement, or no improvement at all. This is consistent with the findings of the JHU workshop on confidence estimation for statistical machine translation 2003 (Blatz et al., 2003), where the word-level confidence measures also did not help to improve the BLEU or NIST scores.

Successively adding higher order n-gram posterior probabilities, the translation quality improves consistently across all evaluation sets. We also performed experiments with n-gram orders beyond four, but these did not result in further improvements.

Adding the sentence length posterior probability feature is also helpful for all evaluation sets. For the development set, the overall improvement is 1.5% for the BLEU score. On the blind evaluation sets, the overall improvement of the translation quality ranges between 1.1% and 1.6% BLEU.

Some translation examples are shown in Table 3.

7 Future Applications

We have shown that the n-gram posterior probabilities are very useful in a rescoring/reranking framework. In addition, there are several other potential applications. In this section, we will describe two of them.

7.1 Iterative Search

The n-gram posterior probability can be used for rescoring as described in Section 5. An alternative is to use them directly during the search. In this second search pass, we use the models from the first pass, i.e. the baseline system, and additionally the n-gram and sentence length posterior probabilities. As the n-gram posterior probabilities are basically a kind of sentence-specific language model, it is straightforward to integrate them. This process can also be iterated. Thus, using the N-best list of the second pass to recompute the n-gram and sentence length posterior probabilities and do a third search pass, etc..

7.2 Computer Assisted Translation

In the computer assisted translation (CAT) framework, the goal is to improve the productivity of human translators. The machine translation system takes not only the current source language sentence but also the already typed partial translation into account. Based on this information, the system suggest completions of the sentence. Word-level posterior probabilities have been used to select the most appropriate completion of the system, for more details see e.g. (Gandrabur and Foster, 2003; Ueffing and Ney, 2005). The n-gram based posterior probabilities as described in this work, might be better suited for this task as they explicitly model the dependency on the previous words, i.e. the given prefix.

8 Conclusions

We introduced n-gram and sentence length posterior probabilities and demonstrated their usefulness for rescoring purposes. We performed systematic experiments on the Chinese-English NIST task and showed significant improvements of the translation quality. The improvements were consistent among several evaluation sets.

An interesting property of the introduced methods is that they do not require additional knowledge sources. Thus the given knowledge sources are better exploited. Our intuition is that the posterior models prefer hypotheses with n-grams that are common in the N-best list.

The achieved results are promising. Despite that, there are several ways to improve the approach.

Table 2: Case-sensitive translation results for several evaluation sets of the Chinese-English NIST task.

Evaluation set	2002 (dev)		2003		2004		2005	
System	NIST	BLEU[%]	NIST	BLEU[%]	NIST	BLEU[%]	NIST	BLEU[%]
Baseline	8.49	30.5	8.04	29.5	8.14	29.0	8.01	28.2
+ 1-grams	8.51	30.5	8.08	29.5	8.17	29.0	8.03	28.2
+ 2-grams	8.47	30.8	8.03	29.7	8.12	29.2	7.98	28.1
+ 3-grams	8.73	31.6	8.25	30.1	8.45	30.0	8.20	28.6
+ 4-grams	8.74	31.7	8.26	30.1	8.47	30.1	8.20	28.6
+ length	8.87	32.0	8.42	30.9	8.60	30.6	8.34	29.3

Table 3: Translation examples for the Chinese-English NIST task.

Baseline	At present, there is no organization claimed the attack.
Rescored	At present, there is no organization claimed responsibility for the attack.
Reference	So far, no organization whatsoever has claimed responsibility for the attack.
Baseline	FIFA to severely punish football fraud
Rescored	The International Football Federation (FIFA) will severely punish football's deception
Reference	FIFA will severely punish all cheating acts in the football field
Baseline	In more than three months of unrest, a total of more than 60 dead and 2000 injured.
Rescored	In more than three months of unrest, a total of more than 60 people were killed and more than 2000 injured.
Reference	During the unrest that lasted more than three months, a total of more than 60 people died and over 2,000 were wounded.

For the decision rule in Equation 3, the model scaling factors λ_1^M can be multiplied with a constant factor without changing the result. This global factor would affect the proposed posterior probabilities. So far, we have not tuned this parameter, but a proper adjustment might result in further improvements.

Currently, the posterior probabilities are computed on an N-best list. Using word graphs instead should result in more reliable estimates, as the number of hypotheses in a word graph is some orders of a magnitude larger than in an N-best list.

Acknowledgments

This material is partly based upon work supported by the Defense Advanced Research Projects Agency (DARPA) under Contract No. HR0011-06-C-0023, and was partly funded by the European Union under the integrated project TC-STAR (Technology and Corpora for Speech to Speech Translation, IST-2002-FP6-506738, http://www.tc-star.org).

References

J. Blatz, E. Fitzgerald, G. Foster, S. Gandrabur, C. Goutte, A. Kulesza, A. Sanchis, and N. Ueffing. 2003. Confidence estimation for machine translation. Final report, JHU/CLSP Summer Workshop. `http://www.clsp.jhu.edu/ws2003/groups/estimate/`.

J. Blatz, E. Fitzgerald, G. Foster, S. Gandrabur, C. Goutte, A. Kulesza, A. Sanchis, and N. Ueffing. 2004. Confidence estimation for machine translation. In *Proc. 20th Int. Conf. on Computational Linguistics (COLING)*, pages 315–321, Geneva, Switzerland, August.

P. F. Brown, J. Cocke, S. A. Della Pietra, V. J. Della Pietra, F. Jelinek, J. D. Lafferty, R. L. Mercer, and P. S. Roossin. 1990. A statistical approach to machine translation. *Computational Linguistics*, 16(2):79–85, June.

G. Doddington. 2002. Automatic evaluation of machine translation quality using n-gram co-occurrence statistics. In *Proc. ARPA Workshop on Human Language Technology*.

S. Gandrabur and G. Foster. 2003. Confidence estimation for text prediction. In *Proc. Conf. on Natural Lan-*

guage Learning (CoNLL), pages 95–102, Edmonton, Canada, May.

P. Koehn. 2004. Pharaoh: a beam search decoder for phrase-based statistical machine translation models. In *6th Conf. of the Association for Machine Translation in the Americas (AMTA 04)*, pages 115–124, Washington DC, September/October.

NIST. 2005. NIST 2005 machine translation evaluation official results. `http://www.nist.gov/speech/tests/mt/mt05eval_official_results_release_20050801_v3.html`, August.

F. J. Och and H. Ney. 2002. Discriminative training and maximum entropy models for statistical machine translation. In *Proc. of the 40th Annual Meeting of the Association for Computational Linguistics (ACL)*, pages 295–302, Philadelphia, PA, July.

F. J. Och, C. Tillmann, and H. Ney. 1999. Improved alignment models for statistical machine translation. In *Proc. Joint SIGDAT Conf. on Empirical Methods in Natural Language Processing and Very Large Corpora*, pages 20–28, University of Maryland, College Park, MD, June.

F. J. Och, D. Gildea, S. Khudanpur, A. Sarkar, K. Yamada, A. Fraser, S. Kumar, L. Shen, D. Smith, K. Eng, V. Jain, Z. Jin, and D. Radev. 2004. A smorgasbord of features for statistical machine translation. In *Proc. Human Language Technology Conf. / North American Chapter of the Association for Computational Linguistics Annual Meeting (HLT-NAACL)*, pages 161–168, Boston,MA.

F. J. Och. 2003. Minimum error rate training in statistical machine translation. In *Proc. of the 41th Annual Meeting of the Association for Computational Linguistics (ACL)*, pages 160–167, Sapporo, Japan, July.

K. Papineni, S. Roukos, T. Ward, and W. J. Zhu. 2002. Bleu: a method for automatic evaluation of machine translation. In *Proc. of the 40th Annual Meeting of the Association for Computational Linguistics (ACL)*, pages 311–318, Philadelphia, PA, July.

W. H. Press, S. A. Teukolsky, W. T. Vetterling, and B. P. Flannery. 2002. *Numerical Recipes in C++*. Cambridge University Press, Cambridge, UK.

A. Stolcke. 2002. SRILM – an extensible language modeling toolkit. In *Proc. Int. Conf. on Speech and Language Processing (ICSLP)*, volume 2, pages 901–904, Denver, CO, September.

N. Ueffing and H. Ney. 2005. Application of word-level confidence measures in interactive statistical machine translation. In *Proc. of the 10th Annual Conf. of the European Association for Machine Translation (EAMT)*, pages 262–270, Budapest, Hungary, May.

N. Ueffing, K. Macherey, and H. Ney. 2003. Confidence Measures for Statistical Machine Translation. In *Proc. MT Summit IX*, pages 394–401, New Orleans, LA, September.

F. Wessel. 2002. *Word Posterior Probabilities for Large Vocabulary Continuous Speech Recognition*. Ph.D. thesis, RWTH Aachen University, Aachen, Germany, January.

R. Zens and H. Ney. 2004. Improvements in phrase-based statistical machine translation. In *Proc. Human Language Technology Conf. / North American Chapter of the Association for Computational Linguistics Annual Meeting (HLT-NAACL)*, pages 257–264, Boston, MA, May.

R. Zens, O. Bender, S. Hasan, S. Khadivi, E. Matusov, J. Xu, Y. Zhang, and H. Ney. 2005. The RWTH phrase-based statistical machine translation system. In *Proceedings of the International Workshop on Spoken Language Translation (IWSLT)*, pages 155–162, Pittsburgh, PA, October.

Partitioning Parallel Documents Using Binary Segmentation

Jia Xu and **Richard Zens** and **Hermann Ney**
Chair of Computer Science 6
Computer Science Department
RWTH Aachen University
D-52056 Aachen Germany
{xujia,zens,ney}@cs.rwth-aachen.de

Abstract

In statistical machine translation, large numbers of parallel sentences are required to train the model parameters. However, plenty of the bilingual language resources available on web are aligned only at the document level. To exploit this data, we have to extract the bilingual sentences from these documents.

The common method is to break the documents into segments using predefined anchor words, then these segments are aligned. This approach is not error free, incorrect alignments may decrease the translation quality.

We present an alternative approach to extract the parallel sentences by partitioning a bilingual document into two pairs. This process is performed recursively until all the sub-pairs are short enough.

In experiments on the Chinese-English FBIS data, our method was capable of producing translation results comparable to those of a state-of-the-art sentence aligner. Using a combination of the two approaches leads to better translation performance.

1 Introduction

Current statistical machine translation systems use bilingual sentences to train the parameters of the translation models. The exploitation of more bilingual sentences automatically and accurately as well as the use of these data with the limited computational requirements become crucial problems.

The conventional method for producing parallel sentences is to break the documents into sentences and to align these sentences using dynamic programming. Previous investigations can be found in works such as (Gale and Church, 1993) and (Ma, 2006). A disadvantage is that only the monotone sentence alignments are allowed.

Another approach is the binary segmentation method described in (Simard and Langlais, 2003), (Xu et al., 2005) and (Deng et al., 2006), which separates a long sentence pair into two sub-pairs recursively. The binary reordering in alignment is allowed but the segmentation decision is only optimum in each recursion step.

Hence, a combination of both methods is expected to produce a more satisfying result. (Deng et al., 2006) performs a two-stage procedure. The documents are first aligned at level using dynamic programming, the initial alignments are then refined to produce shorter segments using binary segmentation. But on the Chinese-English FBIS training corpus, the alignment accuracy and recall are lower than with Champollion (Ma, 2006).

We refine the model in (Xu et al., 2005) using a log-linar combination of different feature functions and combine it with the approach of (Ma, 2006). Here the corpora produced using both approaches are concatenated, and each corpus is assigned a weight. During the training of the word alignment models, the counts of the lexicon entries

Proceedings of the Workshop on Statistical Machine Translation, pages 78–85,
New York City, June 2006.

are linear interpolated using the corpus weights. In the experiments on the Chinese-English FBIS corpus the translation performance is improved by 0.4% of the BLEU score compared to the performance only with Champollion.

The remainder of this paper is structured as follows: First we will briefly review the baseline statistical machine translation system in Section 2. Then, in Section 3, we will describe the refined binary segmentation method. In Section 4.1, we will introduce the methods to extract bilingual sentences from document aligned texts. The experimental results will be presented in Section 4.

2 Review of the Baseline Statistical Machine Translation System

In this section, we briefly review our translation system and introduce the word alignment models.

In statistical machine translation, we are given a source language sentence $f_1^J = f_1 \ldots f_j \ldots f_J$, which is to be translated into a target language sentence $e_1^I = e_1 \ldots e_i \ldots e_I$. Among all possible target language sentences, we will choose the sentence with the highest probability:

$$\begin{aligned} \hat{e}_1^{\hat{I}} &= \underset{I, e_1^I}{\text{argmax}} \left\{ Pr(e_1^I | f_1^J) \right\} \\ &= \underset{I, e_1^I}{\text{argmax}} \left\{ Pr(e_1^I) \cdot Pr(f_1^J | e_1^I) \right\} \end{aligned} \quad (1)$$

The decomposition into two knowledge sources in Equation 1 allows independent modeling of target language model $Pr(e_1^I)$ and translation model $Pr(f_1^J|e_1^I)$[1]. The translation model can be further extended to a statistical alignment model with the following equation:

$$Pr(f_1^J|e_1^I) = \sum_{a_1^J} Pr(f_1^J, a_1^J|e_1^I)$$

The alignment model $Pr(f_1^J, a_1^J|e_1^I)$ introduces a 'hidden' word alignment $\mathbf{a} = a_1^J$, which describes a mapping from a source position j to a target position a_j.

[1]The notational convention will be as follows: we use the symbol $Pr(\cdot)$ to denote general probability distributions with (nearly) no specific assumptions. In contrast, for model-based probability distributions, we use the generic symbol $p(\cdot)$.

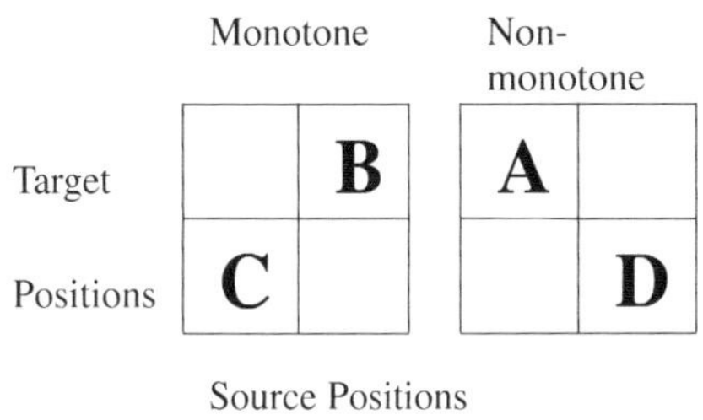

Figure 1: Two Types of Alignment

The IBM model 1 (IBM-1) (Brown et al., 1993) assumes that all alignments have the same probability by using a uniform distribution:

$$p(f_1^J|e_1^I) = \frac{1}{I^J} \cdot \prod_{j=1}^{J} \sum_{i=1}^{I} p(f_j|e_i) \quad (2)$$

We use the IBM-1 to train the lexicon parameters $p(f|e)$, the training software is GIZA++ (Och and Ney, 2003).

To incorporate the context into the translation model, the phrase-based translation approach (Zens et al., 2005) is applied. Pairs of source and target language phrases are extracted from the bilingual training corpus and a beam search algorithm is implemented to generate the translation hypothesis with maximum probability.

3 Binary Segmentation Method

3.1 Approach

Here a document or sentence pair (f_1^J, e_1^I) [2] is represented as a matrix. Every element in the matrix contains a lexicon probability $p(f_j|e_i)$, which is trained on the original parallel corpora. Each position divides a matrix into four parts as shown in Figure 1: the bottom left (C), the upper left (A), the bottom right (D) and the upper right (B). We use m to denote the alignment direction, $m = 1$ means that the alignment is monotone, i.e. the bottom left part is connected with the upper right part, and $m = 0$ means the alignment is non-monotone, i.e. the upper left part is connected with the bottom right part, as shown in Figure 1.

3.2 Log-Linear Model

We use a log-linear interpolation to combine different models: the IBM-1, the inverse IBM-1, the an-

[2]Sentences are equivalent to segments in this paper.

chor words model as well as the IBM-4. K denotes the total number of models.

We go through all positions in the bilingual sentences and find the best position for segmenting the sentence:

$$(\hat{i}, \hat{j}, \hat{m}) = \underset{i,j,m}{\operatorname{argmax}} \left\{ \sum_{k=1}^{K} \lambda_k h_k(j, i, m | f_1^J, e_1^I) \right\},$$

where $i \in [1, I-1]$ and $j \in [1, J-1]$ are positions in the source and target sentences respectively. The feature functions are described in the following sections. In most cases, the sentence pairs are quite long and even after one segmentation we may still have long sub-segments. Therefore, we separate the sub-segment pairs recursively until the length of each new segment is less than a defined value.

3.3 Normalized IBM-1

The function in Equation 2 can be normalized by the source sentence length with a weighting β as described in (Xu et al., 2005):

The monotone alignment is calculated as

$$\begin{aligned} h_1(j, i, 1 | f_1^J, e_1^I) &= \log(p(f_1^j | e_1^i)^{\beta \cdot \frac{1}{j} + (1-\beta)} \quad (3) \\ &\cdot p(f_{j+1}^J | e_{i+1}^I)^{\beta \cdot \frac{1}{J-j} + (1-\beta)}), \end{aligned}$$

and the non-monotone alignment is formulated in the same way.

We also use the inverse IBM-1 as a feature, by exchanging the place of e_1^i and f_1^j its monotone alignment is calculated as:

$$\begin{aligned} h_2(j, i, 1 | f_1^J, e_1^I) &= \log(p(e_1^i | f_1^j)^{\beta \cdot \frac{1}{i} + (1-\beta)} \quad (4) \\ &\cdot p(e_{i+1}^I | f_{j+1}^J)^{\beta \cdot \frac{1}{I-i} + (1-\beta)}) \end{aligned}$$

3.4 Anchor Words

In the task of extracting parallel sentences from the paragraph-aligned corpus, selecting some anchor words as preferred segmentation positions can effectively avoid the extraction of incomplete segment pairs. Therefore we use an anchor words model to prefer the segmentation at the punctuation marks, where the source and target words are identical:

$$h_3(j, i, m | f_1^J, e_1^I) = \begin{cases} 1 : f_j = e_i \wedge e_i \in \mathcal{A} \\ 0 : \text{otherwise} \end{cases}$$

$\mathcal{A}$ is a user defined anchor word list, here we use $\mathcal{A}$={.,"?;}. If the corresponding model scaling factor λ_3 is assigned a high value, the segmentation positions are mostly after anchor words.

3.5 IBM-4 Word Alignment

If we already have the IBM-4 Viterbi word alignments for the parallel sentences and need to retrain the system, for example to optimize the training parameters, we can include the Viterbi word alignments trained on the original corpora into the binary segmentation. In the monotone case, the model is represented as

$$h_4(j, i, 1 | f_1^J, e_1^I) = \log \left(\frac{N(f_1^j, e_1^i) + N(f_{j+1}^J, e_{i+1}^I)}{N(f_1^J, e_1^I)} \right),$$

where $N(f_1^j, e_1^i)$ denotes the number of the alignment links inside the matrix $(1, 1)$ and (j, i). In the non-monotone case the model is formulated in the same way.

3.6 Word Alignment Concatenation

As described in Section 2, our translation is based on phrases, that means for an input sentence we extract all phrases matched in the training corpus and translate with these phrase pairs. Although the aim of segmentation is to split parallel text into translated segment pairs, but the segmentation is still not perfect. During sentence segmentation we might separate a phrase into two segments, so that the whole phrase pair can not be extracted.

To avoid this, we concatenate the word alignments trained with the segmentations of one sentence pair. During the segmentation, the position of each segmentation point in the sentence is memorized. After training the word alignment model with the segmented sentence pairs, the word alignments are concatenated again according to the positions of their segments in the sentences. The original sentence pairs and the concatenated alignments are then used for the phrase extraction.

Table 1: Corpus Statistics: NIST

		Chinese	English
Train	Sentences	8.64 M	
	Running Words	210 M	226 M
	Average Sentence Length	24.4	26.3
	Vocabulary	224 268	359 623
	Singletons	98 842	156 493
Segmentation	Sentences	17.9 M	
	Running Words	210 M	226 M
	Average Sentence Length	11.7	12.6
	Vocabulary	221 517	353 148
	Singletons	97 062	152 965
Segmentation with Additional Data	Sentences	19.5 M	
	Running Words	230 M	248 M
	Added Running Words	8.0%	8.2%
Evaluation	Sentences	878	3 512
	Running Words	24 111	105 516
	Vocabulary	4 095	6 802
	OOVs (Running Words)	8	658

4 Translation Experiments

4.1 Bilingual Sentences Extraction Methods

In this section, we describe the different methods to extract the bilingual sentence pairs from the document aligned corpus.

Given each document pair, we assume that the paragraphs are aligned one to one monotone if both the source and target language documents contain the same number of paragraphs; otherwise the paragraphs are aligned with the Champollion tool.

Starting from the parallel paragraphs we extract the sentences using three methods:

1. Binary segmentation

   The segmentation method described in Section 3 is applied by treating the paragraph pairs as long sentence pairs. We can use the anchor words model described in Section 3.4 to prefer splitting at punctuation marks.

   The lexicon parameters $p(f|e)$ in Equation 2 are estimated as follows: First the sentences are aligned roughly using the dynamic programming algorithm. Training on these aligned sentences, we get the initial lexicon parameters. Then the binary segmentation algorithm is applied to extract the sentences again.

2. Champollion

   After a paragraph is divided into sentences at punctuation marks, the Champollion tool (Ma, 2006) is used, which applies dynamic programming for the sentence alignment.

3. Combination

   The bilingual corpora produced by the binary segmentation and Champollion methods are concatenated and are used in the training of the translation model. Each corpus is assigned a weight. During the training of the word alignment models, the counts of the lexicon entries are linearly interpolated using the corpus weights.

4.2 Translation Tasks

We will present the translation results on two Chinese-English tasks.

1. On the large data track NIST task (NIST, 2005), we will show improvements using the refined binary segmentation method.

Table 2: Corpus Statistics: FBIS

		Segmentation		Champollion	
		Chinese	English	Chinese	English
Train	Sentences	739 899		177 798	
	Running Words	8 588 477	10 111 752	7 659 776	9 801 257
	Average Sentence Length	11.6	13.7	43.1	55.1
	Vocabulary	34 896	56 573	34 377	55 775
	Singletons	4 775	19 283	4 588	19 004
Evaluation	Sentences	878	3 513	878	3 513
	Running Words	24 111	105 516	24 111	105 516
	Vocabulary	4 095	6 802	4 095	6 802
	OOVs (Running Words)	109	2 257	119	2 309

2. On the FBIS corpus, we will compare the different sentence extraction methods described in Section 4.1 with respect to translation performance. We do not apply the extraction methods on the whole NIST corpora, because some corpora provided by the LDC (LDC, 2005) are sentence aligned but not document aligned.

4.3 Corpus Statistics

The training corpora used in NIST task are a set of individual corpora including the FBIS corpus. These corpora are provided by the Linguistic Data Consortium (LDC, 2005), the domains are news articles. The translation experiments are carried out on the NIST 2002 evaluation set.

As shown in Table 1, there are 8.6 million sentence pairs in the original corpora of the NIST task. The average sentence length is about 25. After segmentation, there are twice as many sentence pairs, i.e. 17.9 million, and the average sentence length is around 12. Due to a limitation of GIZA++, sentences consisting of more than one hundred words are filtered out. Segmentation of long sentences circumvents this restriction and allows us include more data. Here we were able to add 8% more Chinese and 8.2% more English running words to the training data. The training time is also reduced.

Table 2 presents statistics of the FBIS data. After the paragraph alignment described in Section 4.1 we have nearly 81 thousand paragraphs, 8.6 million Chinese and 10.1 million English running words. One of the advantages of the binary segmentation is that we do not loose words during the bilingual sentences extraction. However, we produce sentence pairs with very different lengths. Using Champollion we loose 10.8% of the Chinese and 3.1% of the English words.

4.4 Segmentation Parameters

We did not optimize the log-linear model scaling factors for the binary segmentation but used the following fixed values: $\lambda_1 = \lambda_2 = 0.5$ for the IBM-1 models in both directions; $\lambda_3 = 10^8$, if the anchor words model is is used; $\lambda_4 = 30$, if the IBM-4 model is used. The maximum sentence length is 25.

4.5 Evaluation Criteria

We use four different criteria to evaluate the translation results automatically:

- WER (word error rate):
  The WER is computed as the minimum number of substitution, insertion and deletion operations that have to be performed to convert the generated sentence into the reference sentence, divided by the reference sentence length.

- PER (position-independent word error rate):
  A shortcoming of the WER is that it requires a perfect word order. The word order of an acceptable sentence can be differ from that of the target sentence, so that the WER measure alone could be misleading. The PER compares the words in the two sentences ignoring the word order.

- BLEU score:
  This score measures the precision of unigrams,

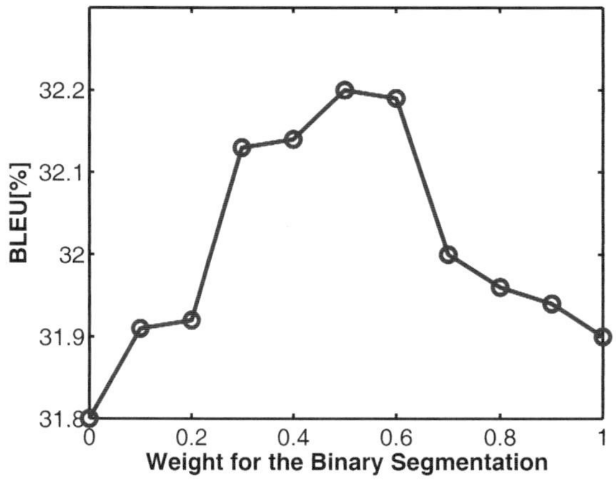

Figure 2: Translation performance as a function of the weight for the binary segmentation α (weight for Champollion: $1 - \alpha$)

bigrams, trigrams and fourgrams with a penalty for too short sentences. (Papineni et al., 2002).

- NIST score:
  This score is similar to BLEU, but it uses an arithmetic average of N-gram counts rather than a geometric average, and it weights more heavily those N-grams that are more informative. (Doddington, 2002).

The BLEU and NIST scores measure accuracy, i.e. larger scores are better. In our evaluation the scores are measured as case insensitive and with respect to multiple references.

4.6 Translation Results

For the segmentation of long sentences into short segments, we performed the experiments on the NIST task. Both in the baseline and the segmentation systems we obtain 4.7 million bilingual phrases during the translation. The method of alignment concatenation increases the number of the extracted bilingual phrase pairs from 4.7 million to 4.9 million, the BLEU score is improved by 0.1%. By including the IBM-4 Viterbi word alignment, the NIST score is improved. The training of the baseline system requires 5.9 days, after the sentence segmentation it requires only 1.5 days. Moreover, the segmentation allows the inclusion of long sentences that are filtered out in the baseline system. Using the added data, the translation performance is enhanced by 0.3% in the BLEU score. Because of the long translation period, the translation parameters are only optimized on the baseline system with respect to the BLEU score, we could expect a further improvement if the parameters were also optimized on the segmentation system.

Our major objective here is to introduce another approach to parallel sentence extraction: binary segmentation of the bilingual texts recursively. We use the paragraph-aligned corpus as a starting point. Table 4 presents the translation results on the training corpora generated by the different methods described in Section 4.1. The translation parameters are optimized with the respect to the BLEU score. We observe that the binary segmentation methods are comparable to Champollion and the segmentation with anchors outperforms the one without anchors. By combining the methods of Champollion and the binary segmentation with anchors, the BLEU score is improved by 0.4% absolutely.

We optimized the weightings for the binary segmentation method, the sum of the weightings for both methods is one. As shown in Figure 2, using one of the methods alone does not produce the best result. The maximum BLEU score is attained when both methods are combined with equal weightings.

5 Discussion and Future Work

We successfully applied the binary sentence segmentation method to extract bilingual sentence pairs from the document aligned texts. The experiments on the FBIS data show an enhancement of 0.4% of the BLEU score compared to the score obtained using a state-of-art sentence aligner. In addition to the encouraging results obtained, further improvements could be achieved in the following ways:

1. By extracting bilingual paragraphs from the documents, we lost running words using Champollion. Applying the segmentation approach to paragraph alignment might avoid the loss of this data.

2. We combined a number of different models in the binary segmentation, such as IBM-1, and anchor words. The model weightings could be optimized with respect to translation quality.

Table 3: Translation Results using Refined Segmentation Methods on NIST task

	Error Rate[%]		Accuracy	
	WER	PER	NIST	BLEU[%]
Baseline	62.7	42.1	8.95	33.5
Segmentation	62.6	42.4	8.80	33.5
Segmentation + concatenation	62.4	42.3	8.84	33.6
Segmentation + concatenation + IBM-4	62.8	42.4	8.91	33.6
Segmentation + added data	62.9	42.5	9.00	33.9

Table 4: Translation Results on Sentence Alignment Task with FBIS Training Corpus

	Error Rate[%]		Accuracy	
	WER	PER	NIST	BLEU[%]
Champollion	64.2	43.7	8.61	31.8
Segmentation without Anchors	64.3	44.4	8.57	31.8
Segmentation with Anchors	64.0	43.9	8.58	31.9
Champollion + Segmentation with Anchors	64.3	44.2	8.57	32.2

3. In the binary segmentation method, an incorrect segmentation results in further mistakes in the segmentation decisions of all its subsegments. An alternative method (Wu, 1997) makes decisions at the end but has a high computational requirement. A restricted expansion of the search space might better balance segmentation accuracy and the efficiency.

6 Acknowledgments

This work was supported by the European Union under the integrated project TC-Star (Technology and Corpora for Speech to Speech Translation, IST-2002-FP6-506738, http://www.tc-star.org) and the Defense Advanced Research Projects Agency (DARPA) under Contract No. HR0011-06-C-0023.

References

P. F. Brown, S. A. Della Pietra, V. J. Della Pietra, and R. L. Mercer. 1993. The mathematics of statistical machine translation: Parameter estimation. *Computational Linguistics*, 19(2):263–311, June.

Y. Deng, S. Kumar, and W. Byrne. 2006. Segmentation and alignment of parallel text for statistical machine translation. *Natural Language Engineering*, Accepted. To appear.

G. Doddington. 2002. Automatic evaluation of machine translation quality using n-gram co-occurrence statistics. In *Proceedings of Human Language Technology*, pages 128–132, San Diego, California, March.

W. A. Gale and K. W. Church. 1993. A program for aligning sentences in bilingual corpora. *Computational Linguistics*, 19(1):75–90.

LDC. 2005. Linguistic data consortium resource home page. http://www.ldc.upenn.edu/Projects/TIDES.

X. Ma. 2006. Champollion: A robust parallel text sentence aligner. In *Proceedings of the fifth international conference on Language Resources and Evaluation (LREC)*, Genoa, Italy, Accepted. To appear.

NIST. 2005. Machine translation home page. http://www.nist.gov/speech/tests/mt/index.htm.

F. J. Och and H. Ney. 2003. A systematic comparison of various statistical alignment models. *Computational Linguistics*, 29(1):19–51, March.

K. A. Papineni, S. Roukos, T. Ward, and W. J. Zhu. 2002. Bleu: a method for automatic evaluation of machine translation. In *Proceedings of the 40th Annual Meeting of the Association for Computational Linguistics*, pages 311–318, Philadelphia, July.

M. Simard and P. Langlais. 2003. Statistical translation alignment with compositionality constraints. In *NAACL 2003 Workshop on Building and Using Parallel Texts: Data Driven Machine Translation and Beyond*, Edmonton, Canada, May.

D. Wu. 1997. Stochastic inversion transduction grammars and bilingual parsing of parallel corpora. *Computational Linguistics*, 23(3):377–403, September.

J. Xu, R. Zens, and H. Ney. 2005. Sentence segmentation using IBM word alignment model 1. In *Proceedings of EAMT 2005 (10th Annual Conference of the European Association for Machine Translation)*, pages 280–287, Budapest, Hungary, May.

R. Zens, O. Bender, S. Hasan, S. Khadivi, E. Matusov, J. Xu, Y. Zhang, and H. Ney. 2005. The RWTH phrase-based statistical machine translation system. In *Proceedings of the International Workshop on Spoken Language Translation (IWSLT)*, pages 155–162, Pittsburgh, PA, October.

Contextual Bitext-Derived Paraphrases in Automatic MT Evaluation

Karolina Owczarzak **Declan Groves** **Josef Van Genabith** **Andy Way**
National Centre for Language Technology
School of Computing
Dublin City University
Dublin 9, Ireland
{owczarzak,dgroves,josef,away}@computing.dcu.ie

Abstract

In this paper we present a novel method for deriving paraphrases during automatic MT evaluation using only the source and reference texts, which are necessary for the evaluation, and word and phrase alignment software. Using target language paraphrases produced through word and phrase alignment a number of alternative reference sentences are constructed automatically for each candidate translation. The method produces lexical and low-level syntactic paraphrases that are relevant to the domain in hand, does not use external knowledge resources, and can be combined with a variety of automatic MT evaluation system.

1 Introduction

Since their appearance, BLEU (Papineni et al., 2002) and NIST (Doddington, 2002) have been the standard tools used for evaluating the quality of machine translation. They both score candidate translations on the basis of the number of n-grams it shares with one or more reference translations provided. Such automatic measures are indispensable in the development of machine translation systems, because they allow the developers to conduct frequent, cost-effective, and fast evaluations of their evolving models.

These advantages come at a price, though: an automatic comparison of n-grams measures only the string similarity of the candidate translation to one or more reference strings, and will penalize any divergence from them. In effect, a candidate translation expressing the source meaning accurately and fluently will be given a low score if the lexical choices and syntactic structure it contains, even though perfectly legitimate, are not present in at least one of the references. Necessarily, this score would not reflect a much more favourable human judgment that such a translation would receive.

The limitations of string comparison are the reason why it is advisable to provide multiple references for a candidate translation in the BLEU- or NIST-based evaluation in the first place. While (Zhang and Vogel, 2004) argue that increasing the size of the test set gives even more reliable system scores than multiple references, this still does not solve the inadequacy of BLEU and NIST for sentence-level or small set evaluation. On the other hand, in practice even a number of references do not capture the whole potential variability of the translation. Moreover, often it is the case that multiple references are not available or are too difficult and expensive to produce: when designing a statistical machine translation system, the need for large amounts of training data limits the researcher to collections of parallel corpora like Europarl (Koehn, 2005), which provides only one reference, namely the target text; and the cost of creating additional reference translations of the test set, usually a few thousand sentences long, often exceeds the resources available. Therefore, it would be desirable to find a way to automatically generate legitimate translation alternatives not present in the reference(s) already available.

Proceedings of the Workshop on Statistical Machine Translation, pages 86–93,
New York City, June 2006.

In this paper, we present a novel method that automatically derives paraphrases using only the source and reference texts involved in for the evaluation of French-to-English Europarl translations produced by two MT systems: statistical phrase-based Pharaoh (Koehn, 2004) and rule-based Logomedia.[1] In using what is in fact a miniature bilingual corpus our approach differs from the mainstream paraphrase generation based on monolingual resources. We show that paraphrases produced in this way are more relevant to the task of evaluating machine translation than the use of external lexical knowledge resources like thesauri or WordNet[2], in that our paraphrases contain both lexical equivalents and low-level syntactic variants, and in that, as a side-effect, evaluation bitext-derived paraphrasing naturally yields domain-specific paraphrases. The paraphrases generated from the evaluation bitext are added to the existing reference sentences, in effect creating multiple references and resulting in a higher score for the candidate translation. Our hypothesis, confirmed by the experiments in this paper, is that the scores raised by additional references produced in this way will correlate better with human judgment than the original scores.

The remainder of this paper is organized as follows: Section 2 describes related work; Section 3 describes our method and presents examples of derived paraphrases; Section 4 presents the results of the comparison between the BLUE and NIST scores for a single-reference translation and the same translation using the paraphrases automatically generated from the bitext, as well as the correlations between the scores and human judgment; Section 5 discusses ongoing work; Section 6 concludes.

2 Related work

2.1 Word and phrase alignment

Several researchers noted that the word and phrase alignment used in training translation models in Statistical MT can be used for other purposes as well. (Diab and Resnik, 2002) use second language alignments to tag word senses. Working on an assumption that separate senses of a L1 word can be distinguished by its different translations in L2, they also note that a set of possible L2 translations for a L1 word may contain many synonyms. (Bannard and Callison-Burch, 2005), on the other hand, conduct an experiment to show that paraphrases derived from such alignments can be semantically correct in more than 70% of the cases.

2.2 Automatic MT evaluation

The insensitivity of BLEU and NIST to perfectly legitimate variation has been raised, among others, in (Callison-Burch et al., 2006), but the criticism is widespread. Even the creators of BLEU point out that it may not correlate particularly well with human judgment at the sentence level (Papineni et al., 2002), a problem also noted by (Och et al., 2003) and (Russo-Lassner et al., 2005). A side effect of this phenomenon is that BLEU is less reliable for smaller data sets, so the advantage it provides in the speed of evaluation is to some extent counterbalanced by the time spent by developers on producing a sufficiently large test data set in order to obtain a reliable score for their system.

Recently a number of attempts to remedy these shortcomings have led to the development of other automatic machine translation metrics. Some of them concentrate mainly on the word reordering aspect, like Maximum Matching String (Turian et al., 2003) or Translation Error Rate (Snover et al., 2005). Others try to accommodate both syntactic and lexical differences between the candidate translation and the reference, like CDER (Leusch et al., 2006), which employs a version of edit distance for word substitution and reordering; METEOR (Banerjee and Lavie, 2005), which uses stemming and WordNet synonymy; and a linear regression model developed by (Russo-Lassner et al., 2005), which makes use of stemming, WordNet synonymy, verb class synonymy, matching noun phrase heads, and proper name matching.

A closer examination of these metrics suggests that the accommodation of lexical equivalence is as difficult as the appropriate treatment of syntactic variation, in that it requires considerable external knowledge resources like WordNet, verb class databases, and extensive text preparation: stemming, tagging, etc. The advantage of our method is that it produces relevant paraphrases with nothing more than the evaluation bitext and a widely available word and phrase alignment software, and therefore can be used with any existing evaluation metric.

[1] http://www.lec.com/

[2] http://wordnet.princeton.edu/

3 Contextual bitext-derived paraphrases

The method presented in this paper rests on a combination of two simple ideas. First, the components necessary for automatic MT evaluation like BLEU or NIST, a source text and a reference text, constitute a miniature parallel corpus, from which word and phrase alignments can be extracted automatically, much like during the training for a statistical machine translation system. Second, target language words $e_{i1}, \ldots, e_{in}$ aligned as the likely translations to a source language word f_i are often synonyms or near-synonyms of each other. This also holds for phrases: target language phrases $ep_{i1}, \ldots, ep_{in}$ aligned with a source language phrase fp_i are often paraphrases of each other. For example, in our experiment, for the French word *question* the most probable automatically aligned English translations are *question*, *matter*, and *issue*, which in English are practically synonyms. Section 3.2 presents more examples of such equivalent expressions.

3.1 Experimental design

For our experiment, we used two test sets, each consisting of 2000 sentences, drawn randomly from the test section of the Europarl parallel corpus. The source language was French and the target language was English. One of the test sets was translated by Pharaoh trained on 156,000 French-English sentence pairs. The other test set was translated by Logomedia, a commercially available rule-based MT system. Each test set consisted therefore of three files: the French source file, the English translation file, and the English reference file.

Each translation was evaluated by the BLEU and NIST metrics first with the single reference, then with the multiple references for each sentence using the paraphrases automatically generated from the source-reference mini corpus. A subset of a 100 sentences was randomly extracted from each test set and evaluated by two independent human judges with respect to accuracy and fluency; the human scores were then compared to the BLEU and NIST scores for the single-reference and the automatically generated multiple-reference files.

3.2 Word alignment and phrase extraction

We used the GIZA++ word alignment software[3] to produce initial word alignments for our miniature bilingual corpus consisting of the source French file and the English reference file, and the refined word alignment strategy of (Och and Ney, 2003; Koehn et al., 2003; Tiedemann, 2004) to obtain improved word and phrase alignments.

For each source word or phrase f_i that is aligned with more than one target words or phrases, its possible translations $e_{i1}, \ldots, e_{in}$ were placed in a list as equivalent expressions (i.e. synonyms, near-synonyms, or paraphrases of each other). A few examples are given in (1).

```
(1) agreement - accordance
    adopted - implemented
    matter - lot - case
    funds - money
    arms - weapons
    area - aspect
    question - issue - matter
    we would expect - we cer-
    tainly expect
    bear on - are centred
    around
```

Alignment divides target words and phrases into equivalence sets; each set corresponds to one source word/phrase that was originally aligned with the target elements. For example, for the French word *citoyens* three English words were deemed to be the most appropriate translations: *people*, *public*, and *citizens*; therefore these three words constitute an equivalence set. Another French word *population* was aligned with two English translations: *population* and *people*; so the word *people* appears in two equivalence set (this gives rise to the question of equivalence transitivity, which will be discussed in Section 3.3). From the 2000-sentence evaluation bitext we derived 769 equivalence sets, containing in total 1658 words or phrases. Each set contained on average two or three elements. In effect, we produced at least one equivalent expression for 1658 English words or phrases.

An advantage of our method is that the target paraphrases and words come ordered with re-

---

[3] http://www.fjoch.com/GIZA++

spect to their likelihood of being the translation of the source word or phrase – each of them is assigned a probability expressing this likelihood, so we are able to choose only the most likely translations, according to some experimentally established threshold. The experiment reported here was conducted without such a threshold, since the word and phrase alignment was of a very high quality.

3.3 Domain-specific lexical and syntactic paraphrases

It is important to notice here how the paraphrases produced are more appropriate to the task at hand than synonyms extracted from a general-purpose thesaurus or WordNet. First, our paraphrases are contextual - they are restricted to only those *relevant to the domain* of the text, since they are derived from the text itself. Given the context provided by our evaluation bitext, the word *area* in (1) turns out to be only synonymous with *aspect*, and not with *land*, *territory*, *neighbourhood*, *division*, or other synonyms a general-purpose thesaurus or WordNet would give for this entry. This allows us to limit our multiple references only to those that are likely to be useful in the context provided by the source text. Second, the phrase alignment captures something neither a thesaurus nor WordNet will be able to provide: a certain amount of syntactic variation of paraphrases. Therefore, we know that a string such as *we would expect* in (1), with the sequence *noun-aux-verb*, might be paraphrased by *we certainly expect*, a sequence of *noun-adv-verb*.

3.4 Open and closed class items

One important conclusion we draw from analysing the synonyms obtained through word alignment is that equivalence is limited mainly to words that belong to open word classes, i.e. nouns, verbs, adjectives, adverbs, but is unlikely to extend to closed word classes like prepositions or pronouns. For instance, while the French preposition *à* can be translated in English as *to*, *in*, or *at*, depending on the context, it is not the case that these three prepositions are synonymous in English. The division is not that clear-cut, however: within the class of pronouns, *he*, *she*, and *you* are definitely not synonymous, but the demonstrative pronouns *this* and *that* might be considered equivalent for some purposes. Therefore, in our experiment we exclude prepositions and in future work we plan to examine the word alignments more closely to decide whether to exclude any other words.

3.5 Creating multiple references

After the list of synonyms and paraphrases is extracted from the evaluation bitext, for each reference sentence a string search replaces every eligible word or phrase with its equivalent(s) from the paraphrase list, one at a time, and the resulting string is added to the array of references. The original string is added to the array as well. This process results in a different number of reference sentences for every test sentence, depending on whether there was anything to replace in the reference and how many paraphrases we have available for the original substring. One example of this process is shown in (2).

(2) *Original reference:*
`i admire the` **`answer`** `mrs parly gave this morning` **`but`** `we have turned a blind eye to` **`that`**
Paraphrase 1:
`i admire the` **`reply`** `mrs parly gave this morning but we have turned a blind eye to that`
Paraphrase 2:
`i admire the answer mrs parly gave this morning` **`however`** `we have turned a blind eye to that`
Paraphrase 3:
`i admire the answer mrs parly gave this morning but we have turned a blind eye to` **`it`**

Transitivity

As mentioned before, an interesting question that arises here is the potential transitivity of our automatically derived synonyms/paraphrases. It could be argued that if the word *people* is equivalent to *public* according to one set from our list, and to the word *population* according to another set, then *public* can be thought of as equivalent to *population*. In this case, the equivalence is not controversial. However, consider the following relation: if *sure* in one of the equivalence sets is synonymous to *certain*, and *certain* in a different set is listed as equivalent to *some*, then treating *sure* and *some* as synonyms is a mistake. In our experiment we do not allow synonym transitivity; we only use the paraphrases from equivalence sets containing the word/phrase we want to replace.

Multiple simultaneous substitution

Note that at the moment the references we are producing do not contain multiple simultaneous substitutions of equivalent expressions; for example, in (2) we currently do not produce the following versions:

(3) *Paraphrase 4:*
`i admire the` **`reply`** `mrs parly gave this morning` **`however`** `we have turned a blind eye to` **`that`**
Paraphrase 5:
`i admire the` **`answer`** `mrs parly gave this morning` **`however`** `we have turned a blind eye to` **`it`**
Paraphrase 6:
`i admire the` **`reply`** `mrs parly gave this morning` **`but`** `we have turned a blind eye to` **`it`**

This can potentially prevent higher n-grams being successfully matched if two or more equivalent expressions find themselves within the range of n-grams being tested by BLEU and NIST. To avoid combinatorial problems, implementing multiple simultaneous substitutions could be done using a lattice, much like in (Pang et al., 2003).

4 Results

As expected, the use of multiple references produced by our method raises both the BLEU and NIST scores for translations produced by Pharaoh (test set PH) and Logomedia (test set LM). The results are presented in Table 1.

	BLEU	NIST
PH single ref	0.2131	6.1625
PH multi ref	0.2407	7.0068
LM single ref	0.1782	5.5406
LM multi ref	0.2043	6.3834

Table 1. Comparison of single-reference and multi-reference scores for test set PH and test set LM

The hypothesis that the multiple-reference scores reflect better human judgment is also confirmed. For 100-sentence subsets (Subset PH and Subset LM) randomly extracted from our test sets PH and LM, we calculated Pearson's correlation between the average accuracy and fluency scores that the translations in this subset received from two human judges (for each subset) and the single-reference and multiple-reference sentence-level BLEU and NIST scores.

There are two issues that need to be noted at this point. First, BLEU scored many of the sentences as zero, artificially leveling many of the weaker translations.[4] This explains the low, although still statistically significant (p value < 0.01[5]) correlation with BLEU for both single and multiple reference translations. Using a version of BLEU with add-one smoothing we obtain considerably higher correlations. Table 2 shows Pearson's correlation coefficient for BLEU, BLEU with add-one smoothing, NIST, and human judgments for Subsets PH. Multiple paraphrase references produced by our method consistently lead to a higher correlation with human judgment for every metric.[6]

Subset PH / Metric	single ref	multi ref
H & BLEU	0.297	0.307
H & BLEU smoothed	0.396	0.404
H & NIST	0.323	0.355

Table 2. Pearson's correlation between human judgment and single-reference and multiple-reference BLEU, smoothed BLEU, and NIST for subset PH (of test set PH)

The second issue that requires explanation is the lower general scores Logomedia's translation received on the full set of 2000 sentences, and the extremely low correlation of its automatic evaluation with human judgment, irrespective of the number of references. It has been noticed (Calli-

[4] BLEU uses a geometric average while calculating the sentence-level score and will score a sentence as 0 if it does not have at least one 4-gram.
[5] A critical value for Pearson's correlation coefficient for the sample size between 90 and 100 is 0.267, with $p < 0.01$.
[6] The significance of the rise in scores was confirmed in a resampling/bootstrapping test, with $p < 0.0001$.

son-Burch et al., 2006) that BLEU and NIST favour n-gram based MT models such as Pharaoh, so the translation produced by Logomedia scored lower on the automatic evaluation, even though the human judges rated Logomedia output higher than Pharaoh's translation. Both human judges consistently gave very high scores to most sentences in subset LM (Logomedia), and as a consequence there was not enough variation in the scores assigned by them to create a good correlation with the BLEU and NIST scores. The average human scores for the subsets PH and LM and the coefficients of variation are presented in Table 3. It is easy to see that Logomedia's translation received a higher mean score (on a scale 0 to 5) from the human judges and with less variance than Pharaoh.

	Mean score	Variation
Subset PH	3.815	19.1%
Subset LM	4.005	16.25%

Table 3. Human judgment mean scores and coefficients of variation for Subset PH and Subset LM

As a result of the consistently high human scores for Logomedia, none of the Pearson's correlations computed for Subset LM is high enough to be significant. The values are lower than the critical value 0.164 corresponding to $p < 0.10$.

Metric \ Subset LM	single ref	multi ref
H & BLEU	0.046*	0.067*
H & BLEU smoothed	0.163*	0.151*
H & NIST	0.078*	0.116*

Table 4. Pearson's correlation between human judgment and single-reference and multiple-reference BLEU, smoothed BLEU, and NIST for subset LM (of test set LM). * denotes values with $p > 0.10$.

5 Current and future work

We would like to experiment with the way in which the list of equivalent expressions is produced. One possible development would be to derive the expressions from a very large training corpus used by a statistical machine translation system, following (Bannard and Callison-Burch, 2005), for instance, and use it as an external wider-purpose knowledge resource (rather than a current domain-tailored resource as in our experiment), which would be nevertheless improve on a thesaurus in that it would also include phrase equivalents with some syntactic variation. According to (Bannard and Callison-Burch, 2005), who derived their paraphrases automatically from a corpus of over a million German-English Europarl sentences, the baseline syntactic and semantic accuracy of the best paraphrases (those with the highest probability) reaches 48.9% and 64.5%, respectively. That is, by replacing a phrase with its one most likely paraphrase the sentence remained syntactically well-formed in 48.9% of the cases and retained its meaning in 65% of the cases.

In a similar experiment we generated paraphrases from a French-English Europarl corpus of 700,000 sentences. The data contained a considerably higher level of noise than our previous experiment on the 2000-sentence test set, even though we excluded any non-word entities from the results. Like (Bannard and Callison-Burch, 2005), we used the product of probabilities $p(f_i|e_{i1})$ and $p(e_{i2}|f_i)$ to determine the best paraphrase for a given English word e_{i1}. We then compared the accuracy across four samples of data. Each sample contained 50 randomly drawn words/phrases and their paraphrases. For the first two samples, the paraphrases were derived from the initial 2000-sentence corpus; for the second two, the paraphrases were derived from the 700,000-sentence corpus. For each corpus, one of the two samples contained only one best paraphrase for each entry, while the other listed all possible paraphrases. We then evaluated the quality of each paraphrase with respect to its syntactic and semantic accuracy. In terms of syntax, we considered the paraphrase accurate either if it had the same category as the original word/phrase; in terms of semantics, we relied on human judgment of similarity. Tables 5 and 6 summarize the syntactic and semantic accuracy levels in the samples.

Derived from \ Paraphrases	Best	All
2000-sent. corpus	59%	60%
700,000-sent. corpus	70%	48%

Table 5. Syntactic accuracy of paraphrases

Derived from \ Paraphrases	Best	All
2000-sent. corpus	83%	74%
700,000-sent. corpus	76%	68%

Table 6. Semantic accuracy of paraphrases

Although it has to be kept in mind that these percentages were taken from relatively small samples, an interesting pattern emerges from comparing the results. It seems that the average syntactic accuracy of all paraphrases decreases with increased corpus size, but the syntactic accuracy of the one best paraphrase improves. This reflects the idea behind word alignment: the bigger the corpus, the more potential alignments there are for a given word, but at the same time the better their order in terms of probability and the likelihood to obtain the correct translation. Interestingly, the same pattern is not repeated for semantic accuracy, but again, these samples are quite small. In order to address this issue, we plan to repeat the experiment with more data.

Additionally, it should be noted that certain expressions, although not completely correct syntactically, could be retained in the paraphrase lists for the purposes of machine translation evaluation. Consider the case where our equivalence set looks like this:

```
(4) abandon - abandoning -
abandoned
```

The words in (4) are all inflected forms of the verb *abandon*, and although they would produce rather ungrammatical paraphrases, those ungrammatical paraphrases still allow us to score our translation higher in terms of BLEU or NIST if it contains one of the forms of *abandon* than when it contains some unrelated word like *piano* instead. This is exactly what other scoring metrics mentioned in Section 2 attempt to obtain with the use of stemming or prefix matching.

6 Conclusions

In this paper we present a novel combination of existing ideas from statistical machine translation and paraphrase generation that leads to the creation of multiple references for automatic MT evaluation, using only the source and reference files that are required for the evaluation. The method uses simple word and phrase alignment software to find possible synonyms and paraphrases for words and phrases of the target text, and uses them to produce multiple reference sentences for each test sentence, raising the BLEU and NIST evaluation scores and reflecting human judgment better. The advantage of this method over other ways to generate paraphrases is that (1) unlike other methods, it does not require extensive parallel monolingual paraphrase corpora, but it extracts equivalent expressions from the miniature bilingual corpus of the source and reference evaluation files; (2) unlike other ways to accommodate synonymy in automatic evaluation, it does not require external lexical knowledge sources like thesauri or WordNet; (3) it extracts only synonyms that are relevant to the domain in hand; and (4) the equivalent expressions it produces include a certain amount of syntactic paraphrases.

The method is general and it can be used with any automatic evaluation metric that supports multiple references. In our future work, we plan to apply it to newly developed evaluation metrics like CDER and TER that aim to allow for syntactic variation between the candidate and the reference, therefore bringing together solutions for the two shortcomings of automatic evaluation systems: insensitivity to allowable lexical differences and syntactic variation.

References

Satanjeev Banerjee and Alon Lavie. 2005. METEOR: An Automatic Metric for MT Evaluation with Improved Correlation with Human Judgments. *Proceedings of the ACL 2005 Workshop on Intrinsic and Extrinsic Evaluation Measures for MT and/or Summarization*: 65-73.

Colin Bannard and Chris Callison-Burch. 2005. Paraphrasing with Bilingual Parallel Corpora. *Proceedings of the 43rd Annual Meeting of the Association for Computational Linguistics (ACL 2005): 597-604.*

Chris Callison-Burch, Miles Osborne and Philipp Koehn. 2006. Re-evaluating the role of BLEU in Machine Translation Research. To appear in *Proceedings of EACL-2006.*

Mona Diab and Philip Resnik. 2002. An unsupervised Method for Word Sense Tagging using Parallel Corpora. *Proceedings of the 40th Annual Meeting of the*

Association for Computational Linguistics, Philadelphia, PA.

George Doddington. 2002. Automatic Evaluation of MT Quality using N-gram Co-occurrence Statistics. *Proceedings of Human Language Technology Conference 2002*: 138–145.

Philipp Koehn, Franz Och and Daniel Marcu. 2003. Statistical Phrase-Based Translation. *Proceedings of the Human Language Technology Conference (HLT-NAACL 2003)*: 48-54.

Philipp Koehn. 2004. Pharaoh: a beam search decoder for phrase-based statistical machine translation models. *Machine translation: From real users to research. 6th Conference of the Association for Machine Translation in the Americas (AMTA 2004)*: 115-124.

Philipp Koehn. 2005. Europarl: A Parallel Corpus for Statistical Machine Translation. *Proceedings of MT Summit 2005*: 79-86.

Gregor Leusch, Nicola Ueffing and Hermann Ney. 2006. CDER: Efficient MT Evaluation Using Block Movements. To appear in *Proceedings of the 11th Conference of the European Chapter of the Association for Computational Linguistics (EACL 2006).*

Franz Josef Och and Hermann Ney. 2003. A Systematic Comparison of Various Statistical Alignment Modes. *Computational Linguistics*, 29:19—51.

Franz Josef Och, Daniel Gildea, Sanjeev Khudanpur, Anoop Sarkar, Kenji Yamada, Alex Fraser, Shankar Kumar, Libin Shen, David Smith, Katherine Eng, Viren Jain, Zhen Jin, and Dragomir Radev. 2003. *Syntax for statistical machine translation.* Technical report, Center for Language and Speech Processing, John Hopkins University, Baltimore, MD.

Bo Pang, Kevin Knight and Daniel Marcu. 2003. Syntax-based Alignment of Multiple Translations: Extracting Paraphrases and Generating New Sentences. *Proceedings of Human Language Technology-North American Chapter of the Association for Computational Linguistics (HLT-NAACL) 2003: 181—188.*

Kishore Papineni, Salim Roukos, Todd Ward, and Wei-Jing Zhu. 2002. BLEU: a method for automatic evaluation of machine translation. In *Proceedings of ACL*: 311-318.

Grazia Russo-Lassner, Jimmy Lin, and Philip Resnik. 2005. *A Paraphrase-based Approach to Machine Translation Evaluation.* Technical Report LAMP-TR-125/CS-TR-4754/UMIACS-TR-2005-57, University of Maryland, College Park, MD.

Mathew Snover, Bonnie Dorr, Richard Schwartz, John Makhoul, Linnea Micciula and Ralph Weischedel. 2005. *A Study of Translation Error Rate with Targeted Human Annotation.* Technical Report LAMP-TR-126, CS-TR-4755, UMIACS-TR-2005-58, University of Maryland, College Park. MD.

Jörg Tiedemann. 2004. Word to word alignment strategies. *Proceedings of the 20th International Conference on Computational Linguistics (COLING 2004)*: 212-218.

Joseph P. Turian, Luke Shen, and I. Dan Melamed. 2003. Evaluation of Machine translation and Its Evaluation. *Proceedings of MT Summit 2003*: 386-393.

Ying Zhang and Stephan Vogel. 2004. Measuring confidence intervals for the machine translation evaluation metrics. *TMI-2004: Proceedings of the 10th Conference on Theoretical and Methodological Issues in Machine Translation*: 85-94.

How Many Bits Are Needed To Store Probabilities for Phrase-Based Translation?

Marcello Federico and Nicola Bertoldi
ITC-irst - Centro per la Ricerca Scientifica e Tecnologica
38050 Povo - Trento, Italy
{federico,bertoldi}@itc.it

Abstract

State of the art in statistical machine translation is currently represented by phrase-based models, which typically incorporate a large number of probabilities of phrase-pairs and word n-grams. In this work, we investigate data compression methods for efficiently encoding n-gram and phrase-pair probabilities, that are usually encoded in 32-bit floating point numbers. We measured the impact of compression on translation quality through a phrase-based decoder trained on two distinct tasks: the translation of European Parliament speeches from Spanish to English, and the translation of news agencies from Chinese to English. We show that with a very simple quantization scheme all probabilities can be encoded in just 4 bits with a relative loss in BLEU score on the two tasks by 1.0% and 1.6%, respectively.

1 Introduction

In several natural language processing tasks, such as automatic speech recognition and machine translation, state-of-the-art systems rely on the statistical approach.

Statistical machine translation (SMT) is based on parametric models incorporating a large number of observations and probabilities estimated from monolingual and parallel texts. The current state of the art is represented by the so-called phrase-based translation approach (Och and Ney, 2004; Koehn et al., 2003). Its core components are a translation model that contains probabilities of phrase-pairs, and a language model that incorporates probabilities of word n-grams.

Due to the intrinsic data-sparseness of language corpora, the set of observations increases almost linearly with the size of the training data. Hence, to efficiently store observations and probabilities in a computer memory the following approaches can be tackled: designing compact data-structures, pruning rare or unreliable observations, and applying data compression.

In this paper we only focus on the last approach. We investigate two different quantization methods to encode probabilities and analyze their impact on translation performance. In particular, we address the following questions:

- How does probability quantization impact on the components of the translation system, namely the language model and the translation model?
- Which is the optimal trade-off between data compression and translation performance?
- How do quantized models perform under different data-sparseness conditions?
- Is the impact of quantization consistent across different translation tasks?

Experiments were performed with our phrase-based SMT system (Federico and Bertoldi, 2005) on two large-vocabulary tasks: the translation of European Parliament Plenary Sessions from Spanish to

Proceedings of the Workshop on Statistical Machine Translation, pages 94–101,
New York City, June 2006.

English, and the translation of news agencies from Chinese to English, according to the set up defined by the 2005 NIST MT Evaluation Workshop.

The paper is organized as follows. Section 2 reviews previous work addressing efficiency in speech recognition and information retrieval. Section 3 introduces the two quantization methods considered in this paper, namely the Lloyd's algorithm and the Binning method. Section 4 briefly describes our phrase-based SMT system. Sections 5 reports and discusses experimental results addressing the questions in the introduction. Finally, Section 6 draws some conclusions.

2 Previous work

Most related work can be found in the area of speech recognition, where n-gram language models have been used for a while.

Efforts targeting efficiency have been mainly focused on pruning techniques (Seymore and Rosenfeld, 1996; Gao and Zhang, 2002), which permit to significantly reduce the amount of n-grams to be stored at a negligible cost in performance. Moreover, very compact data-structures for storing back-off n-gram models have been recently proposed by Raj and Whittaker (2003).

Whittaker and Raj (2001) discuss probability encoding as a means to reduce memory requirements of an n-gram language model. Quantization of a 3-gram back-off model was performed by applying the *k-means* Lloyd-Max algorithm at each n-gram level. Experiments were performed on several large-vocabulary speech recognition tasks by considering different levels of compression. By encoded probabilities in 4 bits, the increase in word-error-rate was only around 2% relative with respect to a baseline using 32-bit floating point probabilities.

Similar work was carried out in the field of information retrieval, where memory efficiency is instead related to the indexing data structure, which contains information about frequencies of terms in all the individual documents. Franz and McCarley (2002) investigated quantization of term frequencies by applying a binning method. The impact on retrieval performance was analyzed against different quantization levels. Results showed that 2 bits are sufficient to encode term frequencies at the cost of a negligible loss in performance.

In our work, we investigate both data compression methods, namely the Lloyd's algorithm and the binning method, in a SMT framework.

3 Quantization

Quantization provides an effective way of reducing the number of bits needed to store floating point variables. The quantization process consists in partitioning the real space into a finite set of k *quantization levels* and identifying a center c_i for each level, $i = 1, \ldots, k$. A function $q(x)$ maps any real-valued point x onto its unique center c_i. Cost of quantization is the approximation error between x and c_i.

If $k = 2^h$, h bits are enough to represent a floating point variable; as a floating point is usually encoded in 32 bits (4 byte), the *compression ratio* is equal to $32/h$[1] . Hence, the compression ratio also gives an upper bound for the relative reduction of memory use, because it assumes an optimal implementation of data structures without any memory waste. Notice that memory consumption for storing the k-entry codebook is negligible ($k * 32$ bits).

As we will apply quantization on probabilistic distribution, we can restrict the range of real values between 0 and 1. Most quantization algorithms require a fixed (although huge) amount of points in order to define the quantization levels and their centers. Probabilistic models used in SMT satisfy this requirement because the set of parameters larger than 0 is always limited.

Quantization algorithms differ in the way partition of data points is computed and centers are identified. In this paper we investigate two different quantization algorithms.

Lloyd's Algorithm

Quantization of a finite set of real-valued data points can be seen as a clustering problem. A large family of clustering algorithms, called *k-means* algorithms (Kanungo et al., 2002), look for optimal *centers* c_i which minimize the mean squared distance from each data point to its nearest center. The map between points and centers is trivially derived.

[1]In the computation of the compression ratio we take into account only the memory needed to store the probabilities of the observations, and not the memory needed to store the observations themselves which depends on the adopted data structures.

As no efficient exact solution to this problem is known, either polynomial-time approximation or heuristic algorithms have been proposed to tackle the problem. In particular, Lloyd's algorithm starts from a feasible set of centers and iteratively moves them until some convergence criterion is satisfied. Finally, the algorithm finds a local optimal solution. In this work we applied the version of the algorithm available in the K-MEANS package[2].

Binning Method

The binning method partitions data points into uniformly populated intervals or *bins*. The center of each bin corresponds to the mean value of all points falling into it. If N_i is the number of points of the i-th bin, and x_i the smallest point in the i-th bin, a partition $[x_i, x_{i+1}]$ results such that N_i is constant for each $i = 0, \ldots, k-1$, where $x_k = 1$ by default. The following map is thus defined:

$$q(x) = c_i \text{ if } x_i <= x < x_{i+1}.$$

Our implementation uses the following *greedy* strategy: bins are build by uniformly partition all different points of the data set.

4 Phrase-based Translation System

Given a string $\mathbf{f}$ in the source language, our SMT system (Federico and Bertoldi, 2005; Cettolo et al., 2005), looks for the target string $\mathbf{e}$ maximizing the posterior probability $\Pr(\mathbf{e}, \mathbf{a} \mid \mathbf{f})$ over all possible word alignments $\mathbf{a}$. The conditional distribution is computed with the log-linear model:

$$p_{\boldsymbol{\lambda}}(\mathbf{e}, \mathbf{a} \mid \mathbf{f}) \quad \propto \quad \exp\left\{\sum_{r=1}^{R} \lambda_r h_r(\mathbf{e}, \mathbf{f}, \mathbf{a})\right\},$$

where $h_r(\mathbf{e}, \mathbf{f}, \mathbf{a}), r = 1 \ldots R$ are real valued feature functions.

The log-linear model is used to score translation hypotheses $(\mathbf{e}, \mathbf{a})$ built in terms of strings of phrases, which are simple sequences of words. The translation process works as follows. At each step, a target phrase is added to the translation whose corresponding source phrase within $\mathbf{f}$ is identified through three random quantities: the *fertility* which establishes its length; the *permutation* which sets its first position; the *tablet* which tells its word string. Notice that target phrases might have fertility equal to zero, hence they do not translate any source word. Moreover, untranslated words in $\mathbf{f}$ are also modeled through some random variables.

The choice of permutation and tablets can be constrained in order to limit the search space until performing a monotone phrase-based translation. In any case, local word reordering is permitted by phrases.

The above process is performed by a beam-search decoder and is modeled with twelve feature functions (Cettolo et al., 2005) which are either estimated from data, e.g. the target n-gram language models and the phrase-based translation model, or empirically fixed, e.g. the permutation models. While feature functions exploit statistics extracted from monolingual or word-aligned texts from the training data, the scaling factors λ of the log-linear model are empirically estimated on development data.

The two most memory consuming feature functions are the phrase-based Translation Model (TM) and the n-gram Language Model (LM).

Translation Model

The TM contains phrase-pairs statistics computed on a parallel corpus provided with word-alignments in both directions. Phrase-pairs up to length 8 are extracted and singleton observations are pruned off. For each extracted phrase-pair $(\tilde{f}, \tilde{e})$, four translation probabilities are estimated:

– a smoothed frequency of $\tilde{f}$ given $\tilde{e}$
– a smoothed frequency of $\tilde{e}$ given $\tilde{f}$
– an IBM model 1 based probability of $\tilde{e}$ given $\tilde{f}$
– an IBM model 1 based probability of $\tilde{f}$ given $\tilde{e}$

Hence, the number of parameters of the translation models corresponds to 4 times the number of extracted phrase-pairs. From the point of view of quantization, the four types of probabilities are considered separately and a specific codebook is generated for each type.

Language Model

The LM is a 4-gram back-off model estimated with the *modified Kneser-Ney smoothing* method (Chen and Goodman, 1998). Singleton pruning is applied on 3-gram and 4-gram statistics. In terms of num-

[2]www.cs.umd.edu/~mount/Projects/KMeans.

task	parallel resources		mono resources	LM				TM
	src	trg	words	1-gram	2-gram	3-gram	4-gram	phrase pairs
NIST	82,168	88,159	463,855	1,408	20,475	29,182	46,326	10,410
EPPS	34,460	32,951	3,2951	110	2,252	2,191	2,677	3,877
EPPS-800	23,611	22,520	22,520	90	1,778	1,586	1,834	2,499
EPPS-400	11,816	11,181	11,181	65	1,143	859	897	1,326
EPPS-200	5,954	5,639	5,639	47	738	464	439	712
EPPS-100	2,994	2,845	2,845	35	469	246	213	387

Table 1: Figures (in thousand) regarding the training data of each translation task.

ber of parameters, each n-gram, with $n < 4$, has two probabilities associated with: the probability of the n-gram itself, and the back-off probability of the corresponding $n + 1$-gram extensions. Finally, 4-grams have only one probability associated with.

For the sake of quantization, two separate codebooks are generated for each of the first three levels, and one codebook is generated for the last level. Hence, a total of 7 codebooks are generated. In all discussed quantized LMs, unigram probabilities are always encoded with 8 bits. The reason is that unigram probabilities have indeed the largest variability and do not contribute significantly to the total number of parameters.

5 Experiments

Data and Experimental Framework

We performed experiments on two large vocabulary translation tasks: the translation of European Parliamentary Plenary Sessions (EPPS) (Vilar et al., 2005) from Spanish to English, and the translation of documents from Chinese to English as proposed by the NIST MT Evaluation Workshops[3].

Translation of EPPS is performed on the so-called final text editions, which are prepared by the translation office of the European Parliament. Both the training and testing data were collected by the TC-STAR[4] project and were made freely available to participants in the 2006 TC-STAR Evaluation Campaign. In order to perform experiments under different data sparseness conditions, four subsamples of the training data with different sizes were generated, too.

Training and test data used for the NIST task are

[3]www.nist.gov/speech/tests/mt/.

[4]www.tc-star.org

task	sentences	src words	ref words
EPPS	840	22725	23066
NIST	919	25586	29155

Table 2: Statistics of test data for each task.

available through the Linguistic Data Consortium[5]. Employed training data meet the requirements set for the Chinese-English large-data track of the 2005 NIST MT Evaluation Workshop. For testing we used instead the NIST 2003 test set.

Table 1 reports statistics about the training data of each task and the models estimated on them. That is, the number of running words of source and target languages, the number of n-grams in the language model and the number phrase-pairs in the translation model. Table 2 reports instead statistics about the test sets, namely, the number of source sentences and running words in the source part and in the gold reference translations.

Translation performance was measured in terms of BLEU score, NIST score, word-error rate (WER), and position independent error rate (PER). Score computation relied on two and four reference translations per sentence, respectively, for the EPPS and NIST tasks. Scores were computed in case-insensitive modality with punctuation. In general, none of the above measures is alone sufficiently informative about translation quality, however, in the community there seems to be a preference toward reporting results with BLEU. Here, to be on the safe side and to better support our findings we will report results with all measures, but will limit discussion on performance to the BLEU score.

In order to just focus on the effect of quantiza-

[5]www.ldc.upenn.edu

	LM-h						
	32	8	6	5	4	3	2
32	54.78	54.75	54.73	54.65	54.49	54.24	53.82
8	54.78	54.69	54.69	54.79	54.55	54.18	53.65
6	54.57	54.49	54.76	54.57	54.63	54.26	53.60
TM-h 5	54.68	54.68	54.56	54.61	54.60	54.10	53.39
4	54.37	54.36	54.47	54.44	54.23	54.06	53.26
3	54.28	54.03	54.22	53.96	53.75	53.69	53.03
2	53.58	53.51	53.47	53.35	53.39	53.41	52.41

Table 3: BLEU scores in the EPPS task with different quantization levels of the LM and TM.

tion, all reported experiments were performed with a plain configuration of the ITC-irst SMT system. That is, we used a single decoding step, no phrase re-ordering, and task-dependent weights of the log-linear model.

Henceforth, LMs and TM quantized with h bits are denoted with `LM-h` and `TM-h`, respectively. Non quantized models are indicated with `LM-32` and `TM-32`.

Impact of Quantization on LM and TM

A first set of experiments was performed on the EPPS task by applying probability quantization either on the LM or on the TMs. Figures 1 and 2 compare the two proposed quantization algorithms (`LLOYD` and `BINNING`) against different levels of quantization, namely 2, 3, 4, 5, 6, and 8 bits. The scores achieved by the non quantized models (`LM-32` and `TM-32`) are reported as reference.

The following considerations can be drawn from these results. The Binning method works slightly, but not significantly, better than the Lloyd's algorithm, especially with the highest compression ratios.

In general, the LM seems less affected by data compression than the TM. By comparing quantization with the binning method against no quantization, the BLEU score with LM-4 is only 0.42% relative worse (54.78 vs 54.55). Degradation of BLEU score by TM-4 is 0.77% (54.78 vs 54.36). For all the models, encoding with 8 bits does not affect translation quality at all.

In following experiments, binning quantization was applied to both LM and TM. Figure 3 plots all scores against different levels of quantization. As references, the curves corresponding to only

LM-h	TM-h	BLEU	NIST	WER	PER
32	32	28.82	8.769	62.41	42.30
8	8	28.87	8.772	62.39	42.19
4	4	28.36	8.742	62.94	42.45
2	2	25.95	8.491	65.87	44.04

Table 4: Translation scores on the NIST task with different quantization levels of the LM and TM.

LM quantization (`LM-h`) and only TM quantization (`TM-h`) are shown. Independent levels of quantization of the LM and TM were also considered. BLEU scores related to several combinations are reported in Table 3.

Results show that the joint impact of LM and TM quantization is almost additive. Degradation with 4 bits quantization is only about 1% relative (from 54.78 to 54.23). Quantization with 2 bits is surprisingly robust: the BLEU score just decreases by 4.33% relative (from 54.78 to 52.41).

Quantization vs. Data Sparseness

Quantization of LM and TM was evaluated with respect to data-sparseness. Quantized and not quantized models were trained on four subset of the EPPS corpus with decreasing size. Statistics about these sub-corpora are reported in Table 1. Quantization was performed with the binning method using 2, 4, and 8 bit encodings. Results in terms of BLEU score are plotted in Figure 4. It is evident that the gap in BLEU score between the quantized and not quantized models is almost constant under different training conditions. This result suggests that performance of quantized models is not affected by data sparseness.

Consistency Across Different Tasks

A subset of quantization settings tested with the EPPS tasks was also evaluated on the NIST task. Results are reported in Table 4.

Quantization with 8 bits does not affect performance, and gives even slightly better scores. Also quantization with 4 bits produces scores very close to those of non quantized models, with a loss in BLEU score of only 1.60% relative. However, pushing quantization to 2 bits significantly deteriorates performance, with a drop in BLEU score of 9.96% relative.

In comparison to the EPPS task, performance degradation due to quantization seems to be twice as large. In conclusion, consistent behavior is observed among different degrees of compression. Absolute loss in performance, though quite different from the EPPS task, remains nevertheless very reasonable.

Performance vs. Compression

From the results of single versus combined compression, we can reasonably assume that performance degradation due to quantization of LM and TM probabilities is additive. Hence, as memory savings on the two models are also independent we can look at the optimal trade-off between performance and compression separately. Experiments on the NIST and EPPS tasks seem to show that encoding of LM and TM probabilities with 4 bits provides the best trade-off, that is a compression ratio of 8 with a relative loss in BLEU score of 1% and 1.6%. It can be seen that score degradation below 4 bits grows generally faster than the corresponding memory savings.

6 Conclusion

In this paper we investigated the application of data compression methods to the probabilities stored by a phrase-based translation model. In particular, probability quantization was applied on the n-gram language model and on the phrase-pair translation model. Experimental results confirm previous findings in speech recognition: language model probabilities can be encoded in just 4 bits at the cost of a very little loss in performance. The same resolution level seems to be a good compromise even for the translation model. Remarkably, the impact of quantization on the language model and translation model seems to be additive with respect to performance. Finally, quantization does not seems to be affected by data sparseness and behaves similarly on different translation tasks.

References

M Cettolo, M. Federico, N. Bertoldi, R. Cattoni, and B. Chen. 2005. A Look Inside the ITC-irst SMT System. In *Proc. of MT Summit X*, pp. 451–457, Pukhet, Thailand.

S. F. Chen and J. Goodman. 1998. An Empirical Study of Smoothing Techniques for Language Modeling. Technical Report TR-10-98, Computer Science Group, Harvard University, Cambridge, MA, USA.

M. Federico and N. Bertoldi. 2005. A Word-to-Phrase Statistical Translation Model. *ACM Transaction on Speech Language Processing*, 2(2):1–24.

M. Franz and J. S. McCarley. 2002. How Many Bits are Needed to Store Term Frequencies. In *Proc. of ACM SIGIR*, pp. 377–378, Tampere, Finland.

J. Gao and M. Zhang. 2002. Improving Language Model Size Reduction using Better Pruning Criteria. In *Proc. of ACL*, pp. 176–182, Philadelphia, PA.

T. Kanungo, D. M. Mount, N. Netanyahu, C. Piatko, R. Silverman, , and A. Y. Wu. 2002. An Efficient K-Means Clustering Algorithm: Analysis and Implementation. *IEEE Transaction on Pattern Analysis and Machine Intelligence*, 24(7):881–892.

P. Koehn, F. J. Och, and D. Marcu. 2003. Statistical Phrase-Based Translation. In *Proc. of HLT/NAACL 2003*, pp. 127–133, Edmonton, Canada.

F. J. Och and H. Ney. 2004. The Alignment Template Approach to Statistical Machine Translation. *Computational Linguistics*, 30(4):417–449.

B. Raj and E. W. D. Whittaker. 2003. Lossless Compression of Language Model Structure and Word Identifiers. In *Proc. of ICASSP*, pp. 388–391, Honk Kong.

K. Seymore and R. Rosenfeld. 1996. Scalable Backoff Language Models. In *Proc. of ICSLP*, vol. 1, pp. 232–235, Philadelphia, PA.

D. Vilar, E. Matusov, S. Hasan, R . Zens, , and H. Ney. 2005. Statistical Machine Translation of European Parliamentary Speeches. In *Proc. of MT Summit X*, pp. 259–266, Pukhet, Thailand.

E. W. D. Whittaker and B. Raj. 2001. Quantization-based Language Model Compression. In *Proc. of Eurospeech*, pp. 33–36, Aalborg, Denmark.

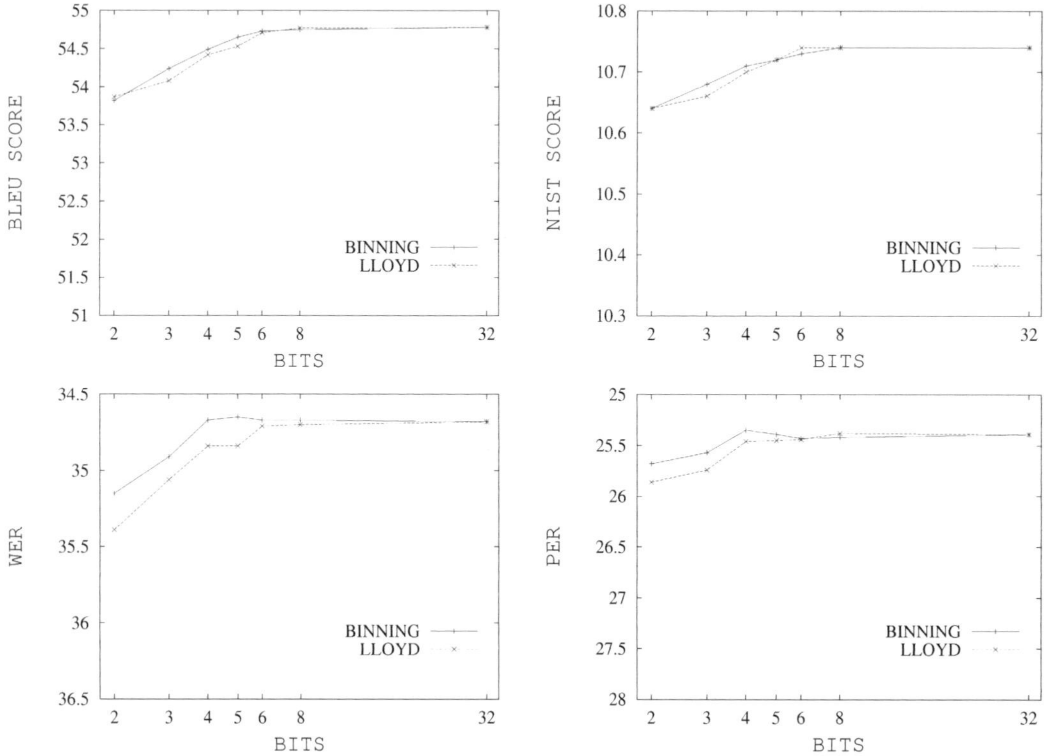

Figure 1: EPPS task: translation scores vs. quantization level of LM. TM is not quantized.

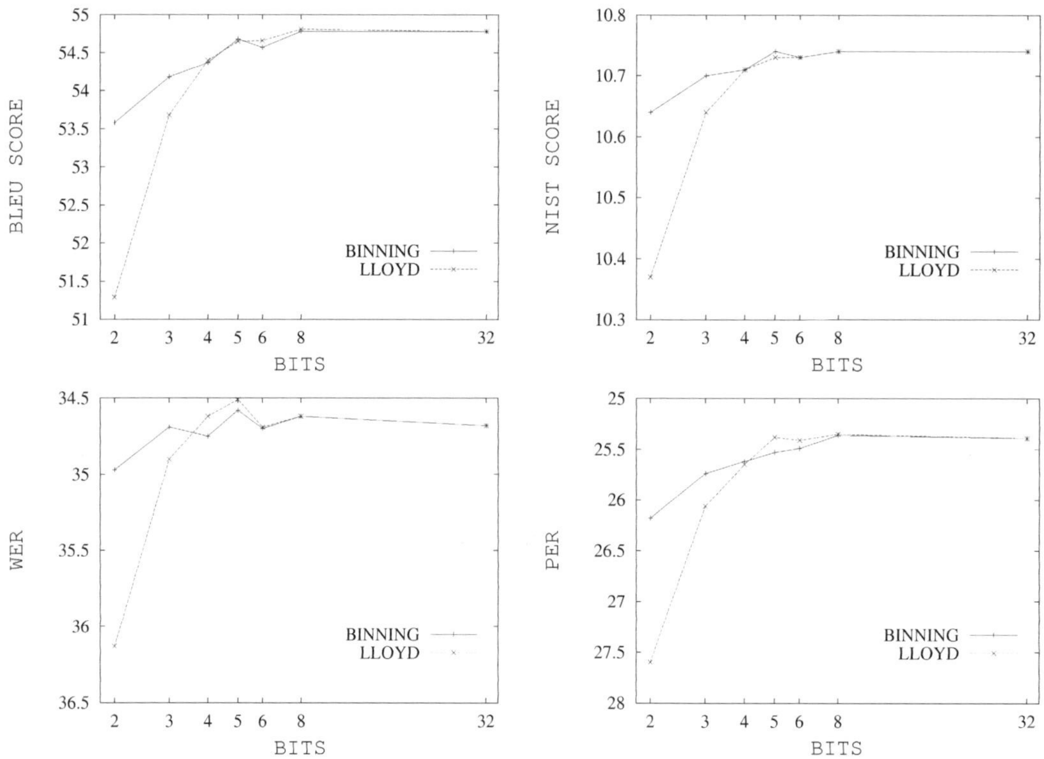

Figure 2: EPPS task: translation scores vs. quantization level of TM. LM is not quantized.

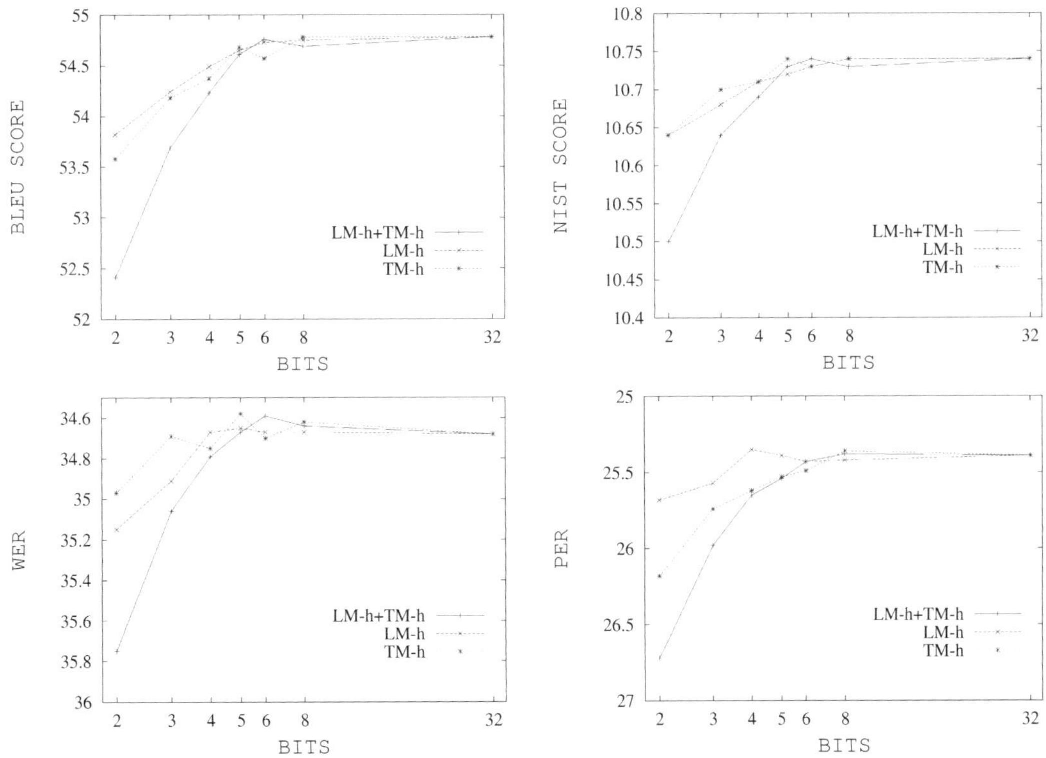

Figure 3: EPPS task: translation scores vs. quantization level of LM and TM. Quantization was performed with the Binning algorithm.

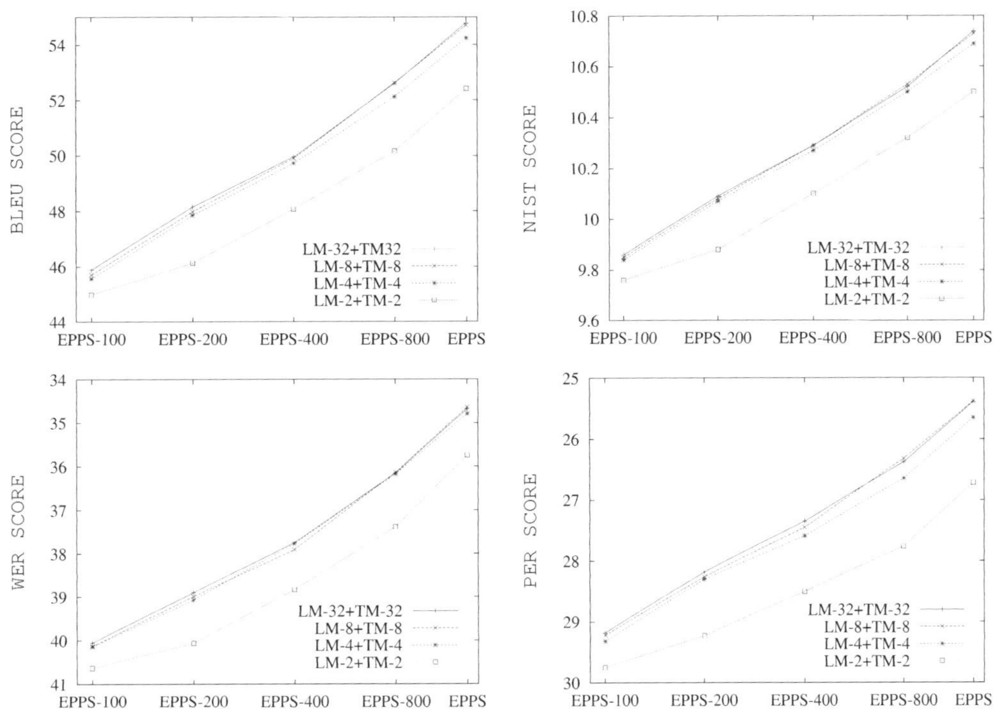

Figure 4: EPPS task: translation scores vs. amount of training data. Different levels of quantization were generated with the Binning algorithm.

Manual and Automatic Evaluation of Machine Translation between European Languages

Philipp Koehn
School of Informatics
University of Edinburgh
pkoehn@inf.ed.ac.uk

Christof Monz
Department of Computer Science
Queen Mary, University of London
christof@dcs.qmul.ac.uk

Abstract

We evaluated machine translation performance for six European language pairs that participated in a shared task: translating French, German, Spanish texts to English and back. Evaluation was done automatically using the BLEU score and manually on *fluency* and *adequacy*.

For the 2006 NAACL/HLT Workshop on Machine Translation, we organized a shared task to evaluate machine translation performance. 14 teams from 11 institutions participated, ranging from commercial companies, industrial research labs to individual graduate students.

The motivation for such a competition is to establish baseline performance numbers for defined training scenarios and test sets. We assembled various forms of data and resources: a baseline MT system, language models, prepared training and test sets, resulting in actual machine translation output from several state-of-the-art systems and manual evaluations. All this is available at the workshop website[1].

The shared task is a follow-up to the one we organized in the previous year, at a similar venue (Koehn and Monz, 2005). As then, we concentrated on the translation of European languages and the use of the Europarl corpus for training. Again, most systems that participated could be categorized as statistical phrase-based systems. While there is now a number of competitions — DARPA/NIST (Li, 2005), IWSLT (Eck and Hori, 2005), TC-Star — this one focuses on text translation between various European languages.

This year's shared task changed in some aspects from last year's:

- We carried out a manual evaluation in addition to the automatic scoring. Manual evaluation was done by the participants. This revealed interesting clues about the properties of automatic and manual scoring.
- We evaluated translation *from* English, in addition to *into* English. English was again paired with German, French, and Spanish. We dropped, however, one of the languages, Finnish, partly to keep the number of tracks manageable, partly because we assumed that it would be hard to find enough Finnish speakers for the manual evaluation.
- We included an out-of-domain test set. This allows us to compare machine translation performance in-domain and out-of-domain.

1 Evaluation Framework

The evaluation framework for the shared task is similar to the one used in last year's shared task. Training and testing is based on the Europarl corpus. Figure 1 provides some statistics about this corpus.

1.1 Baseline system

To lower the barrier of entrance to the competition, we provided a complete baseline MT system, along with data resources. To summarize, we provided:

- sentence-aligned, tokenized training corpus
- a development and development test set
- trained language models for each language
- the phrase-based MT decoder Pharaoh
- a training script to build models for Pharaoh

The performance of the baseline system is similar to the best submissions in last year's shared task. We are currently working on a complete open source implementation of a training and decoding system, which should become available over the summer.

[1] http://www.statmt.org/wmt06/

Proceedings of the Workshop on Statistical Machine Translation, pages 102–121,
New York City, June 2006.

Training corpus

	Spanish ↔ English	French ↔ English	German ↔ English
Sentences	730,740	688,031	751,088
Foreign words	15,676,710	15,323,737	15,256,793
English words	15,222,105	13,808,104	16,052,269
Distinct foreign words	102,886	80,349	195,291
Distinct English words	64,123	61,627	65,889

Language model data

	English	Spanish	French	German
Sentence	1,003,349	1,070,305	1,066,974	1,078,141
Words	27,493,499	29,129,720	31,604,879	26,562,167

In-domain test set

	English	Spanish	French	German
Sentences	2,000			
Words	59,307	61,824	66,783	55,533
Unseen words	141	206	164	387
Ratio of unseen words	0.23%	0.40%	0.24%	0.70%
Distinct words	6,031	7,719	7,230	8,812
Distinct unseen words	139	203	163	385

Out-of-domain test set

	English	Spanish	French	German
Sentences	1,064			
Words	25,919	29,826	31,937	26,818
Unseen words	464	368	839	913
Ratio of unseen words	1.79%	1.23%	2.62%	3.40%
Distinct words	5,166	5,689	5,728	6,594
Distinct unseen words	340	267	375	637

Figure 1: Properties of the training and test sets used in the shared task. The training data is the Europarl corpus, from which also the in-domain test set is taken. There is twice as much language modelling data, since training data for the machine translation system is filtered against sentences of length larger than 40 words. Out-of-domain test data is from the Project Syndicate web site, a compendium of political commentary.

ID	Participant
cmu	Carnegie Mellon University, USA (Zollmann and Venugopal, 2006)
lcc	Language Computer Corporation, USA (Olteanu et al., 2006b)
ms	Microsoft, USA (Menezes et al., 2006)
nrc	National Research Council, Canada (Johnson et al., 2006)
ntt	Nippon Telegraph and Telephone, Japan (Watanabe et al., 2006)
rali	RALI, University of Montreal, Canada (Patry et al., 2006)
systran	Systran, France
uedin-birch	University of Edinburgh, UK — Alexandra Birch (Birch et al., 2006)
uedin-phi	University of Edinburgh, UK — Philipp Koehn (Birch et al., 2006)
upc-jg	University of Catalonia, Spain — Jesús Giménez (Giménez and Màrquez, 2006)
upc-jmc	University of Catalonia, Spain — Josep Maria Crego (Crego et al., 2006)
upc-mr	University of Catalonia, Spain — Marta Ruiz Costa-jussà (Costa-jussà et al., 2006)
upv	University of Valencia, Spain (Sánchez and Benedí, 2006)
utd	University of Texas at Dallas, USA (Olteanu et al., 2006a)

Figure 2: Participants in the shared task. Not all groups participated in all translation directions.

1.2 Test Data

The test data was again drawn from a segment of the Europarl corpus from the fourth quarter of 2000, which is excluded from the training data. Participants were also provided with two sets of 2,000 sentences of parallel text to be used for system development and tuning.

In addition to the Europarl test set, we also collected 29 editorials from the Project Syndicate website[2], which are published in all the four languages of the shared task. We aligned the texts at a sentence level across all four languages, resulting in 1064 sentence per language. For statistics on this test set, refer to Figure 1.

The out-of-domain test set differs from the Europarl data in various ways. The text type are editorials instead of speech transcripts. The domain is general politics, economics and science. However, it is also mostly political content (even if not focused on the internal workings of the European Union) and opinion.

1.3 Participants

We received submissions from 14 groups from 11 institutions, as listed in Figure 2. Most of these groups follow a phrase-based statistical approach to machine translation. Microsoft's approach uses dependency trees, others use hierarchical phrase models. Systran submitted their commercial rule-based system that was not tuned to the Europarl corpus.

About half of the participants of last year's shared task participated again. The other half was replaced by other participants, so we ended up with roughly the same number. Compared to last year's shared task, the participants represent more long-term research efforts. This may be the sign of a maturing research environment.

While building a machine translation system is a serious undertaking, in future we hope to attract more newcomers to the field by keeping the barrier of entry as low as possible.

For more on the participating systems, please refer to the respective system description in the proceedings of the workshop.

2 Automatic Evaluation

For the automatic evaluation, we used BLEU, since it is the most established metric in the field. The BLEU metric, as all currently proposed automatic metrics, is occasionally suspected to be biased towards statistical systems, especially the phrase-based systems currently in use. It rewards matches of n-gram sequences, but measures only at most indirectly overall grammatical coherence.

The BLEU score has been shown to correlate well with human judgement, when statistical ma-

[2] `http://www.project-syndicate.com/`

chine translation systems are compared (Doddington, 2002; Przybocki, 2004; Li, 2005). However, a recent study (Callison-Burch et al., 2006), pointed out that this correlation may not always be strong. They demonstrated this with the comparison of statistical systems against (a) manually post-edited MT output, and (b) a rule-based commercial system.

The development of automatic scoring methods is an open field of research. It was our hope that this competition, which included the manual and automatic evaluation of statistical systems and one rule-based commercial system, will give further insight into the relation between automatic and manual evaluation. At the very least, we are creating a data resource (the manual annotations) that may the basis of future research in evaluation metrics.

2.1 Computing BLEU Scores

We computed BLEU scores for each submission with a single reference translation. For each sentence, we counted how many n-grams in the system output also occurred in the reference translation. By taking the ratio of matching n-grams to the total number of n-grams in the system output, we obtain the precision p_n for each n-gram order n. These values for n-gram precision are combined into a BLEU score:

$$\text{BLEU} = \text{BP} \cdot \exp\left(\sum_{n=1}^{4} \log p_n\right) \tag{1}$$

$$\text{BP} = \min(1, e^{1-r/c}) \tag{2}$$

The formula for the BLEU metric also includes a brevity penalty for too short output, which is based on the total number of words in the system output c and in the reference r.

BLEU is sensitive to tokenization. Because of this, we retokenized and lowercased submitted output with our own tokenizer, which was also used to prepare the training and test data.

2.2 Statistical Significance

Confidence Interval: Since BLEU scores are not computed on the sentence level, traditional methods to compute statistical significance and confidence intervals do not apply. Hence, we use the bootstrap resampling method described by Koehn (2004).

Following this method, we repeatedly — say, 1000 times — sample sets of sentences from the output of each system, measure their BLEU score, and use these 1000 BLEU scores as basis for estimating a confidence interval. When dropping the top and bottom 2.5% the remaining BLEU scores define the range of the confidence interval.

Pairwise comparison: We can use the same method to assess the statistical significance of one system outperforming another. If two systems' scores are close, this may simply be a random effect in the test data. To check for this, we do pairwise bootstrap resampling: Again, we repeatedly sample sets of sentences, this time from both systems, and compare their BLEU scores on these sets. If one system is better in 95% of the sample sets, we conclude that its higher BLEU score is statistically significantly better.

The bootstrap method has been critized by Riezler and Maxwell (2005) and Collins et al. (2005), as being too optimistic in deciding for statistical significant difference between systems. We are therefore applying a different method, which has been used at the 2005 DARPA/NIST evaluation.

We divide up each test set into blocks of 20 sentences (100 blocks for the in-domain test set, 53 blocks for the out-of-domain test set), check for each block, if one system has a higher BLEU score than the other, and then use the sign test.

The sign test checks, how likely a sample of better and worse BLEU scores would have been generated by two systems of equal performance.

Let say, if we find one system doing better on 20 of the blocks, and worse on 80 of the blocks, is it significantly worse? We check, how likely only up to $k = 20$ better scores out of $n = 100$ would have been generated by two equal systems, using the binomial distribution:

$$\begin{aligned} p(0..k; n, p) &= \sum_{i=0}^{k} \binom{i}{n} p^i p^{n-i} \\ &= 0.5^n \sum_{i=0}^{k} \binom{i}{n} \end{aligned} \tag{3}$$

If $p(0..k; n, p) < 0.05$, or $p(0..k; n, p) > 0.95$ then we have a statistically significant difference between the systems.

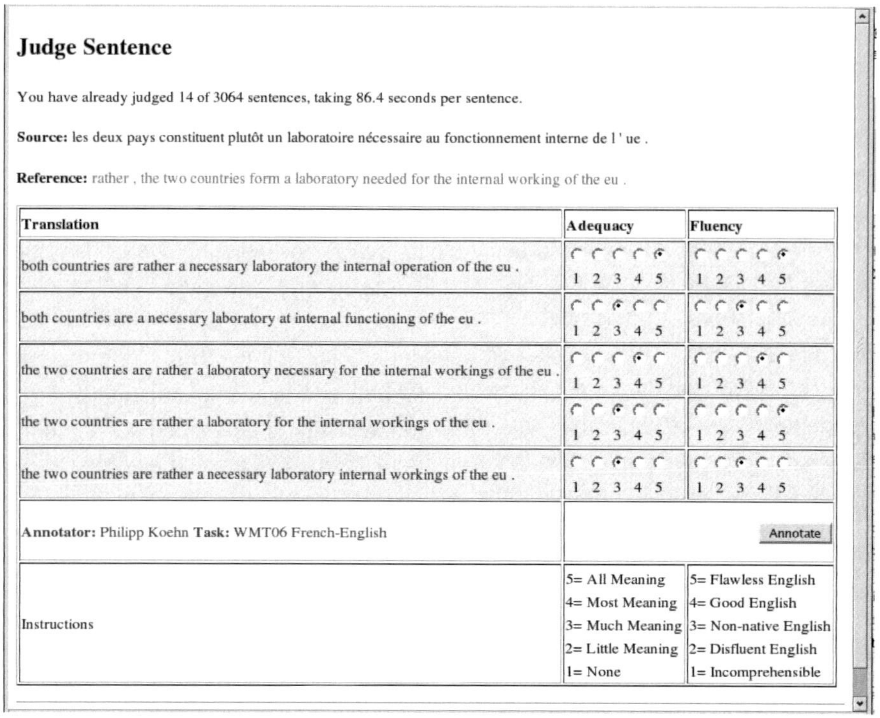

Figure 3: Annotation tool for manual judgement of *adequacy* and *fluency* of the system output. Translations from 5 randomly selected systems for a randomly selected sentence is presented. No additional information beyond the instructions on this page are given to the judges. The tool tracks and reports annotation speed.

3 Manual Evaluation

While automatic measures are an invaluable tool for the day-to-day development of machine translation systems, they are only a imperfect substitute for human assessment of translation quality, or as the acronym BLEU puts it, a bilingual evaluation *understudy*.

Many human evaluation metrics have been proposed. Also, the argument has been made that machine translation performance should be evaluated via task-based evaluation metrics, i.e. how much it assists performing a useful task, such as supporting human translators or aiding the analysis of texts.

The main disadvantage of manual evaluation is that it is time-consuming and thus too expensive to do frequently. In this shared task, we were also confronted with this problem, and since we had no funding for paying human judgements, we asked participants in the evaluation to share the burden. Participants and other volunteers contributed about 180 hours of labor in the manual evaluation.

3.1 Collecting Human Judgements

We asked participants to each judge 200–300 sentences in terms of fluency and adequacy, the most commonly used manual evaluation metrics. We settled on contrastive evaluations of 5 system outputs for a single test sentence. See Figure 3 for a screenshot of the evaluation tool.

Presenting the output of several system allows the human judge to make more informed judgements, contrasting the quality of the different systems. The judgements tend to be done more in form of a ranking of the different systems. We assumed that such a contrastive assessment would be beneficial for an evaluation that essentially pits different systems against each other.

While we had up to 11 submissions for a translation direction, we did decide against presenting all 11 system outputs to the human judge. Our initial experimentation with the evaluation tool showed that this is often too overwhelming.

Making the ten judgements (2 types for 5 systems) takes on average 2 minutes. Typically, judges initially spent about 3 minutes per sentence, but then accelerate with experience. Judges where excluded from assessing the quality of MT systems that were submitted by their institution. Sentences and systems were randomly selected and randomly shuffled for presentation.

We collected around 300–400 judgements per judgement type (adequacy or fluency), per system, per language pair. This is less than the 694 judgements 2004 DARPA/NIST evaluation, or the 532 judgements in the 2005 DARPA/NIST evaluation. This decreases the statistical significance of our results compared to those studies. The number of judgements is additionally fragmented by our break-up of sentences into in-domain and out-of-domain.

3.2 Normalizing the judgements

The human judges were presented with the following definition of *adequacy* and *fluency*, but no additional instructions:

	Adequacy	**Fluency**
5	All Meaning	Flawless English
4	Most Meaning	Good English
3	Much Meaning	Non-native English
2	Little Meaning	Disfluent English
1	None	Incomprehensible

Judges varied in the average score they handed out. The average fluency judgement per judge ranged from 2.33 to 3.67, the average adequacy judgement ranged from 2.56 to 4.13. Since different judges judged different systems (recall that judges were excluded to judge system output from their own institution), we normalized the scores.

The **normalized judgement per judge** is the raw judgement plus (3 minus average raw judgement for this judge). In words, the judgements are normalized, so that the average *normalized judgement per judge* is 3.

Another way to view the judgements is that they are less quality judgements of machine translation systems per se, but rankings of machine translation systems. In fact, it is very difficult to maintain consistent standards, on what (say) an adequacy judgement of 3 means even for a specific language pair.

The way judgements are collected, human judges tend to use the scores to rank systems against each other. If one system is perfect, another has slight flaws and the third more flaws, a judge is inclined to hand out judgements of 5, 4, and 3. On the other hand, when all systems produce muddled output, but one is better, and one is worse, but not completely wrong, a judge is inclined to hand out judgements of 4, 3, and 2. The judgement of 4 in the first case will go to a vastly better system output than in the second case.

We therefore also normalized judgements on a per-sentence basis. The **normalized judgement per sentence** is the raw judgement plus (0 minus average raw judgement for this judge on this sentence).

Systems that generally do better than others will receive a positive average *normalized judgement per sentence*. Systems that generally do worse than others will receive a negative one.

One may argue with these efforts on normalization, and ultimately their value should be assessed by assessing their impact on inter-annotator agreement. Given the limited number of judgements we received, we did not try to evaluate this.

3.3 Statistical Significance

Confidence Interval: To estimate confidence intervals for the average mean scores for the systems, we use standard significance testing.

Given a set of n sentences, we can compute the sample mean $\bar{x}$ and sample variance s^2 of the individual sentence judgements x_i:

$$\bar{x} = \frac{1}{n}\sum_{i=1}^{n} x_i \quad (4)$$

$$s^2 = \frac{1}{n-1}\sum_{i=1}^{n}(x_i - \bar{x})^2 \quad (5)$$

The extend of the confidence interval $[\bar{x}-d, \bar{x}+d]$ can be computed by

$$d = 1.96 \cdot \frac{s}{\sqrt{n}} \quad (6)$$

Pairwise Comparison: As for the automatic evaluation metric, we want to be able to rank different systems against each other, for which we need assessments of statistical significance on the differences between a pair of systems.

Unfortunately, we have much less data to work with than with the automatic scores. The way we

Basis	Diff.	Ratio
Sign test on BLEU	331	75%
Bootstrap on BLEU	348	78%
Sign test on Fluency	224	50%
Sign test on Adequacy	225	51%

Figure 4: Number and ratio of statistically significant distinction between system performance. Automatic scores are computed on a larger tested than manual scores (3064 sentences vs. 300–400 sentences).

collected manual judgements, we do not necessarily have the same sentence judged for both systems (judges evaluate 5 systems out of the 8–10 participating systems).

Still, for about good number of sentences, we do have this direct comparison, which allows us to apply the sign test, as described in Section 2.2.

4 Results and Analysis

The results of the manual and automatic evaluation of the participating system translations is detailed in the figures at the end of this paper. The scores and confidence intervals are detailed first in the Figures 7–10 in table form (including ranks), and then in graphical form in Figures 11–16. In the graphs, system scores are indicated by a point, the confidence intervals by shaded areas around the point.

In all figures, we present the per-sentence normalized judgements. The normalization on a per-judge basis gave very similar ranking, only slightly less consistent with the ranking from the pairwise comparisons.

The confidence intervals are computed by bootstrap resampling for BLEU, and by standard significance testing for the manual scores, as described earlier in the paper.

Pairwise comparison is done using the sign test. Often, two systems can not be distinguished with a confidence of over 95%, so there are ranked the same. This actually happens quite frequently (more below), so that the rankings are broad estimates. For instance: if 10 systems participate, and one system does better than 3 others, worse then 2, and is not significant different from the remaining 4, its rank is in the interval 3–7.

Domain	BLEU	Fluency	Adequacy
in-domain	26.63	3.17	3.58
out-of-domain	20.37	2.74	3.08

Figure 5: Evaluation scores for in-domain and out-of-domain test sets, averaged over all systems

4.1 Close results

At first glance, we quickly recognize that many systems are scored very similar, both in terms of manual judgement and BLEU. There may be occasionally a system clearly at the top or at the bottom, but most systems are so close that it is hard to distinguish them.

In Figure 4, we displayed the number of system comparisons, for which we concluded statistical significance. For the automatic scoring method BLEU, we can distinguish three quarters of the systems. While the Bootstrap method is slightly more sensitive, it is very much in line with the sign test on text blocks.

For the manual scoring, we can distinguish only half of the systems, both in terms of fluency and adequacy. More judgements would have enabled us to make better distinctions, but it is not clear what the upper limit is. We can check, what the consequences of less manual annotation of results would have been: With half the number of manual judgements, we can distinguish about 40% of the systems, 10% less.

4.2 In-domain vs. out-of-domain

The test set included 2000 sentences from the Europarl corpus, but also 1064 sentences out-of-domain test data. Since the inclusion of out-of-domain test data was a very late decision, the participants were not informed of this. So, this was a surprise element due to practical reasons, not malice.

All systems (except for Systran, which was not tuned to Europarl) did considerably worse on out-of-domain training data. This is demonstrated by average scores over all systems, in terms of BLEU, *fluency* and *adequacy*, as displayed in Figure 5.

The manual scores are averages over the raw unnormalized scores.

Language Pair	BLEU	Fluency	Adequacy
French-English	26.09	3.25	3.61
Spanish-English	28.18	3.19	3.71
German-English	21.17	2.87	3.10
English-French	28.33	2.86	3.16
English-Spanish	27.49	2.86	3.34
English-German	14.01	3.15	3.65

Figure 6: Average scores for different language pairs. Manual scoring is done by different judges, resulting in a not very meaningful comparison.

4.3 Language pairs

It is well know that language pairs such as English-German pose more challenges to machine translation systems than language pairs such as French-English. Different sentence structure and rich target language morphology are two reasons for this.

Again, we can compute average scores for all systems for the different language pairs (Figure 6). The differences in difficulty are better reflected in the BLEU scores than in the raw un-normalized manual judgements. The easiest language pair according to BLEU (English-French: 28.33) received worse manual scores than the hardest (English-German: 14.01). This is because different judges focused on different language pairs. Hence, the different averages of manual scores for the different language pairs reflect the behaviour of the judges, not the quality of the systems on different language pairs.

4.4 Manual judgement vs. BLEU

Given the closeness of most systems and the wide over-lapping confidence intervals it is hard to make strong statements about the correlation between human judgements and automatic scoring methods such as BLEU.

We confirm the finding by Callison-Burch et al. (2006) that the rule-based system of Systran is not adequately appreciated by BLEU. In-domain Systran scores on this metric are lower than all statistical systems, even the ones that have much worse human scores. Surprisingly, this effect is much less obvious for out-of-domain test data. For instance, for out-of-domain English-French, Systran has the best BLEU and manual scores.

Our suspicion is that BLEU is very sensitive to jargon, to selecting exactly the right words, and not synonyms that human judges may appreciate as equally good. This is can not be the only explanation, since the discrepancy still holds, for instance, for out-of-domain French-English, where Systran receives among the best adequacy and fluency scores, but a worse BLEU score than all but one statistical system.

This data set of manual judgements should provide a fruitful resource for research on better automatic scoring methods.

4.5 Best systems

So, who won the competition? The best answer to this is: many research labs have very competitive systems whose performance is hard to tell apart. This is not completely surprising, since all systems use very similar technology.

For some language pairs (such as German-English) system performance is more divergent than for others (such as English-French), at least as measured by BLEU.

The statistical systems seem to still lag behind the commercial rule-based competition when translating into morphological rich languages, as demonstrated by the results for English-German and English-French.

The predominate focus of building systems that translate into English has ignored so far the difficult issues of generating rich morphology which may not be determined solely by local context.

4.6 Comments on Manual Evaluation

This is the first time that we organized a large-scale manual evaluation. While we used the standard metrics of the community, the we way presented translations and prompted for assessment differed from other evaluation campaigns. For instance, in the recent IWSLT evaluation, first fluency annotations were solicited (while withholding the source sentence), and then adequacy annotations.

Almost all annotators reported difficulties in maintaining a consistent standard for fluency and adequacy judgements, but nevertheless most did not explicitly move towards a ranking-based evaluation. Almost all annotators expressed their preference to move to a ranking-based evaluation in the future. A few pointed out that adequacy should be broken up into two criteria: (a) are all source words covered? (b) does the translation have the same meaning, including connotations?

Annotators suggested that long sentences are almost impossible to judge. Since all long sentence translation are somewhat *muddled*, even a contrastive evaluation between systems was difficult. A few annotators suggested to break up long sentences into clauses and evaluate these separately.

Not every annotator was fluent in both the source and the target language. While it is essential to be fluent in the target language, it is not strictly necessary to know the source language, if a reference translation was given. However, ince we extracted the test corpus automatically from web sources, the reference translation was not always accurate — due to sentence alignment errors, or because translators did not adhere to a strict sentence-by-sentence translation (say, using pronouns when referring to entities mentioned in the previous sentence). Lack of correct reference translations was pointed out as a short-coming of our evaluation. One annotator suggested that this was the case for as much as 10% of our test sentences. Annotators argued for the importance of having correct and even multiple references.

It was also proposed to allow annotators to skip sentences that they are unable to judge.

5 Conclusions

We carried out an extensive manual and automatic evaluation of machine translation performance on European language pairs. While many systems had similar performance, the results offer interesting insights, especially about the relative performance of statistical and rule-based systems.

Due to many similarly performing systems, we are not able to draw strong conclusions on the question of correlation of manual and automatic evaluation metrics. The bias of automatic methods in favor of statistical systems seems to be less pronounced on out-of-domain test data.

The manual evaluation of scoring translation on a graded scale from 1–5 seems to be very hard to perform. Replacing this with an ranked evaluation seems to be more suitable. Human judges also pointed out difficulties with the evaluation of long sentences.

Acknowledgements

The manual evaluation would not have been possible without the contributions of the manual annotators: Jesus Andres Ferrer, Abhishek Arun, Amittai Axelrod, Alexandra Birch, Chris Callison-Burch, Jorge Civera, Marta Ruiz Costa-jussà, Josep Maria Crego, Elsa Cubel, Chris Irwin Davis, Loic Dugast, Chris Dyer, Andreas Eisele, Cameron Fordyce, Jesús Giménez, Fabrizio Gotti, Hieu Hoang, Eric Joanis Howard Johnson, Philipp Koehn, Beata Kouchnir, Roland Kuhn, Elliott Macklovitch, Arul Menezes, Marian Olteanu, Chris Quirk, Reinhard Rapp, Fatiha Sadat, Joan Andreu Sànchez, Germán Sanchis, Michel Simard, Ashish Venugopal, and Taro Watanabe.

This work was supported in part under the GALE program of the Defense Advanced Research Projects Agency, Contract No. HR0011-06-C-0022.

References

Birch, A., Callison-Burch, C., Osborne, M., and Koehn, P. (2006). Constraining the phrase-based, joint probability statistical translation model. In *Proceedings on the Workshop on Statistical Machine Translation*, pages 154–157, New York City. Association for Computational Linguistics.

Callison-Burch, C., Osborne, M., and Koehn, P. (2006). Re-evaluating the role of BLEU in machine translation research. In *Proceedings of EACL*.

Collins, M., Koehn, P., and Kucerova, I. (2005). Clause restructuring for statistical machine translation. In *Proceedings of ACL*.

Costa-jussà, M. R., Crego, J. M., de Gispert, A., Lambert, P., Khalilov, M., Mariño, J. B., Fonollosa, J. A. R., and Banchs, R. (2006). Talp phrase-based statistical translation system for european language pairs. In *Proceedings on the Workshop on Statistical Machine Translation*, pages 142–145, New York City. Association for Computational Linguistics.

Crego, J. M., de Gispert, A., Lambert, P., Costa-jussà, M. R., Khalilov, M., Banchs, R., Mariño, J. B., and Fonollosa, J. A. R. (2006). N-gram-based smt system enhanced with reordering patterns. In *Proceedings on the Workshop on Statis-*

tical Machine Translation, pages 162–165, New York City. Association for Computational Linguistics.

Doddington, G. (2002). The NIST automated measure and its relation to IBM's BLEU. In *Proceedings of LREC-2002 Workshopon Machine Translation Evaluation: Human Evaluators Meet Automated Metrics*, Gran Canaria, Spain.

Eck, M. and Hori, C. (2005). Overview of the iwslt 2005 evaluation campaign. In *Proc. of the International Workshop on Spoken Language Translation*.

Giménez, J. and Màrquez, L. (2006). The ldv-combo system for smt. In *Proceedings on the Workshop on Statistical Machine Translation*, pages 166–169, New York City. Association for Computational Linguistics.

Johnson, H., Sadat, F., Foster, G., Kuhn, R., Simard, M., Joanis, E., and Larkin, S. (2006). Portage: with smoothed phrase tables and segment choice models. In *Proceedings on the Workshop on Statistical Machine Translation*, pages 134–137, New York City. Association for Computational Linguistics.

Koehn, P. (2004). Statistical significance tests for machine translation evaluation. In Lin, D. and Wu, D., editors, *Proceedings of EMNLP 2004*, pages 388–395, Barcelona, Spain. Association for Computational Linguistics.

Koehn, P. and Monz, C. (2005). Shared task: Statistical machine translation between European languages. In *Proceedings of the ACL Workshop on Building and Using Parallel Texts*, pages 119–124, Ann Arbor, Michigan. Association for Computational Linguistics.

Li, A. (2005). Results of the 2005 NIST machine translation evaluation. In *Machine Translation Workshop*.

Menezes, A., Toutanova, K., and Quirk, C. (2006). Microsoft research treelet translation system: Naacl 2006 europarl evaluation. In *Proceedings on the Workshop on Statistical Machine Translation*, pages 158–161, New York City. Association for Computational Linguistics.

Olteanu, M., Davis, C., Volosen, I., and Moldovan, D. (2006a). Phramer - an open source statistical phrase-based translator. In *Proceedings on the Workshop on Statistical Machine Translation*, pages 146–149, New York City. Association for Computational Linguistics.

Olteanu, M., Suriyentrakorn, P., and Moldovan, D. (2006b). Language models and reranking for machine translation. In *Proceedings on the Workshop on Statistical Machine Translation*, pages 150–153, New York City. Association for Computational Linguistics.

Patry, A., Gotti, F., and Langlais, P. (2006). Mood at work: Ramses versus pharaoh. In *Proceedings on the Workshop on Statistical Machine Translation*, pages 126–129, New York City. Association for Computational Linguistics.

Przybocki, M. (2004). NIST machine translation 2004 evaluation – summary of results. In *Machine Translation Evaluation Workshop*.

Riezler, S. and Maxwell, J. T. (2005). On some pitfalls in automatic evaluation and significance testing for MT. In *Proceedings of the ACL Workshop on Intrinsic and Extrinsic Evaluation Measures for Machine Translation and/or Summarization*, pages 57–64, Ann Arbor, Michigan. Association for Computational Linguistics.

Sánchez, J. A. and Benedí, J. M. (2006). Stochastic inversion transduction grammars for obtaining word phrases for phrase-based statistical machine translation. In *Proceedings on the Workshop on Statistical Machine Translation*, pages 130–133, New York City. Association for Computational Linguistics.

Watanabe, T., Tsukada, H., and Isozaki, H. (2006). Ntt system description for the wmt2006 shared task. In *Proceedings on the Workshop on Statistical Machine Translation*, pages 122–125, New York City. Association for Computational Linguistics.

Zollmann, A. and Venugopal, A. (2006). Syntax augmented machine translation via chart parsing. In *Proceedings on the Workshop on Statistical Machine Translation*, pages 138–141, New York City. Association for Computational Linguistics.

French-English (In Domain)

	Adequacy (rank)	Fluency (rank)	BLEU (rank)
upc-jmc	+0.19±0.08 (1-7)	+0.09±0.08 (1-8)	30.42±0.86 (1-6)
lcc	+0.14±0.07 (1-6)	+0.13±0.06 (1-7)	30.81±0.85 (1-4)
utd	+0.13±0.08 (1-7)	+0.14±0.07 (1-6)	30.53±0.87 (2-7)
upc-mr	+0.13±0.08 (1-8)	+0.13±0.07 (1-6)	30.33±0.88 (1-7)
nrc	+0.12±0.10 (1-7)	+0.06±0.11 (2-6)	29.62±0.84 (8)
ntt	+0.11±0.08 (1-8)	+0.14±0.08 (2-8)	30.72±0.87 (1-7)
cmu	+0.10±0.08 (3-7)	+0.05±0.07 (4-8)	30.18±0.80 (2-7)
rali	-0.02±0.08 (5-8)	+0.00±0.08 (3-9)	30.39±0.91 (3-7)
systran	-0.08±0.09 (9)	-0.17±0.09 (8-9)	21.44±0.65 (10)
upv	-0.76±0.09 (10)	-0.52±0.09 (10)	24.10±0.89 (9)

Spanish-English (In Domain)

	Adequacy (rank)	Fluency (rank)	BLEU (rank)
upc-jmc	+0.15±0.08 (1-7)	+0.18±0.08 (1-6)	31.01±0.97 (1-5)
ntt	+0.10±0.08 (1-7)	+0.10±0.08 (1-8)	31.29±0.88 (1-5)
lcc	+0.08±0.07 (1-8)	+0.04±0.06 (2-8)	31.46±0.87 (1-4)
utd	+0.08±0.06 (1-8)	+0.08±0.07 (2-7)	31.10±0.89 (1-5)
nrc	+0.06±0.10 (2-8)	+0.08±0.07 (1-9)	30.04±0.79 (6)
upc-mr	+0.06±0.07 (1-8)	+0.08±0.07 (1-6)	29.43±0.83 (7)
uedin-birch	+0.03±0.11 (1-8)	-0.07±0.15 (2-10)	29.01±0.81 (8)
rali	+0.00±0.07 (3-9)	-0.02±0.07 (3-9)	30.80±0.87 (2-5)
upc-jg	-0.10±0.07 (7-9)	-0.11±0.07 (6-9)	28.03±0.83 (9)
upv	-0.45±0.10 (10)	-0.41±0.10 (9-10)	23.91±0.83 (10)

German-English (In Domain)

	Adequacy (rank)	Fluency (rank)	BLEU (rank)
uedin-phi	+0.30±0.09 (1-2)	+0.33±0.08 (1)	27.30±0.86 (1)
lcc	+0.15±0.07 (2-7)	+0.12±0.07 (2-7)	25.97±0.81 (2)
nrc	+0.12±0.07 (2-7)	+0.14±0.07 (2-6)	24.54±0.80 (5-7)
utd	+0.08±0.07 (3-7)	+0.01±0.08 (2-8)	25.44±0.85 (3-4)
ntt	+0.07±0.08 (2-9)	+0.06±0.09 (2-8)	25.64±0.83 (3-4)
upc-mr	+0.00±0.09 (3-9)	-0.21±0.09 (6-9)	23.68±0.79 (8)
rali	-0.01±0.06 (4-9)	+0.00±0.07 (3-9)	24.60±0.80 (5-7)
upc-jmc	-0.02±0.09 (2-9)	-0.04±0.09 (3-9)	24.43±0.86 (5-7)
systran	-0.05±0.10 (3-9)	-0.05±0.09 (3-9)	15.86±0.59 (10)
upv	-0.55±0.09 (10)	-0.38±0.08 (10)	18.08±0.77 (9)

Figure 7: Evaluation of translation to English on in-domain test data

English-French (In Domain)

	Adequacy (rank)	Fluency (rank)	BLEU (rank)
nrc	+0.08±0.09 (1-5)	+0.09±0.09 (1-5)	31.75±0.83 (1-6)
upc-mr	+0.08±0.08 (1-4)	+0.04±0.07 (1-5)	31.50±0.76 (1-6)
upc-jmc	+0.03±0.09 (1-6)	+0.02±0.08 (1-6)	31.75±0.78 (1-5)
systran	-0.01±0.12 (2-7)	+0.06±0.12 (1-6)	25.07±0.71 (7)
utd	-0.03±0.07 (3-7)	-0.05±0.07 (3-7)	31.42±0.85 (3-6)
rali	-0.08±0.09 (1-7)	-0.09±0.09 (2-7)	31.79±0.85 (1-6)
ntt	-0.09±0.09 (4-7)	-0.06±0.08 (4-7)	31.92±0.84 (1-5)

English-Spanish (In Domain)

	Adequacy (rank)	Fluency (rank)	BLEU (rank)
ms	+0.23±0.09 (1-5)	+0.13±0.09 (1-7)	29.76±0.82 (7-8)
upc-mr	+0.20±0.09 (1-4)	+0.17±0.09 (1-5)	31.06±0.86 (1-4)
utd	+0.18±0.08 (1-5)	+0.15±0.08 (1-6)	30.73±0.90 (1-4)
nrc	+0.12±0.09 (2-7)	+0.17±0.08 (1-6)	29.97±0.86 (5-6)
ntt	+0.10±0.09 (3-7)	+0.14±0.08 (1-6)	30.93±0.85 (1-4)
upc-jmc	+0.04±0.10 (2-7)	+0.01±0.08 (2-7)	30.44±0.86 (1-4)
rali	-0.05±0.08 (5-8)	-0.03±0.08 (6-8)	29.38±0.85 (5-6)
uedin-birch	-0.18±0.14 (6-9)	-0.17±0.13 (6-10)	28.49±0.87 (7-8)
upc-jg	-0.32±0.11 (9)	-0.37±0.09 (8-10)	27.46±0.78 (9)
upv	-0.83±0.15 (9-10)	-0.59±0.15 (8-10)	23.17±0.73 (10)

English-German (In Domain)

	Adequacy (rank)	Fluency (rank)	BLEU (rank)
upc-mr	+0.28±0.08 (1-3)	+0.14±0.08 (1-5)	17.24±0.81 (3-5)
ntt	+0.19±0.08 (1-5)	+0.09±0.06 (2-6)	18.15±0.89 (1-3)
upc-jmc	+0.17±0.08 (1-5)	+0.13±0.08 (1-4)	17.73±0.81 (1-3)
nrc	+0.17±0.08 (2-4)	+0.11±0.08 (1-5)	17.52±0.78 (4-5)
rali	+0.08±0.10 (3-6)	+0.03±0.09 (2-6)	17.93±0.85 (1-4)
systran	-0.08±0.11 (5-6)	+0.00±0.10 (3-6)	9.84±0.52 (7)
upv	-0.84±0.12 (7)	-0.51±0.10 (7)	13.37±0.78 (6)

Figure 8: Evaluation of translation from English on in-domain test data

French-English (Out of Domain)

	Adequacy (rank)	Fluency (rank)	BLEU (rank)
upc-jmc	+0.23±0.09 (1-5)	+0.13±0.11 (1-8)	21.79±0.92 (1-4)
cmu	+0.22±0.11 (1-8)	+0.13±0.09 (1-9)	21.15±0.86 (4-7)
systran	+0.19±0.15 (1-8)	+0.15±0.14 (1-7)	19.42±0.82 (9)
lcc	+0.13±0.12 (1-9)	+0.11±0.11 (1-9)	21.77±0.88 (1-5)
upc-mr	+0.12±0.12 (2-8)	+0.11±0.10 (1-7)	21.95±0.94 (1-3)
utd	+0.04±0.10 (1-9)	+0.01±0.10 (1-8)	21.39±0.94 (3-7)
ntt	-0.02±0.12 (3-9)	+0.08±0.11 (1-9)	21.34±0.85 (3-7)
nrc	-0.03±0.14 (3-8)	+0.00±0.11 (3-9)	21.15±0.86 (3-7)
rali	-0.09±0.12 (4-9)	-0.10±0.11 (5-9)	20.17±0.85 (8)
upv	-0.76±0.16 (10)	-0.58±0.14 (10)	15.55±0.79 (10)

Spanish-English (Out of Domain)

	Adequacy (rank)	Fluency (rank)	BLEU (rank)
upc-jmc	+0.28±0.10 (1-2)	+0.17±0.10 (1-6)	27.92±0.94 (1-3)
uedin-birch	+0.25±0.16 (1-7)	+0.18±0.19 (1-6)	25.20±0.91 (5-8)
nrc	+0.18±0.16 (2-8)	+0.09±0.09 (1-8)	25.40±0.94 (5-7)
ntt	+0.11±0.10 (2-7)	+0.17±0.10 (2-6)	26.85±0.89 (3-4)
upc-mr	+0.08±0.11 (2-8)	+0.10±0.10 (1-7)	25.62±0.87 (5-8)
lcc	+0.04±0.10 (4-9)	+0.07±0.11 (3-7)	27.18±0.92 (1-4)
utd	+0.03±0.11 (2-9)	+0.03±0.10 (2-8)	27.41±0.96 (1-3)
upc-jg	-0.09±0.11 (4-9)	-0.09±0.09 (7-9)	23.42±0.87 (9)
rali	-0.09±0.11 (4-9)	-0.15±0.11 (6-9)	25.03±0.91 (6-8)
upv	-0.63±0.14 (10)	-0.47±0.11 (10)	19.17±0.78 (10)

German-English (Out of Domain)

	Adequacy (rank)	Fluency (rank)	BLEU (rank)
systran	+0.30±0.12 (1-4)	+0.21±0.12 (1-4)	15.56±0.71 (7-9)
uedin-phi	+0.22±0.09 (1-6)	+0.21±0.10 (1-7)	18.87±0.84 (1)
lcc	+0.18±0.10 (1-6)	+0.20±0.10 (1-7)	17.96±0.79 (2-3)
utd	+0.08±0.09 (2-7)	+0.07±0.08 (2-6)	16.97±0.76 (4-6)
ntt	+0.07±0.12 (1-9)	+0.21±0.13 (1-7)	17.37±0.76 (3-5)
nrc	+0.04±0.10 (3-8)	+0.04±0.09 (2-8)	15.93±0.76 (7-8)
upc-mr	+0.02±0.10 (4-8)	-0.11±0.09 (6-8)	16.89±0.79 (4-6)
upc-jmc	-0.01±0.10 (4-8)	-0.04±0.11 (3-9)	17.57±0.80 (2-5)
rali	-0.14±0.08 (8-9)	-0.14±0.08 (8-9)	15.22±0.69 (8-9)
upv	-0.64±0.11 (10)	-0.54±0.09 (10)	11.78±0.71 (10)

Figure 9: Evaluation of translation to English on out-of-domain test data

English-French (Out of Domain)

	Adequacy (rank)	Fluency (rank)	BLEU (rank)
systran	+0.50±0.20 (1)	+0.41±0.18 (1)	25.31±0.88 (1)
upc-jmc	+0.09±0.11 (2-5)	+0.09±0.11 (2-4)	23.30±0.75 (2-6)
upc-mr	+0.09±0.11 (2-4)	+0.04±0.09 (2-4)	23.21±0.75 (2-6)
utd	-0.02±0.11 (2-6)	-0.05±0.09 (2-6)	22.79±0.86 (7)
rali	-0.12±0.12 (4-7)	-0.17±0.12 (5-7)	23.34±0.89 (2-6)
nrc	-0.13±0.13 (4-7)	-0.16±0.10 (4-7)	23.66±0.91 (2-5)
ntt	-0.23±0.12 (4-7)	-0.06±0.10 (4-7)	22.99±0.96 (3-6)

English-Spanish (Out of Domain)

	Adequacy (rank)	Fluency (rank)	BLEU (rank)
upc-mr	+0.35±0.11 (1-3)	+0.19±0.10 (1-6)	26.62±0.92 (1-2)
ms	+0.33±0.16 (1-7)	+0.15±0.13 (1-8)	26.15±0.88 (6-7)
utd	+0.21±0.13 (2-6)	+0.13±0.11 (1-7)	25.26±0.78 (3-5)
nrc	+0.18±0.12 (1-6)	+0.07±0.11 (2-7)	25.58±0.85 (3-5)
upc-jmc	+0.17±0.15 (2-7)	+0.24±0.12 (1-6)	25.59±0.95 (3-5)
ntt	+0.12±0.13 (2-7)	+0.12±0.13 (1-7)	26.52±0.90 (1-2)
rali	-0.17±0.16 (6-8)	-0.05±0.13 (4-8)	24.03±0.83 (6-8)
uedin-birch	-0.36±0.24 (6-10)	-0.16±0.16 (5-9)	23.18±0.88 (7-8)
upc-jg	-0.45±0.13 (8-9)	-0.42±0.10 (9-10)	22.04±0.84 (9)
upv	-1.09±0.21 (9)	-0.64±0.19 (8-9)	16.83±0.72 (10)

English-German (Out of Domain)

	Adequacy (rank)	Fluency (rank)	BLEU (rank)
systran	+0.47±0.15 (1)	+0.39±0.15 (1-2)	10.78±0.69 (1-6)
upc-mr	+0.31±0.13 (2-3)	+0.21±0.11 (1-3)	10.96±0.70 (1-5)
upc-jmc	+0.22±0.14 (2-3)	+0.01±0.10 (3-6)	10.64±0.66 (1-6)
rali	+0.13±0.12 (4-6)	-0.06±0.10 (4-6)	10.57±0.65 (1-6)
nrc	+0.00±0.11 (4-6)	+0.05±0.09 (2-6)	10.64±0.65 (2-6)
ntt	-0.03±0.12 (4-6)	+0.08±0.11 (3-5)	10.51±0.64 (1-6)
upv	-0.94±0.13 (7)	-0.57±0.10 (7)	6.55±0.53 (7)

Figure 10: Evaluation of translation from English on out-of-domain test data

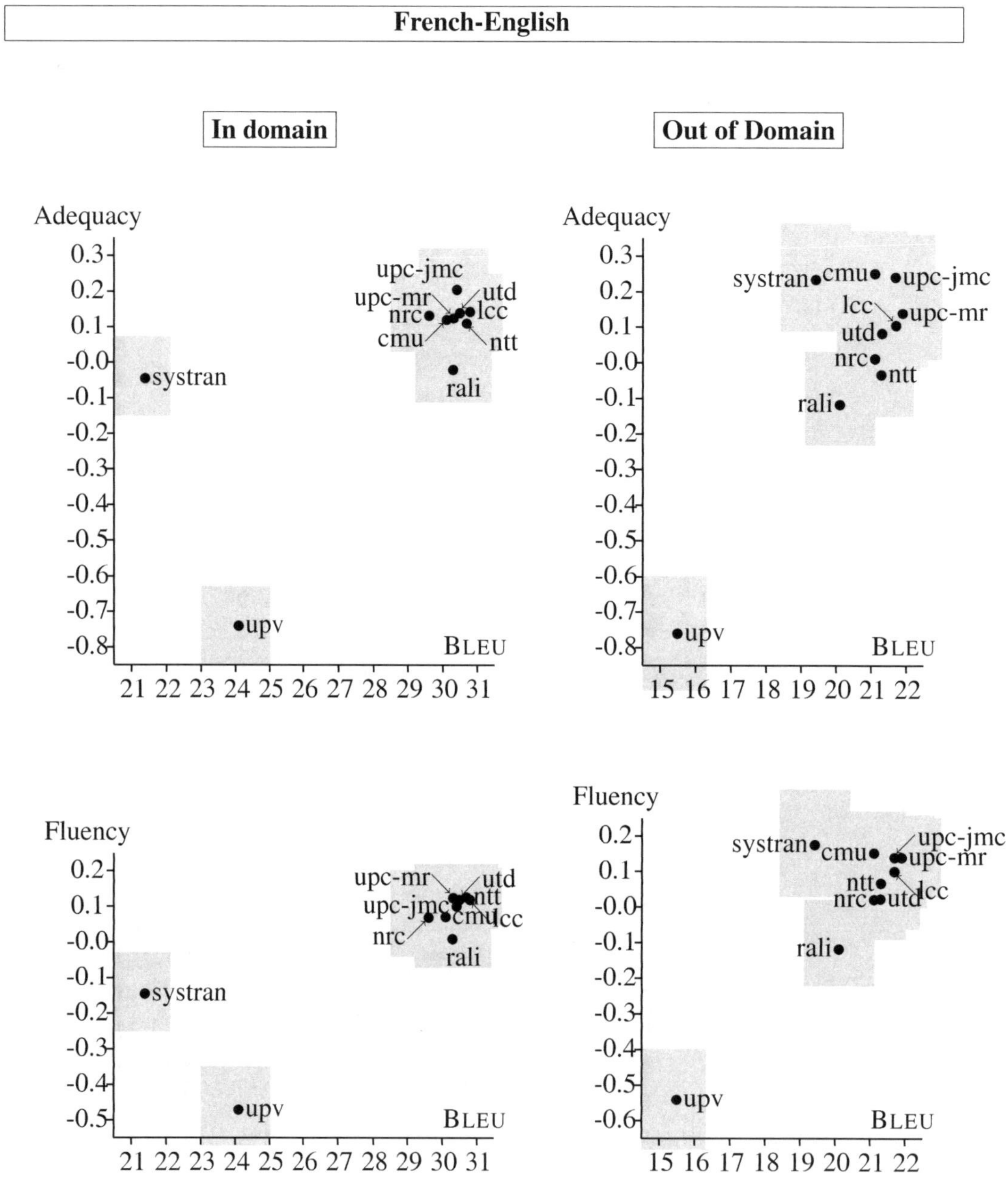

Figure 11: Correlation between manual and automatic scores for French-English

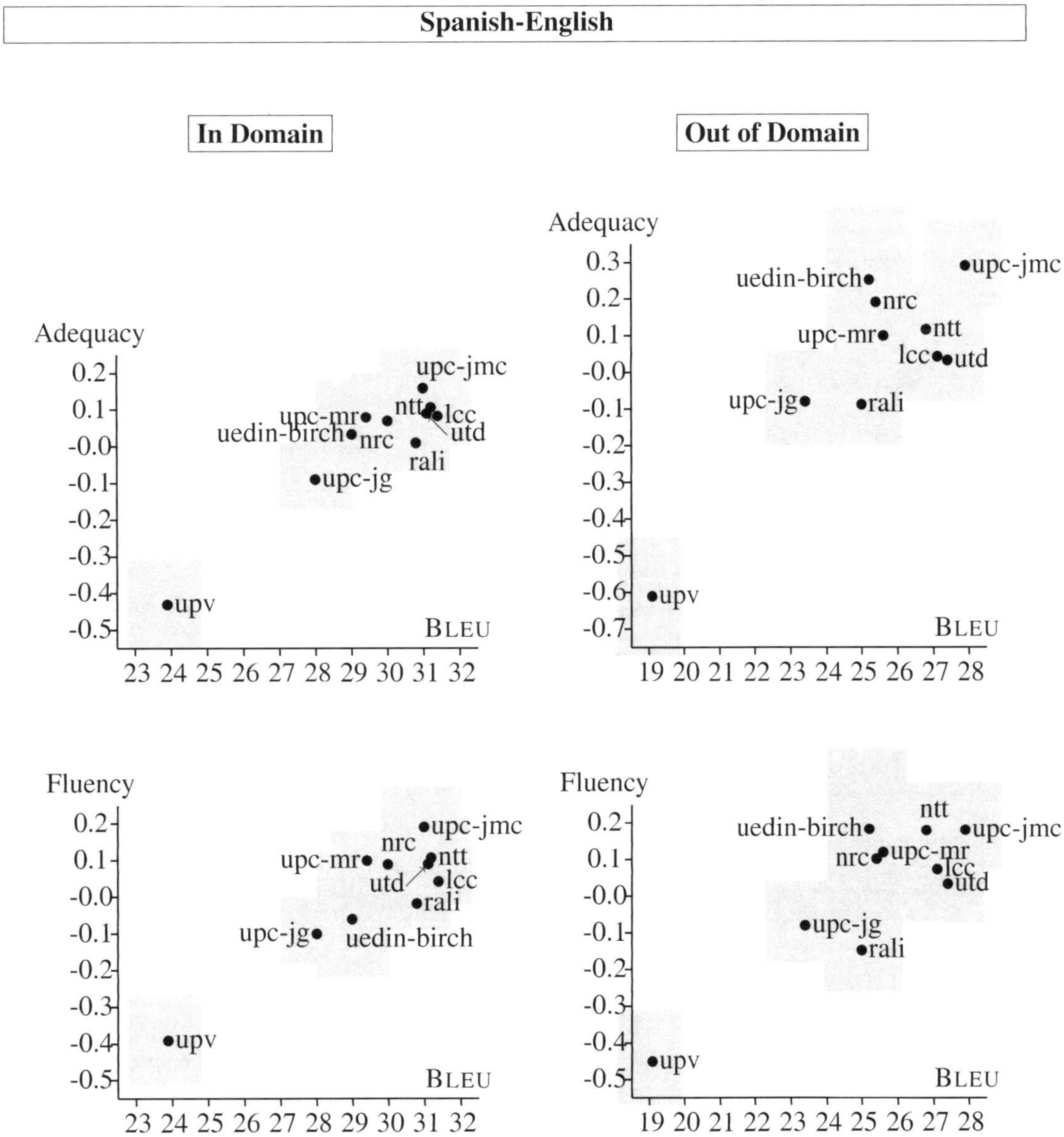

Figure 12: Correlation between manual and automatic scores for Spanish-English

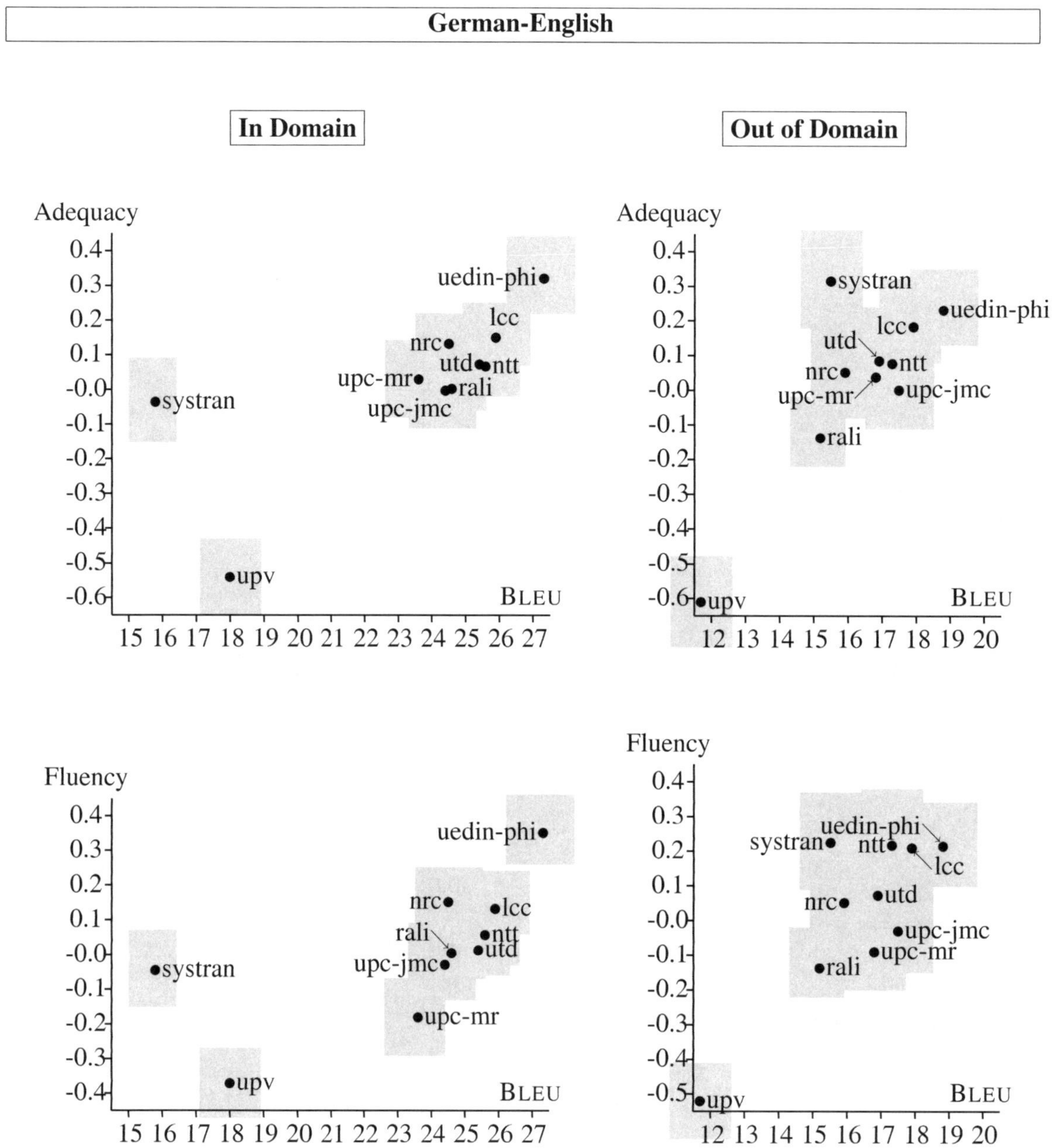

Figure 13: Correlation between manual and automatic scores for German-English

English-French

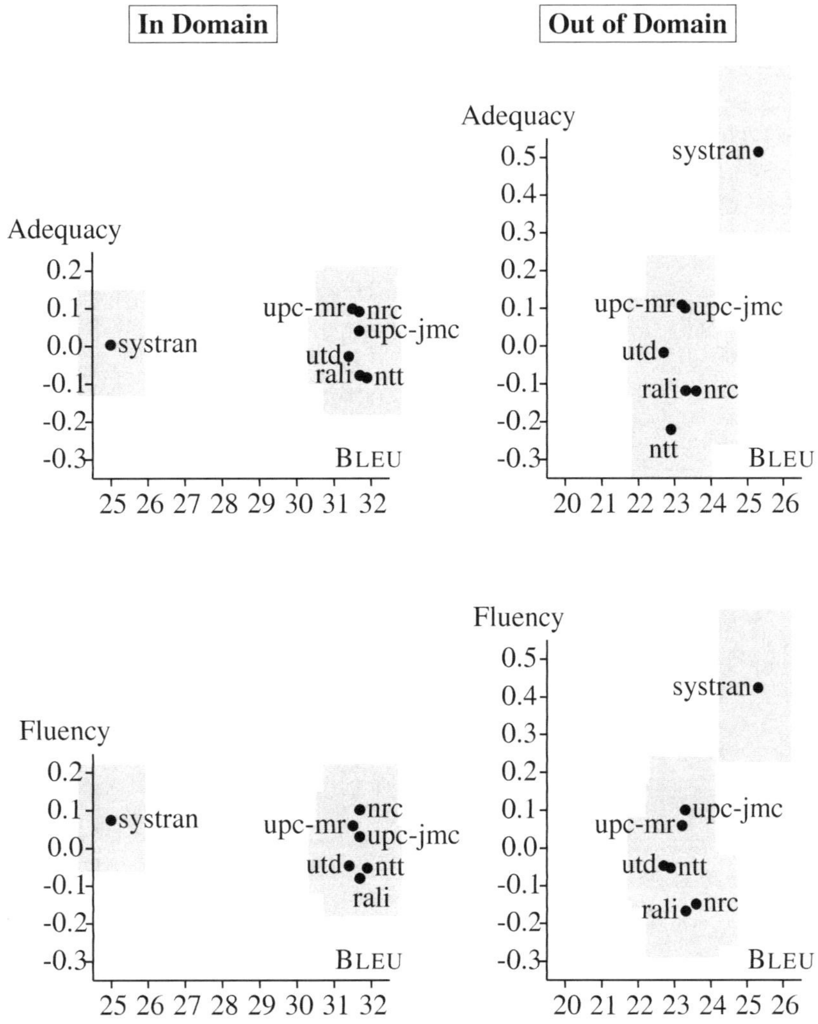

Figure 14: Correlation between manual and automatic scores for English-French

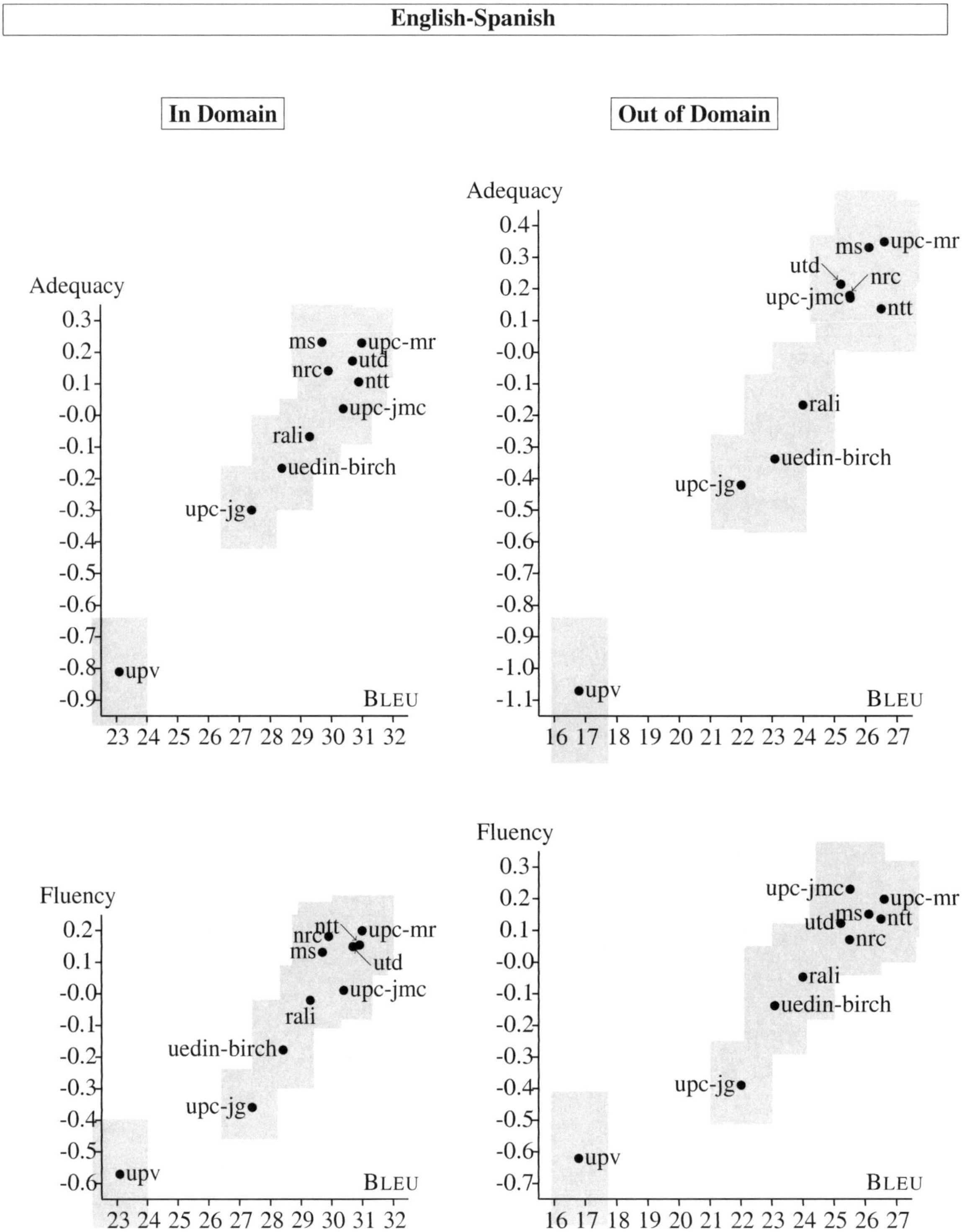

Figure 15: Correlation between manual and automatic scores for English-Spanish

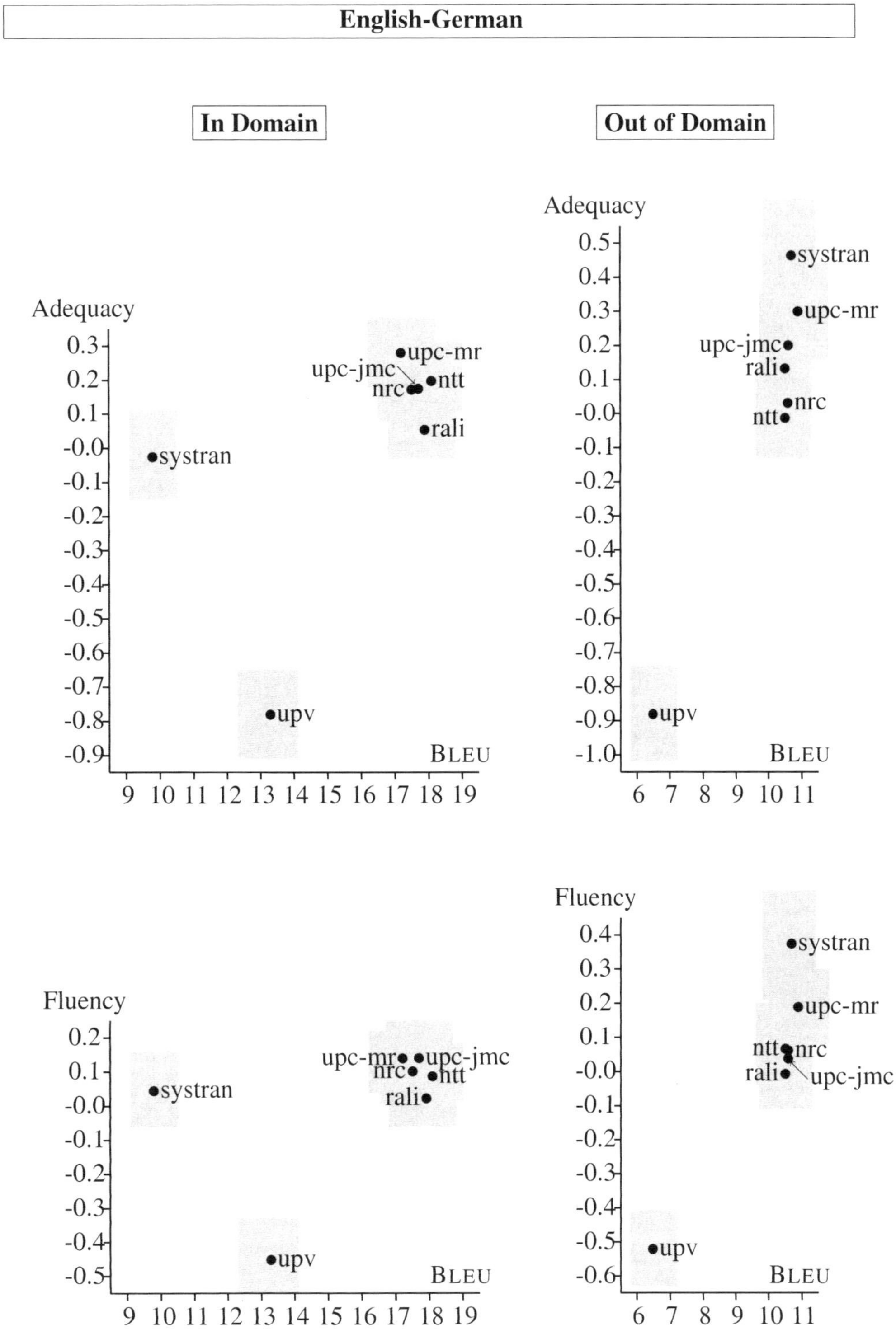

Figure 16: Correlation between manual and automatic scores for English-German

NTT System Description for the WMT2006 Shared Task

Taro Watanabe **Hajime Tsukada** **Hideki Isozaki**
NTT Communication Science Laboratories
2-4 Hikaridai, Seika-cho, Soraku-gun,
Kyoto, Japan 619-0237
{taro,tsukada,isozaki}@kecl.ntt.co.jp

Abstract

We present two translation systems experimented for the shared-task of "Workshop on Statistical Machine Translation," a phrase-based model and a hierarchical phrase-based model. The former uses a phrasal unit for translation, whereas the latter is conceptualized as a synchronous-CFG in which phrases are hierarchically combined using non-terminals. Experiments showed that the hierarchical phrase-based model performed very comparable to the phrase-based model. We also report a phrase/rule extraction technique differentiating tokenization of corpora.

1 Introduction

We contrasted two translation methods for the Workshop on Statistical Machine Translation (WMT2006) shared-task. One is a phrase-based translation in which a phrasal unit is employed for translation (Koehn et al., 2003). The other is a hierarchical phrase-based translation in which translation is realized as a set of paired production rules (Chiang, 2005). Section 2 discusses those two models and details extraction algorithms, decoding algorithms and feature functions.

We also explored three types of corpus pre-processing in Section 3. As expected, different tokenization would lead to different word alignments which, in turn, resulted in the divergence of the extracted phrase/rule size. In our method, phrase/rule translation pairs extracted from three distinctly word-aligned corpora are aggregated into one large phrase/rule translation table. The experiments and the final translation results are presented in Section 4.

2 Translation Models

We used a log-linear approach (Och and Ney, 2002) in which a foreign language sentence $f_1^J = f_1, f_2, ...f_J$ is translated into another language, i.e. English, $e_1^I = e_1, e_2, ..., e_I$ by seeking a maximum likelihood solution of

$$\hat{e}_1^I = \operatorname*{argmax}_{e_1^I} Pr(e_1^I|f_1^J) \tag{1}$$

$$= \operatorname*{argmax}_{e_1^I} \frac{\exp\left(\sum_{m=1}^M \lambda_m h_m(e_1^I, f_1^J)\right)}{\sum_{e'^{I'}_1} \exp\left(\sum_{m=1}^M \lambda_m h_m(e'^{I'}_1, f_1^J)\right)} \tag{2}$$

In this framework, the posterior probability $Pr(e_1^I|f_1^J)$ is directly maximized using a log-linear combination of feature functions $h_m(e_1^I, f_1^J)$, such as a ngram language model or a translation model. When decoding, the denominator is dropped since it depends only on f_1^J. Feature function scaling factors λ_m are optimized based on a maximum likelihood approach (Och and Ney, 2002) or on a direct error minimization approach (Och, 2003). This modeling allows the integration of various feature functions depending on the scenario of how a translation is constituted.

In a phrase-based statistical translation (Koehn et al., 2003), a bilingual text is decomposed as K phrase translation pairs $(\bar{e}_1, \bar{f}_{\bar{a}_1}), (\bar{e}_2, \bar{f}_{\bar{a}_2}), ...$: The input foreign sentence is segmented into phrases $\bar{f}_1^K$,

Proceedings of the Workshop on Statistical Machine Translation, pages 122–125,
New York City, June 2006.

mapped into corresponding English $\bar{e}_1^K$, then, reordered to form the output English sentence according to a phrase alignment index mapping $\bar{a}$.

In a hierarchical phrase-based translation (Chiang, 2005), translation is modeled after a weighted synchronous-CFG consisting of production rules whose right-hand side is paired (Aho and Ullman, 1969):

$$X \rightarrow \langle \gamma, \alpha, \sim \rangle$$

where X is a non-terminal, γ and α are strings of terminals and non-terminals. $\sim$ is a one-to-one correspondence for the non-terminals appeared in γ and α. Starting from an initial non-terminal, each rule rewrites non-terminals in γ and α that are associated with $\sim$.

2.1 Phrase/Rule Extraction

The phrase extraction algorithm is based on those presented by Koehn et al. (2003). First, many-to-many word alignments are induced by running a one-to-many word alignment model, such as GIZA++ (Och and Ney, 2003), in both directions and by combining the results based on a heuristic (Och and Ney, 2004). Second, phrase translation pairs are extracted from the word aligned corpus (Koehn et al., 2003). The method exhaustively extracts phrase pairs (f_j^{j+m}, e_i^{i+n}) from a sentence pair (f_1^J, e_1^I) that do not violate the word alignment constraints a.

In the hierarchical phrase-based model, production rules are accumulated by computing "holes" for extracted contiguous phrases (Chiang, 2005):

1. A phrase pair $(\bar{f}, \bar{e})$ constitutes a rule:

$$X \rightarrow \left\langle \bar{f}, \bar{e} \right\rangle$$

2. A rule $X \rightarrow \langle \gamma, \alpha \rangle$ and a phrase pair $(\bar{f}, \bar{e})$ s.t. $\gamma = \gamma' \bar{f} \gamma''$ and $\alpha = \alpha' \bar{e} \alpha''$ constitutes a rule:

$$X \rightarrow \left\langle \gamma' \; X_{\boxed{k}} \; \gamma'', \alpha' \; X_{\boxed{k}} \; \alpha'' \right\rangle$$

2.2 Decoding

The decoder for the phrase-based model is a left-to-right generation decoder with a beam search strategy synchronized with the cardinality of already translated foreign words. The decoding process is very similar to those described in (Koehn et al., 2003): It starts from an initial empty hypothesis. From an existing hypothesis, new hypothesis is generated by consuming a phrase translation pair that covers untranslated foreign word positions. The score for the newly generated hypothesis is updated by combining the scores of feature functions described in Section 2.3. The English side of the phrase is simply concatenated to form a new prefix of English sentence.

In the hierarchical phrase-based model, decoding is realized as an Earley-style top-down parser on the foreign language side with a beam search strategy synchronized with the cardinality of already translated foreign words (Watanabe et al., 2006). The major difference to the phrase-based model's decoder is the handling of non-terminals, or holes, in each rule.

2.3 Feature Functions

Our phrase-based model uses a standard pharaoh feature functions listed as follows (Koehn et al., 2003):

- Relative-count based phrase translation probabilities in both directions.
- Lexically weighted feature functions in both directions.
- The supplied trigram language model.
- Distortion model that counts the number of words skipped.
- The number of words in English-side and the number of phrases that constitute translation.

For details, please refer to Koehn et al. (2003).

In addition, we added three feature functions to restrict reorderings and to represent globalized insertion/deletion of words:

- Lexicalized reordering feature function scores whether a phrase translation pair is monotonically translated or not (Och et al., 2004):

$$h_{lex}(\bar{a}_1^K | \bar{f}_1^K, \bar{e}_1^K) = \log \prod_{k=1}^{K} p_r(\delta_k | \bar{f}_{\bar{a}_k}, \bar{e}_k) \quad (3)$$

  where $\delta_k = 1$ iff $\bar{a}_k - \bar{a}_{k-1} = 1$ otherwise $\delta_k = 0$.

- Deletion feature function penalizes words that do not constitute a translation according to a

Table 1: Number of word alignment by different preprocessings.

	de-en	es-en	fr-en	en-de	en-es	en-fr
lower	17,660,187	17,221,890	16,176,075	17,596,764	17,237,723	16,220,520
stem	17,110,890	16,601,306	15,635,900	17,052,808	16,597,274	15,658,940
prefix4	16,975,398	16,540,767	15,610,319	16,936,710	16,530,810	15,613,755
intersection	12,203,979	12,677,192	11,645,404	12,218,997	12,688,773	11,653,242
union	23,186,379	21,709,212	20,760,539	23,066,052	21,698,267	20,789,570

Table 2: Number of phrases extracted from differently preprocessed corpora.

	de-en	es-en	fr-en	en-de	en-es	en-fr
lower	37,711,217	61,161,868	56,025,918	38,142,663	60,619,435	55,198,497
stem	46,550,101	75,610,696	68,210,968	46,749,195	75,473,313	67,733,045
prefix4	53,429,522	78,193,818	70,514,377	53,647,033	78,223,236	70,378,947
merged	80,260,191	111,153,303	103,523,206	80,666,414	110,787,982	102,940,840

lexicon model $t(f|e)$ (Bender et al., 2004):

$$h_{del}(e_1^I, f_1^J) = \sum_{j=1}^{J} \left[\max_{0 \le i \le I} t(f_j|e_i) < \tau_{del} \right] \quad (4)$$

The deletion model simply counts the number of words whose lexicon model probability is lower than a threshold τ_{del}. Likewise, we also added an insertion model $h_{ins}(e_1^I, f_1^J)$ that penalizes the spuriously inserted English words using a lexicon model $t(e|f)$.

For the hierarchical phrase-based model, we employed the same feature set except for the distortion model and the lexicalized reordering model.

3 Phrase Extraction from Different Word Alignment

We prepared three kinds of corpora differentiated by tokenization methods. First, the simplest preprocessing is lower-casing (lower). Second, corpora were transformed by a Porter's algorithm based multilingual stemmer (stem) [1]. Third, mixed-cased corpora were truncated to the prefix of four letters of each word (prefix4). For each differently tokenized corpus, we computed word alignments by a HMM translation model (Och and Ney, 2003) and by a word alignment refinement heuristic of "grow-diag-final" (Koehn et al., 2003). Different preprocessing yields quite divergent alignment points as illustrated in Table 1. The table also shows the numbers for the intersection and union of three alignment annotations.

The (hierarchical) phrase translation pairs are extracted from three distinctly word aligned corpora. In this process, each word is recovered into its lower-cased form. The associated counts are aggregated to constitute relative count-based feature functions. Table 2 summarizes the size of phrase tables induced from the corpora. The number of rules extracted for the hierarchical phrase-based model was roughly twice as large as those for the phrase-based model. Fewer word alignments resulted in larger phrase translation table size as observed in the "prefix4" corpus. The size is further increased by our aggregation step (merged).

Different induction/refinement algorithms or preprocessings of a corpus bias word alignment. We found that some word alignments were consistent even with different preprocessings, though we could not justify whether such alignments would match against human intuition. If we could trust such consistently aligned words, reliable (hierarchical) phrase translation pairs would be extracted, which, in turn, would result in better estimates for relative count-based feature functions. At the same time, differently biased word alignment annotations suggest alternative phrase translation pairs that is useful for increasing the coverage of translations.

4 Results

Table 3 shows the open test translation results on 2005 and 2006 test set (the development-test set and the final test set) [2]. We used the merged (hierarchical) phrase tables for decoding. Feature function scaling factors were optimized on BLEU score using the supplied development set that is identical to the 2005's development set. We observed that our

[1] We used the Snowball stemmer from http://snowball.tartarus.org

[2] We did not differetiated in-domain or out-of-domain for 2006 test set.

Table 3: Open test on the 2005/2006 test sets (BLEU [%]).

		de-en	es-en	fr-en	en-de	en-es	en-fr
test2005	Phrase	25.72	30.97	30.97	18.08	30.48	32.14
	Rule	25.14	30.11	30.31	17.96	27.96	31.04
	2005's best	24.77	30.95	30.27			
test2006	Phrase	23.16	29.90	27.89	15.79	29.54	29.19
	Rule	22.74	28.80	27.28	15.99	26.56	27.86

results are very comparable to the last year's best results in test2005. Also found that our hierarchical phrase-based translation (Rule) performed slightly inferior to the phrase-based translation (Phrase) in both test sets. The hierarchically combined phrases seem to be too flexible to represent the relationship of similar language pairs. Note that our hierarchical phrase-based model performed better in the English-to-German translation task. Those language pair requires rather distorted reordering, which could be represented by hierarchically combined phrases.

We also conducted additional studies on how differently aligned corpora might affect the translation quality on Spanish-to-English task for the 2005 test set. Using our phrase-based model, the BLEU scores for lower/stem/prefix4 were 30.90/30.89/30.76, respectively. The differences of translation qualities were statistically significant at the 95% confidence level. Our phrase translation pairs aggregated from all the differently preprocessed corpora improved the translation quality.

5 Conclusion

We presented two translation models, a phrase-based model and a hierarchical phrase-based model. The former performed as well as the last year's best system, whereas the latter performed comparable to our phrase-based model. We are going to experiment new feature functions to restrict the too flexible reordering represented by our hierarchical phrase-based model.

We also investigated different word alignment annotations, first using lower-cased corpus, second performing stemming, and third retaining only 4-letter prefix. Differently preprocessed corpora resulted in quite divergent word alignment. Large phrase/rule translation tables were accumulated from three distinctly aligned corpora, which in turn, increased the translation quality.

References

Alfred V. Aho and Jeffrey D. Ullman. 1969. Syntax directed translations and the pushdown assembler. *J. Comput. Syst. Sci.*, 3(1):37–56.

Oliver Bender, Richard Zens, Evgeny Matusov, and Hermann Ney. 2004. Alignment templates: the RWTH SMT system". In *Proc. of IWSLT 2004*, pages 79–84, Kyoto, Japan.

David Chiang. 2005. A hierarchical phrase-based model for statistical machine translation. In *Proc. of ACL 2005*, pages 263–270, Ann Arbor, Michigan, June.

Philipp Koehn, Franz Josef Och, and Daniel Marcu. 2003. Statistical phrase-based translation. In *Proc. of NAACL 2003*, pages 48–54, Edmonton, Canada.

Franz Josef Och and Hermann Ney. 2002. Discriminative training and maximum entropy models for statistical machine translation. In *Proc. of ACL 2002*, pages 295–302.

Franz Josef Och and Hermann Ney. 2003. A systematic comparison of various statistical alignment models. *Computational Linguistics*, 29(1):19–51, March.

Franz Josef Och and Hermann Ney. 2004. The alignment template approach to statistical machine translation. *Comput. Linguist.*, 30(4):417–449.

Franz Josef Och, Daniel Gildea, Sanjeev Khudanpur, Anoop Sarkar, Kenji Yamada, Shankar Fraser, Alex a nd Kumar, Libin Shen, David Smith, Katherine Eng, Viren Jain, Zhen Jin, and Dragomir Radev. 2004. A smorgasbord of features for statistical machine translation. In *HLT-NAACL 2004: Main Proceedings*, pages 161–168, Boston, Massachusetts, USA, May 2 - May 7.

Franz Josef Och. 2003. Minimum error rate training in statistical machine translation. In *Proc. of ACL 2003*, pages 160–167.

Taro Watanabe, Hajime Tsukada, and Hideki Isozaki. 2006. Left-to-right target generation for hierarchical phrase-based translation. In *Proc. of COLING-ACL 2006 (to appear)*, Sydney, Australia, July.

Mood at work: Ramses versus Pharaoh

Alexandre Patry, Fabrizio Gotti and Philippe Langlais

RALI — DIRO
Université de Montréal
{patryale,gottif,felipe}@iro.umontreal.ca

Abstract

We present here the translation system we used in this year's WMT shared task. The main objective of our participation was to test RAMSES, an open source phrase-based decoder. For that purpose, we used the baseline system made available by the organizers of the shared task[1] to build the necessary models. We then carried out a pair-to-pair comparison of RAMSES with PHARAOH on the six different translation directions that we were asked to perform. We present this comparison in this paper.

1 Introduction

Phrase-based (PB) machine translation (MT) is now a popular paradigm, partly because of the relative ease with which we can automatically create an acceptable translation engine from a bitext. As a matter of fact, deriving such an engine from a bitext consists in (more or less) gluing together dedicated software modules, often freely available. Word-based models, or the so-called IBM models, can be trained using the GIZA or GIZA++ toolkits (Och and Ney, 2000). One can then train phrase-based models using the THOT toolkit (Ortiz-Martínez et al., 2005). For their part, language models currently in use in SMT systems can be trained using packages such as SRILM (Stolcke, 2002) and the CMU-SLM toolkit (Clarkson and Rosenfeld, 1997).

[1] www.statmt.org/wmt06/shared-task/baseline.html

Once all the models are built, one can choose to use PHARAOH (Koehn, 2004), an efficient full-fledged phrase-based decoder. We only know of one major drawback when using PHARAOH: its licensing policy. Indeed, it is available for non-commercial use in its binary form only. This severely limits its use, both commercially and scientifically (Walker, 2005).

For this reason, we undertook the design of a generic architecture called MOOD (Modular Object-Oriented Decoder), especially suited for instantiating SMT decoders. Two major goals directed our design of this package: offering open source, state-of-the-art decoders and providing an architecture to easily build these decoders. This effort is described in (Patry et al., 2006).

As a proof of concept that our framework (MOOD) is viable, we attempted to use its functionalities to implement a clone of PHARAOH, based on the comprehensive user manual of the latter. This clone, called RAMSES, is now part of the MOOD distribution, which can be downloaded freely from the page http://smtmood.sourceforge.net.

We conducted a pair-to-pair comparison between the two engines that we describe in this paper. We provide an overview of the MOOD architecture in Section 2. Then we describe briefly RAMSES in Section 3. The comparison between the two decoders in terms of automatic metrics is analyzed in Section 4. We confirm this comparison by presenting a manual evaluation we conducted on an random sample of the translations produced by both decoders. This is reported in Section 5. We conclude in Section 6.

Proceedings of the Workshop on Statistical Machine Translation, pages 126–129,
New York City, June 2006. ©2006 Association for Computational Linguistics

2 The MOOD Framework

A decoder must implement a specific combination of two elements: a model representation and a search space exploration strategy. MOOD is a framework designed precisely to allow such a combination, by clearly separating its two elements. The design of the framework is described in (Patry et al., 2006).

MOOD is implemented with the C++ programming language and is licensed under the Gnu General Public License (GPL)[2]. This license grants the right to anybody to use, modify and distribute the program and its source code, provided that any modified version be licensed under the GPL as well. As explained in (Walker, 2005), this kind of license stimulates new ideas and research.

3 MOOD at work: RAMSES

As we said above, in order to test our design, we reproduced the most popular phrase-based decoder, PHARAOH (Koehn, 2004), by following as faithfully as possible its detailed user manual. The command-line syntax RAMSES recognizes is compatible with that of PHARAOH. The output produced by both decoders are compatible as well and RAMSES can also output its n-best lists in the same format as PHARAOH does, i.e. in a format that the CARMEL toolkit can parse (Knight and Al-Onaizan, 1999). Switching decoders is therefore straightforward.

4 RAMSES versus PHARAOH

To compare the translation performances of both decoders in a meaningful manner, RAMSES and PHARAOH were given the exact same language model and translation table for each translation experiment. Both models were produced with the scripts provided by the organizers. This means in practice that the language model was trained using the SRILM toolkit (Stolcke, 2002). The word alignment required to build the phrase table was produced with the GIZA++ package. A Viterbi alignment computed from an IBM model 4 (Brown et al., 1993) was computed for each translation direction. Both alignments were then combined in a heuristic way (Koehn et al.,). Each pair of phrases in the model is given 5 scores, described in the PHARAOH training manual.[3]

To tune the coefficients of the log-linear combination that both PHARAOH and RAMSES use when decoding, we used the organizers' `minimum-error-rate-training.perl` script. This tuning step was performed on the first 500 sentences of the dedicated development corpora. Inevitably, RAMSES differs slightly from PHARAOH, because of some undocumented embedded heuristics. Thus, we found appropriate to tune each decoder separately (although with the same material). In effect, each decoder does slightly better (with BLEU) when it uses its own best parameters obtained from tuning, than when it uses the parameters of its counterpart.

Eight coefficents were adjusted this way: five for the translation table (one for each score associated to each pair of phrases), and one for each of the following models: the language model, the so-called word penalty model and the distortion model (word reordering model). Each parameter is given a starting value and a range within which it is allowed to vary. For instance, the language model coefficient's starting value is 1.0 and the coefficient is in the range [0.5–1.5]. Eventually, we obtained two optimal configurations (one for each decoder) with which we translated the TEST material.

We evaluated the translations produced by both decoders with the organizers' `multi-bleu.perl` script, which computes a BLEU score (and displays the n-gram precisions and brevity penalty used). We report the scores we gathered on the test corpus of 2000 pairs of sentences in Table 1. Overall, both decoders offer similar performances, down to the n-gram precisions. To assess the statistical significance of the observed differences in BLEU, we used the bootstrapping technique described in (Zhang and Vogel, 2004), randomly selecting 500 sentences from each test set, 1000 times. Using a 95% confidence interval, we determined that the small differences between the two decoders are not statistically significant, except for two tests. For the direction English to French, RAMSES outperforms PHARAOH, while in the German to English direc-

[2] `http://www.gnu.org/copyleft/gpl.html`

[3] `http://www.statmt.org/wmt06/shared-task/training-release-1.3.tgz`

tion, PHARAOH is better. Whenever a decoder is better than the other, Table 1 shows that it is attributable to higher n-gram precisions; not to the brevity penalty.

We further investigated these two cases by calculating BLEU for subsets of the test corpus sharing similar sentence lengths (Table 2). We see that both decoders have similar performances on short sentences, but can differ by as much as 1% in BLEU on longer ones. In contrast, on the Spanish-to-English translation direction, where the two decoders offer similar performances, the difference between BLEU scores never exceeds 0.23%.

Expectedly, Spanish and French are much easier to translate than German. This is because, in this study, we did not apply any pre-processing strategy that we know can improve performances, such as clause reordering or compound-word splitting (Collins et al., 2005; Langlais et al., 2005).

Table 2 shows that it does not seem much more difficult to translate into English than from English. This is surprising: translating into a morphologically richer language should be more challenging. The opposite is true for German here: without doing anything specific for this language, it is much easier to translate from German to English than the other way around. This may be attributed in part to the language model: for the test corpus, the perplexity of the language models provided is 105.5 for German, compared to 59.7 for English.

D	BLEU	p_1	p_2	p_3	p_4	BP
			es → en			
P	30.65	64.10	36.52	23.70	15.91	1.00
R	30.48	64.08	36.30	23.52	15.76	1.00
			fr → en			
P	30.42	64.28	36.45	23.39	15.64	1.00
R	30.43	64.58	36.59	23.54	15.73	0.99
			de → en			
P	25.15	61.19	31.32	18.53	11.61	0.99
R	24.49	61.06	30.75	17.73	10.81	1.00
			en → es			
P	29.40	61.86	35.32	22.77	15.02	1.00
R	28.75	62.23	35.03	22.32	14.58	0.99
			en → fr			
P	30.96	61.10	36.56	24.49	16.80	1.00
R	31.79	61.57	37.38	25.30	17.53	1.00
			en → de			
P	18.03	52.77	22.70	12.45	7.25	0.99
R	18.14	53.38	23.15	12.75	7.47	0.98

Table 1: Performance of RAMSES and PHARAOH on the provided test set of 2000 pairs of sentences per language pair. **P** stands for PHARAOH, **R** for RAMSES. All scores are percentages. p_n is the n-gram precision and BP is the brevity penalty used when computing BLEU.

5 Human Evaluation

In an effort to correlate the objective metrics with human reviews, we undertook the blind evaluation of a sample of 100 pairwise translations for the three Foreign language-to-English translation tasks. The pairs were randomly selected from the 3064 translations produced by each engine. They had to be different for each decoder and be no more than 25 words long.

Each evaluator was presented with a source sentence, its reference translation and the translation produced by each decoder. The last two were in random order, so the evaluator did not know which engine produced the translation. The evaluator's task was two-fold. (1) He decided whether one translation was better than the other. (2) If he replied 'yes' in test (1), he stated whether the best translation was satisfactory while the other was not. Two evaluators went through the 3×100 sentence pairs. None of them understands German; subject B understands Spanish, and both understand French and English. The results of this informal, yet informative exercise are reported in Table 3.

Overall, in many cases (64% and 48% for subject A and B respectively), the evaluators did not prefer one translation over the other. On the Spanish- and French-to-English tasks, both subjects slightly preferred the translations produced by RAMSES. In about one fourth of the cases where one translation was preferred did the evaluators actually flag the selected translation as significantly better.

6 Discussion

We presented a pairwise comparison of two decoders, RAMSES and PHARAOH. Although RAMSES is roughly twice as slow as PHARAOH, both de-

Test set		[0,15]	[16,25]	[26,∞[
en → fr	(**P**)	33.52	30.65	30.39
en → fr	(**R**)	33.78	31.19	31.35
de → en	(**P**)	29.74	24.30	24.76
de → en	(**R**)	29.85	23.92	23.78
es → en	(**P**)	34.23	28.32	30.60
es → en	(**R**)	34.46	28.39	30.40

Table 2: BLEU scores on subsets of the test corpus filtered by sentence length ([min words, max words] intervals), for **P**haraoh and **R**amses.

	Preferred			Improved	
	P	R	No	P	R
		es → en			
subject A	13	16	71	6	1
subject B	23	31	46	3	8
		fr → en			
subject A	18	19	63	5	3
subject B	20	21	59	8	8
		de → en			
subject A	24	18	58	5	9
subject B	30	31	39	3	3
Total	128	136	336	30	32

Table 3: Human evaluation figures. The column `Preferred` indicates the preference of the subject (**P**haraoh, **R**amses or **No** preference). The column `Improved` shows when a subject did prefer a translation and also said that the preferred translation was correct while the other one was not.

coders offer comparable performances, according to automatic and informal human evaluations.

Moreover, RAMSES is the product of clean framework: MOOD, a solid tool for research projects. Its code is open source and the architecture is modular, making it easier for researchers to experiment with SMT. We hope that the availability of the source code and the clean design of MOOD will make it a useful platform to implement new decoders.

Acknowledgments

We warmly thanks Elliott Macklovitch for his participation in the manual annotation task. This work has been partially funded by an NSERC grant.

References

P.F. Brown, S.A. Della Pietra, V.J. Della Pietra, and R.L. Mercer. 1993. The Mathematics of Statistical Machine Translation: Parameter Estimation. *Computational Linguistics*, 19(2):263–311.

P. Clarkson and R. Rosenfeld. 1997. Statistical language modeling using the CMU-cambridge toolkit. In *Proc. of Eurospeech*, pages 2707–2710, Rhodes, Greece.

M. Collins, P. Koehn, and I. Kucerova. 2005. Clause restructuring for statistical machine translation. In *Proc. of the 43rd ACL*, pages 531–540, Ann Arbor, MI.

K. Knight and Y. Al-Onaizan, 1999. *A Primer on Finite-State Software for Natural Language Processing*. www.isi.edu/licensed-sw/carmel.

P. Koehn, F. Joseph Och, and D. Marcu. Statistical Phrase-Based Translation. In *Proc. of HLT*, Edmonton, Canada.

P. Koehn. 2004. Pharaoh: a Beam Search Decoder for Phrase-Based SMT. In *Proc. of the 6th AMTA*, pages 115–124, Washington, DC.

P. Langlais, G. Cao, and F. Gotti. 2005. RALI: SMT shared task system description. In *2nd ACL workshop on Building and Using Parallel Texts*, pages 137–140, Ann Arbor, MI.

F.J. Och and H. Ney. 2000. Improved Statistical Alignment Models. In *Proc. of ACL*, pages 440–447, Hongkong, China.

D. Ortiz-Martínez, I. Garciá-Varea, and F. Casacuberta. 2005. Thot: a toolkit to train phrase-based statistical translation models. In *Proc. of MT Summit X*, pages 141–148, Phuket, Thailand.

A. Patry, F. Gotti, and P. Langlais. 2006. MOOD a modular object-oriented decoder for statistical machine translation. In *Proc. of LREC*, Genoa, Italy.

A. Stolcke. 2002. SRILM - an Extensible Language Modeling Toolkit. In *Proc. of ICSLP*, Denver, USA.

D.J. Walker. 2005. The open "a.i." kit^{TM}: General machine learning modules from statistical machine translation. In *Workshop of MT Summit X, "Open-Source Machine Translation"*, Phuket, Thailand.

Ying Zhang and Stephan Vogel. 2004. Measuring confidence intervals for the machine translation evaluation metrics. In *Proc. of the 10th TMI*, Baltimore, MD.

Stochastic Inversion Transduction Grammars for Obtaining Word Phrases for Phrase-based Statistical Machine Translation

J.A. Sánchez and J.M. Benedí
Departamento de Sistemas Informáticos y Computación
Universidad Politécnica de Valencia
Valencia, Spain
`jandreu@dsic.upv.es` `jbenedi@dsic.upv.es`

Abstract

An important problem that is related to phrase-based statistical translation models is the obtaining of word phrases from an aligned bilingual training corpus. In this work, we propose obtaining word phrases by means of a Stochastic Inversion Translation Grammar. Experiments on the shared task proposed in this workshop with the Europarl corpus have been carried out and good results have been obtained.

1 Introduction

Phrase-based statistical translation systems are currently providing excellent results in real machine translation tasks (Zens et al., 2002; Och and Ney, 2003; Koehn, 2004). In phrase-based statistical translation systems, the basic translation units are word phrases.

An important problem that is related to phrase-based statistical translation is to automatically obtain bilingual word phrases from parallel corpora. Several methods have been defined for dealing with this problem (Och and Ney, 2003). In this work, we study a method for obtaining word phrases that is based on Stochastic Inversion Transduction Grammars that was proposed in (Wu, 1997).

Stochastic Inversion Transduction Grammars (SITG) can be viewed as a restricted Stochastic Context-Free Syntax-Directed Transduction Scheme. SITGs can be used to carry out a simultaneous parsing of both the input string and the output string. In this work, we apply this idea to obtain aligned word phrases to be used in phrase-based translation systems (Sánchez and Benedí, 2006).

In Section 2, we review the phrase-based machine translation approach. SITGs are reviewed in Section 3. In Section 4, we present experiments on the shared task proposed in this workshop with the Europarl corpus.

2 Phrase-based Statistical Machine Transduction

The translation units in a phrase-based statistical translation system are bilingual phrases rather than simple paired words. Several systems that follow this approach have been presented in recent works (Zens et al., 2002; Koehn, 2004). These systems have demonstrated excellent translation performance in real tasks.

The basic idea of a phrase-based statistical machine translation system consists of the following steps (Zens et al., 2002): first, the source sentence is segmented into phrases; second, each source phrase is translated into a target phrase; and third, the target phrases are reordered in order to compose the target sentence.

Bilingual translation phrases are an important component of a phrase-based system. Different methods have been defined to obtain bilingual translations phrases, mainly from word-based alignments and from syntax-based models (Yamada and Knight, 2001).

In this work, we focus on learning bilingual word phrases by using Stochastic Inversion Transduction Grammars (SITGs) (Wu, 1997). This formalism al-

Proceedings of the Workshop on Statistical Machine Translation, pages 130–133,
New York City, June 2006.

lows us to obtain bilingual word phrases in a natural way from the bilingual parsing of two sentences. In addition, the SITGs allow us to easily incorporate many desirable characteristics to word phrases such as length restrictions, selection according to the word alignment probability, bracketing information, etc. We review this formalism in the following section.

3 Stochastic Inversion Transduction Grammars

Stochastic Inversion Transduction Grammars (SITGs) (Wu, 1997) can be viewed as a restricted subset of Stochastic Syntax-Directed Transduction Grammars. They can be used to simultaneously parse two strings, both the source and the target sentences. SITGs are closely related to Stochastic Context-Free Grammars.

Formally, a SITG in Chomsky Normal Form[1] τ_s can be defined as a tuple (N, S, W_1, W_2, R, p), where: N is a finite set of non-terminal symbols; $S \in N$ is the axiom of the SITG; W_1 is a finite set of terminal symbols of language 1; and W_2 is a finite set of terminal symbols of language 2. R is a finite set of: lexical rules of the type $A \rightarrow x/\epsilon$, $A \rightarrow \epsilon/y$, $A \rightarrow x/y$; direct syntactic rules that are noted as $A \rightarrow [BC]$; and inverse syntactic rules that are noted as $A \rightarrow \langle BC \rangle$, where $A, B, C \in N$, $x \in W_1$, $y \in W_2$, and ϵ is the empty string. When a direct syntactic rule is used in a parsing, both strings are parsed with the syntactic rule $A \rightarrow BC$. When an inverse rule is used in a parsing, one string is parsed with the syntactic rule $A \rightarrow BC$, and the other string is parsed with the syntactic rule $A \rightarrow CB$. Term p of the tuple is a function that attaches a probability to each rule.

An efficient Viterbi-like parsing algorithm that is based on a Dynamic Programing Scheme is proposed in (Wu, 1997). The proposed algorithm has a time complexity of $O(|x|^3|y|^3|R|)$. It is important to note that this time complexity restricts the use of the algorithm to real tasks with short strings.

If a bracketed corpus is available, then a modified version of the parsing algorithm can be defined to take into account the bracketing of the strings. The modifications are similar to those proposed in (Pereira and Schabes, 1992) for the *inside* algorithm. Following the notation that is presented in (Pereira and Schabes, 1992), we can define a partially bracketed corpus as a set of sentence pairs that are annotated with parentheses that mark constituent frontiers. More precisely, a bracketed corpus Ω is a set of tuples (x, B_x, y, B_y), where x and y are strings, B_x is the bracketing of x, and B_y is the bracketing of y. Let d_{xy} be a parsing of x and y with the SITG τ_s. If the SITG does not have useless symbols, then each non-terminal that appears in each sentential form of the derivation d_{xy} generates a pair of substrings $x_i \dots x_j$ of x, $1 \leq i \leq j \leq |x|$, and $y_k \dots y_l$ of y, $1 \leq k \leq l \leq |y|$, and defines a *span* (i, j) of x and a *span* (k, l) of y. A derivation of x and y is compatible with B_x and B_y if all the spans defined by it are compatible with B_x and B_y. This compatibility can be easily defined by the function $c(i, j, k, l)$, which takes a value of 1 if (i, j) does not overlap any $b \in B_x$ and, if (k, l) does not overlap any $b \in B_y$; otherwise it takes a value of 0. This function filters those derivations (or partial derivations) whose parsing is not compatible with the bracketing defined in the sample (Sánchez and Benedí, 2006).

The algorithm can be implemented to compute only those subproblems in the Dynamic Programing Scheme that are compatible with the bracketing. Thus, the time complexity is $O(|x|^3|y|^3|R|)$ for an unbracketed string, while the time complexity is $O(|x||y||R|)$ for a fully bracketed string. It is important to note that the last time complexity allows us to work with real tasks with longer strings.

Moreover, the parse tree can be efficiently obtained. Each node in the tree relates two word phrases of the strings being parsed. The related word phrases can be considered to be the translation of each other. These word phrases can be used to compute the translation table of a phrase-based machine statistical translation system.

4 Experiments

The experiments in this section were carried out for the shared task proposed in this workshop. This consisted of building a probabilistic phrase translation table for phrase-based statistical machine translation. Evaluation was translation quality on an unseen test set. The experiments were carried out using

[1] A Normal Form for SITGs can be defined (Wu, 1997) by analogy to the Chomsky Normal Form for Stochastic Context-Free Grammars.

the Europarl corpus (Koehn, 2005). Table 1 shows the language pairs and some figures of the training corpora. The test set had $3,064$ sentences.

Languages	Sentences	# words (input/output)
De-En	751,088	15,257,871 / 16,052,702
Es-En	730,740	15,725,136 / 15,222,505
Fr-En	688,031	15,599,184 / 13,808,505

Table 1: Figures of the training corpora. The languages are English (En), French (Fr), German (De) and Spanish (Es)

A common framework was provided to all the participants so that the results could be compared. The material provided comprised of: a training set, a language model, a baseline translation system (Koehn, 2004), and a word alignment. The participants could augment these items by using: their own training corpus, their own sentence alignment, their own language model, or their own decoder. We only used the provided material for the experiments reported in this work. The BLEU score was used to measure the results.

A SITG was obtained for every language pair in this section as described below. The SITG was used to parse paired sentences in the training sample by using the parsing algorithm described in Section 3. All pairs of word phrases that were derived from each internal node in the parse tree, except the root node, were considered for the phrase-based machine translation system. A translation table was obtained from paired word phrases by placing them in the adequate order and counting the number of times that each pair appeared in the phrases. These values were then appropriately normalized (Sánchez and Benedí, 2006).

4.1 Obtaining a SITG from an aligned corpus

For this experiment, a SITG was constructed for every language pair as follows. The alignment was used to compose lexical rules of the form $A \rightarrow e/f$. The probability of each rule was obtained by counting. Then, two additional rules of the form $A \rightarrow [AA]$ and $A \rightarrow \langle AA \rangle$ were added. It is important to point out that the constructed SITG did not parse all the training sentences. Therefore, the model was *smoothed* by adding all the rules of the form $A \rightarrow e/\epsilon$ and $A \rightarrow \epsilon/f$ with low probability, so that all the training sentences could be parsed. The rules were then adequately normalized.

This SITG was used to obtain word phrases from the training corpus. Then, these word phrases were used by the Pharaoh system (Koehn, 2004) to translate the test set. We used word phrases up to a given length. In these experiments several lengths were tested and the best values ranged from 6 to 10. Table shows 2 the obtained results and the size of the translation table.

Lang.	BLEU	Lang.	BLEU
De-En	15.91 (8.7)	En-De	11.20 (9.7)
Es-En	22.85 (6.5)	En-Es	21.18 (8.6)
Fr-En	21.30 (7.3)	En-Fr	20.12 (8.1)

Table 2: Obtained results for different pairs and directions. The value in parentheses is the number of word phrases in the translation table (in millions).

Note that better results were obtained when English was the target language.

4.2 Using bracketing information in the parsing

As Section 3 describes, the parsing algorithm for SITGs can be adequately modified in order to take bracketed sentences into account. If the bracketing respects linguistically motivated structures, then aligned phrases with linguistic information can be used. Note that this approach requires having quality parsed corpora available. This problem can be reduced by using automatically learned parsers.

This experiment was carried out to determine the performance of the translation when some kind of structural information was incorporated in the parsing algorithm described in Section 3. We bracketed the English sentences of the Europarl corpus with an automatically learned parser. This automatically learned parser was trained with bracketed strings obtained from the UPenn Treebank corpus. We then obtained word phrases according to the bracketing by using the same SITG that was described in the previous section. The obtained phrases were used with the Pharaoh system. Table 3 shows the results obtained in this experiment.

Note that the results decreased slightly in all

Lang.	BLEU	Lang.	BLEU
De-En	15.13 (7.1)	En-De	10.40 (9.2)
Es-En	21.61 (6.6)	En-Es	19.86 (9.6)
Fr-En	20.57 (6.3)	En-Fr	18.95 (8.3)

Table 3: Obtained results for different pairs and directions when word phrases were obtained from a parsed corpus.The value in parentheses is the number of word phrases in the translation table (in millions).

cases. This may be due to the fact that the bracketing incorporated hard restrictions to the paired word phrases and some of them were too forced. In addition, many sentences could not be parsed (up to 5% on average) due to the bracketing. However, it is important to point out that incorporating bracketing information to the English sentences notably accelerated the parsing algorithm, thereby accelerating the process of obtaining word phrases, which is an important detail given the magnitude of this corpus.

4.3 Combining word phrases

Finally, we considered the combination of both kinds of segments. The results can be seen in Table 4. This table shows that the results improved the results of Table 2 when English was the target language. However, the results did not improve when English was the source language. The reason for this could be that both kinds of segments were different in nature, and, therefore, the number of word phrases increased notably, specially in the English part.

Lang.	BLEU	Lang.	BLEU
De-En	16.39 (17.1)	En-De	11.02 (15.3)
Es-En	22.96 (11.7)	En-Es	20.86 (14.1)
Fr-En	21.73 (17.0)	En-Fr	19.93 (14.9)

Table 4: Obtained results for different pairs and directions when word phrases were obtained from a non-parsed corpus and a parsed corpus.The value in parentheses is the number of word phrases in the translation table (in millions).

5 Conclusions

In this work, we have explored the problem of obtaining word phrases for phrase-based machine translation systems from SITGs. We have described how the parsing algorithms for this formalism can be modified in order to take into account a bracketed corpus. If bracketed corpora are used the time complexity can decrease notably and large tasks can be considered. Experiments were reported for the Europarl corpus, and the results obtained were competitive.

For future work, we propose to work along different lines: first, to incorporate new linguistic information in both the parsing algorithm and in the aligned corpus; second, to obtain better SITGs from aligned bilingual corpora; an third, to improve the SITG by estimating the syntactic rules. We also intend to address other machine translation tasks.

Acknowledgements

This work has been partially supported by the *Universidad Politécnica de Valencia* with the ILETA project.

References

P. Koehn. 2004. Pharaoh: a beam search decoder for phrase-based statistical machine translation models. In *Proc. of AMTA*.

P. Koehn. 2005. Europarl: A parallel corpus for statistical machine translation. In *Proc. of MT Summit*.

F.J. Och and H. Ney. 2003. A systematic comparison of various statistical alignment models. *Computational Linguistics*, 29(1):19–52.

F. Pereira and Y. Schabes. 1992. Inside-outside reestimation from partially bracketed corpora. In *Proceedings of the 30th Annual Meeting of the Association for Computational Linguistics*, pages 128–135. University of Delaware.

J.A. Sánchez and J.M. Benedí. 2006. Obtaining word phrases with stochastic inversion transduction grammars for phrase-based statistical machine translation. In *Proc. 11th Annual conference of the European Association for Machine Translation*, page Accepted, Oslo, Norway.

D. Wu. 1997. Stochastic inversion transduction grammars and bilingual parsing of parallel corpora. *Computational Linguistics*, 23(3):377–404.

K. Yamada and K. Knight. 2001. A syntax-based statistical translation model. In *Proc. of the 39th Annual Meeting of the Association of Computational Linguistics*, pages 523–530.

R. Zens, F.J. Och, and H. Ney. 2002. Phrase-based statistical machine translation. In *Proc. of the 25th Annual German Conference on Artificial Intelligence*, pages 18–32.

PORTAGE: with Smoothed Phrase Tables and Segment Choice Models

Howard Johnson
National Research Council
Institute for Information Technology
Interactive Information
1200 Montreal Road
Ottawa, ON, Canada K1A 0R6
Howard.Johnson@cnrc-nrc.gc.ca

Fatiha Sadat, George Foster, Roland Kuhn, Michel Simard, Eric Joanis and Samuel Larkin
National Research Council
Institute for Information Technology
Interactive Language Technologies
101 St-Jean-Bosco Street
Gatineau, QC, Canada K1A 0R6
firstname.lastname@cnrc-nrc.gc.ca

Abstract

Improvements to Portage and its participation in the shared task of NAACL 2006 Workshop on Statistical Machine Translation are described. Promising ideas in phrase table smoothing and global distortion using feature-rich models are discussed as well as numerous improvements in the software base.

1 Introduction

The statistical machine translation system Portage is participating in the NAACL 2006 Workshop on Statistical Machine Translation. This is a good opportunity to do benchmarking against a publicly available data set and explore the benefits of a number of recently added features.

Section 2 describes the changes that have been made to Portage in the past year that affect the participation in the 2006 shared task. Section 3 outlines the methods employed for this task and extensions of it. In Section 4 the results are summarized in tabular form. Following these, there is a conclusions section that highlights what can be gleaned of value from these results.

2 Portage

Because this is the second participation of Portage in such a shared task, a description of the base system can be found elsewhere (Sadat et al, 2005). Briefly, Portage is a research vehicle and development prototype system exploiting the state-of-the-art in statistical machine translation (SMT). It uses a custom built decoder followed by a rescoring module that adjusts weights based on a number of features defined on the source sentence. We will devote space to discussing changes made since the 2005 shared task.

2.1 Phrase-Table Smoothing

Phrase-based SMT relies on conditional distributions $p(s|t)$ and $p(t|s)$ that are derived from the joint frequencies $c(s,t)$ of source/target phrase pairs observed in an aligned parallel corpus. Traditionally, relative-frequency estimation is used to derive conditional distributions, ie $p(s|t) = c(s,t)/\sum_s c(s,t)$. However, relative-frequency estimation has the well-known problem of favouring rare events. For instance, any phrase pair whose constituents occur only once in the corpus will be assigned a probability of 1, almost certainly higher than the probabilities of pairs for which much more evidence exists. During translation, rare pairs can directly compete with overlapping frequent pairs, so overestimating their probabilities can significantly degrade performance.

To address this problem, we implemented two simple smoothing strategies. The first is based on the Good-Turing technique as described in (Church and Gale, 1991). This replaces each observed joint frequency c with $c_g = (c+1)n_{c+1}/n_c$, where n_c is the number of distinct pairs with frequency c (smoothed for large c). It also assigns a total count mass of n_1 to unseen pairs, which we distributed in proportion to the frequency of each conditioning

Proceedings of the Workshop on Statistical Machine Translation, pages 134–137,
New York City, June 2006.

phrase. The resulting estimates are:

$$p_g(s|t) = \frac{c_g(s,t)}{\sum_s c_g(s,t) + p(t)n_1},$$

where $p(t) = c(t)/\sum_t c(t)$. The estimates for $p_g(t|s)$ are analogous.

The second strategy is Kneser-Ney smoothing (Kneser and Ney, 1995), using the interpolated variant described in (Chen and Goodman., 1998):[1]

$$p_k(s|t) = \frac{c(s,t) - D + D\, n_{1+}(*,t)\, p_k(s)}{\sum_s c(s,t)}$$

where $D = n_1/(n_1 + 2n_2)$, $n_{1+}(*,t)$ is the number of distinct phrases s with which t co-occurs, and $p_k(s) = n_{1+}(s,*)/\sum_s n_{1+}(s,*)$, with $n_{1+}(s,*)$ analogous to $n_{1+}(*,t)$.

Our approach to phrase-table smoothing contrasts to previous work (Zens and Ney, 2004) in which smoothed phrase probabilities are constructed from word-pair probabilities and combined in a log-linear model with an unsmoothed phrase-table. We believe the two approaches are complementary, so a combination of both would be worth exploring in future work.

2.2 Feature-Rich DT-based distortion

In a recent paper (Kuhn et al, 2006), we presented a new class of probabilistic "Segment Choice Models" (SCMs) for distortion in phrase-based systems. In some situations, SCMs will assign a better distortion score to a drastic reordering of the source sentence than to no reordering; in this, SCMs differ from the conventional penalty-based distortion, which always favours less rather than more distortion.

We developed a particular kind of SCM based on decision trees (DTs) containing both questions of a positional type (e.g., questions about the distance of a given phrase from the beginning of the source sentence or from the previously translated phrase) and word-based questions (e.g., questions about the presence or absence of given words in a specified phrase).

The DTs are grown on a corpus consisting of segment-aligned bilingual sentence pairs. This segment-aligned corpus is obtained by training a phrase translation model on a large bilingual corpus and then using it (in conjunction with a distortion penalty) to carry out alignments between the phrases in the source-language sentence and those in the corresponding target-language sentence in a second bilingual corpus. Typically, the first corpus (on which the phrase translation model is trained) is the same as the second corpus (on which alignment is carried out). To avoid overfitting, the alignment algorithm is leave-one-out: statistics derived from a particular sentence pair are not used to align that sentence pair.

Note that the experiments reported in (Kuhn et al, 2006) focused on translation of Chinese into English. The interest of the experiments reported here on WMT data was to see if the feature-rich DT-based distortion model could be useful for MT between other language pairs.

3 Application to the Shared Task: Methods

3.1 Restricted Resource Exercise

The first exercise that was done is to replicate the conditions of 2005 as closely as possible to see the effects of one year of research and development. The second exercise was to replicate all three of these translation exercises using the 2006 language model, and to do the three exercises of translating out of English into French, Spanish, and German. This was our baseline for other studies. A third exercise involved modifying the generation of the phrase-table to incorporate our Good-Turing smoothing. All six language pairs were re-processed with these phrase-tables. The improvement in the results on the devtest set were compelling. This became the baseline for further work. A fourth exercise involved replacing penalty-based distortion modelling with the feature-rich decision-tree based distortion modelling described above. A fifth exercise involved the use of a Kneser-Ney phrase-table smoothing algorithm as an alternative to Good-Turing.

For all of these exercises, 1-best results after decoding were calculated as well as rescoring on 1000-best lists of results using 12 feature functions (13 in the case of decision-tree based distortion modelling). The results submitted for the shared task

[1] As for Good-Turing smoothing, this formula applies only to pairs s, t for which $c(s,t) > 0$, since these are the only ones considered by the decoder.

were the results of the third and fourth exercises where rescoring had been applied.

3.2 Open Resource Exercise

Our goal in this exercise was to conduct a comparative study using additional training data for the French-English shared task. Results of WPT 2005 showed an improvement of at least 0.3 BLEU point when exploiting different resources for the French-English pair of languages. In addition to the training resources used in WPT 2005 for the French-English task, i.e. Europarl and Hansard, we used a bilingual dictionary, *Le Grand Dictionnaire Terminologique* (GDT) [2] to train translation models and the English side of the UN parallel corpus (LDC2004E13) to train an English language model. Integrating terminological lexicons into a statistical machine translation engine is not a straightforward operation, since we cannot expect them to come with attached probabilities. The approach we took consists on viewing all translation candidates of each source term or phrase as equiprobable (Sadat et al, 2006).

In total, the data used in this second part of our contribution to WMT 2006 is described as follows: (1) A set of 688,031 sentences in French and English extracted from the *Europarl parallel corpus* (2) A set of 6,056,014 sentences in French and English extracted from the *Hansard parallel corpus*, the official record of Canada's parliamentary debates. (3) A set of 701,709 sentences in French and English extracted from the bilingual dictionary *GDT*. (4) Language models were trained on the French and English parts of the Europarl and Hansard. We used the provided Europarl corpus while omitting data from Q4/2000 (October-December), since it is reserved for development and test data. (5) An additional English language model was trained on 128 million words of the *UN Parallel corpus*.

For the supplied Europarl corpora, we relied on the existing segmentation and tokenization, except for French, which we manipulated slightly to bring into line with our existing conventions (e.g., converting l ' an into l' an, aujourd ' hui into aujourd'hui).

For the Hansard corpus used to supplement our French-English resources, we used our own alignment based on Moore's algorithm, segmentation, and tokenization procedures. English preprocessing simply included lower-casing, separating punctuation from words and splitting off 's.

[2] http://www.granddictionnaire.com/

4 Results

The results are shown in Table 1. The numbers shown are BLEU scores. The MC rows correspond to the multi-corpora results described in the open resource exercise section above. All other rows are from the restricted resource exercise.

The devtest results are the scores computed before the shared-task submission and were used to drive the choice of direction of the research. The test results were computed after the shared-task submission and serve for validation of the conclusions.

We believe that our use of multiple training corpora as well as our re-tokenization for French and an enhanced language model resulted in our overall success in the English-French translation track. The results for the in-domain test data puts our group at the top of the ranking table drawn by the organizers (first on Adequacy and fluency and third on BLEU scores).

5 Conclusion

Benchmarking with same language model and parameters as WPT05 reproduces the results with a tiny improvement. The larger language model used in 2006 for English yields about half a BLEU. Good-Turing phrase table smoothing yields roughly half a BLEU point. Kneser-Ney phrase table smoothing yields between a third and half a BLEU point more than Good-Turing. Decision tree based distortion yields a small improvement for the devtest set when rescoring was not used but failed to show improvement on the test set.

In summary, the results from phrase-table smoothing are extremely encouraging. On the other hand, the feature-rich decision tree distortion modelling requires additional work before it provides a good pay-back. Fortunately we have some encouraging avenues under investigation. Clearly there is more work needed for both of these areas.

Acknowledgements

We wish to thank Aaron Tikuisis and Denis Yuen for important contributions to the Portage code base

Table 1: Restricted and open resource results

	fr ⟶ en	es ⟶ en	de ⟶ en	en ⟶ fr	en ⟶ es	en ⟶ de
			devtest: with rescoring			
WPT05	29.32	29.08	23.21			
LM-2005	29.30	29.21	23.41			
LM-2006	29.88	29.54	23.94	30.43	28.81	17.33
GT-PTS	30.35	29.84	24.60	30.89	29.54	17.62
GT-PTS+DT-dist	30.09	29.44	24.62	31.06	29.46	**17.84**
KN-PTS	**30.55**	**30.12**	**24.66**	**31.28**	**29.90**	17.78
MC WPT05	29.63					
MC	30.09			31.30		
MC+GT-PTS	**30.75**			**31.37**		
			devtest: 1-best after decoding			
LM-2006	28.59	28.45	23.22	29.22	28.30	16.94
GT-PTS	29.23	28.91	**23.67**	30.07	28.86	17.32
GT-PTS+DT-dist	29.48	29.07	23.50	30.22	29.46	17.42
KN-PTS	**29.77**	**29.76**	23.27	**30.73**	**29.62**	**17.78**
MC WPT05	28.71					
MC	29.63			31.01		
MC+GT-PTS	**29.90**			**31.22**		
			test: with rescoring			
LM-2006	26.64	28.43	21.33	28.06	28.01	15.19
GT-PTS	27.19	28.95	21.91	28.60	28.83	15.38
GT-PTS+DT-dist	26.84	28.56	21.84	28.56	28.59	15.45
KN-PTS	**27.40**	**29.07**	**21.98**	**28.96**	**29.06**	**15.64**
MC	26.95			29.12		
MC+GT-PTS	**27.10**			**29.46**		
			test: 1-best after decoding			
LM-2006	25.35	27.25	20.46	27.20	27.18	14.60
GT-PTS	25.95	28.07	21.06	27.85	27.96	15.05
GT-PTS+DT-dist	25.86	28.04	20.74	27.85	27.97	14.92
KN-PTS	**26.83**	**28.66**	**21.36**	**28.62**	**28.71**	**15.42**
MC	26.70			28.74		
MC+GT-PTS	**26.81**			**29.03**		

and the OQLF (Office Québécois de la Langue Française) for permission to use the GDT.

References

S. F. Chen and J. T. Goodman. 1998. An empirical study of smoothing techniques for language modeling. Technical Report TR-10-98, Computer Science Group, Harvard University.

K. Church and W. Gale. 1991. A comparison of the enhanced Good-Turing and deleted estimation methods for estimating probabilities of English bigrams. *Computer speech and language*, 5(1):19–54.

R. Kneser and H. Ney. 1995. Improved backing-off for m-gram language modeling. In *Proc. International Conference on Acoustics, Speech, and Signal Processing (ICASSP) 1995*, pages 181–184, Detroit, Michigan. IEEE.

R. Kuhn, D. Yuen, M. Simard, G. Foster, P. Paul, E. Joanis and J. H. Johnson. 2006. Segment Choice Models: Feature-Rich Models for Global Distortion in Statistical Machine Translation (accepted for publication in HLT-NAACL conference, to be held June 2006).

F. Sadat, J. H. Johnson, A. Agbago, G. Foster, R. Kuhn, J. Martin and A. Tikuisis. 2005. PORTAGE: A Phrase-based Machine Translation System In *Proc. ACL 2005 Workshop on building and using parallel texts.* Ann Arbor, Michigan.

F. Sadat, G. Foster and R. Kuhn. 2006. Système de traduction automatique statistique combinant différentes ressources. In *Proc. TALN 2006 (Traitement Automatique des Langues Naturelles).* Leuven, Belgium, April 10-13, 2006.

R. Zens and H. Ney. 2004. Improvements in phrase-based statistical machine translation. In *Proc. Human Language Technology Conference / North American Chapter of the ACL*, Boston, May.

Syntax Augmented Machine Translation via Chart Parsing

Andreas Zollmann and **Ashish Venugopal**
School of Computer Science
Carnegie Mellon University
{zollmann,ashishv}@cs.cmu.edu

Abstract

We present translation results on the shared task "Exploiting Parallel Texts for Statistical Machine Translation" generated by a chart parsing decoder operating on phrase tables augmented and generalized with target language syntactic categories. We use a target language parser to generate parse trees for each sentence on the target side of the bilingual training corpus, matching them with phrase table lattices built for the corresponding source sentence. Considering phrases that correspond to syntactic categories in the parse trees we develop techniques to augment (declare a syntactically motivated category for a phrase pair) and generalize (form mixed terminal and nonterminal phrases) the phrase table into a synchronous bilingual grammar. We present results on the French-to-English task for this workshop, representing significant improvements over the workshop's baseline system. Our translation system is available open-source under the GNU General Public License.

1 Introduction

Recent work in machine translation has evolved from the traditional word (Brown et al., 1993) and phrase based (Koehn et al., 2003a) models to include hierarchical phrase models (Chiang, 2005) and bilingual synchronous grammars (Melamed, 2004). These advances are motivated by the desire to integrate richer knowledge sources within the translation process with the explicit goal of producing more fluent translations in the target language. The hierarchical translation operations introduced in these methods call for extensions to the traditional beam decoder (Koehn et al., 2003a). In this work we introduce techniques to generate syntactically motivated generalized phrases and discuss issues in chart parser based decoding in the statistical machine translation environment.

(Chiang, 2005) generates synchronous context-free grammar (SynCFG) rules from an existing phrase translation table. These rules can be viewed as phrase pairs with mixed lexical and non-terminal entries, where non-terminal entries (occurring as pairs in the source and target side) represent placeholders for inserting additional phrases pairs (which again may contain nonterminals) at decoding time. While (Chiang, 2005) uses only two nonterminal symbols in his grammar, we introduce multiple syntactic categories, taking advantage of a target language parser for this information. While (Yamada and Knight, 2002) represent syntactical information in the decoding process through a series of transformation operations, we operate directly at the phrase level. In addition to the benefits that come from a more structured hierarchical rule set, we believe that these restrictions serve as a syntax driven language model that can guide the decoding process, as n-gram context based language models do in traditional decoding. In the following sections, we describe our phrase annotation and generalization process followed by the design and pruning decisions in our chart parser. We give results on the French-English Europarl data and conclude with prospects for future work.

Proceedings of the Workshop on Statistical Machine Translation, pages 138–141,
New York City, June 2006.

2 Rule Generation

We start with phrase translations on the parallel training data using the techniques and implementation described in (Koehn et al., 2003a). This phrase table provides the purely lexical entries in the final hierarchical rule set that will be used in decoding. We then use Charniak's parser (Charniak, 2000) to generate the most likely parse tree for each English target sentence in the training corpus. Next, we determine all phrase pairs in the phrase table whose source and target side occur in each respective source and target sentence pair defining the scope of the initial rules in our SynCFG.

Annotation If the target side of any of these initial rules correspond to a syntactic category C of the target side parse tree, we label the phrase pair with that syntactic category. This label corresponds to the left-hand side of our synchronous grammar. Phrase pairs that do not correspond to a span in the parse tree are given a default category "X", and can still play a role in the decoding process. In work done after submission to the 2006 data track, we assign such phrases an extended category of the form $C_1 + C_2$, C_1/C_2, or $C_2\backslash C_1$, indicating that the phrase pair's target side spans two adjacent syntactic categories (e.g., *she went: NP+V*), a partial syntactic category C_1 missing a C_2 to the right (e.g., *the great: NP/NN*), or a partial C_1 missing a C_2 to the left (e.g., *great wall: DT\NP*), respectively.

Generalization In order to mitigate the effects of sparse data when working with phrase and n-gram models we would like to generate generalized phrases, which include non-terminal symbols that can be filled with other phrases. Therefore, after annotating the initial rules from the current training sentence pair, we adhere to (Chiang, 2005) to recursively generalize each existing rule; however, we abstract on a per-sentence basis. The grammar extracted from this evaluation's training data contains 75 nonterminals in our standard system, and 4000 nonterminals in the extended-category system. Figure 1 illustrates the annotation and generalization process.

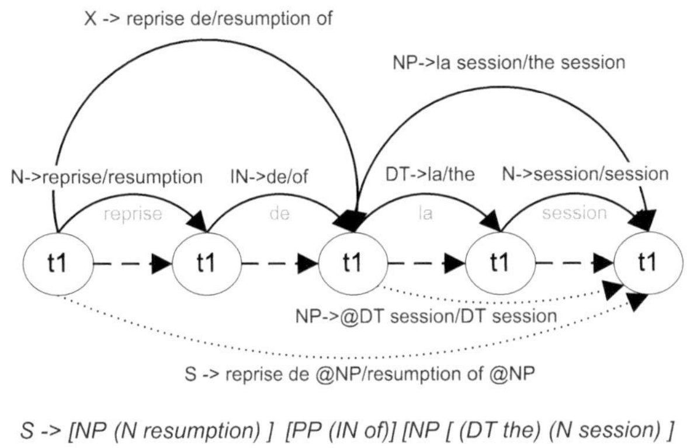

Figure 1: *Selected annotated and generalized (dotted arc) rules for the first sentence of Europarl.*

3 Scoring

We employ a log-linear model to assign costs to the SynCFG. Given a source sentence f, the preferred translation output is determined by computing the lowest-cost derivation (combination of hierarchical and glue rules) yielding f as its source side, where the cost of a derivation $R_1 \circ \cdots \circ R_n$ with respective feature vectors $v^1, \ldots, v^n \in \mathbb{R}^m$ is given by

$$\sum_{i=1}^{m} \lambda_i \sum_{j=1}^{n} (v^j)_i \, .$$

Here, $\lambda_1, \ldots, \lambda_m$ are the parameters of the log-linear model, which we optimize on a held-out portion of the training set (2005 development data) using minimum-error-rate training (Och, 2003). We use the following features for our rules:

- source- and target-conditioned neg-log lexical weights as described in (Koehn et al., 2003b)
- neg-log relative frequencies: left-hand-side-conditioned, target-phrase-conditioned, source-phrase-conditioned
- Counters: n.o. rule applications, n.o. target words
- Flags: IsPurelyLexical (i.e., contains only terminals), IsPurelyAbstract (i.e., contains only nonterminals), IsXRule (i.e., non-syntactical span), IsGlueRule

- Penalties: rareness penalty $\exp(1 - \mathit{RuleFrequency})$; unbalancedness penalty $|\mathit{MeanTargetSourceRatio} * \text{'n.o. source words'} - \text{'n.o. target words'}|$

4 Parsing

Our SynCFG rules are equivalent to a probabilistic context-free grammar and decoding is therefore an application of chart parsing. Instead of the common method of converting the CFG grammar into Chomsky Normal Form and applying a CKY algorithm to produce the most likely parse for a given source sentence, we avoided the explosion of the rule set caused by the introduction of new non-terminals in the conversion process and implemented a variant of the CKY+ algorithm as described in (J.Earley, 1970).

Each cell of the parsing process in (J.Earley, 1970) contains a set of hypergraph nodes (Huang and Chiang, 2005). A hypergraph node is an equivalence class of complete hypotheses (derivations) with identical production results (left-hand sides of the corresponding applied rules). Complete hypotheses point directly to nodes in their backwards star, and the cost of the complete hypothesis is calculated with respect to each back pointer node's best cost.

This structure affords efficient parsing with minimal pruning (we use a single parameter to restrict the number of hierarchical rules applied), but sacrifices effective management of unique language model states contributing to significant search errors during parsing. At initial submission time we simply re-scored a K-Best list extracted after first best parsing using the lazy retrieval process in (Huang and Chiang, 2005).

Post-submission After our workshop submission, we modified the K-Best list extraction process to integrate an n-gram language model during K-Best extraction. Instead of expanding each derivation (complete hypothesis) in a breadth-first fashion, we expand only a single back pointer, and score this new derivation with its translation model scores and a language model cost estimate, consisting of an accurate component, based on the words translated so far, and an estimate based on each remaining (not expanded) back pointer's top scoring hypothesis.

To improve the diversity of the final K-Best list, we keep track of partially expanded hypotheses that have generated identical target words and refer to the same hypergraph nodes. Any arising twin hypothesis is immediately removed from the K-Best extraction beam during the expansion process.

5 Results

We present results that compare our system against the baseline Pharaoh implementation (Koehn et al., 2003a) and MER training scripts provided for this workshop. Our results represent work done before the submission due date as well as after with the following generalized phrase systems.

- Baseline - Pharaoh with phrases extracted from IBM Model 4 training with maximum phrase length 7 and extraction method 'diag-growth-final' (Koehn et al., 2003a)
- Lex - Phrase-decoder simulation: using only the initial lexical rules from the phrase table, all with LHS X, the Glue rule, and a binary reordering rule with its own reordering-feature
- XCat - All nonterminals merged into a single X nonterminal: simulation of the system Hiero (Chiang, 2005).
- Syn - Syntactic extraction using the Penn Treebank parse categories as nonterminals; rules containing up to 4 nonterminal abstraction sites.
- SynExt - Syntactic extraction using the extended-category scheme, but with rules only containing up to 2 nonterminal abstraction sites.

We also explored the impact of longer initial phrases by training another phrase table with phrases up to length 12. Our results are presented in Table 1. While our submission time system (Syn using LM for rescoring only) shows no improvement over the baseline, we clearly see the impact of integrating the language model into the K-Best list extraction process. Our final system shows at statistically significant improvement over the baseline (0.78 BLEU points is the 95 confidence level). We also see a trend towards improving translation quality as we

System	Dev: w/o LM	Dev: LM-rescoring	Test: LM-r.	Dev: integrated LM	Test: int. LM
Baseline - max. phr. length 7	–	–	–	31.11	30.61
Lex - max. phrase length 7	27.94	29.39	29.95	28.96	29.12
XCat - max. phrase length 7	27.56	30.27	29.81	30.89	31.01
Syn - max. phrase length 7	29.20	**30.95**	**30.58**	31.52	31.31
SynExt - max. phrase length 7	–	–	–	31.73	31.41
Baseline - max. phr. length 12	–	–	–	31.16	30.90
Lex - max. phr. length 12	–	–	–	29.30	29.51
XCat - max. phr. length 12	–	–	–	30.79	30.59
SynExt - max. phr. length 12	–	–	–	31.07	31.76

Table 1: *Translation results (IBM BLEU) for each system on the Fr-En '06 Shared Task 'Development Set' (used for MER parameter tuning) and '06 'Development Test Set' (identical to last year's Shared Task's test set). The system submitted for evaluation is highlighted in bold.*

employ richer extraction techniques. The relatively poor performance of Lex with LM in K-Best compared to the baseline shows that we are still making search errors during parsing despite tighter integration of the language model.

We also ran an experiment with CMU's phrase-based decoder (Vogel et al., 2003) using the length-7 phrase table. While its development-set score was only 31.01, the decoder achieved 31.42 on the test set, placing it at the same level as our extended-category system for that phrase table.

6 Conclusions

In this work we applied syntax based resources (the target language parser) to annotate and generalize phrase translation tables extracted via existing phrase extraction techniques. Our work reaffirms the feasibility of parsing approaches to machine translation in a large data setting, and illustrates the impact of adding syntactic categories to drive and constrain the structured search space. While no improvements were available at submission time, our subsequent performance highlights the importance of tight integration of n-gram language modeling within the syntax driven parsing environment. Our translation system is available open-source under the GNU General Public License at: `www.cs.cmu.edu/~zollmann/samt`

References

Peter F. Brown, Vincent J. Della Pietra, Stephen A. Della Pietra, and Robert L. Mercer. 1993. The mathematics of statistical machine translation: parameter estimation. *Comput. Linguist.*, 19(2):263–311.

Eugene Charniak. 2000. A maximum entropy-inspired parser. In *Proceedings of the North American Association for Computational Linguistics (HLT/NAACL)*.

David Chiang. 2005. A hierarchical phrase-based model for statistical machine translation. In *Proc. of the Association for Computational Linguistics*.

Liang Huang and David Chiang. 2005. Better k-best parsing. In *Proceedings of the 9th International Workshop on Parsing Technologies*.

J.Earley. 1970. An efficient context-free parsing algorithm. *Communications of the Assocation for Computing Machinery*, 13(2):94–102.

Philipp Koehn, Franz Josef Och, and Daniel Marcu. 2003a. Pharaoh: A beam search decoder for phrase-base statistical machine translation models. In *Proceedings of the Sixth Confernence of the Association for Machine Translation in the Americas*, Edomonton, Canada, May 27-June 1.

Philipp Koehn, Franz Josef Och, and Daniel Marcu. 2003b. Statistical phrase-based translation. In *Proceedings of the Human Language Technology and North American Association for Computational Linguistics Conference (HLT/NAACL)*, Edomonton, Canada, May 27-June 1.

I. Dan Melamed. 2004. Statistical machine translation by parsing. In *ACL*, pages 653–660.

Franz Josef Och. 2003. Minimum error rate training in statistical machine translation. In *Proc. of the Association for Computational Linguistics*, Sapporo, Japan, July 6-7.

Stephan Vogel, Ying Zhang, Fei Huang, Alicia Tribble, Ashish Venogupal, Bing Zhao, and Alex Waibel. 2003. The CMU statistical translation system. In *Proceedings of MT Summit IX*, New Orleans, LA, September.

Kenji Yamada and Kevin Knight. 2002. A decoder for syntax-based statistical mt. In *Proc. of the Association for Computational Linguistics*.

TALP Phrase-based statistical translation system for European language pairs

Marta R. Costa-jussà **Josep M. Crego** **Adrià de Gispert**
Patrik Lambert **Maxim Khalilov** **Rafael E. Banchs**
José B. Mariño **José A. R. Fonollosa**
Department of Signal Theory and Communications
TALP Research Center (UPC)
Barcelona 08034, Spain
(mruiz,jmcrego,agispert,lambert,khalilov,canton,adrian, rbanchs)@gps.tsc.upc.edu

Abstract

This paper reports translation results for the "Exploiting Parallel Texts for Statistical Machine Translation" (HLT-NAACL Workshop on Parallel Texts 2006). We have studied different techniques to improve the standard Phrase-Based translation system. Mainly we introduce two reordering approaches and add morphological information.

1 Introduction

Nowadays most Statistical Machine Translation (SMT) systems use phrases as translation units. In addition, the decision rule is commonly modelled through a log-linear maximum entropy framework which is based on several feature functions (including the translation model), h_m. Each feature function models the probability that a sentence e in the target language is a translation of a given sentence f in the source language. The weights, λ_i, of each feature function are typically optimized to maximize a scoring function. It has the advantage that additional features functions can be easily integrated in the overall system.

This paper describes a Phrase-Based system whose baseline is similar to the system in Costa-jussà and Fonollosa (2005). Here we introduce two reordering approaches and add morphological information. Translation results for all six translation directions proposed in the shared task are presented and discussed. More specifically, four different languages are considered: English (en), Spanish (es), French (fr) and German (de); and both translation directions are considered for the pairs: **EnEs**, **EnFr**, and **EnDe**. The paper is organized as follows: Section 2 describes the system; Section 3 presents the shared task results; and, finally, in Section 4, we conclude.

[0]This work has been supported by the European Union under grant FP6-506738 (TC-STAR project) and the TALP Research Center (under a TALP-UPC-Recerca grant).

2 System Description

This section describes the system procedure followed for the data provided.

2.1 Alignment

Given a bilingual corpus, we use GIZA++ (Och, 2003) as word alignment core algorithm. During word alignment, we use 50 classes per language estimated by 'mkcls', a freely-available tool along with GIZA++. Before aligning we work with lowercase text (which leads to an Alignment Error Rate reduction) and we recover truecase after the alignment is done.

In addition, the alignment (in specific pairs of languages) was improved using two strategies:

Full verb forms The morphology of the verbs usually differs in each language. Therefore, it is interesting to classify the verbs in order to address the rich variety of verbal forms. Each verb is reduced into its base form and reduced POS tag as explained in (de Gispert, 2005). This transformation is only done for the alignment, and its goal is to simplify the work of the word alignment improving its quality.

Block reordering (*br*) The difference in word order between two languages is one of the most significant sources of error in SMT. Related works either deal with reordering in general as (Kanthak et al., 2005) or deal with local reordering as (Tillmann and Ney, 2003). We report a local reordering technique, which is implemented as a preprocessing stage, with two applications: (1) to improve only alignment quality, and (2) to improve alignment quality and to infer reordering in translation. Here, we present a short explanation of the algorithm, for further details see Costa-jussà and Fonollosa (2006).

Proceedings of the Workshop on Statistical Machine Translation, pages 142–145,
New York City, June 2006. ©2006 Association for Computational Linguistics

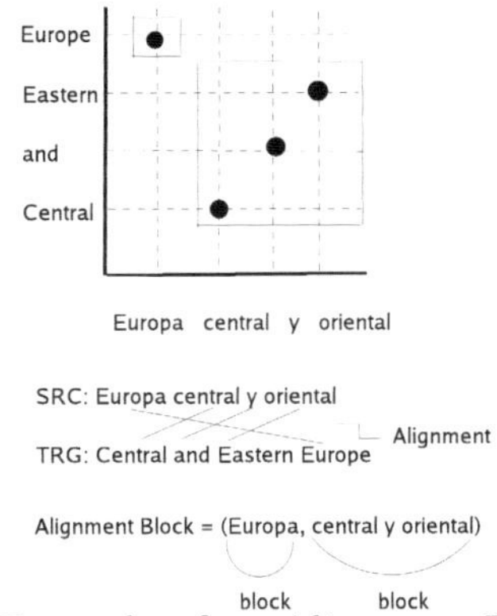

Figure 1: *Example of an Alignment Block, i.e. a pair of consecutive blocks whose target translation is swapped*

This reordering strategy is intended to infer the most probable reordering for sequences of words, which are referred to as blocks, in order to monotonize current data alignments and generalize reordering for unseen pairs of blocks.

Given a word alignment, we identify those pairs of consecutive source blocks whose translation is swapped, i.e. those blocks which, if swapped, generate a correct monotone translation. Figure 1 shows an example of these pairs (hereinafter called Alignment Blocks).

Then, the list of Alignment Blocks (LAB) is processed in order to decide whether two consecutive blocks have to be reordered or not. By using the classification algorithm, see the Appendix, we divide the LAB in groups ($G_n, n = 1 \ldots N$). Inside the same group, we allow new internal combination in order to generalize the reordering to unseen pairs of blocks (i.e. new Alignment Blocks are created). Based on this information, the source side of the bilingual corpora are reordered.

In case of applying the reordering technique for purpose (1), we modify only the source training corpora to realign and then we recover the original order of the training corpora. In case of using Block Reordering for purpose (2), we modify all the source corpora (both training and test), and we use the new training corpora to realign and build the final translation system.

2.2 Phrase Extraction

Given a sentence pair and a corresponding word alignment, phrases are extracted following the criterion in Och and Ney (2004). A phrase (or bilingual phrase) is any pair of m source words and n target words that satisfies two basic constraints: words are consecutive along both sides of the bilingual phrase, and no word on either side of the phrase is aligned to a word out of the phrase. We limit the maximum size of any given phrase to 7. The huge increase in computational and storage cost of including longer phrases does not provide a significant improvement in quality (Koehn et al., 2003) as the probability of reappearance of larger phrases decreases.

2.3 Feature functions

Conditional and posterior probability (*cp, pp*) Given the collected phrase pairs, we estimate the phrase translation probability distribution by relative frequency in both directions.

The target language model (*lm*) consists of an n-gram model, in which the probability of a translation hypothesis is approximated by the product of word n-gram probabilities. As default language model feature, we use a standard word-based 5-gram language model generated with Kneser-Ney smoothing and interpolation of higher and lower order n-grams (Stolcke, 2002).

The POS target language model (*tpos*) consists of an N-gram language model estimated over the same target-side of the training corpus but using POS tags instead of raw words.

The forward and backwards lexicon models (*ibm1, ibm1*$^{-1}$) provide lexicon translation probabilities for each phrase based on the word IBM model 1 probabilities. For computing the forward lexicon model, IBM model 1 probabilities from GIZA++ source-to-target alignments are used. In the case of the backwards lexicon model, target-to-source alignments are used instead.

The word bonus model (*wb*) introduces a sentence length bonus in order to compensate the system preference for short output sentences.

The phrase bonus model (*pb*) introduces a constant bonus per produced phrase.

2.4 Decoding

The search engine for this translation system is described in Crego et al. (2005) which takes into account the features described above.

Using reordering in the decoder (*rgraph*) A highly constrained reordered search is performed by means of a set of reordering patterns (linguistically motivated rewrite patterns) which are used to extend the monotone search graph with additional arcs. See the details in Crego et al. (2006).

2.5 Optimization

It is based on a simplex method (Nelder and Mead, 1965). This algorithm adjusts the log-linear weights in order to maximize a non-linear combination of translation BLEU and NIST: $10 * log10((BLEU * 100) + 1) + NIST$. The maximization is done over the provided development set for each of the six translation directions under consideration. We have experimented an improvement in the coherence between all the automatic figures by integrating two of these figures in the optimization function.

3 Shared Task Results

3.1 Data

The data provided for this shared task corresponds to a subset of the official transcriptions of the European Parliament Plenary Sessions, and it is available through the shared task website at: `http://www.statmt.org/wmt06/shared-task/`. The development set used to tune the system consists of a subset (500 first sentences) of the official development set made available for the Shared Task.

We carried out a morphological analysis of the data. The English POS-tagging has been carried out using freely available TNT tagger (Brants, 2000). In the Spanish case, we have used the $Freeling$ (Carreras et al., 2004) analysis tool which generates the POS-tagging for each input word.

3.2 Systems configurations

The baseline system is the same for all tasks and includes the following features functions: *cp, pp, lm, ibm1*, $ibm1^{-1}$, *wb, pb*. The POStag target language model has been used in those tasks for which the tagger was available. Table 1 shows the reordering configuration used for each task.

The Block Reordering (application 2) has been used when the source language belongs to the Romanic family. The length of the block is limited to 1 (i.e. it allows the swapping of single words). The main reason is that specific errors are solved in the tasks from a Romanic language to a Germanic language (as the common reorder of $Noun + Adjective$ that turns into $Adjective + Noun$). Although the Block Reordering approach does not depend on the task, we have not done the corresponding experiments to observe its efficiency in all the pairs used in this evaluation.

Task	Reordering Configuration
Es2En	*br2*
En2Es	*br1 + rgraph*
Fr2En	*br2*
En2Fr	*br1 + rgraph*
De2En	-
En2De	-

Table 1: *Additional reordering models for each task: br1 (br2) stands for Block Reordering application 1 (application 2); and rgraph refers to the reordering integrated in the decoder*

The *rgraph* has been applied in those cases where: we do not use *br2* (there is no sense in applying them simultaneously); and we have the tagger for the source language model available.

In the case of the pair GeEn, we have not experimented any reordering, we left the application of both reordering approaches as future work.

3.3 Discussion

Table 2 presents the BLEU scores evaluated on the test set (using TRUECASE) for each configuration. The official results were slightly better because a lowercase evaluation was used, see (Koehn and Monz, 2006).

For both, Es2En and Fr2En tasks, *br* helps slightly. The improvement of the approach depends on the quality of the alignment. The better alignments allow to extract higher quality Alignment Blocks (Costa-jussà and Fonollosa, 2006).

The En2Es task is improved when adding both *br1* and *rgraph*. Similarly, the En2Fr task seems to perform fairly well when using the *rgraph*. In this case, the improvement of the approach depends on the quality of the alignment patterns (Crego et al., 2006). However, it has the advantage of delaying the final decision of reordering to the overall search, where all models are used to take a fully informed decision.

Finally, the *tpos* does not help much when translating to English. It is not surprising because it was used in order to improve the gender and number agreement, and in English there is no need. However, in the direction to Spanish, the *tpos* added to the corresponding reordering helps more as the Spanish language has gender and number agreement.

Task	Baseline	+tpos	+rc	+tpos+rc
Es2En	29.08	29.08	29.89	**29.98**
En2Es	27.73	27.66	28.79	**28.99**
Fr2En	27.05	27.06	27.43	**27.23**
En2Fr	26.16	-	27.80	-
De2En	21.59	**21.33**	-	-
En2De	**15.20**	-	-	-

Table 2: *Results evaluated using* TRUECASE *on the test set for each configuration: rc stands for Reordering Configuration and refers to Table 1. The bold results were the configurations submitted.*

4 Conclusions

Reordering is important when using a Phrase-Based system. Although local reordering is supposed to be included in the phrase structure, performing local reordering improves the translation quality. In fact, local reordering, provided by the reordering approaches, allows for those generalizations which phrases could not achieve. Reordering in the DeEn task is left as further work.

References

T. Brants. 2000. Tnt - a statistical part-of-speech tagger. *Proceedings of the Sixth Applied Natural Language Processing*.

X. Carreras, I. Chao, L. Padró, and M. Padró. 2004. Freeling: An open-source suite of language analyzers. *4th Int. Conf. on Language Resources and Evaluation, LREC'04*.

M. R. Costa-jussà and J.A.R. Fonollosa. 2005. Improving the phrase-based statistical translation by modifying phrase extraction and including new features. *Proceedings of the ACL Workshop on Building and Using Parallel Texts: Data-Driven Machine Translation and Beyond*.

M. R. Costa-jussà and J.A.R. Fonollosa. 2006. Using reordering in statistical machine translation based on alignment block classification. *Internal Report*.

J.M. Crego, J. Mariño, and A. de Gispert. 2005. An Ngram-based statistical machine translation decoder. *Proc. of the 9th Int. Conf. on Spoken Language Processing, ICSLP'05*.

J. M. Crego, A. de Gispert, P. Lambert, M. R. Costa-jussà, M. Khalilov, J. Mariño, J. A. Fonollosa, and R. Banchs. 2006. Ngram-based smt system enhanced with reordering patterns. *HLT-NAACL06 Workshop on Building and Using Parallel Texts: Data-Driven Machine Translation and Beyond*, June.

A. de Gispert. 2005. Phrase linguistic classification for improving statistical machine translation. *ACL 2005 Students Workshop*, June.

S. Kanthak, D. Vilar, E. Matusov, R. Zens, and H. Ney. 2005. Novel reordering approaches in phrase-based statistical machine translation. *Proceedings of the ACL Workshop on Building and Using Parallel Texts: Data-Driven Machine Translation and Beyond*, pages 167–174, June.

P. Koehn and C. Monz. 2006. Manual and automatic evaluation of machine translation between european languages. June.

P. Koehn, F.J. Och, and D. Marcu. 2003. Statistical phrase-based translation. *Proc. of the Human Language Technology Conference, HLT-NAACL'2003*, May.

J.A. Nelder and R. Mead. 1965. A simplex method for function minimization. *The Computer Journal*, 7:308–313.

F.J. Och and H. Ney. 2004. The alignment template approach to statistical machine translation. *Computational Linguistics*, 30(4):417–449, December.

F.J. Och. 2003. Giza++ software. http://www-i6.informatik.rwth-aachen.de/~och/ software/giza++.html.

A. Stolcke. 2002. Srilm - an extensible language modeling toolkit. *Proc. of the 7th Int. Conf. on Spoken Language Processing, ICSLP'02*, September.

C. Tillmann and H. Ney. 2003. Word reordering and a dynamic programming beam search algorithm for statistical machine translation. *Computational Linguistics*, 29(1):97–133, March.

A Appendix

Here we describe the classification algorithm used in Section 1.

1. Initialization: set $n \leftarrow 1$ and $LAB' \leftarrow LAB$.
2. Main part: while LAB' is not empty do
    - $G_n = \{(\alpha_k, \beta_k)\}$ where (α_k, β_k) is any element of LAB', i.e. α_k is the first block and β_k is the second block of the Alignment Block k of the LAB'.
    - Recursively, move elements (α_i, β_i) from LAB' to G_n if there is an element $(\alpha_j, \beta_j) \in G_n$ such that $\alpha_i = \alpha_j$ or $\beta_i = \beta_j$
    - Increase n (i.e. $n \leftarrow n + 1$)
3. Ending: For each G_n, construct the two sets A_n and B_n which consists on the first and second element of the pairs in G_n, respectively.

Phramer - An Open Source Statistical Phrase-Based Translator

Marian Olteanu, Chris Davis, Ionut Volosen and Dan Moldovan
Human Language Technology Research Institute
The University of Texas at Dallas
Richardson, TX 75080
{marian,phoo,volosen,moldovan}@hlt.utdallas.edu

Abstract

This paper describes the open-source Phrase-Based Statistical Machine Translation Decoder - Phramer. The paper also presents the UTD (HLTRI) system build for the WMT06 shared task. Our goal was to improve the translation quality by enhancing the translation table and by preprocessing the source language text

1 Introduction

Despite the fact that the research in Statistical Machine Translation (SMT) is very active, there isn't an abundance of open-source tools available to the community. In this paper, we present Phramer, an open-source system that embeds a phrase-based decoder, a minimum error rate training (Och, 2003) module and various tools related to Machine Translation (MT). The software is released under BSD license and it is available at http://www.phramer.org/.

We also describe our Phramer-based system that we build for the WMT06 shared task.

2 Phramer

Phramer is a phrase-based SMT system written in Java. It includes:

- A decoder that is compatible with Pharaoh (Koehn, 2004),
- A minimum error rate training (MERT) module, compatible with Phramer's decoder, with Pharaoh and easily adaptable to other SMT or non-SMT tasks and
- various tools.

The decoder is fully compatible with Pharaoh 1.2 in the algorithms that are implemented, input files (configuration file, translation table, language models) and command line. Some of the advantages of Phramer over Pharaoh are: (1) source code availability and its permissive license; (2) it is very fast (1.5–3 times faster for most of the configurations); (3) it can work with various storage layers for the translation table (TT) and the language models (LMs): memory, remote (access through TCP/IP), disk (using SQLite databases[1]). Extensions for other storage layers can be very easily implemented; (4) it is more configurable; (5) it accepts compressed data files (TTs and LMs); (6) it is very easy to extend; an example is provided in the package – part-of-speech decoding on either source language, target language or both; support for POS-based language models; (7) it can internally generate n-best lists. Thus no external tools are required.

The MERT module is a highly modular, efficient and customizable implementation of the algorithm described in (Och, 2003). The release has implementations for BLEU (Papineni et al., 2002), WER and PER error criteria and it has decoding interfaces for Phramer and Pharaoh. It can be used to search parameters over more than one million variables. It offers features as resume search, reuse hypotheses from previous runs and various strategies to search for optimal λ weight vectors.

[1] http://www.sqlite.org/

Proceedings of the Workshop on Statistical Machine Translation, pages 146–149,
New York City, June 2006.

The package contains a set of tools that include:

- Distributed decoding (compatible with both Phramer and Pharaoh) – it automatically splits decoding jobs and distributes them to workers and assembles the results. It is compatible with lattice generation, therefore it can also be used during weights search (using MERT).
- Tools to process translation tables – filter the TT based on the input file, flip TT to reuse it for English-to-Foreign translation, filter the TT by phrase length, convert the TT to a database.

3 WMT06 Shared Task

We have assembled a system for participation in the WMT 2006 shared task based on Phramer and other tools. We participated in 5 subtasks: DE→EN, FR→EN, ES→EN, EN→FR and EN→ES.

3.1 Baseline system

3.1.1 Translation table generation

To generate a translation table for each pair of languages starting from a sentence-aligned parallel corpus, we used a modified version of the Pharaoh training software [2]. The software also required GIZA++ word alignment tool(Och and Ney, 2003).

We generated for each phrase pair in the translation table 5 features: phrase translation probability (both directions), lexical weighting (Koehn et al., 2003) (both directions) and phrase penalty (constant value).

3.1.2 Decoder

The Phramer decoder was used to translate the *devtest2006* and *test2006* files. We accelerated the decoding process by using the *distributed decoding* tool.

3.1.3 Minimum Error Rate Training

We determined the weights to combine the models using the MERT component in Phramer. Because of the time constrains for the shared task submission[3], we used Pharaoh + Carmel[4] as the decoder for the MERT algorithm.

3.1.4 Preprocessing

We removed from the source text the words that don't appear either in the source side of the training corpus (thus we know that the translation table will not be able to translate them) or in the language model for the target language (and we estimate that there is a low chance that the untranslated word might actually be part of the reference translation). The purpose of this procedure is to minimize the risk of inserting words into the automatic translation that are not in the reference translation.

We applied this preprocessing step only when the target language was English.

3.2 Enhancements to the baseline systems

Our goal was to improve the translation quality by enhancing the the translation table.

The following enhancements were implemented:

- reduce the vocabulary size perceived by the GIZA++ and preset alignment for certain words
- "normalize" distortion between pairs of languages by reordering noun-adjective constructions

The first enhancement identifies pairs of tokens in the parallel sentences that, with a very high probability, align together and they don't align with other tokens in the sentence. These tokens are replaced with a special identifier, chosen so that GIZA++ will learn the alignment between them easier than before replacement. The targeted token types are proper nouns (detected when the same upper-cased token were present in both the foreign sentence and the English sentence) and numbers, also taking into account the differences between number representation in different languages (i.e.: 399.99 vs. 399,99). Each distinct proper noun to be replaced in the sentence was replaced with a specific identifier, distinct from other replacement identifiers already used in the sentence. The same procedure was applied also for numbers. The specific identifiers were reused in other sentences. This has the effect of reducing the vocabulary, thus it provides a large number of instances for the special token forms. The change in

[2] http://www.iccs.inf.ed.ac.uk/~pkoehn/training.tgz

[3] After the shared task submission, we optimized a lot our decoder. Before the optimizations (LM optimizations, fixing bugs that affected performance), Phramer was 5 to 15 times slower than Pharaoh.

[4] http://www.isi.edu/licensed-sw/carmel/

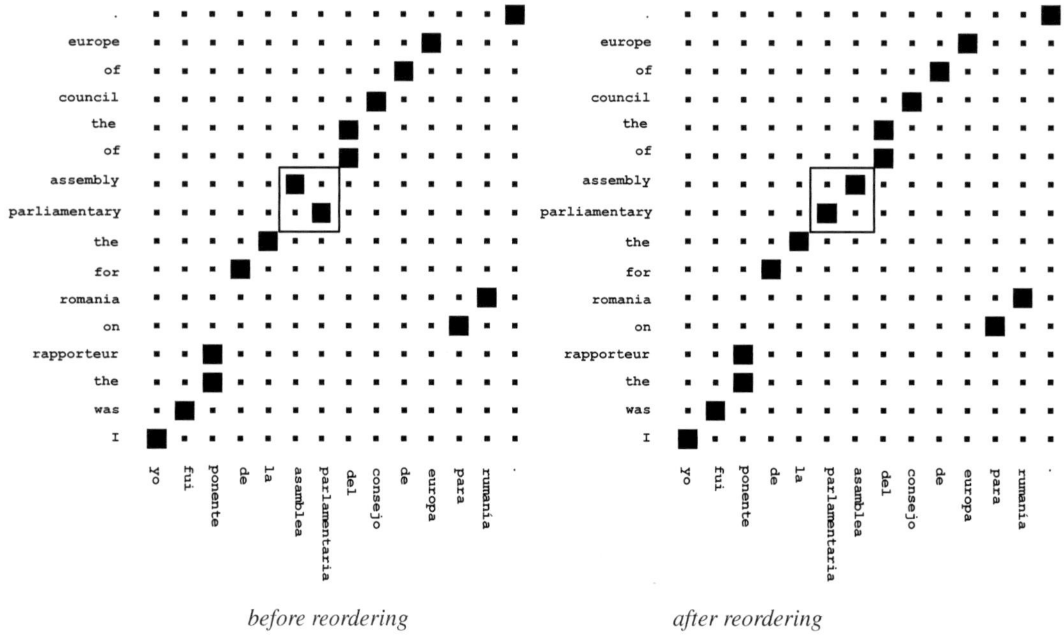

Figure 1: NN-ADJ reordering

Corpus	Before	After
DE	195,290	184,754
FR	80,348	70,623
ES	102,885	92,827

Table 1: Vocabulary size change due to forced alignment

the vocabulary size is shown in Table 1. To simplify the process, we limited the replacement of tokens to one-to-one (one real token to one special token), so that the word alignment file can be directly used together with the original parallel corpus to extract phrases required for the generation of the translation table. Table 2 shows an example of the output.

The second enhancement tries to improve the quality of the translation by rearranging the words in the source sentence to better match the correct word order in the target language (Collins et al., 2005). We focused on a very specific pattern – based on the part-of-speech tags, changing the order of NN-ADJ phrases in the non-English sentences. This process was also applied to the input dev/test files, when the target language was English. Figure 1 shows the reordering process and its effect on the alignment.

The expected benefits are:

- Better word alignment due to an alignment closer to the expected alignment (monotone).
- More phrases extracted from the word aligned corpus. Monotone alignment tends to generate more phrases than a random alignment.
- Higher mixture weight for the monotone distortion model because of fewer reordering constraints during MERT, thus the value of the monotone distortion model increases, "tightening" the translation.

3.3 Experimental Setup

We implemented the first enhancement on ES→EN subtask by part-of-speech tagging the Spanish text using `TreeTagger`[5] followed by a NN-ADJ inversion heuristic.

The language models provided for the task was used.

We used the 1,000 out of the 2,000 sentences in each of the *dev2006* datasets to determine weights for the 8 models used during decoding (one monotone distortion mode, one language model, five translation models, one sentence length model) through MERT. The weights were determined individually for each pair of source-target languages.

[5]http://www.ims.uni-stuttgart.de/projekte/corplex/TreeTagger/DecisionTreeTagger.html

There are **145** settlements in the West Bank , **16** in **Gaza** , **9** in East Jerusalem ; **400,000** people live in them .	Existen **145** asentamientos en Cisjordania , **16** en **Gaza** y **9** en Jerusaln Este ; en ellos viven **400.000** personas .
There are **[x1]** settlements in the West Bank , **[x2]** in **[y1]** , **[x3]** in East Jerusalem ; **[x4]** people live in them .	Existen **[x1]** asentamientos en Cisjordania , **[x2]** en **[y1]** y **[x3]** en Jerusaln Este ; en ellos viven **[x4]** personas .

Table 2: Forced alignment example

Subtask	OOV filtering	forced alignment	NN-ADJ inversion	BLEU score
DE→EN	√	—	—	25.45
	√	√	—	**25.53**
FR→EN	√	—	—	30.70
	√	√	—	**30.70**
ES→EN	√	—	—	30.77
	√	√	—	30.84
	√	√	√	**30.92**
EN→FR	—	—	—	31.67
	—	√	—	**31.79**
EN→ES	—	—	—	30.17
	—	√	—	**30.11**

Table 3: Results on the *devtest2006* files

Subtask	BLEU	1/2/3/4-gram precision (bp)
DE→EN	22.96	58.8/28.8/16.5/9.9 (1.000)
FR→EN	27.78	61.8/33.6/21.0/13.7 (1.000)
ES→EN	29.93	63.5/36.0/23.0/15.2 (1.000)
EN→FR	28.87	60.0/34.7/22.7/15.2 (0.991)
EN→ES	29.00	62.9/35.8/23.0/15.1 (0.975)

Table 4: Results on the *test2006* files

Using these weights, we measured the BLEU score on the *devtest2006* datasets. Based on the model chosen, we decoded the *test2006* datasets using the same weights as for *devtest2006*.

3.4 Results

Table 3 presents the results on the *devtest2006* files using different settings. Bold values represent the result for the settings that were also chosen for the final test. Table 4 shows the results on the submitted files (*test2006*).

3.5 Conclusions

The enhancements that we proposed provide small improvements on the *devtest2006* files. As expected, when we used the NN-ADJ inversion the ratio $\frac{\lambda_D}{\lambda_{LM}}$ increased from 0.545 to 0.675. The LM is the only model that opposes the tendency of the distortion model towards monotone phrase order.

`Phramer` delivers a very good baseline system. Using only the baseline system, we obtain +0.68 on DE→EN, +0.43 on FR→EN and -0.18 on ES→EN difference in BLEU score compared to WPT05's best system (Koehn and Monz, 2005). This fact is caused by the MERT module. This module is capable of estimating parameters over a large development corpus in a reasonable time, thus it is able to generate highly relevant parameters.

References

Michael Collins, Philipp Koehn, and Ivona Kucerova. 2005. Clause restructuring for statistical machine translation. In *Proceedings of the 43rd Annual Meeting of the Association for Computational Linguistics (ACL'05)*, pages 531–540, Ann Arbor, Michigan, June. Association for Computational Linguistics.

Philipp Koehn and Christof Monz. 2005. Shared task: Statistical machine translation between European languages. In *Proceedings of the ACL Workshop on Building and Using Parallel Texts*, pages 119–124, Ann Arbor, Michigan, June. Association for Computational Linguistics.

Philipp Koehn, Franz Josef Och, and Daniel Marcu. 2003. Statistical phrase-based translation. In *Proceedings of HLT/NAACL 2003*, Edmonton, Canada.

Philipp Koehn. 2004. Pharaoh: A beam search decoder for phrase-based statistical machine translation models. In *Proceedings of AMTA*.

Franz Josef Och and Hermann Ney. 2003. A systematic comparison of various statistical alignment models. *Computational Linguistics*, 29(1):19–51.

Franz Josef Och. 2003. Minimum error rate training in statistical machine translation. In Erhard Hinrichs and Dan Roth, editors, *Proceedings of the 41st Annual Meeting of the Association for Computational Linguistics*, pages 160–167.

Kishore Papineni, Salim Roukos, Todd Ward, and Wei-Jing Zhu. 2002. Bleu: a method for automatic evaluation of machine translation. In *Proceedings of the 40th Annual Meeting of the Association for Computational Linguistics (ACL)*, pages 311–318.

Language Models and Reranking for Machine Translation

Marian Olteanu, Pasin Suriyentrakorn and Dan Moldovan
Language Computer Corp.
Richardson, TX 75080
{marian,psuri,moldovan}@languagecomputer.com

Abstract

Complex Language Models cannot be easily integrated in the first pass decoding of a Statistical Machine Translation system – the decoder queries the LM a very large number of times; the search process in the decoding builds the hypotheses incrementally and cannot make use of LMs that analyze the whole sentence. We present in this paper the Language Computer's system for WMT06 that employs LM-powered reranking on hypotheses generated by phrase-based SMT systems

1 Introduction

Statistical machine translation (SMT) systems combine a number of translation models with one or more language models. Adding complex language models in the incremental process of decoding is a very challenging task. Some language models can only score sentences as a whole. Also, SMT decoders generate during the search process a very large number of partial hypotheses and query the language model/models [1].

The solution to these problems is either to use multiple iterations for decoding, to make use of the complex LMs only for complete hypotheses in the search space or to generate n-best lists and to rescore the hypotheses using also the additional LMs. For the WMT 2006 shared task we opted for the reranking solution. This paper describes our solution and results.

2 System Description

We developed for the WMT 2006 shared task a system that is trained on a (a) word-aligned bilingual corpus, (b) a large monolingual (English) corpus and (c) an English treebank and it is capable of translating from a source language (German, Spanish and French) into English.

Our system embeds `Phramer`[2] (used for minimum error rate training, decoding, decoding tools), `Pharaoh` (Koehn, 2004) (decoding), `Carmel` [3] (helper for `Pharaoh` in n-best generation), Charniak's parser (Charniak, 2001) (language model) and SRILM[4] (n-gram LM construction).

2.1 Translation table construction

We developed a component that builds a translation table from a word-aligned parallel corpus. The component generates the translation table according to the process described in the Pharaoh training manual[5]. It generates a vector of 5 numeric values for each phrase pair:

- phrase translation probability:

$$\phi(\bar{f}|\bar{e}) = \frac{count(\bar{f},\bar{e})}{count(\bar{e})}, \phi(\bar{e}|\bar{f}) = \frac{count(\bar{f},\bar{e})}{count(\bar{f})}$$

[1] During the translation of the first 10 sentences of the *devtest2006.de* dataset using Phramer and the configuration described in Section 3, the 3-gram LM was queried 27 million times (3 million distinct queries).

[2] http://www.phramer.org/ – Java-based open-source phrase based SMT system

[3] http://www.isi.edu/licensed-sw/carmel/

[4] http://www.speech.sri.com/projects/srilm/

[5] http://www.iccs.inf.ed.ac.uk/~pkoehn/training.tgz

Proceedings of the Workshop on Statistical Machine Translation, pages 150–153,
New York City, June 2006.

- lexical weighting (Koehn et al., 2003):

$$lex(\bar{f}|\bar{e},a) = \prod_{i=1}^{n} \frac{1}{|\{j|(i,j) \in a\}|} \sum_{\forall(i,j)\in a} w(f_i|e_j)$$

$$lex(\bar{e}|\bar{f},a) = \prod_{j=1}^{m} \frac{1}{|\{i|(i,j) \in a\}|} \sum_{\forall(i,j)\in a} w(e_j|f_i)$$

- phrase penalty: $\tau(\bar{f}|\bar{e}) = e$; $log(\tau(\bar{f}|\bar{e})) = 1$

2.2 Decoding

We used the Pharaoh decoder for both the Minimum Error Rate Training (Och, 2003) and test dataset decoding. Although Phramer provides decoding functionality equivalent to Pharaoh's, we preferred to use Pharaoh for this task because it is much faster than Phramer – between 2 and 15 times faster, depending on the configuration – and preliminary tests showed that there is no noticeable difference between the output of these two in terms of BLEU (Papineni et al., 2002) score.

The log-linear model uses 8 features: one distortion feature, one basic LM feature, 5 features from the translation table and one sentence length feature.

2.3 Minimum Error Rate Training

To determine the best coefficients of the log-linear model ($\bar{\lambda}$) for both the initial stage decoding and the second stage reranking, we used the *unsmoothed Minimum Error Rate Training* (MERT) component present in the Phramer package. The MERT component is highly efficient; the time required to search a set of 200,000 hypotheses is less than 30 seconds per iteration (search from a previous/random $\bar{\lambda}$ to a local maximum) on a 3GHz P4 machine. We also used the *distributed decoding* component from Phramer to speed up the search process.

We generated the n-best lists required for MERT using the Carmel toolkit. Pharaoh outputs a lattice for each input sentence, from which Carmel extracts a specific number of hypotheses. We used the *europarl.en.srilm* language model for decoding the n-best lists.

The weighting vector is calculated individually for each subtask (pair of source and target languages).

No. of sentences	96.7 M
No. of tokens	2.3 B
Vocabulary size	1.6 M
Distinct grams	1 B

Table 1: English Gigaword LM statistics

2.4 Language Models for reranking

We employed both syntactic language models and n-gram based language models extracted from very large corpora for improving the quality of the translation through reranking of the n-best list. These language models add a total of 13 new features to the log-linear model.

2.4.1 English Gigaword

We created large-scale n-gram language models using English Gigaword Second Edition[6] (EGW).

We split the corpus into sentences, tokenized the corpus, lower-cased the sentences, replaced every digit with "9" to cluster different numbers into the same unigram entry, filtered noisy sentences and we collected n-gram counts (up to 4-grams). Table 1 presents the statistics related to this process.

We pruned the unigrams that appeared less than 15 times in the corpus and all the n-grams that contain the pruned unigrams. We also pruned 3-grams and 4-grams that appear only once in the corpus. Based on these counts, we calculated 4 features for each sentence: the logarithm of the probability of the sentence based on unigrams, on bigrams, on 3-grams and on 4-grams. The probabilities of each word in the analyzed translation hypotheses were bounded by 10^{-5} (to avoid overall zero probability of a sentence caused by zero-counts).

Based on the unpruned counts, we calculated 8 additional features: how many of the n-grams in the the hypothesis appear in the EGW corpus and also how many of the n-grams in the hypotheses don't appear in the Gigaword corpus ($n = 1..4$). The two types of counts will have different behavior only when they are used to discriminate between two hypotheses with different length.

The number of n-grams in each of the two cases is presented in Table 2.

[6]http://www.ldc.upenn.edu/Catalog/CatalogEntry.jsp?catalogId=LDC2005T12

	sentence probability model	n-gram hit/miss model
1-grams	310 K	310 K
2-grams	45 M	45 M
3-grams	123 M	283 M
4-grams	235 M	675 M

Table 2: Number of n-gram entries in the EGW LM

2.4.2 Charniak parsing

We used Charniak's parser as an additional LM (Charniak, 2001) in reranking. The parser provides one feature for our model – the log-grammar-probability of the sentence.

We retrained the parser on lowercased Penn Treebank II (Marcus et al., 1993), to match the lowercased output of the MT decoder.

Considering the huge number of hypotheses that needed to be parsed for this task, we set it to parse very fast (using the command-line parameter *-T10*[7]).

2.5 Reranking and voting

A $\overline{\lambda}$ weights vector trained over the 8 basic features ($\overline{\lambda_1}$) is used to decode a n-best list. Then, a λ vector trained over all 21 features ($\overline{\lambda_2}$) is used to rerank the n-best list, potentially generating a new first-best hypothesis.

To improve the results, we generated during training a set of distinct $\overline{\lambda_2}$ weight vectors (4-10 different weight vectors). Each $\overline{\lambda_2}$ picks a preferred hypothesis. The final hypothesis is chosen using a voting mechanism. The computational cost of the voting process is very low - each of the $\overline{\lambda_2}$ is applied on the same set of hypotheses - generated by a single $\overline{\lambda_1}$.

2.6 Preprocessing

The vocabulary of languages like English, French and Spanish is relatively small. Most of the new words that appear in a text and didn't appear in a predefined large text (i.e.: translation table) are abbreviations and proper nouns, that usually don't change their form when they are translated into another language. Thus `Pharaoh` and `Phramer` deal with out-of-vocabulary (OOV) words – words that don't appear in the translation table – by copying them into the output translation. German is a compounding language, thus the German vocabulary is virtually infinite. In order to avoid OOV issues for new text, we applied a heuristic to improve the probability of properly translating compound words that are not present in the translation table. We extracted the German vocabulary from the translation table. Then, for each word in a text to be translated (development set or test set), we checked if it is present in the translation dictionary. If it was not present, we checked if it can be obtained by concatenating two words in the dictionary. If we found at least one variant of splitting the unknown word, we altered the text by dividing the word into the corresponding pieces. If there are multiple ways of splitting, we randomly took one. The minimum length for the generated word is 3 letters.

In order to minimize the risk of inserting words that are not in the reference translation into the output translation, we applied a OOV pruning algorithm (Koehn et al., 2005) – we removed every word in the text to be translated that we know we cannot translate (doesn't appear either in the foreign part of the parallel corpus used for training) or in what we expect to be present in an English text (doesn't appear in the English Gigaword corpus). This method was applied to all the input text that was automatically translated – development and test; German, French and Spanish.

For the German-to-English translation, the compound word splitting algorithm was applied before the unknown word removal process.

3 Experimental Setup

We generated the translation tables for each pair of languages using the alignment provided for this shared task.

We split the *dev2006* files into two halves. The first half was used to determine $\overline{\lambda_1}$. Using $\overline{\lambda_1}$, we created a 500-best list for each sentence in the second half. We calculated the value of the enhanced features (EGW and Charniak) for each of these hypotheses. Over this set of almost 500 K hypotheses, we computed 10 different $\overline{\lambda_2}$ using MERT. The search process was seeded using $\overline{\lambda_1}$ padded with 0 for the new 13 features. We sorted the $\overline{\lambda_2}$s by the BLEU score estimated by the MERT algorithm. We pruned manually the $\overline{\lambda_2}$s that diverge too much from the overall set of $\overline{\lambda_2}$s (based on the observation that

[7]Time factor. Higher is better. Default: 210

	500-best oracle	$\overline{\lambda_1}$	best $\overline{\lambda_2}$	voting $\overline{\lambda_2}$	WPT05 best
DE-EN					
– no split		25.70			
– split	33.63	25.81	26.29	26.28	24.77
FR-EN	37.33	30.90	31.21	31.21	30.27
ES-EN	38.06	31.13	31.15	31.22	30.95

Table 3: BLEU scores on the *devtest2006* datasets. Comparison with WPT05 results

	500-best oracle	$\overline{\lambda_1}$	voting $\overline{\lambda_2}$
DE-EN (split)	30.93	23.03	**23.55**
FR-EN	34.71	27.83	**28.00**
ES-EN	37.68	29.97	**30.12**

Table 4: BLEU scores on the *test2006* datasets. Submitted results are bolded.

these weights are overfitting). We picked from the remaining set the best $\overline{\lambda_2}$ and a preferred subset of $\overline{\lambda_2}$s to be used in voting.

The $\overline{\lambda_1}$ was also used to decode a 500-best list for each sentence in the *devtest2006* and *test2006* sets. After computing value of the enhanced features for each of these hypotheses, we applied the reranking algorithm to pick a new first-best hypothesis – the output of our system.

We used the following parameters for decoding: *-dl 5 -b 0.0001 -ttable-limit 30 -s 200* for French and Spanish and *-dl 9 -b 0.00001 -ttable-limit 30 -s 200* for German.

4 Results

Table 3 presents the detailed results of our system on the *devtest2006* datasets and comparison with WMT 2006 best results [8]. The final results, on the test set of the shared task, are reported in Table 4.

5 Conclusions

By analyzing the results, we observe that a very powerful component of our system is the MERT component of `Phramer`. It provided a very high baseline for the *devtest2006* sets (WPT05 test sets).

The additional language models seem to consistently improve the results, although the increase is not very significant on FR-EN and ES-EN subtasks. The cause might be the specifics of the data involved in this shared task – mostly European Parliament proceedings, which is different than the domain of both Treebank and English Gigaword – newswire. The enhanced LMs compete with the default LM (which is also part of the model) that is trained on European Parliament data.

The word splitting heuristics offers also a small improvement for the performance on DE-EN subtask.

Voting seems to slightly improve the results in some cases (ES-EN subtask). We believe that the voting implementation reduces λ weights overfitting, by combining the output of multiple local maxima of the development set. The size of the development set used to generate $\overline{\lambda_1}$ and $\overline{\lambda_2}$ (1000 sentences) compensates the tendency of the unsmoothed MERT algorithm to overfit (Och, 2003) by providing a high ratio between number of variables and number of parameters to be estimated.

[8] http://www.statmt.org/wpt05/mt-shared-task/

References

Eugene Charniak. 2001. Immediate-head parsing for language models. In *Proceedings of 39th Annual Meeting of the Association for Computational Linguistics*, pages 124–131.

Philipp Koehn, Franz Josef Och, and Daniel Marcu. 2003. Statistical phrase-based translation. In *Proceedings of HLT/NAACL 2003*, Edmonton, Canada.

Philipp Koehn, Amittai Axelrod, Alexandra Birch Mayne, Chris Callison-Burch, Miles Osborne, David Talbot, and Michael White. 2005. Edinburgh system description for the 2005 NIST MT Evaluation.

Philipp Koehn. 2004. Pharaoh: A beam search decoder for phrase-based statistical machine translation models. In *Proceedings of AMTA*.

Mitchell Marcus, Beatrice Santorini, and Mary Ann Marcinkiewicz. 1993. Building a large annotated corpus of English: the Penn Treebank. *Computational Linguistics*, 19(2):313–330.

Franz Josef Och. 2003. Minimum error rate training in statistical machine translation. In Erhard Hinrichs and Dan Roth, editors, *Proceedings of the 41st Annual Meeting of the Association for Computational Linguistics*, pages 160–167.

Kishore Papineni, Salim Roukos, Todd Ward, and Wei-Jing Zhu. 2002. Bleu: a method for automatic evaluation of machine translation. In *Proceedings of the 40th Annual Meeting of the Association for Computational Linguistics (ACL)*, pages 311–318.

Constraining the Phrase-Based, Joint Probability Statistical Translation Model

Alexandra Birch Chris Callison-Burch Miles Osborne Philipp Koehn
School of Informatics
University of Edinburgh
2 Buccleuch Place
Edinburgh, EH8 9LW, UK
a.c.birch-mayne@sms.ed.ac.uk

Abstract

The joint probability model proposed by Marcu and Wong (2002) provides a strong probabilistic framework for phrase-based statistical machine translation (SMT). The model's usefulness is, however, limited by the computational complexity of estimating parameters at the phrase level. We present the first model to use word alignments for constraining the space of phrasal alignments searched during Expectation Maximization (EM) training. Constraining the joint model improves performance, showing results that are very close to state-of-the-art phrase-based models. It also allows it to scale up to larger corpora and therefore be more widely applicable.

1 Introduction

Machine translation is a hard problem because of the highly complex, irregular and diverse nature of natural languages. It is impossible to accurately model all the linguistic rules that shape the translation process, and therefore a principled approach uses statistical methods to make optimal decisions given incomplete data.

The original IBM Models (Brown et al., 1993) learn word-to-word alignment probabilities which makes it computationally feasible to estimate model parameters from large amounts of training data. Phrase-based SMT models, such as the alignment template model (Och, 2003), improve on word-based models because phrases provide local context which leads to better lexical choice and more reliable local reordering. However, most phrase-based models extract their phrase pairs from previously word-aligned corpora using ad-hoc heuristics. These models perform no search for optimal phrasal alignments. Even though this is an efficient strategy, it is a departure from the rigorous statistical framework of the IBM Models.

Marcu and Wong (2002) proposed the joint probability model which directly estimates the phrase translation probabilities from the corpus in a theoretically governed way. This model neither relies on potentially sub-optimal word alignments nor on heuristics for phrase extraction. Instead, it searches the phrasal alignment space, simultaneously learning translation lexicons for both words and phrases. The joint model has been shown to outperform standard models on restricted data sets such as the small data track for Chinese-English in the 2004 NIST MT Evaluation (Przybocki, 2004).

However, considering all possible phrases and all their possible alignments vastly increases the computational complexity of the joint model when compared to its word-based counterpart. In this paper, we propose a method of constraining the search space of the joint model to areas where most of the unpromising phrasal alignments are eliminated and yet as many potentially useful alignments as possible are still explored. The joint model is constrained to phrasal alignments which do not contradict a set high confidence word alignments for each sentence. These high confidence alignments could incorporate information from both statistical and linguistic sources. In this paper we use the points of high confidence from the intersection of the bi-directional Viterbi word alignments to constrain the model, increasing performance and decreasing complexity.

Proceedings of the Workshop on Statistical Machine Translation, pages 154–157,
New York City, June 2006. ©2006 Association for Computational Linguistics

2 Translation Models

2.1 Standard Phrase-based Model

Most phrase-based translation models (Och, 2003; Koehn et al., 2003; Vogel et al., 2003) rely on a pre-existing set of word-based alignments from which they induce their parameters. In this project we use the model described by Koehn et al. (2003) which extracts its phrase alignments from a corpus that has been word aligned. From now on we refer to this phrase-based translation model as the standard model. The standard model decomposes the foreign input sentence F into a sequence of I phrases $\overline{f}_1, \ldots, \overline{f}_I$. Each foreign phrase $\overline{f_i}$ is translated to an English phrase $\overline{e_i}$ using the probability distribution $\theta(\overline{f}_i|\overline{e}_i)$. English phrases may be reordered using a relative distortion probability.

This model performs no search for optimal phrase pairs. Instead, it extracts phrase pairs $(\overline{f}_i, \overline{e}_i)$ in the following manner. First, it uses the IBM Models to learn the most likely word-level Viterbi alignments for English to Foreign and Foreign to English. It then uses a heuristic to reconcile the two alignments, starting from the points of high confidence in the intersection of the two Viterbi alignments and growing towards the points in the union. Points from the union are selected if they are adjacent to points from the intersection and their words are previously unaligned.

Phrases are then extracted by selecting phrase pairs which are 'consistent' with the symmetrized alignment, which means that all words within the source language phrase are only aligned to the words of the target language phrase and vice versa. Finally the phrase translation probability distribution is estimated using the relative frequencies of the extracted phrase pairs.

This approach to phrase extraction means that phrasal alignments are locked into the symmetrized alignment. This is problematic because the symmetrization process will grow an alignment based on arbitrary decisions about adjacent words and because word alignments inadequately represent the real dependencies between translations.

2.2 Joint Probability Model

The joint model (Marcu and Wong, 2002), does not rely on a pre-existing set of word-level alignments. Like the IBM Models, it uses EM to align and estimate the probabilities for sub-sentential units in a parallel corpus. Unlike the IBM Models, it does not constrain the alignments to being single words.

The joint model creates phrases from words and commonly occurring sequences of words. A concept, c_i, is defined as a pair of aligned phrases $< \overline{e}_i, \overline{f}_i >$. A set of concepts which completely covers the sentence pair is denoted by C. Phrases are restricted to being sequences of words which occur above a certain frequency in the corpus. Commonly occurring phrases are more likely to lead to the creation of useful phrase pairs, and without this restriction the search space would be much larger.

The probability of a sentence and its translation is the sum of all possible alignments $\mathcal{C}$, each of which is defined as the product of the probability of all individual concepts:

$$p(F, E) = \sum_{C \in \mathcal{C}} \prod_{<\overline{e}_i, \overline{f}_i> \in C} p(< \overline{e}_i, \overline{f}_i >) \qquad (1)$$

The model is trained by initializing the translation table using Stirling numbers of the second kind to efficiently estimate $p(< \overline{e}_i, \overline{f}_i >)$ by calculating the proportion of alignments which contain $p(< \overline{e}_i, \overline{f}_i >)$ compared to the total number of alignments in the sentence (Marcu and Wong, 2002). EM is then performed by first discovering an initial phrasal alignments using a greedy algorithm similar to the competitive linking algorithm (Melamed, 1997). The highest probability phrase pairs are iteratively selected until all phrases are are linked. Then hill-climbing is performed by searching once for each iteration for all merges, splits, moves and swaps that improve the probability of the initial phrasal alignment. Fractional counts are collected for all alignments visited.

Training the IBM models is computationally challenging, but the joint model is much more demanding. Considering all possible segmentations of phrases and all their possible alignments vastly increases the number of possible alignments that can be formed between two sentences. This number is exponential with relation to the length of the shorter sentence.

3 Constraining the Joint Model

The joint model requires a strategy for restricting the search for phrasal alignments to areas of the alignment space which contain most of the probability mass. We propose a method which examines phrase pairs that are consistent with a set of high confidence word alignments defined for the sentence. The set of alignments are taken from the intersection of the bi-directional Viterbi alignments.

This strategy for extracting phrase pairs is similar to that of the standard phrase-based model and the definition of 'consistent' is the same. However, the constrained joint model does not lock the search into a heuristically derived symmetrized alignment. Joint model phrases must also occur above a certain frequency in the corpus to be considered.

The constraints on the model are binding during the initialization phase of training. During EM, inconsistent phrase pairs are given a small, non-zero probability and are thus not considered unless unaligned words remain after linking together high probability phrase pairs. All words must be aligned, there is no NULL alignment like in the IBM models.

By using the IBM Models to constrain the joint model, we are searching areas in the phrasal alignment space where both models overlap. We combine the advantage of prior knowledge about likely word alignments with the ability to perform a probabilistic search around them.

4 Experiments

All data and software used was from the NAACL 2006 Statistical Machine Translation workshop unless otherwise indicated.

4.1 Constraints

The unconstrained joint model becomes intractable with very small amounts of training data. On a machine with 2 Gb of memory, we were only able to train 10,000 sentences of the German-English Europarl corpora. Beyond this, pruning is required to keep the model in memory during EM. Table 1 shows that the application of the word constraints considerably reduces the size of the space of phrasal alignments that is searched. It also improves the BLEU score of the model, by guiding it to explore the more promising areas of the search space.

4.2 Scalability

Even though the constrained joint model reduces complexity, pruning is still needed in order to scale up to larger corpora. After the initialization phase of the training, all phrase pairs with counts less than 10 million times that of the phrase pair with the highest count, are pruned from the phrase table. The model is also parallelized in order to speed up training.

	Unconstrained	Constrained
No. Concepts	6,178k	1,457k
BLEU	19.93	22.13
Time(min)	299	169

Table 1. The impact of constraining the joint model trained on 10,000 sentences of the German-English Europarl corpora and tested with the Europarl test set used in Koehn et al. (2003)

The translation models are included within a log-linear model (Och and Ney, 2002) which allows a weighted combination of features functions. For the comparison of the basic systems in Table 2 only three features were used for both the joint and the standard model: $p(e|f)$, $p(f|e)$ and the language model, and they were given equal weights.

The results in Table 2 show that the joint model is capable of training on large data sets, with a reasonable performance compared to the standard model. However, here it seems that the standard model has a slight advantage. This is almost certainly related to the fact that the joint model results in a much smaller phrase table. Pruning eliminates many phrase pairs, but further investigations indicate that this has little impact on BLEU scores.

	BLEU	Size
Joint Model	25.49	2.28
Standard Model	26.15	19.04

Table 2. Basic system comparisons: BLEU scores and model size in millions of phrase pairs for Spanish-English

The results in Table 3 compare the joint and the standard model with more features. Apart from including all Pharaoh's default features, we use two new features for both the standard and joint models: a 5-gram language model and a lexicalized reordering model as described in Koehn et al. (2005). The weights of the feature functions, or model components, are set by minimum error rate training provided by David Chiang from the University of Maryland.

On smaller data sets (Koehn et al., 2003) the joint model shows performance comparable to the standard model, however the joint model does not reach the level of performance of the stan-

	EN-ES	ES-EN
Joint		
3-gram, dl4	20.51	26.64
5-gram, dl6	26.34	27.17
+ lex. reordering	26.82	27.80
Standard Model		
5-gram, dl6		
+ lex. reordering	31.18	31.86

Table 3. Bleu scores for the joint model and the standard model showing the effect of the 5-gram language model, distortion length of 6 (dl) and the addition of lexical reordering for the English-Spanish and Spanish-English tasks.

dard model for this larger data set. This could be due to the fact that the joint model results in a much smaller phrase table. During EM only phrase pairs that occur in an alignment visited during hill-climbing are retained. Only a very small proportion of the alignment space can be searched and this reduces the chances of finding optimum parameters. The small number of alignments visited would lead to data sparseness and over-fitting. Another factor could be efficiency trade-offs like the fast but not optimal competitive linking search for phrasal alignments.

4.3 German-English submission

We also submitted a German-English system using the standard approach to phrase extraction. The purpose of this submission was to validate the syntactic reordering method that we previously proposed (Collins et al., 2005). We parse the German training and test corpus and reorder it according to a set of manually devised rules. Then, we use our phrase-based system with standard phrase-extraction, lexicalized reordering, lexical scoring, 5-gram LM, and the Pharaoh decoder.

On the development test set, the syntactic reordering improved performance from 26.86 to 27.70. The best submission in last year's shared task achieved a score of 24.77 on this set.

5 Conclusion

We presented the first attempt at creating a systematic framework which uses word alignment constraints to guide phrase-based EM training. This shows competitive results, to within 0.66 BLEU points for the basic systems, suggesting that a rigorous probabilistic framework is preferable to heuristics for extracting phrase pairs and their probabilities.

By introducing constraints to the alignment space we can reduce the complexity of the joint model and increase its performance, allowing it to train on larger corpora and making the model more widely applicable.

For the future, the joint model would benefit from lexical weighting like that used in the standard model (Koehn et al., 2003). Using IBM Model 1 to extract a lexical alignment weight for each phrase pair would decrease the impact of data sparseness, and other kinds smoothing techniques will be investigated. Better search algorithms for Viterbi phrasal alignments during EM would increase the number and quality of model parameters.

This work was supported in part under the GALE program of the Defense Advanced Research Projects Agency, Contract No. HR0011-06-C-0022.

References

Peter F. Brown, Stephen A. Della Pietra, Vincent J. Della Pietra, and Robert L. Mercer. 1993. The mathematics of machine translation: Parameter estimation. *Computational Linguistics*, 19(2):263–311.

Michael Collins, Philipp Koehn, and Ivona Kucerova. 2005. Clause restructuring for statistical machine translation. In *Proceedings of ACL*.

Philipp Koehn, Franz Och, and Daniel Marcu. 2003. Statistical phrase-based translation. In *Proceedings of HLT/NAACL*, pages 127–133.

Philipp Koehn, Amittai Axelrod, Alexandra Birch Mayne, and Chris Callison-Burch. 2005. Edinburgh system description. In *IWSLT Speech Translation Evaluation*.

Daniel Marcu and William Wong. 2002. A phrase-based, joint probability model for statistical machine translation. In *Proceedings of EMNLP*.

Dan Melamed. 1997. A word-to-word model of translational equivalence. In *Proceedings of ACL*.

Franz Josef Och and Hermann Ney. 2002. Discriminative training and maximum entropy models for statistical machine translation. In *ACL*.

Franz Josef Och. 2003. *Statistical Machine Translation: From Single-Word Models to Alignment Templates*. Ph.D. thesis, RWTH Aachen Department of Computer Science, Aachen, Germany.

Mark Przybocki. 2004. NIST 2004 machine translation evaluation results. Confidential e-mail to workshop participants, May.

Stephan Vogel, Ying Zhang, Fei Huang, Alicia Tribble, Ashish Venugopal, Bing Zhao, and Alex Waibel. 2003. The CMU statistical machine translation system. In *Machine Translation Summit*.

Microsoft Research Treelet Translation System: NAACL 2006 Europarl Evaluation

Arul Menezes, Kristina Toutanova and Chris Quirk

Microsoft Research
One Microsoft Way
Redmond, WA 98052
{arulm,kristout,chrisq}@microsoft.com

Abstract

The Microsoft Research translation system is a syntactically informed phrasal SMT system that uses a phrase translation model based on dependency treelets and a global reordering model based on the source dependency tree. These models are combined with several other knowledge sources in a log-linear manner. The weights of the individual components in the log-linear model are set by an automatic parameter-tuning method. We give a brief overview of the components of the system and discuss our experience with the Europarl data translating from English to Spanish.

1. Introduction

The dependency treelet translation system developed at MSR is a statistical MT system that takes advantage of linguistic tools, namely a source language dependency parser, as well as a word alignment component. [1]

To train a translation system, we require a sentence-aligned parallel corpus. First the source side is parsed to obtain dependency trees. Next the corpus is word-aligned, and the source dependencies are projected onto the target sentences using the word alignments. From the aligned dependency corpus we extract all treelet translation pairs, and train an order model and a bi-lexical dependency model.

To translate, we parse the input sentence, and employ a decoder to find a combination and ordering of treelet translation pairs that cover the source tree and are optimal according to a set of models. In a now-common generalization of the classic noisy-channel framework, we use a log-linear combination of models [2], as in below:

$$translation(S, F, \Lambda) = \underset{T}{\operatorname{argmax}} \left\{ \sum_{f \in F} \lambda_f f(S, T) \right\}$$

Such an approach toward translation scoring has proven very effective in practice, as it allows a translation system to incorporate information from a variety of probabilistic or non-probabilistic sources. The weights $\mathbf{\Lambda} = \{ \lambda_f \}$ are selected by discriminatively training against held out data.

2. System Details

A brief word on notation: s and t represent source and target lexical nodes; **S** and **T** represent source and target trees; **s** and **t** represent source and target treelets (connected subgraphs of the dependency tree). The expression $\forall t \in \mathbf{T}$ refers to all the lexical items in the target language tree **T** and $|\mathbf{T}|$ refers to the count of lexical items in **T**. We use subscripts to indicate selected words: $\mathbf{T}_n$ represents the nth lexical item in an in-order traversal of **T**.

2.1. Training

We use the broad coverage dependency parser NLPWIN [3] to obtain source language dependency trees, and we use GIZA++ [4] to produce word alignments. The GIZA++ training regimen and parameters are tuned to optimize BLEU [5] scores on held-out data. Using the word alignments, we follow a set of dependency tree projection heuristics [1] to construct target dependency trees, producing a word-aligned parallel dependency tree corpus. Treelet translation pairs are extracted by enumerating all source treelets (to a maximum size) aligned to a target treelet.

2.2. Decoding

We use a tree-based decoder, inspired by dynamic programming. It searches for an approximation of

Proceedings of the Workshop on Statistical Machine Translation, pages 158–161,
New York City, June 2006. ©2006 Association for Computational Linguistics

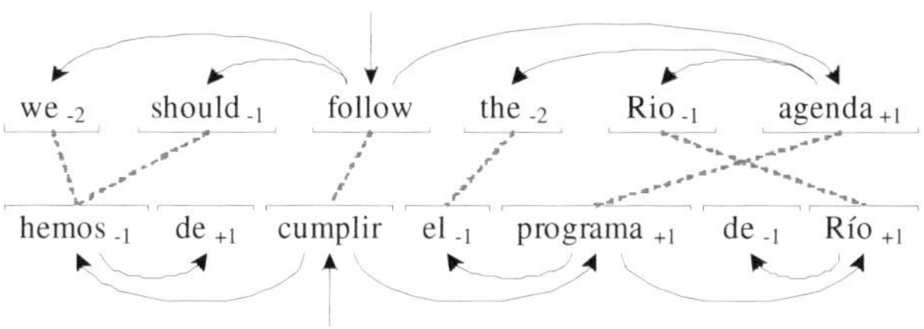

Figure 1: Aligned dependency tree pair, annotated with head-relative positions

the n-best translations of each subtree of the input dependency tree. Translation candidates are composed from treelet translation pairs extracted from the training corpus. This process is described in more detail in [1].

2.3. Models

2.3.1. *Channel models*

We employ several channel models: a direct maximum likelihood estimate of the probability of target given source, as well as an estimate of source given target and target given source using the word-based IBM Model 1 [6]. For MLE, we use absolute discounting to smooth the probabilities:

$$P_{MLE}(t|s)=\frac{c(s,t)-\lambda}{c(s,*)}$$

Here, c represents the count of instances of the treelet pair $\langle \mathbf{s}, \mathbf{t} \rangle$ in the training corpus, and λ is determined empirically.

For Model 1 probabilities we compute the sum over all possible alignments of the treelet without normalizing for length. The calculation of source given target is presented below; target given source is calculated symmetrically.

$$P_{M1}(t|s)=\prod_{t\in t}\sum_{s\in s}P(t|s)$$

2.3.2. *Bilingual n-gram channel models*

Traditional phrasal SMT systems are beset by a number of theoretical problems, such as the ad hoc estimation of phrasal probability, the failure to model the partition probability, and the tenuous connection between the phrases and the underlying word-based alignment model. In string-based SMT systems, these problems are outweighed by the key role played by phrases in capturing "local" order. In the absence of good global ordering models, this has led to an inexorable push towards longer and longer phrases, resulting in serious practical problems of scale, without, in the end, obviating the need for a real global ordering story.

In [13] we discuss these issues in greater detail and also present our approach to this problem. Briefly, we take as our basic unit the Minimal Translation Unit (MTU) which we define as a set of source and target word pairs such that there are no word alignment links between distinct MTUs, and no smaller MTUs can be extracted without violating the previous constraint. In other words, these are the minimal non-compositional phrases. We then build models based on n-grams of MTUs in source string, target string and source dependency tree order. These bilingual n-gram models in combination with our global ordering model allow us to use shorter phrases without any loss in quality, or alternately to improve quality while keeping phrase size constant.

As an example, consider the aligned sentence pair in Figure 1. There are seven MTUs:

m_1 = <*we should / hemos*>
m_2 = <NULL / *de*>
m_3 = <*follow / cumplir*>
m_4 = <*the / el*>
m_5 = <*Rio / Rio*>
m_6 = <*agenda / programa*>
m_7 = <NULL / *de*>

We can then predict the probability of each MTU in the context of (a) the previous MTUs in source order, (b) the previous MTUs in target order, or (c) the ancestor MTUs in the tree. We consider all of these traversal orders, each acting as a separate feature function in the log linear combination. For source and target traversal order we use a trigram model, and a bigram model for tree order.

2.3.3. *Target language models*

We use both a surface level trigram language model and a dependency-based bigram language model [7], similar to the bilexical dependency modes used in some English Treebank parsers (e.g. [8]).

$$P_{surf}(T)=\prod_{i=1}^{|T|}P_{trisurf}(T_i|T_{i-2},T_{i-1})$$

$$P_{bilex}(T)=\prod_{i=1}^{|T|}P_{bidep}(T_i|parent(T_i))$$

$P_{trisurf}$ is a Kneser-Ney smoothed trigram language model trained on the target side of the training corpus, and P_{bilex} is a Kneser-Ney smoothed bigram language model trained on target language dependencies extracted from the aligned parallel dependency tree corpus.

2.3.4. *Order model*

The order model assigns a probability to the position (*pos*) of each target node relative to its head based on information in both the source and target trees:

$$P_{order}(order(T)|S,T) = \prod_{t \in T} P(pos(t, parent(t))|S,T)$$

Here, position is modeled in terms of closeness to the head in the dependency tree. The closest pre-modifier of a given head has position -1; the closest post-modifier has a position 1. Figure 1 shows an example dependency tree pair annotated with head-relative positions.

We use a small set of features reflecting local information in the dependency tree to model P(pos (*t*,parent(*t*)) | **S**, **T**):

- Lexical items of *t* and *parent*(*t*), the parent of *t* in the dependency tree.
- Lexical items of the source nodes aligned to *t* and head(*t*).
- Part-of-speech ("cat") of the source nodes aligned to the head and modifier.
- Head-relative position of the source node aligned to the source modifier.

These features along with the target feature are gathered from the word-aligned parallel dependency tree corpus and used to train a statistical model. In previous versions of the system, we trained a decision tree model [9]. In the current version, we explored log-linear models. In addition to providing a different way of combining information from multiple features, log-linear models allow us to model the similarity among different classes (target positions), which is advantageous for our task.

We implemented a method for automatic selection of features and feature conjunctions in the log-linear model. The method greedily selects feature conjunction templates that maximize the accuracy on a development set. Our feature selection study showed that the part-of-speech labels of the source nodes aligned to the head and the modifier and the head-relative position of the source node corresponding to the modifier were the most important features. It was useful to concatenate the part-of-speech of the source head with every feature. This effectively achieves learning of separate movement models for each source head category. Lexical information on the pairs of head and dependent in the source and target was also very useful.

To model the similarity among different target classes and to achieve pooling of data across similar classes, we added multiple features of the target position. These features let our model know, for example, that position -5 looks more like position -6 than like position 3. We added a feature "positive"/"negative" which is shared by all positive/negative positions. We also added a feature looking at the displacement of a position in the target from the corresponding position in the source and features which group the target positions into bins. These features of the target position are combined with features of the input.

This model was trained on the provided parallel corpus. As described in Section 2.1 we parsed the source sentences, and projected target dependencies. Each head-modifier pair in the resulting target trees constituted a training instance for the order model.

The score computed by the log-linear order model is used as a single feature in the overall log-linear combination of models (see Section 1), whose parameters were optimized using MaxBLEU [2]. This order model replaced the decision tree-based model described in [1].

We compared the decision tree model to the log-linear model on predicting the position of a modifier using reference parallel sentences, independent of the full MT system. The decision tree achieved per decision accuracy of 69% whereas the log-linear model achieved per decision accuracy of 79%.[1] In the context of the full MT system, however, the new order model provided a more modest improvement in the BLEU score of 0.39%.

2.3.5. *Other models*

We include two pseudo-models that help balance certain biases inherent in our other models.

- **Treelet count**. This feature is a count of treelets used to construct the candidate. It acts as a bias toward translations that use a smaller number of treelets; hence toward larger sized treelets incorporating more context.
- **Word count.** We also include a count of the words in the target sentence. This feature

[1] The per-decision accuracy numbers were obtained on different (random) splits of training and test data.

helps to offset the bias of the target language model toward shorter sentences.

3. Discussion

We participated in the English to Spanish track, using the supplied bilingual data only. We used only the target side of the bilingual corpus for the target language model, rather than the larger supplied language model. We did find that increasing the target language order from 3 to 4 had a noticeable impact on translation quality. It is likely that a larger target language corpus would have an impact, but we did not explore this.

	BLEU
Baseline treelet system	27.60
Add bilingual MTU models	28.42
Replace DT order model with log-linear model	28.81

Table 1: Results on development set

We found that the addition of bilingual n-gram based models had a substantial impact on translation quality. Adding these models raised BLEU scores about 0.8%, but anecdotal evidence suggests that human-evaluated quality rose by much more than the BLEU score difference would suggest. In general, we felt that in this corpus, due to the great diversity in translations for the same source language words and phrases, and given just one reference translation, BLEU score correlated rather poorly with human judgments. This was borne out in the human evaluation of the final test results. Humans ranked our system first and second, in-domain and out-of-domain respectively, even though it was in the middle of a field of ten systems by BLEU score. Furthermore, n-gram channel models may provide greater robustness. While our BLEU score dropped 3.61% on out-of-domain data, the average BLEU score of the other nine competing systems dropped 5.11%.

4. References

[1] Quirk, C., Menezes, A., and Cherry, C., "Dependency Tree Translation: Syntactically Informed Phrasal SMT", *Proceedings of ACL 2005*, Ann Arbor, MI, USA, 2005.

[2] Och, F. J., and Ney, H., "Discriminative Training and Maximum Entropy Models for Statistical Machine Translation", *Proceedings of ACL 2002*, Philadelphia, PA, USA, 2002.

[3] Heidorn, G., "Intelligent writing assistance", in Dale et al. *Handbook of Natural Language Processing*, Marcel Dekker, 2000.

[4] Och, F. J., and Ney H., "A Systematic Comparison of Various Statistical Alignment Models", *Computational Linguistics*, 29(1):19-51, March 2003.

[5] Papineni, K., Roukos, S., Ward, T., and Zhu, W.-J., "BLEU: a method for automatic evaluation of machine translation", *Proceedings of ACL 2002*, Philadelphia, PA, USA, 2002.

[6] Brown, P. F., Della Pietra, S., Della Pietra, V. J., and Mercer, R. L., "The Mathematics of Statistical Machine Translation: Parameter Estimation", *Computational Linguistics* 19(2): 263-311, 1994.

[7] Aue, A., Menezes, A., Moore, R., Quirk, C., and Ringger, E., "Statistical Machine Translation Using Labeled Semantic Dependency Graphs." *Proceedings of TMI 2004*, Baltimore, MD, USA, 2004.

[8] Collins, M., "Three generative, lexicalised models for statistical parsing", *Proceedings of ACL 1997*, Madrid, Spain, 1997.

[9] Chickering, D.M., "The WinMine Toolkit", Microsoft Research Technical Report MSR-TR-2002-103, Redmond, WA, USA, 2002.

[10] Och, F. J., Gildea, D., Khudanpur, S., Sarkar, A., Yamada, K., Fraser, A., Kumar, S., Shen, L., Smith, D., Eng, K., Jain, V., Jin, Z., and Radev, D., "A Smorgasbord of Features for Statistical Machine Translation". *Proceedings of HLT/NAACL 2004*, Boston, MA, USA, 2004.

[11] Bender, O., Zens, R., Matsuov, E. and Ney, H., "Alignment Templates: the RWTH SMT System". *IWSLT Workshop at INTERSPEECH 2004*, Jeju Island, Korea, 2004.

[12] Och, F. J., "Minimum Error Rate Training for Statistical Machine Translation", *Proceedings of ACL 2003*, Sapporo, Japan, 2003.

[13] Quirk, C and Menezes, A, "Do we need phrases? Challenging the conventional wisdom in Statistical Machine Translation", *Proceedings of HLT/NAACL 2006*, New York, NY, USA, 2006

N-gram-based SMT System Enhanced with Reordering Patterns

Josep M. Crego
Marta R. Costa-jussà
José B. Mariño

Adrià de Gispert
Maxim Khalilov
José A. R. Fonollosa

Patrik Lambert
Rafael E. Banchs

Department of Signal Theory and Communications
TALP Research Center (UPC)
Barcelona 08034, Spain
{jmcrego,agispert,lambert,mruiz,khalilov,rbanchs,canton,adrian}@gps.tsc.upc.edu

Abstract

This work presents translation results for the three data sets made available in the shared task *"Exploiting Parallel Texts for Statistical Machine Translation"* of the HLT-NAACL 2006 Workshop on Statistical Machine Translation. All results presented were generated by using the N-gram-based statistical machine translation system which has been enhanced from the last year's evaluation with a tagged target language model (using Part-Of-Speech tags). For both Spanish-English translation directions and the English-to-French translation task, the baseline system allows for linguistically motivated source-side reorderings.

1 Introduction

The statistical machine translation approach used in this work implements a log-linear combination of feature functions along with a translation model which is based on bilingual n-grams (de Gispert and Mariño, 2002).

This translation model differs from the well known phrase-based translation approach (Koehn et al., 2003) in two basic issues: first, training data is monotonously segmented into bilingual units; and second, the model considers n-gram probabilities instead of relative frequencies. This translation approach is described in detail in (Mariño et al., 2005).

For those translation tasks with Spanish or English as target language, an additional tagged (using POS information) target language model is used. Additionally a reordering strategy that includes POS information is described and evaluated.

Translation results for all six translation directions proposed in the shared task are presented and discussed. Both translation directions are considered for the pairs: **English-Spanish**, **English-French**, and **English-German**.

The paper is structured as follows: Section 2 briefly outlines the baseline system. Section 3 describes in detail the implemented POS-based reordering strategy. Section 4 presents and discusses the shared task results and, finally, section 5 presents some conclusions and further work.

2 Baseline N-gram-based SMT System

As already mentioned, the translation model used here is based on bilingual n-grams. It actually constitutes a language model of bilingual units, referred to as tuples, which approximates the joint probability between source and target languages by using bilingual n-grams (de Gispert and Mariño, 2002).

Tuples are extracted from a word-to-word aligned corpus according to the following two constraints: first, tuple extraction should produce a monotonic segmentation of bilingual sentence pairs; and second, no smaller tuples can be extracted without violating the previous constraint. See (Crego et al., 2004) for further details.

For all experiments presented here, the translation model consisted of a 4-gram language model of tuples. In addition to this bilingual n-gram translation model, the baseline system implements a log linear combination of five feature functions.

Proceedings of the Workshop on Statistical Machine Translation, pages 162–165,
New York City, June 2006.

These five additional models are:

- A **target language model**. 5-gram of the target side of the bilingual corpus.

- A **word bonus**. Based on the number of target words in the partial-translation hypothesis, to compensate the LM preference for short sentences.

- A **Source-to-target lexicon model**. Based on IBM Model 1 lexical parameters(Brown et al., 1993), providing a complementary probability for each tuple in the translation table. These parameters are obtained from source-to-target alignments.

- A **Target-to-source lexicon model**. Analogous to the previous feature, but obtained from target-to-source alignments.

- A **Tagged (POS) target language model**. This feature implements a 5-gram language model of target POS-tags. In this case, each translation unit carried the information of its target side POS-tags, though this is not used for translation model estimation (only in order to evaluate the target POS language model at decoding time). Due to the non-availability of POS-taggers for French and German, it was not possible to incorporate this feature in all translation tasks considered, being only used for those translation tasks with Spanish and English as target languages.

The search engine for this translation system is described in (Crego et al., 2005) and implements a beam-search strategy based on dynamic programming, taking into account all feature functions described above, along with the bilingual n-gram translation model. Monotone search is performed, including histogram and threshold pruning and hypothesis recombination.

An optimization tool, which is based on a downhill simplex method was developed and used for computing log-linear weights for each of the feature functions. This algorithm adjusts the weights so that a non-linear combination of BLEU *and* NIST scores is maximized over the development set for each of the six translation directions considered.

This baseline system is actually very similar to the system used for last year's shared task *"Exploiting Parallel Texts for Statistical Machine Translation"* of ACL'05 Workshop on Building and Using Parallel Texts: Data-Driven Machine Translation and Beyond (Banchs et al., 2005), whose results are available at: `http://www.statmt.org/wpt05/mt-shared-task/`. A more detailed description of the system can be found in (2005).

The tools used for POS-tagging were Freeling (Carreras et al., 2004) for Spanish and TnT (Brants, 2000) for English. All language models were estimated using the SRI language modeling toolkit. Word-to-word alignments were extracted with GIZA++. Improvements in word-to-word alignments were achieved through verb group classification as described in (de Gispert, 2005).

3 Reordering Framework

In this section we outline the reordering framework used for the experiments (Crego and Mariño, 2006). A highly constrained reordered search is performed by means of a set of reordering patterns (linguistically motivated rewrite patterns) which are used to extend the monotone search graph with additional arcs.

To extract patterns, we use the word-to-word alignments (the union of both alignment directions) and source-side POS tags. The main procedure consists of identifying all crossings produced in the

Figure 1: *Reordering patterns are extracted using word-to-word alignments. The generalization power is achieved through the POS tags. Three instances of different patterns are extracted using the sentences in the example.*

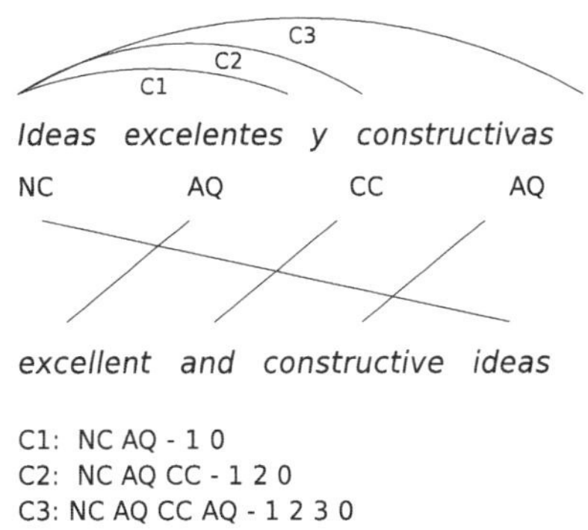

word-to-word alignments. Once a crossing has been detected, its source POS tags and alignments are used to account for a new instance of pattern. The target side of a pattern (source-side positions after reordering), is computed using the original order of the target words to which the source words are aligned. See figure 1 for a clarifying example of pattern extraction.

The monotone search graph is extended with reorderings following the patterns found in training. The procedure identifies first the sequences of words in the input sentence that match any available pattern. Then, each of the matchings implies the addition of an arc into the search graph (encoding the reordering learnt in the pattern). However, this addition of a new arc is not performed if a translation unit with the same source-side words already exists in the training. Figure 2 shows an example of the procedure.

Figure 2: *Three additional arcs have been added to the original monotone graph (bold arcs) given the reordering patterns found matching any of the source POS tags sequence.*

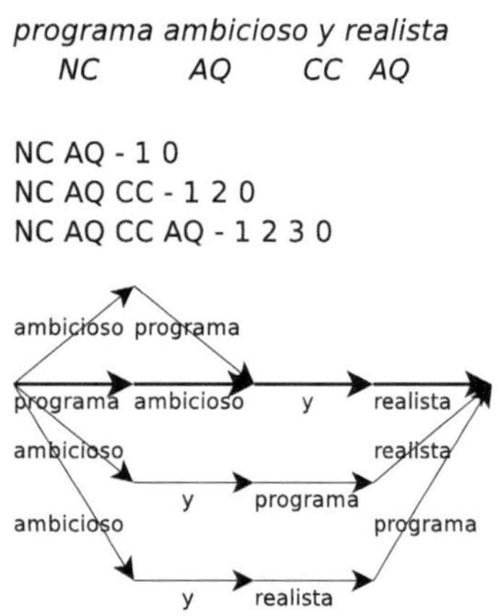

Once the search graph is built, the decoder traverses the graph looking for the best translation. Hence, the winner hypothesis is computed using all the available information (the whole SMT models). The reordering strategy is additionally supported by a **5-gram language model of reordered source POS-tags**. In training, POS-tags are reordered according with the extracted reordering patterns and word-to-word links. The resulting sequence of source POS-tags are used to train the n-gram LM.

Notice that this reordering framework has only been used for some translation tasks (Spanish-to-English, English-to-Spanish and English-to-French). The reason is double: first, because we did not have available a French POS-tagger. Second, because the technique used to learn reorderings (detailed below) does not seem to apply for language pairs like German-English, because the agglutinative characteristic of German (words are formed by joining morphemes together).

Table 1: *BLEU, NIST and mWER scores (computed using* **two** *reference translations) obtained for both translation directions (Spanish-to-English and English-to-Spanish).*

Conf	BLEU	NIST	mWER
Spanish-to-English			
base	55.23	10.69	34.40
+rgraph	55.59	10.70	34.23
+pos	56.39	10.75	33.75
English-to-Spanish			
base	48.03	9.84	41.18
+rgraph	48.53	9.81	41.15
+pos	48.91	9.91	40.29

Table 1 shows the improvement of the original baseline system described in section 2 (**base**), enhanced using reordering graphs (**+rgraph**) and provided the tagged-source language model (**+pos**). The experiments in table 1 were not carried out over the official corpus of this shared task. The Spanish-English corpus of the TC-Star 2005 Evaluation was used. Due to the high similarities between both corpus (this shared task corpus consists of a subset of the whole corpus used in the TC-Star 2005 Evaluation), it makes sense to think that comparable results would be obtained.

It is worth mentioning that the official corpus of the shared task (HLT-NAACL 2006) was used when building and tuning the present shared task system.

4 Shared Task Results

The data provided for this shared task corresponds to a subset of the official transcriptions of the European Parliament Plenary Sessions. The development set used to tune the system consists of a subset (500 first sentences) of the official development set made available for the Shared Task.

Table 2 presents the *BLEU*, *NIST* and *mWER* scores obtained for the development-test data set. The last column shows whether the target POS language model feature was used or not. Computed scores are case sensitive and compare to **one** reference translation. Tasks in bold were conducted allowing for the reordering framework. For French-to-English task, block reordering strategy was used, which is described in (Costa-jussà et al., 2006). As it can be seen, for the English-to-German task we did not use any of the previous enhancements.

Table 2: *Translation results*

Task	BLEU	NIST	mWER	tPOS
en → es	29.50	7.32	58.95	yes
es → en	30.29	7.51	57.72	yes
en → fr	30.23	7.40	59.76	no
fr → en	30.21	7.61	56.97	yes
en → de	17.40	5.61	71.18	no
de → en	23.78	6.70	65.83	yes

Important differences can be observed between the German-English and the rest of translation tasks. They result from the greater differences in word order present in this language pair (the German-English results are obtained under monotone decoding conditions). Also because the greater vocabulary of words of German, which increases sparseness in any task where German is envolved. As expected, differences in translation accuracy between Spanish-English and French-English are smaller.

5 Conclusions and Further Work

As it can be concluded from the presented results, although in principle some language pairs (Spanish-English-French) seem to have very little need for reorderings (due to their similar word order), the use of linguistically-based reorderings proves to be useful to improve translation accuracy.

Additional work is to be conducted to allow for reorderings when translating from/to German.

6 Acknowledgments

This work was partly funded by the European Union under the integrated project TC-STAR[1]: Technology and Corpora for Speech to Speech Translation (IST-2002-FP6-506738) and the European Social Fund.

[1]http://www.tc-star.org

References

R. E. Banchs, J. M. Crego, A. de Gispert, P. Lambert, and J. B. Mariño. 2005. Statistical machine translation of euparl data by using bilingual n-grams. *Proc. of the ACL Workshop on Building and Using Parallel Texts (ACL'05/Wkshp)*, pages 67–72, June.

T. Brants. 2000. TnT – a statistical part-of-speech tagger. In *Proc. of the Sixth Applied Natural Language Processing (ANLP-2000)*, Seattle, WA.

P. Brown, S. Della Pietra, V. Della Pietra, and R. Mercer. 1993. The mathematics of statistical machine translation. *Computational Linguistics*, 19(2):263–311.

X. Carreras, I. Chao, L. Padró, and M. Padró. 2004. Freeling: An open-source suite of language analyzers. *4th Int. Conf. on Language Resources and Evaluation, LREC'04*, May.

M.R. Costa-jussà, J.M. Crego, A. de Gispert, P. Lambert, M. Khalilov, R. Banchs, J.B. Mariño, and J.A.R. Fonollosa. 2006. Talp phrase-based statistical translation system for european language pairs. *Proc. of the HLT/NAACL Workshop on Statistical Machine Translation*, June.

J. M. Crego and J. Mariño. 2006. A reordering framework for statistical machine translation. *Internal Report.*

J. M. Crego, J. Mariño, and A. de Gispert. 2004. Finite-state-based and phrase-based statistical machine translation. *Proc. of the 8th Int. Conf. on Spoken Language Processing, ICSLP'04*, pages 37–40, October.

J. M. Crego, J. Mariño, and A. Gispert. 2005. An ngram-based statistical machine translation decoder. *Proc. of the 9th European Conference on Speech Communication and Technology, Interspeech'05*, September.

A. de Gispert and J. Mariño. 2002. Using X-grams for speech-to-speech translation. *Proc. of the 7th Int. Conf. on Spoken Language Processing, ICSLP'02*, September.

A. de Gispert. 2005. Phrase linguistic classification and generalization for improving statistical machine translation. *Proc. of the ACL Student Research Workshop (ACL'05/SRW)*, June.

P. Koehn, F.J. Och, and D. Marcu. 2003. Statistical phrase-based translation. *Proc. of the Human Language Technology Conference, HLT-NAACL'2003*, May.

J.B. Mariño, R Banchs, J.M. Crego, A. de Gispert, P. Lambert, M. R. Costa-jussà, and J.A.R. Fonollosa. 2005. Bilingual n–gram statistical machine translation. *Proc. of the MT Summit X*, September.

The LDV-COMBO system for SMT

Jesús Giménez and **Lluís Màrquez**
TALP Research Center, LSI Department
Universitat Politècnica de Catalunya
Jordi Girona Salgado 1–3, E-08034, Barcelona
{jgimenez,lluism}@lsi.upc.edu

Abstract

We describe the LDV-COMBO system presented at the Shared Task. Our approach explores the possibility of working with alignments at different levels of abstraction using different degrees of linguistic analysis from the lexical to the shallow syntactic level. Translation models are built on top of combinations of these alignments. We present results for the Spanish-to-English and English-to-Spanish tasks. We show that liniguistic information may be helpful, specially when the target language has a rich morphology.

1 Introduction

The main motivation behind our work is to introduce linguistic information, other than lexical units, to the process of building word and phrase alignments. In the last years, many efforts have been devoted to this matter (Yamada and Knight, 2001; Gildea, 2003).

Following our previous work (Giménez and Màrquez, 2005), we use shallow syntactic information to generate more precise alignments. Far from full syntactic complexity, we suggest going back to the simpler alignment methods first described by IBM (1993). Our approach exploits the possibility of working with alignments at two different levels of granularity, lexical (words) and shallow parsing (chunks). Apart from redefining the scope of the alignment unit, we may use different linguistic data views. We enrich tokens with features further than lexical such as *part-of-speech (PoS)*, *lemma*, and *chunk IOB label*.

For instance, suppose the case illustrated in Figure 1 where the lexical item *'plays'* is seen acting as a verb and as a noun. Considering these two words, with the same lexical realization, as a single token adds noise to the word alignment process. Representing this information, by means of linguistic data views, as *'*$plays_{VBZ}$*'* and *'*$plays_{NNS}$*'* would allow us to distinguish between the two cases. Ideally, one would wish to have still deeper information, moving through syntax onto semantics, such as *word senses*. Therefore, it would be possible to distinguish for instance between two realizations of *'plays'* with different meanings: *'*he_{PRP} $plays_{VBG}$ $guitar_{NN}$*'* and *'*he_{PRP} $plays_{VBG}$ $football_{NN}$*'*. Of course, there is a natural trade-off between the use of linguistic data views and data sparsity. Fortunately, we hava data enough so that statistical parameter estimation remains reliable.

The approach which is closest to ours is that by Schafer and Yarowsky (2003) who suggested a combination of models based on shallow syntactic analysis (part-of-speech tagging and phrase chunking). They followed a backoff strategy in the application of their models. Decoding was based on Finite State Automata. Although no significant improvement in MT quality was reported, results were promising taking into account the short time spent in the development of the linguistic tools utilized.

Our system is further described in Section 2. Results are reported in Section 3. Conclusions and further work are briefly outlined in Section 4.

Proceedings of the Workshop on Statistical Machine Translation, pages 166–169,
New York City, June 2006.

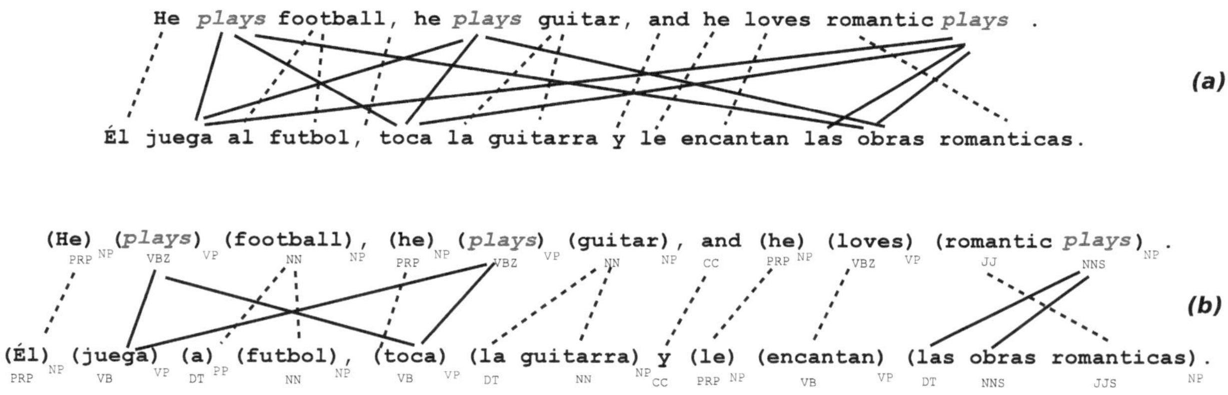

Figure 1: A case of word alignment possibilities on top of lexical units (a) and linguistic data views (b).

2 System Description

The LDV-COMBO system follows the SMT architecture suggested by the workshop organizers. We use the *Pharaoh* beam-search decoder (Koehn, 2004).

First, training data are linguistically annotated. In order to achieve robustness the same tools have been used to linguistically annotate both languages. The *SVMTool*[1] has been used for PoS-tagging (Giménez and Màrquez, 2004). The *Freeling*[2] package (Carreras et al., 2004) has been used for lemmatizing. Finally, the *Phreco* software (Carreras et al., 2005) has been used for shallow parsing. In this paper we focus on data views at the word level. 6 different data views have been built: (W) word, (L) lemma, (WP) word and PoS, (WC) word and chunk IOB label, (WPC) word, PoS and chunk IOB label, (LC) lemma and chunk IOB label.

Then, running *GIZA++* (Och and Ney, 2003), we obtain token alignments for each of the data views. Combined phrase-based translation models are built on top of the Viterbi alignments output by *GIZA++*. Phrase extraction is performed following the phrase-extract algorithm depicted by Och (2002). We do not apply any heuristic refinement. We work with phrases up to 5 tokens. Phrase pairs appearing only once have been discarded. Scoring is performed by relative frequency. No smoothing is applied.

In this paper we focus on the global phrase extraction (GPHEX) method described by Giménez and Màrquez (2005). We build a single translation model from the union of alignments from the 6 data views described above. This model must match the input format. For instance, if the input is annotated with word and PoS (WP), so must be the translation model. Therefore either the input must be enriched with linguistic annotation or translation models must be post-processed in order to remove the additional linguistic annotation. We did not observe significant differences in either alternative. Therefore, we simply adapted translations models to work under the assumption of unannotated inputs (W).

3 Experimental Work

3.1 Setting

We have used only the data sets and language model provided by the organization. For evaluation we have selected a set of 8 metric variants corresponding to seven different families: BLEU ($n = 4$) (Papineni et al., 2001), NIST ($n = 5$) (Lin and Hovy, 2002), GTM F_1-measure ($e = 1, 2$) (Melamed et al., 2003), 1-WER (Nießen et al., 2000), 1-PER (Leusch et al., 2003), ROUGE (ROUGE-S*) (Lin and Och, 2004) and METEOR[3] (Banerjee and Lavie, 2005). Optimization of the decoding parameters (λ_{tm}, λ_{lm}, λ_w) is performed by means of the *Downhill Simplex Method in Multidimensions* (William H. Press and Flannery, 2002) over the BLEU metric.

[1] The SVMTool may be freely downloaded at http://www.lsi.upc.es/~nlp/SVMTool/.

[2] Freeling Suite of Language Analyzers may be downloaded at http://www.lsi.upc.es/~nlp/freeling/

[3] For Spanish-to-English we applied all available modules: exact + stemming + WordNet stemming + WordNet synonymy lookup. However, for English-to-Spanish we were forced to use the exact module alone.

Spanish-to-English

System	1-PER	1-WER	BLEU-4	GTM-1	GTM-2	METEOR	NIST-5	ROUGE-S*
Baseline	**0.5514**	**0.3741**	0.2709	0.6159	0.2579	0.5836	**7.2958**	0.3643
LDV-COMBO	0.5478	0.3657	0.2708	**0.6202**	0.2585	**0.5928**	7.2433	**0.3671**

English-to-Spanish

System	1-PER	1-WER	BLEU-4	GTM-1	GTM-2	METEOR	NIST-5	ROUGE-S*
Baseline	0.5158	**0.3776**	0.2272	0.5673	0.2418	0.4954	6.6835	0.3028
LDV-COMBO	**0.5382**	0.3560	**0.2611**	**0.5910**	**0.2462**	**0.5400**	**7.1054**	**0.3240**

Table 1: MT results comparing the LDV-COMBO system to a baseline system, for the test set both on the Spanish-to-English and English-to-Spanish tasks.

English Reference: *consider* germany , where some leaders [...]
Spanish Reference: **pensemos** en alemania , donde algunos dirigentes [...]

English-to-Spanish		
	Baseline	*estiman* que alemania , donde algunos dirigentes [...]
	LDV-COMBO	**pensemos** en alemania , donde algunos dirigentes [...]

Table 2: A case of error analysis.

3.2 Results

Table 1 presents MT results for the test set both for the Spanish-to-English and English-to-Spanish tasks. The variant of the LDV-COMBO system described in Section 2 is compared to a baseline variant based only on lexical items. In the case of Spanish-to-English performance varies from metric to metric. Therefore, an open issue is which metric should be trusted. In any case, the differences are minor. However, in the case of English-to-Spanish all metrics but '1-WER' agree to indicate that the LDV-COMBO system significantly outperforms the baseline. We suspect this may be due to the richer morphology of Spanish. In order to test this hypothesis we performed an error analysys at the sentence level based on the GTM F-measure. We found many cases where the LDV-COMBO system outperforms the baseline system by choosing a more accurate translation. For instance, in Table 2 we may see a fragment of the case of sentence 2176 in the test set. A better translation for "consider" is provided, "pensemos", which corresponds to the right verb and verbal form (instead of "estiman"). By inspecting translation models we confirmed the better adjustment of probabilities.

Interestingly, LDV-COMBO translation models are between 30% and 40% smaller than the models based on lexical items alone. The reason is that we are working with the union of alignments from different data views, thus adding more constraints into the phrase extraction step. Fewer phrase pairs are extracted, and as a consequence we are also effectively eliminating noise from translation models.

4 Conclusions and Further Work

Many researchers remain sceptical about the usefulness of linguistic information in SMT, because, except in a couple of cases (Charniak et al., 2003; Collins et al., 2005), little success has been reported. In this work we have shown that liniguistic information may be helpful, specially when the target language has a rich morphology (e.g. Spanish).

Moreover, it has often been argued that linguistic information does not yield significant improvements in MT quality, because (i) linguistic processors introduce many errors and (ii) the BLEU score is not specially sensitive to the grammaticality of MT output. We have minimized the impact of the first argument by using highly accurate tools for both languages. In order to solve the second problem more sophisticated metrics are required. Current MT evaluation metrics fail to capture many aspects of MT quality that characterize human translations with respect to those produced by MT systems. We are devoting most of our efforts to the deployment of a new MT evaluation framework which allows to combine several similarity metrics into a single measure of quality (Giménez and Amigó, 2006).

We also leave for further work the experimentation of new data views such as word senses and semantic roles, as well as their natural porting from the alignment step to phrase extraction and decoding.

Acknowledgements

This research has been funded by the Spanish Ministry of Science and Technology (ALIADO TIC2002-04447-C02). Authors are thankful to Patrik Lambert for providing us with the implementation of the Simplex Method used for tuning.

References

Satanjeev Banerjee and Alon Lavie. 2005. METEOR: An Automatic Metric for MT Evaluation with Improved Correlation with Human Judgments. In *Proceedings of ACL Workshop on Intrinsic and Extrinsic Evaluation Measures for Machine Translation and/or Summarization*.

Peter E Brown, Stephen A. Della Pietra, Robert L. Mercer, and Vincent J. Della Pietra. 1993. The Mathematics of Statistical Machine Translation: Parameter Estimation. *Computational Linguistics*, 19(2):263–311.

Xavier Carreras, Isaac Chao, Lluís Padró, and Muntsa Padró. 2004. FreeLing: An Open-Source Suite of Language Analyzers. In *Proceedings of the 4th LREC*.

Xavier Carreras, Lluís Márquez, and Jorge Castro. 2005. Filtering-Ranking Perceptron Learning for Partial Parsing. *Machine Learning*, 59:1–31.

Eugene Charniak, Kevin Knight, and Kenji Yamada. 2003. Syntax-based Language Models for Machine Translation. In *Proceedings of MT SUMMIT IX*.

Michael Collins, Philipp Koehn, and Ivona Kucerová. 2005. Clause Restructuring for Statistical Machine Translation. In *Proceedings of ACL*.

Daniel Gildea. 2003. Loosely Tree-Based Alignment for Machine Translation. In *Proceedings of ACL*.

Jesús Giménez and Enrique Amigó. 2006. IQMT: A Framework for Automatic Machine Translation Evaluation. In *Proceedings of the 5th LREC*.

Jesús Giménez and Lluís Màrquez. 2004. SVMTool: A general POS tagger generator based on Support Vector Machines. In *Proceedings of 4th LREC*.

Jesús Giménez and Lluís Màrquez. 2005. Combining Linguistic Data Views for Phrase-based SMT. In *Proceedings of the Workshop on Building and Using Parallel Texts, ACL*.

Philipp Koehn. 2004. Pharaoh: a Beam Search Decoder for Phrase-Based Statistical Machine Translation Models. In *Proceedings of AMTA*.

G. Leusch, N. Ueffing, and H. Ney. 2003. A Novel String-to-String Distance Measure with Applications to Machine Translation Evaluation. In *Proceedings of MT Summit IX*.

Chin-Yew Lin and E.H. Hovy. 2002. Automatic Evaluation of Machine Translation Quality Using N-gram Co-Occurrence Statistics. Technical report, National Institute of Standards and Technology.

Chin-Yew Lin and Franz Josef Och. 2004. Automatic Evaluation of Machine Translation Quality Using Longest Common Subsequence and Skip-Bigram Statistics. In *Proceedings of ACL*.

I. Dan Melamed, Ryan Green, and Joseph P. Turian. 2003. Precision and Recall of Machine Translation. In *Proceedings of HLT/NAACL*.

S. Nießen, F.J. Och, G. Leusch, and H. Ney. 2000. Evaluation Tool for Machine Translation: Fast Evaluation for MT Research. In *Proceedings of the 2nd International Conference on Language Resources and Evaluation*.

Franz Josef Och and Hermann Ney. 2003. A Systematic Comparison of Various Statistical Alignment Models. *Computational Linguistics*, 29(1):19–51.

Franz Josef Och. 2002. *Statistical Machine Translation: From Single-Word Models to Alignment Templates*. Ph.D. thesis, RWTH Aachen, Germany.

Kishore Papineni, Salim Roukos, Todd Ward, and Wei-Jing Zhu. 2001. Bleu: a method for automatic evaluation of machine translation, rc22176. Technical report, IBM T.J. Watson Research Center.

Charles Schafer and David Yarowsky. 2003. Statistical Machine Translation Using Coercive Two-Level Syntactic Transduction. In *Proceedings of EMNLP*.

William T. Vetterling William H. Press, Saul A. Teukolsky and Brian P. Flannery. 2002. *Numerical Recipes in C++: the Art of Scientific Computing*. Cambridge University Press.

Kenji Yamada and Kevin Knight. 2001. A Syntax-based Statistical Translation Model. In *Proceedings of ACL*.

Author Index